the

BANKING: THE LEGAL ENVIRONMENT

SECOND EDITION

David Palfreman

Pitman

PITMAN PUBLISHING
128 Long Acre, London WC2E 9AN
A Division of Longman Group UK Limited

© David Palfreman 1988, 1991

First published in Great Britain 1988, second edition 1991
Reprinted 1992

British Library Cataloguing in Publication Data
Palfreman, David
    Banking: the legal environment. – (Banking certificate series)
    1. Great Britain. Banking
    I. Title II. Series
    332.10941

    ISBN 0–273–03701 3

Printed and bound in Great Britain

For my father, a remarkable man, sadly missed; also Rula Maria, who never knew him, Chris and Hellen.

Contents

Preface

The Banking Certificate requires students to combine and use relevant skills, knowledge and understanding. Skills are best acquired at work and in the classroom; this book is thus not a substitute for them. Knowledge and understanding it promotes by providing a comprehensive and definitive interpretation of the legal environment of banking. I very much hope that *Banking: the Legal Environment* will enable teachers and students to spend more class time on skills development and less on acquiring information and explanation.

The first edition was a new book for a new course. I endeavoured to write something relevant to bankers and not just another 'general principles of English law book'. Feedback from teachers and students would indicate that I at least partially succeeded. Hence, there are no major changes to the academic structure in this second edition, although it has been completely updated and expanded where extra depth should prove useful. I have resisted two specific temptations: the first to include considerable extra material on the legal system, the second to cover electronic banking. The legal system is covered in sufficient depth for the syllabus and, more importantly, examination questions; electronic banking is not on the syllabus. I hope my book thereby provides more than enough information for the Banking Certificate Course and a firm foundation of legal knowledge for those students who will progress from the Banking Certificate to the Chartered Institute of Bankers' Associateship examination in *Law Relating to Banking Services*.

Those of you familiar with the first edition will notice two obvious changes in this edition: a new layout and the inclusion of numerous 'activities'. I hope the former will make the book more accessible and that the latter will provide the basis for discussion, class and project work.

As with the first edition I have written for bankers, not lawyers, but tried to balance a banking perspective with the traditions of law teaching – where these seemed appropriate. I have attempted to make the book as readable as possible.

I would like to thank Phil Ford, (former Chartered Institute of Bankers' Chief Examiner for this subject) and John Beardshaw. Much of the original text and some of the ideas were based on my long-standing writing partnerships with them. Thanks also to the Chartered Institute of Bankers for permission to reproduce their examination papers.

David Palfreman
1991

Table of cases

Tables of statutes

1 The legal environment: an introduction

OBJECTIVES

After studying this chapter you should be able to:
1 Appreciate some basic ideas about the nature and purpose of law;
2 Be aware of the different types of law;
3 Understand what is meant by the terms 'legislation', 'common law' and 'equity';
4 Appreciate the different forms of legal liability;
5 Explain the role of law in the business of banking.

■ INTRODUCTION

There will be few occasions (if any!) when bankers will sit and discuss the nature of the legal environment. Bankers are practical people and while they may seek to influence the legal environment they will do so in respect to specific aspects which directly affect them; payment systems, securities, consumer credit and insolvency law, for example. They are most unlikely to spend time considering the nature of law itself; the law exists, they have specialists who know all about it and they therefore tend to view the law purely as a framework, albeit important, within which to work. They understand that the law regulates their activities and they know how to use it – a straightforward pragmatic approach.

This is a perfectly acceptable and proper view, one which you no doubt share. However, you have begun a course of legal studies, albeit of law applied to banking, which will inevitably involve some theoretical considerations. For this reason we begin this chapter with a simple discussion of the 'idea of law'. This is something to understand and think about, not something to try to remember. Indeed, much of this chapter is not strictly required by the syllabus but we hope, having read it, that you will find it a useful and interesting background to the rest of your studies.

■ THE IDEA OF LAW

Any attempt to define and explain the 'idea of law' in a book of this nature can do no more than give a very limited introduction to an important philosophical subject. Unlike scientific laws, *law* cannot be objectively defined, let alone proved. It is the product of society, not of nature, and it means different things to different people according to their time, culture and the social structure in which they live.

The greatest of the world's philosophers have considered the 'idea of law', but no one definition has been universally accepted. There are, however, three main kinds of *jurisprudence* (legal theory):

- *historical*, which studies the growth of law, particularly in connection with the development of the state;
- *analytical*, which studies the concepts and structures of the law as they actually are (an approach bankers would most likely take);
- *sociological*, which considers how the workings of the law affect society.

To a greater or lesser extent, all jurisprudence attempts to answer the following questions:

- What is law?
- Why is law necessary?
- What is the purpose of law?
- How just is the law?

We will attempt to answer these questions, but you should always remember that different theories attempt to answer different questions. Some are concerned with the *form* of law, some with its *concept* and others with law's *function*.

Similarly, methods of enquiry differ. An *inductive* approach produces definitions and answers from the observations of actual situations and legal phenomena, while a *deductive* approach involves formulating definitions and answers based on initial assumptions about the nature of law. In our own legal system the *common law* (judge-made law) follows an inductive approach but *legislation* is often the result of a deductive process of law-making. Of greatest importance, perhaps, is the fact that all definitions of law are to a greater or lesser extent, consciously or subconsciously coloured by *value systems* and ideological factors – social, economic and political.

What is law?

Although there is no universally accepted definition of 'law', we can usefully begin our discussion by quoting three well-known jurists (legal writers).

The body of principles recognised and applied by the State in the administration of justice ... In other words the law consists of rules recognised and acted upon by courts of justice. (Salmond)

A law is a general rule of external human action enforced by a sovereign political authority. (Holland)

A social process for settling disputes and securing an ordered existence in the community. (Paton)

We can also put forward our own definition of law: *a set of rules administered and enforced by the state*. This definition is perfectly adequate for our present purposes. We might add that most people would accept that the broad function of law is to regulate conduct within a society.

In all three quotations and our definition, two ideas are either expressly or impliedly involved:

- that law is a *set of rules* by which human conduct within society is ordered and controlled;
- reference to the *state* or other sovereign power within society.

The first of these is largely self-explanatory and non-contentious but reference to the state raises fundamental issues about the nature of the law.

Laws are certainly enforced by the state but does the state impose its own corporate will on its members or is law essentially the will of the people recognised and adopted by the state? Clearly, an individual or bank is unlikely to give money voluntarily to the state to finance its activities, and taxation by law is therefore a necessary imposition. On the other hand the enforcement of the basic criminal law, which protects us all from the anti-social behaviour of the few, is equally clearly the wish of the people. So, the nature of law comes from a combination of factors. Governments use the law to fulfil their policies and serve their political philosophy; banks and other powerful organisations seek to influence the development of law to best serve their own interests, while most ordinary individuals accept the law for what it is, using it when necessary, complaining about what seems 'unfair' and generally knowing little about it.

The concepts of morality and law are closely linked. Virtually all serious crimes are immoral acts, e.g. murder and theft, and some essentially immoral acts are crimes, e.g. perjury (lying on oath) and libel may both be the subject of criminal proceedings; but a vast number of criminal acts committed each year, minor motoring offences in particular, are not usually considered immoral acts but are nevertheless punished. Conversely, many moral offences, adultery for example, go unpunished by the criminal law – at least in this country! (Under some legal systems adultery is a crime, for example, under some Islamic-based codes and, perhaps surprisingly, under the laws of some American states.) The difference between them in legal terms is that laws are enforced by the state while morals are not, *except* when law and morality coincide. In this context, is paying by cheque when you know you have no money in your account and no agreed overdraft facility an immoral act, a criminal act, neither, or both? Does the position differ if you use a cheque guarantee card? What is the position when you knowingly exceed your limit on a credit card or obtain a second mortgage for home improvements and then spend most of the loan on a new car? The legal distinction between law and morality raises an important issue about the purpose of law: should law be used to enforce morals? (This is something you might like to think about – but it would never be an exam question.)

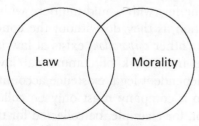

Fig 1.1 Law and morality

ACTIVITY 1.1

The relationship between law and morality is often illustrated using the simple diagram on the previous page. Name other acts or omissions which are (a) exclusively 'illegal', (b) exclusively 'immoral', and (c) both illegal and immoral.

Why do we need law?

Law is central to society. All except anarchists would agree that the existence of law is necessary. Every community has found a need to regulate the rights and duties of individuals in relation to each other and to the state.

A society presupposes order and it would seem that the natural order usually to be found in small primitive communities breaks down as the society becomes larger and more complex. It is clear that controls on powerful bodies and individuals are necessary if the interests of the majority are to be protected. For example, detailed regulation of the consumer credit industry is necessary to protect consumers from the less reputable elements within it, while the Banking Act 1979 (now replaced by the Banking Act 1987) was enacted largely to regulate deposit taking. In a wider context, experience has shown that the absence of health and safety, employment protection and monopoly legislation can have harmful social and economic effects on a society.

ACTIVITY 1.2

There are numerous specific legal rules which regulate the business of banking and many of them are found in Acts of Parliament (statutes). One such statute is the Consumer Credit Act 1974. This and other statutes you will study in Chapter 2. However, think about the regulation of your industry now and list below as many statutes – and legal decisions if you know any – as you can which have such a regulatory function. (Don't forget about statutes which regulate employment and health and safety at work.)

What is the purpose of law?

Law's purpose is usually considered to be the general regulation and control of society, the *criminal law* in particular providing and enforcing minimum standards of social behaviour. The legal system provides means for resolving conflicts and dealing with those who infringe legally enforced *social norms*. However, on the assumption that it is only a small minority of individuals and organisations in society that the law has to positively control, law can equally well be considered as an *enabling medium* for the majority. For example, individuals are able to use and enjoy their land because the *torts* of nuisance and trespass to land restrain the few who would interfere with it. Similarly, banks could not exist or function as they do without the concept of *juristic personality* – that a company (or other *corporation*) exists at law independently from its members – and the framework of commercial law in general. (Incidentally, a company's independent legal existence accounts for the rule that cheques made payable to a company must only be collected for that company's account and cannot, for example, be collected for the account of the only major shareholder/owner.)

ACTIVITY 1.3

Think about this idea of law as an enabling medium and write down as many examples as you can of how the law enables banks to pursue their business activities.

It is not within the scope of this book to argue the validity of different legal theories but one well-known example will illustrate how economic and political ideology can determine theories of the nature and purpose of law. In classic Marxist philosophy, law is viewed as the institutionalisation of the prevailing ideology which the socio-economic elite of a society uses to coerce the masses into obedience in order to preserve its privileged position. Thus, law's purpose is here seen in terms of achieving social, economic and political objectives. This may be a rather too unsophisticated view of law's nature and purpose and extreme, but many of you may often have considered that the government uses law to impose its will upon the individual and that large organisations of all kinds are able to use the law to further their commercial (or other) interests at your expense. It also makes a good contrast with the rather 'cosy' view of law's purpose with which we began this section!

It is clear from just this one example that it is difficult to discuss the ultimate purpose of law without asking fundamental questions about the nature of society as it is and as we might wish it to be. This of course involves questions of political philosophy and the nature of the economic society in which we would choose to live. Such issues merit a book to themselves but we shall examine the specific functions and uses of law in relation to banks and forms of legal liability in general later in this chapter.

Law and justice

The ultimate aim of all law should surely be to promote justice but any attempt to define law in these terms meets two serious obstacles:

- 'justice' is a vague concept, meaning different things to different people;
- law must be considered within its socio-political context and, assuming that law exists to serve society, what may be justice with regard to one individual may not be useful to society.

Theft, for example, is a serious crime. What, however, of people who steal food from supermarkets or milk from doorsteps because they cannot afford to feed themselves or their families? Is justice served by their punishment? Alternatively, a person who is made redundant has a legal right to compensation under the Employment Protection (Consolidation) Act 1978. This is no doubt 'just' but it must be remembered that the rest of us have to contribute towards the compensation through taxation. Is this 'fair' to the rest of us?

You might like to consider the argument that law may always produce injustice unless it is the product of a socially and economically just society. But social and economic justice is, in turn, a matter of personal judgment!

It is possible, however, to talk in more objective terms about the distinction between *procedural justice* and *substantive justice*. The former is concerned with the legal process and the latter, justice in particular cases. At one time the common law was concerned almost solely with procedure and even today the apparent complexity of the legal process seems to act as a positive deterrent to the ordinary person who seeks redress at law.

Justice at law can be assessed in terms of *natural justice*, the assumption being that there exists a perfect code of rules to which human law should aspire. Two basic principles of natural justice are that people must be allowed to speak in their own cause and that resolution of disputes must be by an impartial judge. These are, of course, completely acceptable (at least in our society). However, the weakness of natural justice as an objective criterion for comparison lies in its own human philosophical origins unless, of course, you believe in divine intervention and guidance! Perhaps all that one can say is that according to our conventional criteria some laws and some legal systems promote justice more than others.

■ TYPES OF LAW

Public and private law

This topic can be viewed in a number of ways, it depends on what you are comparing. The most usual division is into *public law* and *private law*, the former concerning matters relating to society as a whole, particularly the relationship between individuals/organisations and the state, and the latter concerning individuals and/or organisations. *Constitutional law*, dealing with the exercise of power in the state, *administrative law*, dealing with the rights and duties of administrative agencies of government, and *criminal law*, dealing with those that break accepted codes of social behaviour, are the most important branches of public law. The first two are, of course, of very little relevance to banking while the third is of some indirect relevance, as you will see.

Of direct relevance are many of the main branches of private law; for example, *contract law*, which regulates agreements between individuals or between organisations, e.g. banks and their customers, *agency*, where one person acts for another, e.g. a bank collecting cheques for its customers; *land law*, covering ownership of land and mortgages among many other things; and the *law of torts*, which determines when compensation is to be paid to a person whose legal rights have been infringed by another – particularly relevant to banking, in the form of the tort of conversion, in the context of safe custody arrangements and the collection and payment of cheques. As a category, private or *civil law* is usually also compared with *criminal law*, and this is done later in the chapter.

A further important division of law is whether its origin lies in *legislation, common law* or *equity*. Understanding this division will be useful to your studies because we will be referring to these terms and discussing examples of these types of law on many occasions in this book.

Legislation

This is law made by Parliament and is to be found in acts of Parliament and orders made under them. Legislation is also referred to as *statute law*. Many acts of Parliament are rather like mini codes of law on particular subjects which the judges use when deciding cases. Most of the business of banking is regulated by statute law. Indeed, legislation is by far the most important type of law in all spheres of business and social activity.

The role of legislation

In the next chapter we shall be introducing a number of statutes which are of direct relevance to banking but at this point it is useful to say something of the role of legislation in society generally.

All British governments use legislation for three main purposes.

1 To regulate and control society. In particular it is used to control antisocial behaviour and protect an individual's basic social rights, e.g. to education, to welfare services and to freedom from discrimination.

2 To raise by taxation the necessary finance for the government's activities, thereby implementing its fiscal policies.

3 To create or repeal, revise or reform the law. New principles can be introduced into the body of law by legislation, e.g. the concept of 'unfair dismissal' by the Industrial Relations Act 1971 (now to be found in the Employment Protection (Consolidation) Act 1978), and 'administration orders' (which protect companies and their assets against legal action by creditors while attempts are made to resurrect their fortunes and avoid their winding-up) by the Insolvency Act 1986. Alternatively, unworkable or out-of-date law can be removed, e.g. the whole of the law on individual insolvency contained in the Bankruptcy Act 1914 was repealed by the Insolvency Act 1985.

Consolidating and codifying Acts

Consolidating and codifying acts are sometimes passed. *Consolidating acts* re-enact a number of statutes on the same subject in one act, sometimes with little amendment but in a rationalised and therefore simpler to use form. For example, the Companies Act 1985 collected into one act all the previous legislation on registered companies and the Insolvency Act 1986 repealed the Insolvency Act 1985 and parts of the Companies Act 1985 and re-enacted them as one coherent statute. (Bad initial planning you might say!)

Codifying acts seek to rationalise both statute and case law on a given subject into a complete and systematic code, although it is the expression rather than the content of the statute which usually differs substantially from the previous law. The classic banking example is the Bills of Exchange Act 1882 which, although somewhat dated in its phraseology and obviously not covering electronic methods of payment (it was designed to regulate paper-based payment systems), has stood the test of time remarkably well. The Insolvency Act 1985 was an important modern example of a codifying statute which means that the Insolvency Act 1986 is in practice something of a hybrid, i.e. both a consolidating and a codifying statute, since it contains the same law as the 1985 Act which it replaced before the latter was fully in force!

ACTIVITY 1.4

ACTIVITY 1.4

Discover at least two other consolidating and two other codifying statutes which affect the business of banking.

Common law

The common law has its origins in the ancient customs of the country, the original basis of all law, and was once administered only in the common law courts. Today, however, we think of the common law as *judge-made law*, that is, the statements of law made by judges when deciding cases. Thus, it is entirely different in kind and concept to legislation although the two types of law are necessarily and inseparably complementary. For example, judges interpret legislation through their decisions where necessary. Common law and equity are also complementary although the latter does presuppose the existence of the former.

Equity

In everyday language equity means justice or fairness and this tells us something about its nature. More formally equity means the principles of law administered before 1875 by the Court of Chancery. (We explain the relevance of the date later.) This, however, tells us little. To understand the nature of equity, you need to know something of the history of the common law.

All actions at common law were begun by a *writ* (a written command in the name of the Sovereign) and by the 14th century its procedure had become so rigid that no action could be brought unless one of a fixed number of writs fitted the plaintiff's claim. This inflexibility was the main reason for the evolution of equity. It became the practice for those with sufficient influence, money and determination to petition the King when the common law offered them no satisfaction of their claim. In time, petitions began to be heard by the Lord Chancellor instead of the King. Finally the Court of Chancery, presided over by the Lord Chancellor, was established to administer the rules of equity. The present Chancery Division of the High Court is a direct descendant of this early judicial function of the Lord Chancellor.

At first the Lord Chancellor decided disputes brought before him purely on the facts of each individual case but gradually a body of case law emerged in the Court of Chancery which was applied almost as strictly as the common law in the common law courts.

Equity's early growth depended above all else on its recognition and protection of one particular interest in property, that of a beneficiary under a trust – equitable ownership. A *trust* is an arrangement whereby legal title to property is given by one person to another (a trustee) with the latter promising to use the property for the benefit of a third person (the beneficiary). Some bank accounts are trust accounts and banks have trustee departments offering professional services in the administration of modern trusts.

Trusts originated in the middle ages. Some of the earliest examples were the arrangements made by knights when they went to fight overseas and wished to ensure that their estates would be maintained and their families provided for, or when a person wished to provide for a monastic order which was forbidden to own property. As neither the knight's wife nor infant heir in the former situation, nor the monks in the latter, could, for different reasons, own a legal estate in land, a straightforward transfer of the legal estate was impossible and a trust had to be employed. Hence, legal title was vested in the trustee(s) but the benefit of the property was vested in the knight's family or monastic order.

The common law only recognised the basic transaction – the transfer of legal title to the trustee(s) – and would not recognise nor protect the beneficiary's interest, e.g. where the trustee used the property for his own benefit. This was clearly unfair and the Lord Chancellor would intervene to compel the trustee, the legal owner of the property, to act according to his conscience and use the property for the benefit of the beneficiary, the owner in equity. In this way Equity supplemented the common law and remedied some of its defects.

Today trusts enable people (or organisations) who are, for one reason or another, unable to hold legal ownership of property to enjoy the benefit of it. For example, minors cannot hold legal estates in land but the land can be held in trust for them. Similarly, since a partnership has no independent legal (corporate) existence, it cannot own property itself and the partnership property of a large firm is usually held by four of the partners (as trustees) on trust for the partners generally.

Equity ceased to be a separately administered system of law in 1875 when a new system of courts was introduced which administered both common law and equity. However, the principles of equity have retained their identity in the modern system and are of considerable importance to banks. A basic principle of equity is that it acts *in personam* (against the person) and not *in rem* (against the property involved). For example, the essential difference to a bank between a legal and an equitable mortgage is that the former gives it various rights against the property mortgaged while the latter only gives it rights of action, e.g. for the debt, against the mortgagor personally.

Perhaps the most relevant example today of equity's original role in supplementing the common law is to be found in its remedies, something which can again be illustrated by banking examples.

If one party to a contract fails to perform their obligations, particularly under a contract involving land, the other party can ask the court for *specific performance* of the contract. This is an order that the contract should be performed as agreed, failure to do so amounting to contempt of court. Banks' equitable mortgages usually contain a clause by which the customer (mortgagor) undertakes to execute a legal mortgage when asked to do so, an undertaking that can be enforced by specific performance. A more general example would be when a contract for the sale of a house has been made and the seller subsequently refuses to execute the conveyance (the deed which transfers the legal estate to the buyer), perhaps because the value of the house has substantially increased in the time since the contract was made. Equity has traditionally taken the view that specific performance of the contract, that is,

9

that the seller must execute the conveyance, is very likely to be the appropriate remedy in this situation.

An *injunction* is a court order which forbids a person from doing something or continuing to do something. An injunction may be used to freeze a bank account where, for example, the ownership of certain funds is disputed; the injunction preventing them from being paid away before ownership is determined by the court. But for these remedies the only action possible would be an action for damages and this might be futile, too late or both.

Unlike common law remedies, where a successful plaintiff has a *right* to their award, all equitable remedies are discretionary. The plaintiff (the person seeking the remedy) must satisfy the court that the common law remedy available, usually an action for damages, would be ineffective or inappropriate. For example, specific performance would be an appropriate remedy where a vendor of land has refused to execute the conveyance because each piece of land is by definition unique and an award of damages can never be adequate compensation.

Other examples of equity that are important to banking are *undue influence*, in connection with guarantees for example, a mortgagor's *equity of redemption* and *trusts*, both trusts themselves and trust accounts. All of these will be covered in this book.

■ DIFFERENT FORMS OF LEGAL LIABILITY

Earlier in this chapter we talked about different types of law. Different types of law involve different types of legal liability, often more than one. You should at least be aware of the differences since banks, their customers and others with which they deal can all incur them in their everyday activities. We will also be involved with them all to a greater or lesser extent in this book.

It is partly according to the type of legal liability involved that a workable distinction can be drawn between various types of legal wrongs. This is because a particular act or omission may constitute more than one type. For example, taking property belonging to another, e.g. a cheque, is both a crime (theft) and a tort (conversion). More complicated examples are possible; the negligent driving of a taxi-driver which causes injury to the passenger is a breach of contract (there is certainly an implied condition in the contract with the passenger that the taxi-driver should drive safely) in addition to being both a crime and a tort. A simple banking illustration is provided in the context of a firm of solicitors' client account — an account that all solicitors must have which should ensure that the money that they hold (on trust) on behalf of their clients is not mixed with the firm's funds and not wrongfully used to benefit the firm or individual partners. Should a bank knowingly allow a partner to withdraw funds from the account for their own purposes, it would be liable in contract to the firm for breach of the banker-customer contract and liable to the clients (the beneficiaries) for breach of trust. Should it knowingly allow a partner to pay into his or her personal account a cheque which should have been paid into the clients' account, it will not only be liable to its customer, the partnership, for breach of contract but also for the tort of conversion (*see* page 14) because it has denied the partnership's right to the money represented by the cheque.

Workable distinctions can also be drawn on the basis of the different functions, procedures and consequences involved in different branches of the law – we looked briefly at public and private law earlier. Under the English legal system the basic distinction affecting individuals and organisations alike is that between criminal and civil law. We will therefore discuss the nature and function of criminal and civil law and then, more specifically, criminal and civil liability. Having done this we will consider the different concepts of fault, strict, and vicarious liability, and their relevance to criminal and civil law.

Criminal and civil law

A *crime* is a breach of a public duty, a legal wrong which affects society in general. The state uses the criminal law to regulate the conduct of its citizens and to protect society. This it endeavours to do by prohibiting certain types of conduct and imposing sanctions on those members of society that disregard the prohibition.

A *civil wrong* is a breach of a private duty which may arise from an agreement between individuals, as in the law of contract, or be imposed by a rule of law as in the law of torts. (By a 'rule of law' we mean a principle derived either from statements made by judges when deciding cases or from the will of Parliament as embodied in statutes.) Thus, the civil law is concerned with protecting and enforcing legal rights and duties between individuals and organisations and, usually, ordering the payment of compensation for damage suffered when they have been infringed or broken.

Since it is impossible to distinguish between crimes and civil wrongs purely on the basis of the act or omission involved, we must use various other criteria.

1 A *functional* distinction. This has already been made but you will no doubt have appreciated that the criminal law indirectly protects private rights by its deterrent effect.

2 The *consequences* of a successfully brought action. A successfully brought prosecution results in conviction of the accused and the imposition of *sanctions*, conventionally in the form of a fine or a term of imprisonment. A successfully brought civil action, however, usually results in the defendant paying *damages* to the plaintiff, although other remedies, as you have seen, may be granted by the court, e.g. an order for the specific performance of a contract or for an injunction to restrain the commission of a tortious (wrongful) act.

3 The *different purpose* of these sanctions and remedies. *Criminal sanctions* are intended to punish and reform the criminal and deter him or her and others from similar activities, thereby protecting society. *Civil remedies* are designed to compensate the individual for the damage suffered as a result of the interference with private rights. For example, in an action for breach of contract an award of damages is generally intended to put the injured party

into the financial position they could reasonably have expected to have enjoyed had the defendant fulfilled their obligations, e.g. the loss of profit on a cancelled order. In an action in tort, damages are designed to restore the injured party to the position they enjoyed before the right was infringed, e.g. the value of a cheque collected in circumstances which prevent the bank from relying on the Cheques Act 1957, s.4. (*See* Chapter 8.) It is obvious, however, that money is poor compensation for many kinds of personal injury, as it would be should a bank wrongly deliver from safe custody, say, family jewels with great sentimental value.

However, civil proceedings may result in 'punishment' and criminal proceedings in 'compensation' but these are always ancillary to the primary purpose of the proceedings. In exceptional circumstances exemplary or punitive damages may be awarded in civil actions, e.g. for defamation. Here the award exceeds the plaintiff's actual loss and is designed to satisfy wounded pride and to act as deterrent to others. Under the Powers of Criminal Courts Act 1973 a criminal court may make a compensation order against a convicted criminal for personal injury, loss or damage resulting from the offence. But here again, the compensation order is ancillary to the main purpose of the criminal proceedings – punishment. In addition, the Crown Court can make a criminal bankruptcy order against a person convicted of causing loss or damage to property of £15,000 or more.

4 There are *different courts* which deal with different infringements of the law. However, as you will see in Chapter 3, most courts exercise both civil and criminal jurisdiction. Nevertheless, there are real differences in the form of trial, procedure and rules of evidence.

5 The role of the *state*. In effect, criminal proceedings are initiated and controlled by the state whereas civil proceedings are initiated and controlled by individuals. Only the state can stop a criminal prosecution once it has begun, while a civil dispute is often resolved by the parties before judgment. However, in so far as the stability of our society depends largely on the protection of individuals' rights, the state has an interest in seeing that they are protected. Thus, it provides means of conflict resolution and enforces civil judgments.

Criminal and civil liability

There are two distinct elements in *criminal liability*:

- a specified act or omission (the *actus reus* or 'guilty act'); and
- a specific state of mind (the *mens rea* or 'guilty mind').

For example, under the Theft Act 1968 the *actus reus* of theft is the appropriation of property belonging to another, and the *mens rea* is a dishonest intention to permanently deprive the other of that property. Similarly, the *actus reus* of burglary is entering a building as a trespasser, and the *mens rea* is the intention to commit certain offences inside, most commonly theft. It follows that it is merely the tort of trespass and not the crime of burglary to unlawfully enter a building without the required unlawful intention.

Both elements are necessary for criminal liability, for where punishment is involved the mere breach of a prohibition should not be a crime. You will see later, however, that there are a range of statutory criminal offences where a 'guilty mind' as such is not required. These are crimes of strict liability.

The *actus reus* embraces not only the specific act or omission required for the offence but also the wider circumstances (if any) which may be specified in the definition. In theft, for example, the property taken must 'belong to another'. Hence, taking abandoned property cannot be theft, no matter how dishonest the intention.

It is common to translate *mens rea* as the 'guilty mind' but this translation is somewhat misleading. Some crimes require 'intention', others 'negligence'. Indeed, a person may quite possibly commit a crime without any sense of guilt and even in the belief that the conduct is justified by law.

Civil liability clearly requires an act or omission but, because the essence of civil law is the protection of rights, it is neither realistic nor necessarily productive to attempt to list and define specific acts or omissions which infringe these rights. In contrast, criminal law specifically defines the acts or omissions which it prohibits. In short, only acts or omissions within the definition of a particular crime can be prosecuted while any act which unlawfully interferes with an individual's right gives grounds for an action at civil law.

The importance and relevance of mental attitudes in civil liability varies but far less emphasis is generally placed upon it than is the case in criminal liability. This is because the purpose and consequences of a civil action is compensation of the injured party and not punishment of the wrongdoer. For example, the reason for awarding compensation to the plaintiff should a bank be in breach of contract is the infringement of the other party's right by the breach itself. The bank's liability does not differ, whether it intended to break the contract, was negligent in its conduct or acted completely innocently. Similarly, a bank's possible liability for conversion should it collect a cheque for a customer not entitled to it is purely because it has denied the true owner's right to it. (We discuss a bank's protection in such circumstances in Chapter 8.) Put another way, it is one thing to make a person compensate another when no fault is involved, it is quite another to impose punishment.

ACTIVITY 1.5

Consider the following statements. Distinguish between them and jot down a few notes. Do this before reading any further.

If A is at fault and injures B, B should be compensated by A.
If B is injured by A, B should be compensated by A.
If B is injured by A, B should be compensated by A's employer.
If B is injured by A, B should be compensated.

Fault, strict and vicarious liability

Liability based upon *fault* is primarily associated with the tort of negligence, for here a person incurs civil liability precisely for failure to exercise reasonable care in his or her activities. Expressed formally, the tort of negligence is committed by the breach of a legal duty of care owed to another person which causes that other person foreseeable damage. As you will see later, it is possible for a bank to incur liability for negligence by giving a negligent opinion on the credit-worthiness of one of its customers. (Note that when the term 'negligence' is used in the Cheques Act 1957, s.4, it does not refer to the tort of negligence but simply to failure to act as a reasonable banker, such failure resulting in loss of statutory protection from liability for conversion; *see* below.)

Where criminal liability is *strict*, the wrongdoer's mental attitude is irrelevant, i.e. proof that the act was committed intentionally or negligently is unnecessary. The wrongdoer is liable merely because the *actus reus* of a particular offence was committed or the plaintiff's right infringed. In criminal law, offences of strict liability include many road traffic offences and offences relating to the sale of food and drugs. Such offences are used as an effective means of social regulation.

Civil liability is strict in contract law; all that is required is a breach of the terms of the contract. Liability in the tort of conversion (essentially denying a person's right to possess and control property) is also strict. Thus, at common law every time a bank quite innocently collects a cheque for or pays a cheque to someone not entitled to it, it commits conversion against the cheque's true owner. You may already know, however, that a bank has limited (but necessary) statutory protection in this respect: the Cheques Act 1957, s.4 in the former case and the Bills of Exchange Act 1882, s.60 in the latter. Needless to say, a bank could not avoid liability for wrongfully delivering property held in safe custody by explaining that it had every reason to think the person to whom it delivered the property was its true owner – liability is strict.

The Consumer Protection Act 1987 adopts strict liability for the principle of *product liability*. It provides that producers of goods are strictly liable for damage caused by defects in their products; they are liable whether or not they were negligent or realised that the goods were defective. This should ensure that producers are liable to the end users of their products with whom there is no contractual relationship and provide a basis for an action for damages by the latter. Such end users may find it difficult to prove breach of a legal duty of care owed to them, as they must if they are to recover compensation by successfully bringing an action for the tort of negligence.

Liability is said to be *vicarious* where one person is liable for the actions of another. Vicarious liability in the law of torts is most important in employment because the common law imposes liability on employers for the torts committed by their employees in the course of their employment. For example, a bank is vicariously liable for the actions of an employee who negligently collects a cheque.

In criminal law one person is not generally liable for the criminal acts of another. There are, however, a number of offences created by statute where vicarious liability is imposed. Here it is necessary to do so to achieve the objective of the statute. For example, under the Consumer Credit Act 1974, it is a criminal offence to send a credit token, for example a credit card, to anybody unless formally requested in writing by that person to do so. It would achieve very little to prosecute the employee responsible; the crime has to be that of the credit card company itself.

■ BANKS AND THE LAW

A conflict?

Law regulates the activities of banks by providing a framework of rules governing every aspect of the business of banking: be it their relationship with customers; the means available to enforce security; responsibilities to their shareholders; or their role as employers. At the same time, however, the regulatory nature and inherent certainty of this framework enables banks to pursue their activities. They use the law to achieve their objectives. For example, contract law enables a bank to acquire in the market place the resources it needs, such as premises and staff, and sell it services, from current accounts to travel insurance to estate agency. The law of agency itself is absolutely fundamental to modern commercial activity and banks both act as and deal with agents all the time. A few simple, specific examples (*see* below) will further illustrate this point but you will come across many others as you read this book.

So, is there a conflict between law's regulatory and enabling roles? If there is, it exists only in an abstract sense. We can explain this quite simply by making a comparison with a game of football or netball. The rules of a game prevent the players from doing certain things but they also enable the game to take place. Without rules, how would the game start and end and how would you determine who had won?

Some specific examples

In theory, customers who want to mortgage their homes to secure loans are free to bargain with the bank as to the exact terms of the mortgage. In reality, of course, this never happens. If the bank grants the loan it will only do so on its own terms; the customer's choice is to accept or reject the standard terms offered by the bank. Thus, the bank is able to include in the contract all the terms which it knows will protect its position. Exactly the same is true of guarantees. Another good example is found in bankers' opinions. In *Hedley Byrne & Co Ltd v Heller Partners Ltd* (1963) the House of Lords indicated that a bank could be liable for causing financial loss through making a negligent statement. However, it held that a disclaimer printed on the opinion protected it from liability. Thus, all opinions have such a disclaimer on them. While you may question the ethics of sheltering behind such disclaimers, the law says banks can do such and therefore they do.

A rather more technical example is a bank's use of a 'floating charge' as part of a security package. When lending to companies banks have usually taken a floating charge (*see* Chapter 7) over the assets. Since the passing of the Insolvency Act 1986 they almost invariably do so. This is because the Act enables an unsecured creditor, a supplier for example, to apply to the court for an administration order against an apparently insolvent company. This effectively prevents any secured creditor, a bank for example, taking steps to enforce its security and puts everything under the control of the court. Such a situation may be desirable from the unsecured creditor's, even the company's, point of view but it is often to a bank's disadvantage. However, holding a floating charge enables the secured creditor to appoint a receiver (technically an 'administrative receiver') – effectively at the first sign of real financial difficulties – and the appointment of a receiver prevents an administration order being made. Thus, by simply taking a floating charge at the time the loan is made, a bank can ensure that it remains firmly in control of the situation. It merely appoints a receiver (it can of course decide not to) as soon as it receives notice, which the court is bound to give, that an application for an administration order has been made.

A final example involves opening an account, a topic we look at in more detail in Chapter 5. The vast majority of accounts are opened with legitimate intentions and with an increasingly competitive environment banks do not always ask for references before opening an account. The risk in not doing so is far outweighed by the cost of doing so. However, in some areas and in some situations references are requested and subsequently checked. While it is still quite possible for a determined rogue to open an account using bogus referees, at least the bank will have done what the law requires and it should be able to rely on the Cheques Act 1957, s.4 (*see* Chapter 8) should it collect a cheque to which its customer has no title.

In this chapter we have discussed various types of law; in the next we discuss the sources of law. We can show how this all fits together diagrammatically – *see* Fig 1.2.

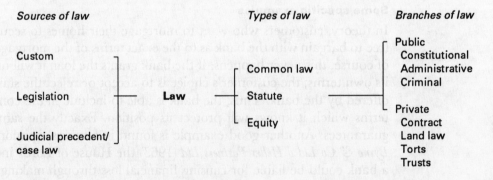

Fig 1.2 Sources, types and branches of law

■ SUMMARY

1 Law can be said to be a set of rules enforced by the state by which human conduct within society is regulated.

2 Governments use the law to implement their policies.

3 The concepts of law and morality are closely linked but our law does not directly seek to enforce morals.

4 Law has both a regulatory and an enabling role.

5 Law and justice are not necessarily the same thing.

6 The distinctions between public law and private law, and between criminal law and civil law are two basic ways of categorising types of law.

7 Legislation is law made by Parliament.

8 Consolidating acts rationalise and re-enact a number of earlier acts on a particular subject in one act.

9 Codifying acts rationalise both statute and case law in a code of law.

10 Common law is judge-made law.

11 Equity is the principles of law originally developed in the Court of Chancery.

12 Legislation, common law and equity are administered together but the three types of law are readily identifiable within the amalgamation.

13 A crime is a breach of a public duty, a legal wrong which affects society in general. A civil wrong is a breach of a private duty owed to an individual or an organisation.

14 The primary purpose of the criminal law is punishment, the civil law compensation.

15 Liability at law can be based on fault, can be strict or can be vicarious.

16 The law regulates all aspects of the business of banking but also enables banks to pursue their activities.

■ SELF-ASSESSMENT QUESTIONS

Please read this carefully!

These self-assessment questions (there are similar ones at the end of each chapter) have a dual purpose: first, they are designed to enable you to test your knowledge and understanding of the chapter; second, learning the answers to them will help you to pass the examination – they are all either previous questions set as part of the compulsory Question 1 or very similar to those that have been set. You will find the answers to them by re-reading the chapter.

You can expect 12 such questions as part of Question 1, comprising:

● three questions on the *sources of law*;
● one question on the *courts* or other *conflict resolving procedures*;
● two questions on general *contract law*;
● two questions on the *banker-customer relationship*;
● two questions on *property* and its use as *security*;
● two questions on *cheques* and other means of *payment*.

1 Define law.

2 What two ideas are usually regarded as the essence of any definition of law?

3 What is the difference between inductive and deductive reasoning?

4 State an example of juristic personality.

5 Distinguish between public law and private law.

6 Give an example of a bank acting as an agent for a customer.

7 What is another name for legislation?

8 For what main purposes do governments use legislation?

9 Explain the difference between a consolidating act and a codifying act. State an example of each.

10 What is meant by common law?

11 What is meant by equity?

12 What was the origin of the common law?

13 Name two equitable remedies.

14 Equity is said to act in personam. Give an example where this principle is relevant to banking.

15 Define a trust.

16 Give an example of how equity supplements the common law.

17 What is an injunction?

18 State two ways in which criminal law and civil law differ.

19 What are the two essential elements of a crime?

20 What is conversion in the law of torts? Explain two ways in which a bank can commit conversion.

21 What is meant by vicarious liability?

22 With the aid of examples, explain how the law has both a regulating and an enabling function in the business of banking.

23 Give an example of how banks use the law in their activities.

2 The sources of English law

OBJECTIVES

After studying this chapter you should be able to:
1 State the sources of law;
2 Explain how the system of case law works and how it affects the business of banking;
3 Explain the different types of legislation and how they affect the business of banking;
4 Understand how and why legislation is interpreted by the courts, with particular reference to banking.

■ INTRODUCTION

The term 'source' has a number of different meanings in the context of English law. We saw in Chapter 1 that the concept of the 'state' is important to the idea of law, as the power that gives rules authority as law. We can call this the *formal source* of law. Under the UK's constitution, the *Queen in Parliament* is the formal source of law and supreme constitutional power in the state. While legislation originates in Parliament, it must receive the Royal Assent before it is enforceable. In theory, the Sovereign could refuse to consent to a particular piece of legislation but in practice it is highly unlikely that this would ever be done – a major constitutional crisis would be the result. In addition, the judges are the Sovereign's judges, deriving their authority from the Royal prerogative and making decisions in the Sovereign's name.

We can also talk of the *literary* sources, the written records of the law, and the *historical* sources. By far the most important, however, are the *legal* sources, the processes by which new principles become part of the body of law. The legal sources are case law, legislation and custom; although custom is perhaps better thought of today as a historical source.

Before we look at the legal sources – those aspects of this topic which you must concentrate on – let us consider the origin of law in custom.

Law's origin in custom

Law has its origins in custom, a far cry from the sophisticated statutory law of today. A custom is nothing more than a group of people doing something in a particular way. It evolves spontaneously and becomes the accepted social norm followed by the members of the community to which it applies. Failure to observe social norms endangers society and breaches of the customary law would be punished. Today we can define a custom as *usage recognised by law*.

Originally, customs controlled the basic aspects of life necessary to preserve and protect a simple society. Custom would regulate marriage, the ban on incest being found in nearly all societies; provide a simple criminal law, e.g. 'thou shalt not kill', 'thou shalt not steal'; and, somewhat later, a method for determining property rights, particularly rights over land and its inheritance. Primogeniture (inheritance by the eldest son) is both an early example of the quest for status in society and recognition that it was not economically desirable to divide land into tiny units. Hence, land was passed from father to eldest son without division among others.

In the earliest communities, as with animal groups, customary rules would be enforced by the physically strongest. Gradually more sophisticated ideas of government and law-making would evolve. In many communities, rule by the eldest or group of elders, or by a 'wiseman' of some kind, emerged. In time certain families attained supreme power and the idea of 'kingship' evolved. Perhaps the final stage in the evolution of law enforcement to date is to be found in a free and democratic system of government, although it is debatable whether a truly democratic system can ever be achieved.

The English legal system is unique in having followed the highly idealised process outlined above more closely than any other system. There has been very little external interference in its development; even the laws and legal system left by the Romans were almost totally destroyed during the Saxon dark ages which followed and in contemporary times joining the EC has had little effect on our purely domestic law.

Clearly, this process of law evolving from custom is of little relevance to banking but there is a direct analogy to banking practice. Many aspects of banking practice have their origins in the 'customs' of the industry and many in turn have been recognised and accepted as law by the courts and Parliament. The use of crossings on cheques is an example. Others have yet to be tested, for example, many accounts are opened without references being taken – if and when tested in the courts, will this 'custom' be accepted as reasonable. At present not taking references is considered to be *prima facie* evidence of negligence at law.

This process can be illustrated diagrammatically.

Fig 2.1 The development of modern law

■ CASE LAW

The nature and operation of case law

As soon as Royal courts were established in England, common custom became the basis of their decisions. From the earliest times judges have referred to the decisions in previous cases for guidance but the present system of case law or *judicial precedent*, as it is technically called, dates from the later part of the nineteenth century and two events in particular. To base decisions on previous cases it is essential to have accurate records of decisions and the legal reasoning by which they were reached. This was made possible in 1865 by the establishment of the Incorporated Society for Law Reporting. Similarly, it is necessary to have a rational and hierarchical court structure so that the avenues of appeal and the authority of each court are settled. The reorganisation of the court structure by the Judicature Acts 1873–5 brought this about.

Today statute law is not only the supreme source of law, it also provides most of our new law. However, much of our older law is found in cases and case law provides the detail which statutes usually cannot; many statutes are also the subject of interpretation by the courts. Traditionally, making the law is not a constitutional function of the judges. Some will argue that this is indeed the case, according to theory they merely 'declare' the law. But others will say that this is a complete fiction, by their very role they must 'make' law. In this book you will come across a number of examples to which this difference of opinion could apply.

Ratio decidendi

Case law is based on the rule that previous decisions of a higher court are followed by lower courts.

Basic to the rule is the concept of the *ratio decidendi*. This can be defined briefly as the 'legal reason for deciding' and consists of three things.

- The judge's statement of the relevant facts, this being used for comparative purposes in later cases.
- An account of the way in which the decision was reached, e.g. which cases and statutes were referred to as 'authority', in other words the process of legal reasoning that was employed.
- The decision the judge made to resolve the dispute between the parties.

Thus, a fuller definition of the *ratio decidendi* is 'the principles of law applied by the court to the facts of the case to reach its decision'.

The *ratio decidendi*, particularly the legal reasoning employed by the judge, becomes part of the common law and can be used as the basis on which to make later decisions.

Binding and persuasive precedents

The English legal system divides *precedents* (previous decisions) into those which have binding authority and those which are of only persuasive authority. The idea of being *bound* by precedents is a principle only found in countries which operate a system of law based on our own, e.g. Commonwealth countries.

Binding precedents are decisions of the House of Lords and the Court of Appeal which have not been overruled by a later case or by legislation. Such decisions *must* be followed whether the judge in the later case approves of them or not.

Two points are worth making here. First, while a judge will carefully consider his or her statement of the law as s/he sees it, ultimately it is up to another court which uses the earlier decision to decide exactly what is the *ratio* of that case. Normally this is a straightforward process but occasionally up to five judges in appellate courts may each explain the law slightly differently or even reach the same conclusion for different legal reasons. Here the later court is presented with a more complicated task. For example, in *Lloyds Bank v Bundy* (1975), one member of the Court of Appeal held that the principle of undue influence was based on inequality in bargaining power; in *National Westminster Bank plc v Morgan* (1985), the House of Lords held that this was neither the *ratio* of the case nor correct. (We discuss both cases in Chapter 4.)

Second, a court may occasionally avoid the doctrine of binding precedent by a process known as *distinguishing*, i.e. finding sufficiently important factual differences between the case before the court and the binding precedent. This can be explained with some simple maths:

$$A = B = C = 1$$

If in the first case the facts were ABC, then the decision would be 1 (ABC = 1).

If in the second case the facts were $(AB)^2C$, mathematically the decision should be the same as the first: 1. However, there is a factual difference: $(AB)^2$. On this ground the court could consider that the earlier case was not binding upon it, supply a different rule and perhaps come to a different decision, say, 1–n!

There are three categories of *persuasive precedents*. The first is very simple: decisions of lower courts, for example, those of the High Court. The second category covers the decisions of courts that operate systems of law very similar to our own: Commonwealth and American courts and the recommendations of the Privy Council. The last of these is interesting because in theory it is not a court at all but an advisory body to the Sovereign, hence the term 'recommendations'. Its recommendations carry great weight because the 'Law Lords' (the judges who hear appeals in the House of Lords, the final appeal court) sit as the Judicial Committee of the Privy Council. It hears appeals from some domestic tribunals and from some of the UK's former overseas territories, including New Zealand.

In *Tai Hing Cotton Mill Ltd v Liu Chong Hing Bank Ltd* (1985), for example, the Privy Council in an appeal from Hong Kong, reaffirmed the customer's duty to draw cheques with reasonable care in order to prevent fraud (*see London Joint Stock Bank v Macmillan & Arthur* (1918)) but held that there is no wider duty to take reasonable precautions in managing their affairs so as to prevent cheques being forged (for example by being careful where they keep their cheque book). Similarly, the customer's duty to inform their bank of any forged cheque drawn on their account of which they were aware was reaffirmed (*see Greenwood v Martins Bank* (1933)) but no duty to check bank statements for unauthorised debit items was recognised. In the case a dishonest employee of the company had forged some 300 of its cheques involving $HK 5.5m over six years. Despite the company's (obviously) lax financial control system and lack of effective supervision of the employee, the bank was held liable to repay to the company the amount of the cheques!

As you will see later, the two principles reaffirmed by *Tai Hing* are established law but the two other arguments of the bank would have extended the customer's duty considerably. Clearly, the decision is of considerable practical importance to all banks and there is no doubt that other courts will treat the decision as the last word on the subject for the foreseeable future, despite it not having the status of a binding precedent. Clearly, the decision was and is very unpopular with banks.

The third category of persuasive precedents are *obiter dicta* statements (things said by the way), that is, statements of law made by a judge when giving judgment which are not strictly relevant to the issue before the court but which must be treated with respect in later cases. For example, if all five Law Lords in the House of Lords are dealing with an appeal where the facts are ABCDE and they then unanimously state the law as they see it on F, a closely related issue, those statements will be *obiter* because F is not relevant to the appeal. But it is likely that they will be treated as true statements of law in later cases involving F.

In some instances important principles have been introduced into the law through *obiter dicta*. The *obiter* statements made by the House of Lords in *Hedley Byrne & Co Ltd v Heller & Partners Ltd* (1963) are examples which directly affect banks. While the appeal held that a disclaimer on a status enquiry protected the bank from liability in the tort of negligence, the House of Lords forcibly stated that in certain circumstances a person can be liable in tort for making negligent statements which cause purely financial loss to a person who relies on them. Here these statements were *obiter* not because they concerned facts which were not the substance of the action, as in our hypothetical example above (*see* the *High Trees Case* (1947) on page 95 for an actual example of this type of *obiter* statement), but because the appeal was decided on a different issue, the validity of the disclaimer, the House did not base their actual decision on whether a duty of care existed and whether the duty had been broken. (In this particular case, however, it is doubtful how far the statements can be considered *obiter* in practice because they reflected the unanimous opinion of all five Law Lords.)

Case law and the court structure

The operation of the system of judicial precedent is very closely tied to the court structure (*see* Chapter 3). Basically, higher courts bind lower courts. The House of Lords binds all other courts and, except in exceptional circumstances, is bound by its own previous decisions – in 1966, in a Practice Statement, it announced that it would depart from (in effect overrule) its previous decisions where it appeared 'right to do so'. (Before 1966 a House of Lords decision could only be changed by an act of Parliament or avoided by the process of 'distinguishing'.) This power has been sparingly used because the House of Lords must bear in mind the danger of retrospectively disturbing financial and property arrangements and the special need for certainty in the criminal law (in fact it did not expressly overrule a previous decision of its own on criminal law until 1986).

Below the House of Lords the Court of Appeal binds the High Court and County Court but is itself bound by the House of Lords and its own previous decisions. However, in all matters relating to the interpretation of the foundation treaties of the EC, and subsidiary legislation made under them, *all* UK courts must follow the decisions of the European Court of Justice which, interestingly enough, does not operate a system of *binding* precedent.

The advantages and disadvantages of case law

We could at this point just present two lists: one of the advantages and one of the disadvantages. As you will quickly see, however, the advantages and disadvantages tend to cancel each other out. All the comments below can be supported and it is largely a question of which view you prefer. Of course, for you to make your own proper objective judgment, you would need to study the issues in far greater detail than is called for in 'Banking: the Legal Environment'.

The system of binding precedent gives the important advantage of *certainty* to the case law system. It is clearly desirable that banks, their customers, and other businesses and individuals are able to pursue their objectives and consider their positions on the basis of definitive legal rules – you have seen above that the House of Lord's power to depart from its own previous decisions is only rarely used. It is equally desirable that legal advisers are in a position to give objective advice on the basis of these rules. However, the operation of binding precedent may at times make the law rather *rigid*. Although unusual, it is possible for a court to have to follow a rule of law of which it disapproves or which it considers leads to an unfair decision on the particular facts purely because it is bound by a decision of a higher court made many years ago when circumstances were perhaps very different. At the very least this means a time-consuming and expensive appeal to a court able to overrule the earlier decision.

There is an equally strong argument for saying that case law is *flexible*. This is because a general principle of law (*ratio decidendi*) stated in one case can be extended to cover a range of different factual situations. The process of distinguishing a case on the facts also contributes to the flexibility of case law although if used excessively would introduce an unwelcome element of uncertainty. Combined with the advantage of flexibility some say that case law *develops in an orderly fashion*, developing to meet the needs of new situations in business and society generally. It has been 'forged slowly on the anvil of reality' (Kiralfy) – it has a practical character. This is in contrast to legislation which frequently is the result of a deliberate, often politically motivated, attempt to make positive changes to legal rules, leading change rather than reflecting norms.

On the other hand case law is criticised for being *haphazard in its development*, and for *reflecting the law as it was* when the dispute arose and not necessarily stating what it will be in the future. The 18th century scientist and philosopher Bentham described the case law as being 'dogs' law', meaning that the law waited until a dispute arose, and then punished or rewarded as it saw fit, rather than lay down codes of rules (as is typically found in other European countries) against which proposed courses of action could be judged to determine the legal position. He saw this as being a much more scientific approach to law-making and, indeed, the Bills of Exchange Act 1882 and the (original) Sale of Goods Act 1893, among others, are (successful) products of his basic approach.

The fact that case law is flexible and can adapt to different situations also means that it is usually very *precise* in that sufficient research and knowledge will usually turn up a precedent which almost exactly matches the issue in question. On the other hand while electronic legal databases have made research far easier and quicker, the proliferation of situations means that the sheer bulk of case law can make it difficult to use and certainly contributes to the considerable time and cost involved in litigation. Indeed, it is perhaps rather anomalous that while only the House of Lords can make a definitive statement of the common law, appeals only reach the House of Lords if the appellant has the desire to pursue the appeal and the financial resources (which must be very considerable) with which to do so, except where an appeal is funded under the legal aid scheme. There is no process by which uncertainties in the law can be referred to the House of Lords at public expense for a definitive ruling. (This contrasts with the position where a point of EC law is disputed. Here a reference to the European Court *must* be made by the House of Lords where the point of law would determine the result of the appeal. A good example of this occurred in mid-1991 where the House of Lords ruled that the dispute over Sunday trading must be referred to the European Court.)

Case law and banking

With the vast output of modern legislation, banks and banking operations are regulated and affected by legislation more than by case law. For example, all the employment, health and safety and tax legislation applies to banks as it does to other organisations, to say nothing of the impact of the annual Finance Act. However, as you read this book you will see that there are many areas of banking where case law has had and still has a major impact. The onus has to be on you to collect your own examples as you read further. Remember that it is as important to understand and explain the specific importance or effect the case had or has on banking operations as the decision itself. Here we give you just a selection of examples on a few topics; they are not necessarily the most important. If you want to find out more about each, look them up in the index. Alternatively, you could wait until you come to the cases in their specific contexts later in the book. You could also look-up the cases in a casebook dealing with banking law. Reading what happened in greater detail brings the cases to life and makes the principle(s) established easier to understand and remember.

Banker-customer

Surprising though it perhaps is, there are no statutory definitions of either a banker or a customer. Case law provides these: *United Dominions Trust Ltd v*

Kirkwood (1966) and *Ladbroke v Todd* (1914) (among others) respectively. The definition of a customer is particularly important because the statutory protection enjoyed by a collecting bank is only available when the bank acts for a customer.

Other important cases on this topic include *Tournier v National Provincial and Union Bank of England* (1924), which clarified the extent of a bank's duty of secrecy in respect of its customer's account; *London Joint Stock Bank v Macmillan & Arthur* (1918), which established the customer's duty to draw cheques with reasonable care to prevent their fraudulent alteration; and *Lloyds Bank v Bundy* (1975), which established that in certain circumstances a bank can owe a particular customer a duty of care over and above that owed under the basic banker-customer contract.

A case with which you will become increasingly familiar is *Devaynes v Noble* (1816), invariably known as *Clayton's Case*. This established the rule for the appropriation of payments where, as is usually the case, there is no specific appropriation of funds by either debtor or creditor.

Securities

Bank lending to a company on the security of a floating charge, i.e. a charge which covers all assets as they may be at any one time and not a specific asset, was made more problematic by the decision in *Aluminium Industrie Vaasen BV v Romalpa Aluminium Ltd* (1976), always referred to as the *Romalpa Case*. Here it was held that a *retention of title* clause in a supplier's contract with a company defeats a receiver's claim to goods subject to the clause. Continuing this subject, in *Standard Chartered Bank Ltd v Walker and another* (1982), it was held that a debenture holder, e.g. a bank, is liable for a receiver's actions if it gives the receiver specific instructions, even though the receiver is specifically appointed as the agent of the company. Clearly a bank must be careful.

The decision in *Williams & Glyn's Bank Ltd v Boland and another* (1980), illustrates just how important it is for a bank (indeed, any mortgagee or purchaser) to make adequate enquiries into possible rights of occupation in land offered as security or for sale, although this case was *distinguished*, much to mortgagees' and purchasers' relief, in *City of London Building Society v Flegg* (1987).

Another decision welcome to banks was *National Westminster Bank Plc v Morgan* (1985). When a customer gives a guarantee as security there is always the possibility that the customer will subsequently seek to set it aside by claiming that the bank exercised undue influence to obtain it. This House of Lords decision, by emphasising that the weaker party must show that they were taken advantage of by the stronger, significantly reduces the likelihood of such an argument succeeding.

Cheques

Here it is really a question of which cases to choose. The following are four of the best known. *Greenwood v Martins Bank* (1933), established that a customer is *estopped* (prevented) from denying that what is in reality a forged cheque is genuine where s/he was aware of the forgery but did not inform the bank. Thus, the bank can debit the account. (We could equally have included this example in the first topic.) *Curtice v London City and Midland Bank Ltd* (1908), established that notice of countermand is ineffective unless and until it comes to the bank's actual attention. In connection with the collection of cheques, *Ladbroke & Co v Todd* (1914), established that a bank is *prima facie* negligent if it opens an account without first making reasonable enquiries and *Midland Bank Ltd v Reckitt* (1938), established that it is similarly *prima facie* negligent for a bank to credit a private account of an agent with a cheque drawn by the agent on the account of their principal.

ACTIVITY 2.1

(a) For each of the cases listed below make sure you can state the *ratio decidendi* or *obiter dicta* (as appropriate) of the case, say whether they are examples of binding or persuasive precedents and explain their relevance to banking. Examination questions quite frequently ask you to do just this. (You may wish to add to your responses after you have considered the cases in full later in your studies. You can of course add to the list – ours contains the more obvious examples.) In no particular order:

Tai Hing Cotton Mill Case (1985)
UDT v Kirkwood (1966)
London Joint Stock Bank v Macmillan & Arthur (1918)
Williams & Glyn's Bank Ltd v Boland (1980)
City of London Building Soc v Flegg (1987)
National Westminster Bank v Morgan (1985)
Tournier's Case (1924)
Curtice v London City and Midland Bank (1908)
Hedley Byrne (1963)
Clayton's Case (1816)
Ladbroke v Todd (1914)

(b) Your college library will almost certainly contain at least one set of law reports. While we don't expect you to read them regularly, you would find it interesting to look up one or two of the leading cases (preferably the more recent ones) we refer to in the law reports and read the summary of the decision and at least part of the judge's statement.

Remember also that *The Times* carries law reports on most days and if you have the opportunity you should read any report that has obvious relevance to banking, similarly the 'Courts' section in *Banking World*.

■ LEGISLATION

The common law – the system of judge-made law originating in custom – was designed to order a socially simple, economically underdeveloped and politically uneducated society. It existed largely to serve the interests and needs of the ruling elite (the nobility and landed gentry) from whose number almost all the judges were drawn. Consequently, the common law clearly reflected their interests in preserving property rights and the social *status quo,* for these were the bastions of their privileged position.

Such a system, reflecting interests and values perfectly typical of underdeveloped societies both before and since, could not survive the tremendous social and economic upheavals brought about by the Industrial Revolution in the 18th and 19th centuries. The population dramatically increased, new towns grew up almost overnight and completely new problems of government associated with urban living and an industrialising society arose. A new, creative type of law-making was needed: Parliamentary legislation.

While there are a number of well-known statutes from earlier centuries, legislation only became an important source of law in the second half of the 19th century. In particular, the basis of commercial law affecting banks and other business organisations today was codified into statutory form in this period, e.g. the Bills of Exchange Act 1882, the Factors Act 1889, the Partnership Act 1890 and the (original) Sale of Goods Act 1893. Since the end of the Second World War in 1945 legislation has been totally dominant as the main source of law and the annual output of acts and orders made under their authority has reached staggering proportions. The structure and regulation of modern British society and, indeed, the business of banking is now very heavily dependent on legislation.

Domestic legislation takes two forms: acts of Parliament and delegated legislation. In addition we must consider EC legislation.

Acts of Parliament

These may be defined as the will of a democratically elected assembly confirmed by the Sovereign. Acts of Parliament are the supreme form of law and they can change, repeal or create law. Since the Bill of Rights 1688, the judges have recognised the supremacy of Parliament and, while they are able to interpret an act when its meaning is ambiguous or obscure, they have no right to challenge the act itself. We have already considered legislation as a 'type' of law in Chapter 1. Re-read the relevant pages now.

How a bill becomes an act

The progress of a typical bill through Parliament is illustrated in Figure 2.1. Study it carefully.

Most bills that run the full course and become law are government sponsored and start off along the 'Green Paper, White Paper' trail. There is only a small amount of time for *private members' bills* and there is actually a lottery to decide who will be allowed to introduce them. Nevertheless, private members' bills have often introduced important non-party political legislation, e.g. reform of the law on homosexuality.

The amount of time a bill takes to pass through Parliament varies enormously; it depends on the amount of opposition to it and the degree of government urgency. For example, the Prevention of Terrorism Act 1974 was introduced into Parliament on the morning of 27 November 1974 and received the Royal Assent at 9.40 am two days later.

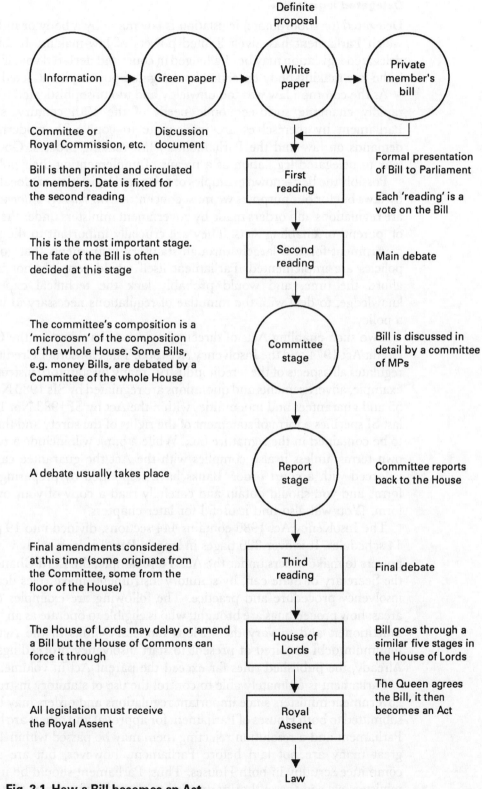

Fig. 2.1 How a Bill becomes an Act

Delegated legislation

Delegated (or subordinate) legislation is law made by a body or individual to which Parliament has given limited powers of law-making. It follows that delegated legislation may be challenged in court and declared void if in making it the law-making body exceeded its delegated powers, i.e. it acted *ultra vires*.

As the common law was too unwieldy and too unsophisticated to serve the rapidly changing socio-economic needs of the 19th century, so acts of Parliament by themselves are inadequate to cope with modern society's demands on law and the Parliamentary law-making process. Governments look to delegated legislation as a means of implementing their policies.

Possibly the best-known examples of delegated legislation are local authority by-laws but for our purposes we must concentrate on *statutory instruments*. These are regulations and orders made by government ministers under the authority of 'parent' or enabling Acts. They are crucially important to the process of government for it is largely through statutory instruments that government policies are implemented. Parliament itself would certainly not be able to afford the time, and would probably lack the technical expertise and knowledge, to deal with the minutiae of regulations necessary to implement a policy.

Two such enabling Acts of direct relevance to banking are the Consumer Credit Act 1974 and the Insolvency Act 1986. The Consumer Credit Act 1974 regulates all aspects of the 'credit industry', many by statutory instrument. For example, advertisements and quotations are regulated by SIs 1980 Nos. 54 and 55 and guarantees and indemnities within the Act by SI 1983 No. 1556. This last SI specifies a form of statement of the rights of the surety and the wording to be contained in the signature box. While a bank will include a range of its own terms, unless it also complies with the Act the guarantee can only be enforced with a court order. Banks have responded by preparing standard forms and you should obtain and carefully read a copy of your own bank's form. (You will also find it useful for later chapters.)

The Insolvency Act 1986 contains 444 sections, divided into 19 parts, and 14 schedules. It is over 320 pages in length. Part 15 deals solely with various powers to make orders under the Act. For example, the Lord Chancellor and the Secretary of State can, by statutory instrument, make rules dealing with insolvency procedure and practice. The following are examples of specific areas: how proceedings are brought; who is eligible to operate as an insolvency practitioner; and to vary the various monetary limits in the Act, e.g. the minimum debt required at present to start insolvency proceedings is £750. Already, the published rules far exceed the parent Act in volume!

Parliament is ultimately able to control the use of statutory instruments by government ministers since important regulations and orders may have to be submitted to both Houses of Parliament for approval and others are laid before Parliament and a resolution rejecting them may be passed within 40 days. A great many are not laid before Parliament, however, but are subject to committee scrutiny in both Houses. Thus, Parliament should be informed if ministers exceed the authority granted to them by the parent Act.

Advantages and disadvantages of legislation

First and foremost, legislation is the only constitutional way of changing the law – as you read above, it can be used to create, alter and repeal law. About this there is no doubt but as with our similar discussion of case law, the advantages and disadvantages tend to counter balance each other. First we deal with legislation generally and then consider delegated legislation specifically.

Legislation is the product of a *democratically elected body*, not the product of decisions of a male-dominated, (arguably) elite handful of judges. Against this we can say that *party politics* greatly influences both the legislative process and the legislation itself. While this is inevitable (law can never be completely divorced from politics), it remains a fact that recent governments have been elected by a minority of the total votes cast. In addition, some legislation is far too technical or specialised for the majority of MPs to fully understand. The virtue of debate in Parliament can therefore be overstated.

Legislation is intended to be *comprehensive* and *definite* and it provides a code against which future conduct can be judged – it is not based on past situations as is case law – and it can deal with hypothetical situations. However, because of the need to be precise and to avoid loopholes, it is often *difficult for non-lawyers to follow* and its sheer *volume* can be daunting. It can also never hope to cover all possible situations. Legislation is *subject to interpretation* by the courts and it can be argued that to a degree this introduces an element of uncertainty. Indeed, on occasions it can result in law somewhat different from that intended by Parliament.

Delegated legislation has a number of very important advantages. For example, it can be *made speedily* – particularly important when Parliament is not in session or unforeseen events occur; it is more *flexible* and it relieves pressure on Parliament's time. It also enables highly complicated issues to be considered by specialists and highly detailed regulations to be made by Ministers where necessary; Parliament cannot, nor should, be expected to do this.

The main disadvantages of delegated legislation are that Parliament's control over legislation is reduced and there is arguably *too much* of it and as it often receives little publicity and it is therefore sometimes difficult to determine what the law actually is! Thus, it is important that delegated legislation is effectively controlled.

EC legislation

In addition to the two forms of domestic legislation, the UK is subject to the supra-national legislation of the European Communities.

Here there is a basic distinction between *primary* and *secondary* legislation and a further distinction between legislation which is directly applicable to the population of each member state and legislation which requires further action by member states for its implementation.

Primary legislation is Community law contained in the Articles of the main treaties, primarily the Treaty of Rome 1957 which established the EC. It takes precedence over domestic law, although domestic legislation may sometimes be required to implement it. Secondary legislation is the law made by the Council of Ministers and the Commission (which together with the European Parliament form the 'government' of the Community) under authority conferred on them by the Treaty of Rome.

The main treaties are not open to review by either the European Court of Justice or our own courts, although both may interpret them. Secondary legislation is open to review on the grounds that it is *ultra vires* (beyond the powers of) the Council of Ministers or the Commission, or because the proper procedures have not been followed.

Types of EC secondary legislation

Secondary legislation takes three forms.

- *Regulations* apply directly to the population of the Community. They automatically form part of the law of member states.
- *Directives* are binding instructions to member states but they are not directly applicable. The member states must take appropriate steps to implement them.
- *Decisions* are directly binding but they are addressed to specific individuals or organisations within the member states and not to the population generally.

In the UK, *directives* are normally implemented by statutory instrument under existing legislation. However, the First Banking Directive (in 1977) was implemented in the UK by Banking Act 1979, although many of its main provisions were not actually required by the Directive, and the Consolidated Supervision Directive (in 1983) was implemented partly by the publication of a Bank of England statement of policy in March 1986.

The First Banking Directive sought to harmonise the law on credit institutions within the Community by the end of 1979. It required Member States to abolish restrictions preventing banks and other financial institutions from establishing themselves or providing services in the host country under the same conditions and with the same rights as nationals of that country, and to abolish administrative practices which discriminated in favour of national institutions. For example, the UK was obliged to abolish the requirement that any company intending to operate as a manager and trustee of a unit trust in the UK must be constituted in the UK. The First Directive was one of the immediate reasons for the passing of the Banking Act 1979.

The Consolidated Supervision Directive requires that the supervision of any credit institution, and any other credit or financial institution in which it has a substantial interest, must be on a consolidated basis, i.e. they must be supervised together. Its rationale is that consolidated supervision enables the authorities supervising a parent credit institution to make a sounder judgment about the financial situation of that credit institution. In practice, the Bank of England was already applying this principle but it was considered that a more systematic system was desirable and additional reporting requirements were introduced by the Bank's policy statement.

The Second Banking Directive (as it is known) was agreed in December 1989 and must be implemented by all Member States by the start of 1993. This Directive is central to the EC's policy relating to banking. Its ultimate aim is to provide, in the long term, full freedom of financial services in the Community. The key feature of the Directive is the 'single banking licence'. It enables any bank validly established and licensed in one Member State to conduct banking business in any other Member State through a branch in the other Member State or, if it has no branches there, directly from its home State without having to obtain further authorisation.

ACTIVITY 2.2

Discover other EC directives relevant to banking.

The effect of Community law in the UK

By the European Communities Act 1972 the UK acceded to the Treaties constituting the European Communities. By so doing a system of supra-national law – often binding upon organisations and individuals without further Parliamentary enactment – was introduced into this country. Law which was inconsistent with Community law was repealed by implication, e.g. laws relating to trade tariffs and customs duties.

The supra-national structure of Community law clearly affects the principle of *Parliamentary supremacy*. This declares that within the UK only Parliament has the right to make law and that no one Parliament can bind its successors, i.e. any Act passed can be repealed. However, for three reasons this effect is not so drastic as it may seem.

- Community law does not affect any of the matters which concern solely the UK – domestic law is unaffected.
- Parliamentary supremacy must be seen in political as well as legal terms. Thus, while the repeal of any Act, including the European Communities Act 1972, is legally possible, political considerations may make it impossible. Britain could hardly repeal the various Acts giving Commonwealth countries their independence and it would be a politically extreme step, and very probably disastrous to the economy, to repeal the 1972 Act.
- Community law affects the sovereignty of all member states and not just the UK – sovereignty can be viewed as a legal and political commodity which can be traded among the members states to (hopefully) the economic benefit of all.

Until 1985 Community law operated on the basis of 'harmonisation' of the relevant law of the Member States, i.e. laws should progressively become the same. This proved to be too complex to be practical and little progress was achieved. Since 1985 the Community has operated on the basis of 'mutual recognition' of each Member State's regulations with only the minimum degree of harmonisation – of the basic ground rules – necessary to make mutual recognition feasible.

Legislation affecting banks

Where do we start? The choice is enormous. We could, for example, spend time considering the various Employment Acts and the Health and Safety at Work Act 1974 since these regulate the banking industry every bit as much as the Consumer Credit Act 1974. However, we will consider just a few examples of legislation which affect aspects of mainstream banking operations. Once again, it is up to you to collect your own additional examples.

Bankers Books Evidence Act 1879

Under the Act any party to legal proceedings is able to obtain a court order enabling them to inspect entries and take copies of those entries in the banker's books. A banker's books include ledgers, day books, cash books, account books and other records used in the course of the bank's ordinary business. These records may be kept in written form, on microfilm, magnetic tape or by any form of mechanical or electronic data retrieval system. Correspondence does not form part of a banker's books and therefore a bank cannot be made to produce it under an order made under the Act. (This would, however, be possible as part of a witness summons.) The Act further provides that a duly authenticated copy of any entry in the books can be used as evidence in all legal proceedings. Thus, the bank is able to produce certified copies of book entries instead of the books themselves.

Bills of Exchange Act 1882

This example of late 19th century commercial law codification is still fundamentally important to banks. Despite the decline in the use of bills of exchange other than cheques, the Act still gives banks limited but vital protection in paying cheques – obviously a mainstream activity. Section 60 is particularly important in this context and we cover it fully in Chapter 8. In addition, the Act defines both bills of exchange generally and cheques specifically, crossings and a 'holder in due course' – an important creature with whom you will become well acquainted in the future. In branches which deal with bills of exchange – those which handle overseas trade – virtually all banking operations in relation to bills are dictated by the Act.

Cheques Act 1957

This act amended the position under the 1882 Act with regard to cheques. In particular, s.4 gives banks limited protection in the collection of cheques and s.1 is important in paying cheques. Again, we cover these topics in Chapter 8. Together with the rules of the Committee of London & Scottish Clearing Banks (now wound up and its work taken over by the British Bankers' Association as from April 1991), this Act, the 1882 Act and the many important cases on their implementation, provide a total regulatory and protective framework within which cheques are collected the paid. (Note, however, that neither this Act nor the 1882 Act provides any legal framework for electronic payment systems or the use of credit and debit cards.)

Consumer Credit Act 1974

This Act merits more detailed consideration and it is convenient to deal with it as a whole at this point. Besides, it provides a good example of how all-embracing a single piece of legislation can be. It is of course an excellent example of statutory intervention in contractual arrangements (*see* Chapters 4 and 5). The Act regulates all credit facilities up to £15,000 provided to private individuals, sole traders, partnerships and other unincorporated bodies (organisations without a legal existence separate from their members), such as societies and associations. Thus, it affects hire purchase and rental companies, moneylenders and pawnbrokers and a host of professional people besides all banks. In addition, it also regulates ancillary businesses such as credit and mortgage brokers, debt collectors, debt adjusters and counsellors, and credit reference agencies.

Purpose of the Act. The main purpose of the Act is to prevent the exploitation of individuals by unscrupulous suppliers of credit by providing an effective means of controlling a wide range of consumer credit transactions. It seeks to do this by:

- supervising all those involved in granting credit through a licensing system;
- regulating the contract between lender and borrower;
- controlling the advertising and canvassing of credit.

For example, the contact must include terms relating to the amount of credit, the credit limit, the rate of interest and the repayments. If such prescribed terms are not included, the agreement is wholly unenforceable. Thus, the debtor is given (statutory) rights which are quite independent of the express terms of the contract.

Remember, however, that the Act does not regulate the provision of credit to registered companies and other corporate bodies, nor credit in excess of £15,000 to anyone.

Major provisions of the Act. 1 *Licensing* All businesses that provide credit, lend money or hire goods within the Act's provisions, or engage in ancillary credit activities must be *licensed*. Licences are issued by the Office of Fair Trading and it is a criminal offence to engage unlicensed in such activities. It follows that you must ensure that any customers who are involved in the industry are properly licensed before making loans to them. For example, advances secured by charges over rental or hire purchase agreements would be put at risk if they were not.

2 *Advertising* The Act imposes restrictions on the mode of advertising for credit and gives potential borrowers the right to ask for quotations of the true cost of the credit available. This enables them to shop around with confidence to get the best terms to suit their requirements. Remember, of course, that while banks compete with each other there is, in practice, very little difference between the terms which they offer borrowers. All banks are subject to the same market forces and the same legal regulations.

3 *Canvassing* This consists of deliberately attempting to persuade an individual

to enter into an agreement for credit facilities and/or to accept an ancillary credit service by making oral representations to the individual when:

- not previously requested to do so in writing; and
- where a visit is made in order to persuade the individual to enter into such an agreement.

Canvassing prohibitions only apply to *debtor-creditor* agreements, that is agreements which only involve the lender and the borrower, not a third party supplier of goods or services (*see* below, *debtor-creditor-supplier agreements*).

In so far as banks are concerned, there are two categories of business covered by the *canvassing prohibitions*. These are:

- almost any type of advance and further advance, including credit cards, that separately do not exceed £15,000; and
- certain brokerage arrangements, debt adjusting and debt counselling.

The prohibitions make it a criminal offence to canvass either type of business when not on *trade premises*. (The canvassing of *overdrafts for existing customers* is permitted.)

Branches and other bank offices are clearly trade premises but problems can arise with the premises of a customer or prospective customer. For example, factories and offices are not the trade premises of the employees working in them and the office of a managing director of a company would not be trade premises in relation to personal business. Canvassing of a private customer must not take place off bank premises without a prior written invitation.

Remember that the restrictions do not apply where the customer or prospective customer is a company or other corporate body, nor where the credit facility under discussion exceeds £15,000. Again, restrictions do not apply to telephone conversations, letters, circulars and leaflets (other than to minors), where the customer or prospective customer initiates the discussion about credit facilities, and to speaking engagements to talk about bank services provided only general references to credit facilities and ancillary services are made.

Particular restrictions apply to canvassing *minors*. It is an offence to send a circular or any document to a minor which invites the minor to borrow money or use other credit facilities, including credit cards, or to apply for information or advice on obtaining credit or credit services.

It is also an offence under the Act to send a credit token, for example a credit card, to anybody unless requested in writing by that person to do so. Cash dispenser cards (unless combined with a charge or credit card with cash withdrawals being debited to the charge or credit card account) and cheque guarantee cards are not credit tokens because they give no automatic entitlement to credit.

4 *Regulated agreements* The Act prescribes the form and content of certain agreements and provides that copies must be supplied to the prospective borrower. These are known as regulated agreements. Loans, overdrafts and credit card facilities are all regulated agreements. One important point is that

a running-account credit facility, e.g. an overdraft, will still qualify as a regulated consumer credit agreement provided the limit is over £15,000 provided the borrower cannot draw, or is unlikely to draw, more than £15,000 at any one time.

While both are regulated agreements, a loan (fixed sum credit) requires a signed written agreement in the prescribed form, but an overdraft facility (running-account credit) is exempt from the documentation requirements of the Act.

A regulated agreement can be cancelled by written notice within the five days (the 'cooling-off period) after receiving a second copy of the agreement or a statutory cancellation notice by post provided that:

- the agreement was *not* signed by the debtor on the bank's (creditor's) premises or on the trade premises of any other party involved in the overall arrangement (technically the supplier of goods and services under a debtor-creditor-supplier agreement: *see* below); or
- there were face-to-face discussions between the bank (the creditor) and the debtor before the debtor signed the agreement. (It follows that prior discussion over the telephone or negotiations by letter do *not* make the agreement cancellable.)

In fact, banks normally regard *any* agreement not signed on bank premises as cancellable.

An agreement secured on land (an example of an exempt agreement, *see* below) is *not* cancellable but the Act allows a customer to *withdraw* from the agreement before it is ever (legally) entered into. A *consideration period* of at least fourteen days is given during which period the bank cannot approach the customer about the proposed loan and during which period the borrower can withdraw from the proposed agreement.

Failure to comply with the Act's regulations renders the agreement unenforceable without a court order. The court can vary or impose terms or suspend the agreement. These powers extend to any securities taken in connection with the loan.

An *exempt agreement* is one which is not regulated by the provisions of the Act. Such agreements important to lending banks are loans secured by mortgages on land and advances to finance the export of goods and services.

5 *Debtor-creditor-supplier agreements* Provided a pre-existing arrangement exists between a lender and the supplier of goods or services to an individual, the lender will be *jointly and severally liable* with the supplier for any *misrepresentation* or *breach of contract* by the latter. In relation to banks, such an agreement must involve an arrangement between the bank and a supplier whereby the bank is prepared to consider providing finance to enable a prospective purchaser to buy goods and/or services from the supplier. Such an agreement may be quite loose, for example, a debtor-creditor-supplier agreement might be held to exist if the bank's advertising materials are displayed in the supplier's premises or if the bank encourages the supplier to send customers to its branches. Classic example of debtor-creditor-supplier agreements are retail-

ers' schemes where purchases are financed by loans from a third party finance company, and credit card schemes.

6 *Charge for credit* The total charge must include not only the *interest payments* but also *all other charges* payable under the agreement or transactions made in connection with it, for example, a security arrangement. The total charge is converted into a rate of total charge for credit, the annual percentage rate of charge or APR. This enables a prospective lender to make objective comparisons among different credit facilities and different financial institutions.

Implementing the Act. Both bankers and lawyers consider the Consumer Credit Act to be a highly technical piece of legislation; very few would claim to be completely conversant with it. Because of this, banks have adopted a centralised approach to implementing its provisions. Branches follow procedures determined by specialists at head offices – there is no room for local interpretation – and in this way are able to comply with the Act without problems. What are your own bank's procedures, particularly in relation to signing, withdrawing from and cancelling agreements? Fortunately, few customers ever ask for explanations of the Act's regulations – they are solely concerned with whether or not they are going to be given credit and how much it is going to cost them!

Sex Discrimination Act 1975

This is important in the employment of staff but it also has important effects in banking operations. A few examples will illustrate this. When opening an account for a married woman, case law requires the bank to obtain details of her husband's employment (*Lloyds Bank Ltd v Savory & Co* (1933)) but not vice versa if the husband opens an account. Similarly, the numerous problems, in particular with undue influence, which have arisen when wives have guaranteed lending to their husbands, or to companies controlled by their husbands, indicate that wives should be asked to sign a *free will* clause. Both these practices are almost certainly contrary to the 1975 Act. What are the practices of your bank in these situations? Find out.

Unfair Contract Terms Act 1977

This is a landmark in consumer protection. It restricts the extent to which liability for breach of contract and negligence can be avoided. With the exception of liability for breach of implied obligations in sales of goods and hire purchase, neither of which need concern us here, the Act regulates only *business liability*, i.e. liability arising from activities in the course of a business or from the occupation of business premises. The purpose of the Act is to allow legitimate disclaimers of liability and exclusion clauses, such as those found in insurance contracts, while protecting consumers (particularly) and businesses from completely unfair practices.

Liability for the sort of loss, that is financial, likely to arise from a bank's *negligence* can only be restricted or excluded under the Act in so far as a disclaimer or relevant exclusion clause (an express term of a contract) satisfies a test of *reasonableness*. The former, for example, covers status enquiries (no contract is involved here); the disclaimer on which the bank successfully relied in *Hedley Byrne & Co Ltd v Heller & Partners Ltd* (1963) would now have been subject to the test and it would now be up to the bank to prove that it was reasonable. (It remains to be established whether a bank can successfully argue that such a blanket disclaimer is 'reasonable'.)

Furthermore, where one party deals as a consumer (for our purposes, a private customer) or on the other's written standard terms of business, any exclusion of liability for *breach of contract* must satisfy the reasonableness test if it is relied on as a defence. Since a bank will invariably seek to contract on its own standard terms in its dealings with business customers, the vast majority of contracts that a bank enters into are covered by this provision.

As a consequence of the Act, any exclusion clause in a bank contract or disclaimer is potentially subject to challenge under the Act. Banks have, however, a strong interest in representing themselves as 'fair' organisations and they take care that such terms are reasonable. It is unlikely, therefore, that a bank contract has been or will be challenged under the Act.

Supply of Goods and Services Act 1982

This Act basically states that a contract for services must be performed with a reasonable degree of care and skill (s.13). This duty takes the form of an unexcludable implied term in the contract, i.e. a term which the parties have not expressly agreed to but which nevertheless forms part of the contract because the Act says so.

It may seem inappropriate to class banks with less than reputable plumbers and garages but it covers the reputable and less reputable alike. Thus, many financial services offered by banks are subject to the Act, the giving of financial advice for example. Actions against banks (or threats of) under the Act must be extremely rare. This is partly because banks offer a high standard of service; partly because it is usually in their interests to offer compensation to prevent an action going to court; and partly because advice is always offered with a 'without responsibility' contractual disclaimer. While such a disclaimer would not protect a bank from liability for breach of s.13, it would, in principle, protect it from legal action for giving poor or inaccurate advice, provided, of course, that it had shown reasonable care and skill. As you have seen, however, such disclaimers can always be challenged under the Unfair Contract Terms Act 1977.

Data Protection Act 1984

All information on individuals (not companies) stored on computer is covered by this Act. Anyone (a data user) holding such information must register with the Data Protection Registrar and his Register must show:

- the source of the information;
- the purpose for which it was obtained;
- to whom it may be disclosed.

Banks hold vast stores of such information but much of it is not computerised at present. However, it is clear that the balance will steadily change and therefore this Act will become of increasing importance to everyday banking.

Data must only be held for a purpose that has been registered, it must be accurate and up-to-date, and it must not be disclosed except as specified in the Register. Opinions on race, sex, religion and politics are not to be recorded and details of an individual's mental or physical health must only be recorded if they are relevant to the bank's relationship with the individual. The moral for banks is clear – they must register all possible purposes for which they may wish to use information on their customers and be very careful what information is held. For example, personal information obtained when an account is opened can only be used for marketing purposes if marketing is a registered use. Remember also that an individual (a data subject) has the right to access to such data and have incorrect information corrected or removed.

Companies Act 1985

This important Act consolidated the statutory law on companies and is the framework within which all companies operate, including banks. You are most concerned with how the Act regulates taking security from companies, guarantees and charges for example, and the steps necessary to protect it.

Note that the Companies Act 1989 amended the 1985 Act in relation to taking charges from companies and virtually abolishes the once important *ultra vires* (beyond the powers of) rule.

Insolvency Act 1986

Since most businesses depend, at least to some extent, on loans from banks, any insolvency – corporate or individual – is likely to involve a bank. Thus, while it is a somewhat specialist area, recovery work (as it is usually known) is an important aspect of the business of banking. We have already explained a more technical aspect of banks' use of the Act in Chapter 1, here we look at its general aims.

The Act aims to establish effective and straightforward procedures which will encourage companies and individuals to recognise their financial difficulties at an early stage and act in the interests of their creditors. It also includes penalties for irresponsible behaviour and malpractice by company managers and introduces licensing for those employed to handle insolvencies – insolvency practitioners.

In addition to involvement through its lending, a bank can easily become involved in an insolvency merely by operating an account for the company or individual. Limited protection is given to a bank that operates a debtor's account in good faith. To go deeper at this point would be too technical; you will study insolvency law in the Associateship examinations should you decide to continue with your studies.

Drug Trafficking Offences Act 1986

This Act added another specific exception to a bank's duty not to disclose information about its customers' affairs. However, it also imposes obligations on banks which may cause practical problems. In an effort to prevent drug traffickers 'laundering' their money, the Act makes it a criminal offence if any person knowing or suspecting that another trafficks, or has trafficked in drugs, or has benefited from drug trafficking, retains or controls the proceeds of drug trafficking or places the funds so obtained at that other's disposal. No offence is committed if the suspicion is disclosed to the police as soon as reasonably possible. Case law makes it clear that suspicion means just that, proof is not required before the obligation to inform the police arises. Bank practice may therefore require a bank to inspect credits as they come in and make enquiries of, for example, large, unexpected or regular cash deposits. This can obviously be a delicate matter.

Financial Services Act 1986

The Financial Services Act 1986 established a system for regulating the conduct of investment business with the aims of encouraging competition among financial organisations and promoting confidence among investors. The Act relies on a system of *self-regulation* by the financial services industry controlled by the Securities and Investment Board (SIB), a private limited company but in effect a government agency. All investment businesses must obtain authorisation for their activities either from the SIB directly or, more usually, by being a member of one of a number of Self Regulatory Organisations (SROs) which the SIB has recognised. It is a criminal offence to conduct investment business without authorisation.

Investments subject to the Act include stocks and shares, debentures, certificates of deposit, government and local authority bonds, unit trusts and long-term life assurance contracts. Bank deposits are excluded. Investment dealing is defined as dealing, arranging deals, managing and advising on any investment product. From this you can see that the modern bank – the 'financial supermarket' – offering, for example, investment, pension fund and unit trusts management, life assurance, insurance broking, trusteeship, the offer of securities and applications for listing, to say nothing of day-to-day advice to customers, is subject to the Act. In some cases, companies within a bank group have had to become members of several SROs because their business spans their remits. (What is the practice of your bank with respect to the Act?)

Banking Act 1987

The Banking Act 1987 was passed as a result of the necessary 'rescue' of Johnson Matthey Bankers in 1984. It replaced the Banking Act 1979 which itself was a response to the secondary banking crisis of 1973–4, caused by a number of 'fringe banks' getting into difficulties by borrowing short and lending long. In doing so it abolishes the previous two-tier system of recognised banks and licensed deposit-takers, replacing it with the single designation of 'authorised institution'.

The main purpose of the Act is *prudential supervision*. It provides a statutory basis for the Bank of England's supervision of banks and other deposit-taking businesses and backs this up with a deposit protection scheme to cover any failures which may still occur. It does not directly regulate day-to-day banking operations.

Deposit taking. All deposit-taking institutions must be authorised by the Bank of England unless an institution falls within one of a number of specific exemptions. Building societies and local authorities, for example, are exempt.

The most important condition for authorisation is that the business must be conducted in a prudent manner. In particular, the institution must have adequate capital and liquidity, make adequate provision for depreciation and doubtful debts and maintain adequate accounting and other record and control systems. The Bank is not bound to follow rigid ratio requirements and it is therefore able to make *qualitative* judgments as to whether a business is adequately capitalised and being prudently run. Any new institution, however, must have net assets of at least £1m at the time of authorisation.

The Act also regulates the issue, form and content of advertisements for deposits and requires overseas banks establishing offices in the UK to give notice to the Bank.

Use of the name 'bank'. This is restricted to larger institutions, those with a capital of £5m or more although this test does not apply to overseas authorised institutions.

The deposit protection scheme. This provides a measure of protection to small depositors if an authorised institution becomes insolvent. All such institutions must contribute to a central fund, the resources of which would be used to pay any depositor who had lost money in a 'bank failure'. Payments to depositors are limited to 75 per cent of the amount lost up to a maximum deposit of £20,000, i.e. they can actually recover a maximum of £15,000. The size of each institution's contribution to the central fund is proportional to the size of its deposit base, that is 0.3 per cent of its deposit base up to a maximum of £300,000, with a minimum contribution of £10,000. The fund's assets total £5–6 million.

Changes in control. The Bank of England has the power to block changes in the controlling shareholders of authorised institutions incorporated in the UK if it considers that the would-be controllers are not 'fit and proper' persons. Specifically, no shareholder may acquire a fifteen per cent or more stake without the Bank's prior consent nor an existing shareholder a majority shareholding.

Law of Property (Miscellaneous Provisions) Act 1989

This Act is an excellent example of how a simple (and sensible) change in the law can result in changes in a bank's procedures – in this case, those for taking security over land and buildings.

Section two of the Act provides that a contract for the sale or other disposition of an interest in land, such as a mortgage, must:

- be made in writing;
- incorporate in one contract all the terms the parties have expressly agreed (if contracts are exchanged, as in the sale of a house, in both);
- be signed by each party.

Before the Act came into force, such a contract could be made orally provided there was written evidence of it, such as a letter, signed by the person it was sought to hold liable on the contract.

The most important consequence of the Act is that security on land cannot be accepted merely by deposit of title deeds, there must be 'memorandum of deposit' of the agreement (the contract) which is signed by the customer *and* the bank. Before the Act the deposit of the deeds alone would create an equitable mortgage over the land and while it was usual to ask for a memorandum of deposit to be signed by the customer, there was no need for the bank to sign it. (Note that a legal mortgage over land must be executed by deed since this actually creates an interest in land, it is not just a contract to do so, *see* Chapter 7.)

A further change is that banks have ceased to grant facilities such as overdrafts on the basis of an oral agreement enforced by a subsequent letter where land is to be the security offered. The customer and the bank must both sign a written contract in which the customer undertakes to provide the security.

Another change made by the Act is to abolish the age old practice of sealing deeds made by *individuals*, a practice which although originally important to authenticate deeds had for a long time been based purely on tradition. A deed must now be signed in the presence of a witness who must in turn attest the signature (sign to confirm that the signature is genuine). If not properly executed, the instrument (document) is void as a deed. Thus, the appearance of deeds used by banks – when taking a legal mortgage over land for example – have changed. (Deeds should never be posted to customers for execution just in case they are inadvertently avoided by not being signed in the presence of the witness.)

Companies Act 1989

This Act makes a number of important changes to company law; here we are concerned with just one, the virtual abolition of the *ultra vires* rule (the principle that a company could not legally act outside the powers which its memorandum of association gave it).

The 1989 Act substitutes a new s.35 into the Companies Act 1985. This states that the validity of an act done by a company cannot be questioned on the grounds of *lack of corporate capacity* irrespective of anything contained within the registered objects of the company. Furthermore, if a person deals with a company in *good faith* the powers of the directors are not limited by anything which might be stated in the company's constitution (its memorandum and articles of association).

The virtual abolition of the rule affects banks in the following way. Banks will always at least have sight, and probably take a file copy, of the memorandum and articles of association of their company customers. It was generally thought that this would prevent a bank establishing that it had acted in good faith if the transaction was *ultra vires* the directors, e.g. loans entered into by directors acting *ultra vires* would be irrecoverable because it would (or should) have known that they had no authority to enter into the agreement. The new s.35 expressly provides that knowledge that the directors acted *ultra vires* does not, of itself, amount to a lack of good faith. This would assist a bank where branch A had knowledge of the memorandum but branch B, which did not, lent the company money for an *ultra vires* purpose. Branch B would here be acting in good faith within the meaning of the Act and could enforce the loan. If branch A lent the money, presumably it would be acting in bad faith and could not. In practice, of course, where large loans are arranged, banks should continue to ensure that they are made for purposes within the objects of the company.

ACTIVITY 2.3

Essentially we want you to repeat the previous activity, but this time in relation to legislation. Write a *short* summary of what each to the Acts listed below do and how they affect the business of banking. Work on the principle that in an examination each would be worth five marks and you need three good points about the Act and two good points about the effect of the Act – an easy way to score good marks don't you think!

Bills of Exchange Act 1882	Cheques Act 1957
Consumer Credit Act 1974	Sex Discrimination Act 1975
Data Protection Act 1984	Drug Trafficking Offences Act 1986
Financial Services Act 1986	Banking Act 1987

Of course, you're not limited to these Acts and in fact the examiners welcome more original ones. For example, you could use various employment Acts or health and safety legislation (if you have information readily available). And don't forget any new legislation – knowledge and understanding of recent legislation impresses greatly.

The interpretation of statutes

Some examples

Under s.75 of the Bills of Exchange Act 1882, a bank's authority to pay a cheque is determined by a 'countermand of payment'. Simple, or is it? In *Curtice v London, City and Midland Bank Ltd* (1908), Curtice, a customer of the defendant bank, purchased some horses from a Mr Jones on the 31 October and issued a cheque for £63 in payment. However, the horses were not delivered as promised and later that day Curtice sent a telegram to the bank instructing it to stop payment of the cheque. On the evening of the same day the telegram was delivered by messenger but as the bank was closed it was put into the branch's letter box.

The following morning, when the letter box was cleared, the telegram was overlooked and it was not brought to the bank's attention until the 2 November when the telegram and confirmation of the stop posted by Curtice were removed from the letter box. In the meantime the cheque had been presented and paid on the 1 November and the bank therefore advised Curtice that the stop instructions had been received too late to be acted upon. Curtice sued the bank claiming that it was not entitled to debit his account with the amount of the cheque.

The court had to determine what amounted to a valid countermand since the Act was not specific. In particular, was delivering it to the bank sufficient or did it have to come to the bank's attention. The court held it to be the latter; hence the rule with which you are probably familiar. As the judge said: 'There is no such thing as constructive countermand in a commercial transaction of this kind.' Applying this to modern banking, what is the rule in your branch on telephone countermands? No doubt written confirmation is requested but what happens if it does not arrive within a reasonable time? Are you then legally protected if the cheque is paid in error?

You will learn in Chapter 8 that for a person to become a 'holder in due course' of a bill of exchange (don't worry about the expression at this stage) the Bills of Exchange Act 1882, s.29 requires that the bill be '... complete and regular on the face of it ...'. In *Arab Bank v Ross* (1952) a bill had not been endorsed properly and this was held to prevent the bank from becoming its holder in due course. The point was that s.29 refers to 'face' while an endorsement is by definition on the back of a bill. The term therefore had to be interpreted. In the event it was held that the 'face' of a bill included the back of it.

In *United Dominions Trust v Kirkwood* (1966), UDT had lent money to Kirkwood's business and received security for the loan from him. The business went into liquidation and UDT sought to enforce the security. Kirkwood's only defence was that UDT were not licensed under the Moneylenders Act 1900 and therefore not entitled to recover the debt. UDT pleaded that they were exempted from the licensing requirement by s.6 because they were bankers, one of the exempt categories within the section. You could be forgiven for thinking that whether or not UDT were bankers was somewhat of a non-question. A banker banks. However, there were (and are) no statutory definitions which use the *functions* of a bank as the determining criteria. Thus, the Court of Appeal had to consider the meaning of the term. In the event, UDT were held to be bankers within s.6 and were therefore able to enforce the security and recover the debt. (We discuss the definition in Chapter 5.)

A case of considerable importance to banks and other mortgagees and purchasers of land is *Williams & Glyn's Bank Ltd v Boland and another* (1980), a case we have already mentioned in this chapter. Mr and Mrs Boland had bought a house with their joint earnings although it was conveyed to Mr Boland alone and he appeared as the sole registered proprietor at the Land Registry. Mr Boland's company borrowed money from the bank and he gave his personal guarantee as security. Without telling his wife he also mortgaged the house to the bank under a registered charge. The bank made no enquiry of either Mr or Mrs Boland as to whether the latter had an interest in the house.

Subsequently, the company ran into difficulties, the bank called upon Mr Boland to pay under his guarantee and when he could not they sought possession of the house. Mrs Boland resisted the bank's action claiming that she had an 'overriding' interest in the property. Without becoming too technical, an overriding interest is good against any purchaser or mortgagee whether or not they know about it and even though no mention of it is made on the Land Registry registers. Mrs Boland claimed the overriding interest by virtue of the Land Registration Act 1925, s.70(1)(g) which states that 'the rights of every person in actual occupation of the land ...' are overriding interests '... save where enquiry is made of such person and the rights are not disclosed'. She undoubtedly had an interest in the property because she had contributed to its purchase (technically she was a beneficiary under an implied trust) but the bank argued that her interest was only a minor interest (another technical term) which meant that the bank's legal charge defeated her interest, reducing it to a claim against whatever money was left after the bank had sold the property and repaid itself. They maintained that 'actual occupation' under s.70 did not include occupation by the spouse of a legal owner who was also in actual occupation.

In the High Court the bank's interpretation of the Act succeeded but the Court of Appeal reversed the decision and the reversal was upheld by the House of Lords. The Act meant what it said, Mrs Boland was in 'actual occupation' and therefore had an overriding interest to which the bank's mortgage was subject.

We can note here that in *City of London Building Society v Flegg* (1987), the House of Lords held that where there are *joint* owners holding property on trust, and not a sole legal owner as in *Boland*, (an example of 'distinguishing') the rights of beneficiaries in actual occupation are overreached (defeated by) a conveyance or mortgage. Specifically, the House held that s.14 of the Law of Property Act 1925 which states that 'This part of the Act shall not prejudicially affect the interest of any person in possession or in actual occupation of land to which he may be entitled ...' did not, despite its clear wording prevent the interests of the beneficiaries being overreached. The Lords so held because any other interpretation would have completely upset the purpose of other sections of the Act which expressly provide that the interests of beneficiaries are overreached on a purchase from or mortgage by two trustees or a trust corporation. (We discuss both cases in the context of security practice in Chapter 7, basically the importance of making adequate enquiries. Accept the explanation as an illustration of statutory interpretation, don't worry about the technical points raised at this point.)

Sometimes the interpretation of a statute can have consequences which reach far beyond the facts of the case. In *Hazell v London Borough of Hammersmith & Fulham* (1991), for example, a case where the Council's interest rate swop transactions on the money market were challenged by the district auditor (Hazell), the Local Government Act 1972, s.111 had to be interpreted. This states that '... subject to the provisions of this Act ... a local authority shall have power to do anything ... which is calculated to facilitate, or is conducive or incidental to, the discharge of any of their functions'. The banks that had entered into swap contracts with the local authorities argued that this section, particularly the words '... calculated to facilitate, or is conducive or incidental to ...' gave local authorities implied power to do so. The House of Lords held, however, that they did not. The financial dealings of local authorities were regulated by Schedule 13 of the Act and this provides a comprehensive code defining and limiting their powers in this respect. In the Law Lords' opinion this was quite inconsistent with any implied power to enter into swap transactions. All such transactions were therefore *ultra vires* and unlawful, and could not be enforced against the Council. Lord Templeman said that the Council had effectively staked the ratepayers' (the transactions preceded the era of the Poll Tax) money on a gamble on interest rates when it owed a duty to them to preserve ratepayers' funds. The decision can perhaps be best understood as a 'policy decision'. Someone had to bear the loss and the House of Lords would seem to have taken the view that the commercial banks involved were in a better position to do so than the residents of the Borough. Be this as it may, the facts and the consequences of the case are worth exploring further.

The 'swap transactions' concerned involved the Council swapping payments on fixed interest rate loans it had obtained from the Public Works Loan Board for payments on variable interest rate loans raised by banks on the capital market. A total of 592 swap deals worth £6 billion between 1987–89 were involved. In essence the Council hoped that the variable rate would fall below the fixed rate, leaving them with a profit. For a time this happened but eventually interest rates moved up and Council were apparently liable to pay far more interest than was due under the fixed interest loans.

About this time, as a result of the district auditor's action, the Council stopped payments due under the transactions because it then accepted that the transactions were *ultra vires* and should not have been entered into in the first place. (It was clearly in its interests to do so since the payments on the variable interest loans were now higher than those on the fixed interest loans.) A sum of about £140m was involved, the amount the Council owed to the banks to make up the difference in the interest payments. Thus, as a result of the case the Council avoided payment of this sum leaving the banks with a corresponding loss. (It was estimated that somewhere between £500 and £1bn was involved if all similar activities of other councils were included in the calculation of the loss.)

Although there was evidence that banks had encouraged local authorities to enter swap transactions, the banks warned that local authorities could lose their status as 'blue chip' borrowers and would in future be charged higher interest rates on normal borrowing. This could cause a rise in poll tax payments – a contemporary estimate was that a 1% rise in interest rates charged on total English and Welsh local authority borrowing of some £450 billion per year would cost £15 per year per poll tax payer. The Government pointed out that since normal local authority borrowing is protected by law there was no reason to alter local authority ratings.

A wider consequence is that the judgment wipes out other swaps contracts between many of the world's largest banks and 130 local authorities and destroyed an important section of one of the City's fastest-growing markets – quite apart from the enormous loss incurred by the banks. The banks fear that the decision has attacked the basis of contract law and damaged the City's international reputation as a safe business centre. In particular, it would seem to attack the City's flexible regulatory framework which has traditionally allowed such markets to develop and flourish in comparison with the more rigid systems on the Continent. Indeed there was some early evidence that foreign institutions began to do business elsewhere in Europe as a result of the decision when all their business had previously been done in the City.

Another daunting prospect is that the banks declared that they were not going to take the ruling lying down. This could mean appeals to the European Court of Justice and many hundreds of individual actions for restitution on a contract by contract basis. (A claim for restitution may possibly succeed even where the contract under which money was paid is a nullity.)

ACTIVITY 2.4

(a) Why should five Law Lords be able to outlaw transactions on an 'apparent' technicality when they had become accepted by all parties and had come to form the basis of an important international money market? A difficult question this. Discuss it with your colleagues and put forward some reasons. Do you support the Law Lords' decision?

(b) Up-date your notes with any future developments in this matter.

Rules of statutory interpretation

Parliament makes the law but the courts enforce it and it is sometimes necessary to ascertain the intention of Parliament before this can be done. The cases above are all examples of statutes where this was necessary because particular words or phrases used in them were unclear or ambiguous, or failed to achieve the objective of the legislation when applied to the facts. However, it is essential to remember that the courts cannot challenge Parliament's authority to legislate and that if the words of the statute are clear and unambiguous the need for judicial interpretation does not arise.

A thorough study of statutory interpretation uncovers a considerable diversity of rules, judicial attitudes and precedents, so much so that at times it seems that there are no real rules of interpretation. Nevertheless, a general summary should always be included in any consideration of legislation for, through their power of interpretation, the courts may be able to affect the meaning and application of some statutes.

Conventionally there are said to be three basic judicial approaches to statutory interpretation: the 'literal' rule, the 'golden' rule and the 'mischief' rule.

The literal rule. The role of the judges is to ascertain the intention of Parliament from the Act itself. Thus, if the words of the statute are capable of only one meaning, this is the meaning the court will take and the statute will be enforced accordingly, even if the result is unlikely or harsh. The remedy for a harsh law lies in an amending act and not with the courts. However, in the great majority of cases a literal interpretation of the statute produces the desired result. The *Boland Case* can be considered as an example of the literal rule being applied.

The golden rule. This is said to be a modification of the literal rule. It is used either where a literal interpretation would produce an obviously absurd or unwanted result, provided a reasonable alternative interpretation is possible, or where the statute is capable of more than one literal meaning, i.e. it is ambiguous. In the latter situation the literal rule has no place and the golden rule is applied to effect the most reasonable of the alternative meanings possible. This latter use of the rule is more common than the former. If the reverse was true, the court could be usurping Parliament's function and exceeding its constitutional role as the interpreter and enforcer of legislation.

Arab Bank v Ross (1952) can be considered an example of the golden rule being applied because in the context of the case 'face' could have had two possible meanings: the front of the bill only or its surface, front and back. Given that endorsement is essential to the negotiation of all order bills of exchange it would be contrary to reason if the irregularity of an endorsement could be ignored because it was on the back of the bill and 'face' referred to the front of the bill only. Thus, the more reasonable of the meanings was adopted. *Flegg's Case* can also be considered an example of the golden rule being applied, any other interpretation would have frustrated the purpose of other important sections of the Act.

The mischief rule. This rule has a long history, dating from *Heydon's Case* (1584). It can be applied where the statute under consideration was passed to remedy a defect or 'mischief' in the law, most commonly where the statute passed to do this is ambiguous. The rule is used to promote the interpretation which remedies the defect. Occasionally, however, it is applied in preference to the literal rule where an application of the latter would not remedy the defect in the law.

An example for you, nothing to do with banking we hasten to add! The Street Offences Act 1959, s. 1 provides that 'It shall be an offence for a common prostitute to loiter or solicit in a street or public place for the purpose of prostitution.' In *Smith v Hughes* (1960), a prostitute was charged under s. 1 after she had been observed soliciting men from behind the windows of a house and from a balcony. In *Behrendt v Burridge* (1970) the defendant was similarly charged after she was observed for about an hour sitting on a high stool in a bay window, illuminated by a red light, dressed in a low-cut top and mini-skirt. At no time was she seen to communicate actively with any person in the street. Problems for the prosecution; in *Smith v Hughes* (1960), the accused was not in a street nor in a public place and in *Behrendt v Burridge* (1970), there was no active soliciting. Clearly if the Act was interpreted literally no offence would have been committed in either case but nor would the purpose of the legislation have been implemented. The question was whether the accused women had been 'soliciting' for the purposes of the Act. In each case the accused were held to have been doing so. By putting this wider interpretation on s. 1, the purpose of the Act, the control of prostitution, was promoted.

The mischief rule is notable for providing the sole exception to another basic principle of statutory interpretation: that the intention of Parliament is to be ascertained only from the words of the Act itself and not from external sources, e.g. Parliamentary debates or reports of Royal Commissions. When applying the mischief rule the court can look outside the statute to discover the defect in the law which the statute was designed to remedy and hence interpret the statute to 'suppress the mischief and advance the remedy'.

Other rules and presumptions. A number of other rules, or maxims, are also employed.

The *ejusdem generis* (of the same type) rule applies to general words of summary which follow particular words. The general words are limited to the category of things or persons identified by the particular words. For example, in *Brownsea Haven Properties Ltd v Poole Corporation* (1958) it was held that the Corporation's powers to make orders for the direction of traffic '... in all times of public processions, rejoicings, or illuminations, and in any other case when the streets are thronged or liable to be obstructed ...' did not extend to creating a one-way traffic system for the duration of the summer holiday season. Under the Consumer Credit Act 1984, s.14 a credit token is defined as '... a card, check, voucher, coupon stamp, form, booklet or *other document or thing* (our italics) given to an individual by a person carrying on a consumer credit business ...', clearly intending the Act to cover every conceivable item, thereby preventing avoidance of the Act on a question of construction.

Where specific words are not followed be general words the *expresso unius est exclusio alterius* rule applies (the expression of one thing implies the exclusion of another). Thus, the Act will apply only to the specific things mentioned. For example, an Act which repeals one or more other named Acts is not presumed to repeal other Acts even though they are associated with them.

The *noscitur a sociis* (the meaning of a word can be gathered from its context) rule states simply that where the meaning of a word is doubtful, its meaning should be determined from the words and phrases with which it is associated.

Many statutes contain an interpretation section which specifically defines the meaning of, possibly, debatable words or phrases used in the Act or where Parliament wishes to give a precise meaning to them. For example, the Bills of Exchange Act 1882, s.2 (the Act's interpretation section) defines a ' holder' of a bill as 'The payee or endorsee of a bill who is in possession of it, or the bearer therefore.' In addition, the Interpretation Act 1978 defines many general words and terms used in Acts. For example, unless it is clearly not the case, singular words include the plural and *vice versa* and masculine words or expressions include the feminine.

It is presumed that an act of Parliament applies to the UK only; that it does not bind the Crown; that it is not to be retrospective (to have any effect before the date it is brought into force); and that it does not alter the common law.

Interpreting community legislation

You have already seen that the legislation of the European Community is somewhat different from our own. In particular, Community legislation tends to enact broad principles rather than detailed provisions. Consequently, English courts must play a far more active role to affect the aims of Community legislation than they need or can do with our own domestic legislation. They must look to the intent and purpose of the legislation and not be concerned to examine the words in meticulous detail or argue about their precise grammatical sense. If there is a gap in the legislation they must fill it as they think the European legislators would have wished. This is in sharp contrast to domestic legislation where any gap must be filled by Parliament.

Thus, in following the European pattern far more use will be made of the golden and mischief rules than the literal rule. In addition, statements made on behalf of the Community, and Community publications which reflect the substance of and attitudes in the negotiations which led to the conclusion of the treaties (the *travaux préparatoires*), may be consulted to resolve any ambiguity or uncertainty in an enactment. This again is in sharp contrast with English principles of interpretation.

■ THE LITERARY SOURCES

These are the written records of the law. There are three main literary sources.

The Statute Books

These contain the Acts of Parliament. Two original copies of each act are signed by the Sovereign or her representative, one being kept at the Public Records Office and the other in the House of Lords. However, for all practical purposes the Queen's Printer's copies, the sort you may have at work, are acceptable.

The law reports

These contain records of the facts, legal arguments and decisions in important court cases. Today, nearly all important cases are reported. However, the courts have never created a methodical system for producing reports and it has been left entirely in the hands of private organisations. Consequently, there is still an element of chance and individual preference as to whether a case is reported or not.

In 1865 the Incorporated Council of Law Reporting in England and Wales was founded and by convention since then its *Law Reports* are always cited in court when they contain a report of the required case. A few series of private reports are still published, of which the best-known and most comprehensive are the *All England Reports*. In addition, *The Times* newspaper carries reports of the previous day's cases and these are sometimes cited in court when the decision is too recent to have been published in the more formal series.

New technology is now having an impact on law reporting and the preparation of cases. LEXIS, a computer data base of leading cases, including some unreported in the conventional reports, and statute law is now fairly widely used. It can drastically reduce the time taken to find a relevant legal authority merely by inputing details of the issue concerned. However, some leading judges have seen it as a mixed blessing. Sir John Donaldson (the Master of the Rolls – head of the Civil Division of the Court of Appeal) said in one 1983 case that 'the profession was afflicted, or assisted, as the case may be, by electronic data processing appliances'. The problem he foresaw was of judges being bombarded with numerous unnecessary and often otherwise unreported decisions just because the data base had spewed them out. Later the same year, the House of Lords stated that unreported decisions could generally not be cited in an appeal to the House. This is a significant change to ancient practice: formerly any decision could be cited which was vouched for by a barrister.

Textbooks

Modern textbooks, no matter how well-respected, are not authority for legal rules until and unless a particular passage or passages have been accepted and adopted by the court as true statements of the law. This happens infrequently. An example from banking law where a court more or less accepted a textbook writer's view is *United Dominions Trust v Kirkwood* (1966), 1 All E.R. 968, which we have already used to illustrate statutory interpretation. Here the Court of Appeal cited the three characteristics of a banker stated in Paget's *Law of Banking* (6th ed, 1961), as being the basis of its criteria for determining who was a banker within the meaning of the Moneylenders Act 1960, s.6. (The reference after the case indicates that it is reported in the first volume of the *All England Reports* of 1966 at page 968.) Nevertheless, leading textbook writers influence successive generations of judges and lawyers and in this way they are an influence on the evolution of the law. (This textbook is unlikely to influence any judge!)

■ HISTORICAL SOURCES

Custom

We have already seen in this chapter how law began in custom. We have also seen how custom can, very occasionally be a 'legal' source of law. How does this relate to the English legal system?

Before the Norman Conquest in 1066, there was no centralised English state, let alone a United Kingdom. The Normans began the process of creating a single nation. From time to time the Norman kings would send tax officials and government administrators around the country to collect the King's revenues and to look after his interests. It became common for these royal officials, who were not trained lawyers, to resolve local disputes and try those accused of crimes. It became the practice for their decisions to be based on the customs of the locality.

Over the years a body of customs emerged which were either to be found in all parts of the country or which the royal officials, or justices as they began to be called, thought should be applied everywhere. Such customs became known as *common customs* or *customs of the realm* (as opposed to local customs), and formed the basis of the common law which was enforced in the common law courts (the King's courts).

Today, common customs have long since been absorbed into case law and statute and are only of historical interest. However, local customs (applying to a particular place, group of people, or both) which satisfy a number of legal requirements are occasionally recognised as *exceptions* to the general law and enforced accordingly. A particularly well-known example was the custom of *Gavelkind* which was still found in Kent in the 19th century. Under it, land was inherited by all sons in equal shares and not by the eldest son alone.

Equity

We discussed the origin and nature of equity in Chapter 1. We saw there that the principles of equity are very much alive in our modern law but that equity ceased to be administered separately in 1875. For this reason, equity is usually classified as a historical source of law.

The Law Merchant

In the same way as the rigidity and inadequacy of the common law caused the growth of equity, so too did it cause the development in the 13th and 14th centuries of a body of rules serving the needs of merchants. They were interested in law which recognised the realities of commerce and offered speedy settlement of their disputes. The rules were often brought to England in the form of *mercantile customs* by the foreign merchants who dominated our trade in the days when the country's economy was based on the production of raw materials such as wool. Unlike equity, however, many of these customs became judicially incorporated into the common law from the 17th century onwards and the merchants' courts fell into disuse. Some eventually became codified as legislation by Parliament, for example, the Bills of Exchange Act 1882, the Partnership Act 1890 and the (original) Sale of Goods Act 1893.

Mercantile custom is the origin of the present law on cheques and other negotiable instruments. The principle of *negotiability* was first introduced in the 17th century and the principles of transfer by endorsement, presumption of consideration (value) and the rule that a *bona fide* holder's title is not invalidated by defects in the title of the person transferring the bill were formulated in the 18th century. (*See* Chapter 8.) Partnership, agency and insurance law are all branches of law affecting banking whose origins lie in mercantile custom. The law on the sale of goods (now found in the Sale of Goods Act 1979), another branch with the same origins, affects us all.

■ SUMMARY

1 The Queen in Parliament is the formal source of law in the UK.

2 Law has its origins in custom, defined as usage recognised by law.

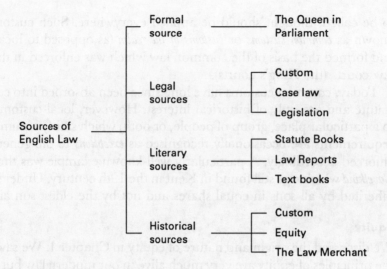

Fig 2.3 The sources of English Law.

3 The legal sources of law today are:
 ● case law (judicial precedent); and
 ● legislation.

4 The *ratio decidendi* is the legal reason for deciding a case. It consists of:
 ● a statement of the relevant facts;
 ● a summary of the process of legal reasoning;
 ● the judgment, together with the award made or sanction imposed.

5 Binding precedents are decisions of the House of Lords and the Court of Appeal which have not been overruled by a later case or by legislation.

6 Persuasive precedents are:
 ● decisions of lower courts;
 ● decisions of Commonwealth and American courts, and the recommendations of the Privy Council;
 ● *obiter dicta* statements.

7 The operation of judicial precedent closely follows the hierarchical structure of the court system.

8 Legislation is law made by act of Parliament or under the authority of an act of Parliament – delegated legislation.

9 Statutory instruments are the form of delegated legislation most relevant to banking.

10 EC legislation is supra-national law.

11 The primary legislation of the EC is found in the founding Treaties of the Community.

12 Secondary legislation of the EC is made by the Council of Ministers or the Commission under the authority of the main Treaties. It takes the form of:
 ● regulations;

THE SOURCES OF ENGLISH LAW

- directives;
- decisions.

13 EC legislation does not affect our purely domestic law.

14 The courts have the power to interpret legislation where its words are unclear, ambiguous or when applied literally would result in an absurd result.

15 The main principles of statutory interpretation are the:
- literal rule;
- golden rule; and
- mischief rule.

16 The literary sources of law are the Statute Books, the law reports and, to some extent, textbooks.

17 Important historical sources of law are custom, equity and the Law Merchant.

■ SELF-ASSESSMENT QUESTIONS

1 What is the formal source of law in the UK?

2 Can the Sovereign refuse to give her consent to a piece of legislation?

3 What are the legal sources of law?

4 Do judges make law?

5 What importance has the date 1875 to the operation of judicial precedent?

6 Explain the term *ratio decidendi* and illustrate it with examples relevant to banking.

7 Explain the term *obiter dicta* and illustrate it with examples relevant to banking.

8 What are binding precedents?

9 The decisions of which English courts are binding precedents?

10 Which decisions have only persuasive authority? Give examples.

11 Explain the process of distinguishing.

12 Explain how the decisions in three cases have affected banking operations.

13 When is the golden rule used in the interpretation of statutes?

14 What is delegated legislation?

15 Give examples of how delegated legislation affects banking operations.

16 What is meant by EC legislation being supra-national law?

17 Choose three Acts of Parliament and specifically explain how they affect banking operations.

18 What do you understand by the Law Merchant?

19 What is the maximum amount of a credit agreement regulated by the Consumer Credit Act 1974?

20 Is the canvassing of overdrafts to existing customers a criminal offence?

21 Loans and overdrafts can both be regulated agreements but they are treated differently by the 1974 Act. Explain this different treatment.

22 When can a regulated agreement be cancelled?

23 What is a debtor-creditor-supplier agreement? What important consequence does it have?

24 What are the aims of the Financial Services Act 1986?

25 On what mechanism does the Financial Services Act rely?

26 Briefly explain the main rules of statutory interpretation.

27 Explain how two examples of statutory interpretation affected banking operation.

28 What are the literary sources of law?

29 Why is custom better considered as an historical rather than as a legal source of law?

30 Explain why the Law Merchant is important to modern banking operations?

■ MULTIPLE-CHOICE QUESTIONS

Please read this carefully!

In all the examinations that have been set in Banking: the Legal Environment there have been a number of multiple-choice questions (MCQs) included in the compulsory Question 1. There are usually eight, comprising:

- one question on the *sources* of law;
- one question on the *courts* and other conflict resolving procedures;
- one question on general *contract law*;
- one question on the *banker-customer* contract;
- two questions on *property* and its use as security;
- two questions on *cheques/methods of payment*.

Students have tended to score very poorly on this question in the past. This is rather surprising and has been commented upon by the Chief Examiner because each multiple choice question tests the knowledge and understanding which underpins the subject, almost always in a very straightforward way. There is a simple solution to this weakness. We have reproduced at the end of each chapter every MCQ set on that topic and collected the answers at the end of the book. *Learn them!* You will both be greatly improving your chances of success in the examination and acquiring the job-related knowledge and understanding that the Banking Certificate is meant to give you.

One thing to remember: setting good MCQs is not easy and, in practice, there are only a limited number of questions that can be set. This means that the

MCQs tend to repeated, sometimes with a subtle variation. This is turn means that if you have taken the sensible step of learning the answers to previous MCQs, *do read the questions carefully* in case they have been changed in this way.

The MCQs below cover both Chapter 1 and Chapter 2.

1 Which of the following is an equitable remedy?
A an action for damages
B foreclosure of a mortgage
C an injunction
D a banker's lien

2 The Companies Act 1985 was enacted primarily:
A as a consolidating statute
B as a codifying statute
C as an enabling Act
D to implement an EC Directive

3 Which of the following best defines the term *ratio decidendi*?
A The evidence brought before the court on which it makes its decision
B The court's judgment in the dispute
C The rules of law on which the court makes its decision
D The reasons for the court's decision

4 The decisions of which of the following bodies are of only persuasive authority in later cases?
A House of Lords
B Privy Council
C Court of Appeal (Civil Division)
D Court of Appeal (Criminal Division)

5 The 'Golden Rule' of statutory interpretation is said to be used where the courts:
A apply the natural meaning of the words in the statute
B consider documents other than the statute itself to determine what was the intention of Parliament
C avoid an interpretation which would lead to an absurd result
D choose not to apply the natural meaning of the words in order to better implement Parliament's intention

6 Which is the principal rule applied by the courts when the meaning of legislation is disputed?
A the Golden rule
B the Ejusdem generis rule
C the Literal rule
D the Mischief rule?

7 The concept of negotiability has its origins in:
A mercantile custom
B the principles of law developed in the Court of Chancery
C common law
D the Bills of Exchange Act 1882

8 The rules of modern equity have their origin in the decisions of the:
A Court of Common Pleas

B Court of Chancery
C Ecclesiastical courts
D Admiralty Court

9 Which of the following is *not* a legal 'source' of law?
A local custom
B decisions of judges in the Court of Appeal
C regulations and Orders made under the Insolvency Act 1986
D reports of cases recorded in the 'Law Reports'

3 Conflict resolving

OBJECTIVES

After studying this chapter you should be able to:
1 **Appreciate factors that banks consider before bringing or defending a legal action;**
2 **Be aware of the differences between judicial and quasi-judicial processes;**
3 **Outline the role and jurisdiction of the major civil and criminal courts;**
4 **Explain the process and use of arbitration;**
5 **Outline the role of administrative tribunals;**
6 **Explain the role of the Bank Ombudsman.**

■ A BANK'S PERSPECTIVE

Conflict always upsets people and most of us seek to avoid it. In business particularly, conflict can usually be measured financially, whether this is exactly quantifiable in terms of lost orders or compensation paid, or less quantifiable in terms of lost time and opportunities and general hassle. Disputes must be investigated, specialists consulted, reports prepared, letters written and meetings arranged and attended. Conflict ties up staff resources that could be more profitably used elsewhere. Businesses do not take legal action unless they must; they exist to pursue profit, not to sue people. Experience often dictates that it is better to write-off some debts rather than pursue a tortuous path through the courts in the hope of recovering something. Legal action is frequently not cost-effective, you can spend thousands to recover hundreds! Generally, only where substantial sums of money or issues important to their activities are involved will banks and other business organisations readily resort to the law. In the latter instance it may be vital to obtain a ruling, as in the *Boland* and *Tai Hing* cases that we discussed in the previous chapter.

Banks will often go to great lengths to avoid court action, even when their claim would be likely to succeed. They have a prominent 'High Street' profile and such cases as *Williams & Glyn's Bank Ltd v Boland* (1980) and *Lloyds Banks Ltd v Bundy* (1975), are hardly likely to endear them to the general public! They must always consider their *image*. Conversely, publicity may occasionally be a motive for bringing an action, for example, where the action involves fraud or other activity which the bank wishes to discourage. Professional judgment is required; it is seldom a simple matter of who is right and who is wrong. Writing-off £1,000 is one thing, writing-off £1m is another. On the other hand, a mortgage is a mortgage and a guarantee is a guarantee. The customer presumably knew what s/he was doing, entered into the contract freely and for their own benefit and knew – or should have been made clearly aware of – the consequences of failure to pay. Banks are not charities.

Despite all this, by the very nature and scale of their activities banks frequently find themselves involved in civil legal action, both as plaintiff (the person bringing the action) and as defendant. Even if transactions (of all kinds) are only disputed at the rate of 0.001 per cent (1:100,000), assuming 1 million transactions per day, this still amounts to a great many disputes over the course of a year.

As plaintiff, such actions will normally be for the recovery of a debt or enforcement of security. As defendant, a bank may be defending an action brought by a customer alleging breach of contract through wrongfully refusing to pay a cheque, or an action in tort for conversion brought by the true owner of a cheque for negligently collecting the cheque on behalf of a customer who was not entitled to receive payment. Banks are infrequently involved in criminal cases.

■ THE JUDICIAL AND QUASI-JUDICIAL PROCESSES

The judicial process

The judicial process consists of an independent adjudicator (a judge) making a reasoned decision according to known rules of law on the basis of the evidence available to both parties and offered to the court. Each party, usually through their legal representatives, can test the evidence tendered by the other and each may put forward factual or legal arguments in support of their claim. In conflicts where a jury sits with a judge, i.e. on the trial of indictable offences in the Crown Court and in some civil actions tried in the Queen's Bench Division of the High Court, the judge decides disputed points of law and the jury determines questions of fact. If the plaintiff succeeds, a civil jury will also determine the amount of damages (if any) that the defendant must pay.

The judicial process assumes that there is an applicable legal rule which will resolve the conflict and that this can be discovered by a rigorous examination of *authority*: statutes and cases. As a consequence of this, the judge can very seldom exercise completely unfettered discretion, in most cases a judge is bound to follow *precedent* (*see* Chapter 2).

By tradition, the English judicial process is an adversarial and not an inquisitorial system. Hence, the court plays a largely passive role and the case is conducted by the parties (usually through their lawyers) with the judge as 'umpire' to ensure that the procedural rules are observed and to adjudicate in the dispute at the end of the process.

The main advantages of the judicial process are said to be:

- an independent adjudicator with an open mind;
- a clearly determined issue to be decided;
- a full and equal opportunity for both sides to present their cases;

- the production of the best available evidence;
- the exclusion of all irrelevant material;
- the application of known legal rules to resolve the dispute; and
- a statement of reasons for the decision made.

Impressive though these advantages undoubtedly are, the process does have a number of disadvantages:

- many would argue that the process resembles a gladiatorial combat where might – in the form of superior legal representation – can overcome right;
- inherent in this is the high cost of the process, perhaps its major detraction;
- a lay person will usually find that the technicality of legal procedure and the formality of the process effectively bar access to the courts unless a professional lawyer is employed, and yet the sheer expense which this involves may cause all hope of redress at law to be abandoned;
- even where legal representation is readily available, considerable delay is inevitable before the conflict is resolved;
- the adversarial system allows the parties to control the process and the truth may not be fully uncovered because the court is unable to enquire into the facts;
- it is argued by some that the isolation of judges from the 'real world' makes it difficult for them to appreciate fully the background to many of the conflicts that they must resolve.

The quasi-judicial process

'Quasi' means similar to and the quasi-judicial process is indeed similar to the judicial process. Each involves establishing facts and applying rules of law but the quasi-judicial process tends to have less rigid rules of procedure and evidence. It is also generally cheaper, less formal and tends to produce decisions rather more quickly than the judicial process; all significant advantages. However, perhaps the true distinction is that a judicial process is used in the courts, properly so called, while a quasi-judicial process is used in those conflict resolving bodies which are not part of the 'official' court system.

Use of the processes

The judicial process, whether with or without a jury, is better suited to the criminal law (indeed only the judicial process is used in matters involving the criminal law), where the full 'majesty of the law' is probably an advantage, and to civil disputes involving questions of 'pure law' where little discretion is needed, such as the construction of an Act of Parliament, conflicts involving an alleged breach of contract or the protection of an individual's legal rights. However, civil conflicts are increasingly being resolved by arbitration and administrative tribunals rather than by the formal judicial process.

Administrative tribunals and formal arbitration bodies are *quasi-judicial bodies*. These may be defined as public bodies which have the power by law to establish facts and apply legal rules without being constituted as parts of the ordinary court system or following the strict rules of evidence and procedure

61

which bind the courts.

To some extent the decline of the judicial process in civil disputes is inevitable. Quasi-judicial conflict resolving is far better suited to some increasingly important branches of the law, such as welfare and employment law, and could be usefully extended into other areas where wider discretionary powers would be an advantage. Welfare law is largely determined by socio-political policy, and while tribunals must reach their decisions judicially, i.e. according to the relevant law and procedure and not purely on policy, their composition and informal procedure make them far better able to deal with the often complicated combination of factual circumstances, policy and socio-legal problems involved. In the commercial world quasi-judicial processes are far from new, for centuries arbitration has been used to resolve conflicts between business people. In fact the process of arbitration has been recognised and supported by the courts since the first Arbitration Act in 1698. Perhaps above all else it is the informality in procedure and the relevant expertise of the decision-makers involved that has brought quasi-judicial conflict resolving processes to a position of such prominence in the legal system.

■ THE COURT SYSTEM

Historically, the administration of justice is a prerogative of the Crown, but the Crown has long since ceased to play an active role in this function of the state. Nevertheless, all English courts derive their jurisdiction directly or indirectly from the Crown and the administration of justice is still formally undertaken in the Sovereign's name. For example, writs in civil actions are issued in the Queen's name and all criminal proceedings are brought on her behalf, the judges are 'Her Majesty's Judges' and they sit in the 'Queen's Courts'.

Classifying the courts

English courts may be classified in various ways. One possible classification is into those which have *criminal* and those which have *civil* jurisdiction. Unfortunately, this simple functional distinction is unsatisfactory; while some courts may have exclusively civil or exclusively criminal jurisdiction, most exercise both. A functional classification according to *original* (trial) or *appellate* jurisdiction is unsatisfactory for the same reason.

The one valid classification of practical importance is according to status and not jurisdiction. English courts may be divided into *superior* and *inferior* courts, the two characteristics of the latter being:

- that their jurisdiction is limited both by the value of the disputed subject-matter and geographically; and
- that they are subject to the supervisory jurisdiction of the High Court (*see* below).

The main *superior* courts are the House of Lords, Court of Appeal, High Court and Crown Court. The main *inferior* courts are the county and magistrates' courts. On the basis of the sheer number of cases with which they deal, the inferior courts are undoubtedly the backbones of the administration of civil and criminal justice respectively.

The European Court of Justice, which has jurisdiction in this country in conflicts involving Community law, clearly does not fit into even this classification. In addition, in September 1989 The Court of First Instance of the European Communities was established because the Court of Justice was unable to keep up with the number of cases being referred to it, a situation made worse by the many cases resulting from moves to complete the Single Market by the end of 1992.

Figure 3.1 shows the structure of the courts, including the European Court of Justice, in terms of their primary functions as criminal or civil, trial or appellate courts. (Refer to Fig. 3.1 as you read through the text.)

■ THE WORK OF THE COURTS

Appeal courts

The House of Lords and the Court of Appeal (Civil and Criminal Divisions) have only appellate jurisdiction. In matters involving purely domestic law, the House of Lords is the final appeal court in the UK for both civil and criminal cases.

High court

The High Court sits in three separate divisions, Queen's Bench, Chancery and Family, and has virtually unlimited original jurisdiction in civil matters. Trial is by a single judge, although a jury will sometimes sit in the Queen's Bench Division to hear actions involving defamation or fraud.

Queen's Bench is the largest of the three divisions and deals mainly with common law disputes involving the law of contract or the law of torts. The Division also exercises the criminal jurisdiction of the High Court. This latter jurisdiction is entirely appellate and consists of deciding points of law stated to it from magistrates' courts and from the Crown Court, the latter when it hears appeals against summary conviction or sentence in a magistrates' court. It also has minor appellate jurisdiction in some civil matters originally heard in the magistrates' courts and certain tribunals. In addition the Division exercises the supervisory jurisdiction of the High Court over quasi-judicial decision making (*see* below) by the issue of the prerogative orders of *certiorari*, *mandamus* and *prohibition*.

The Division also operates the Commercial Court of the High Court staffed by judges with extensive commercial knowledge and experience, to hear cases of a commercial nature, e.g. insurance disputes. The Court uses a simplified procedure which, together with the commercial experience of the judge, is designed to overcome the traditional reluctance of business people to resort to court action instead of arbitration. Indeed a judge of the Court can sit as an arbitrator in a private arbitration and a majority of the Court's work is now in this field rather than in cases heard by the Court itself.

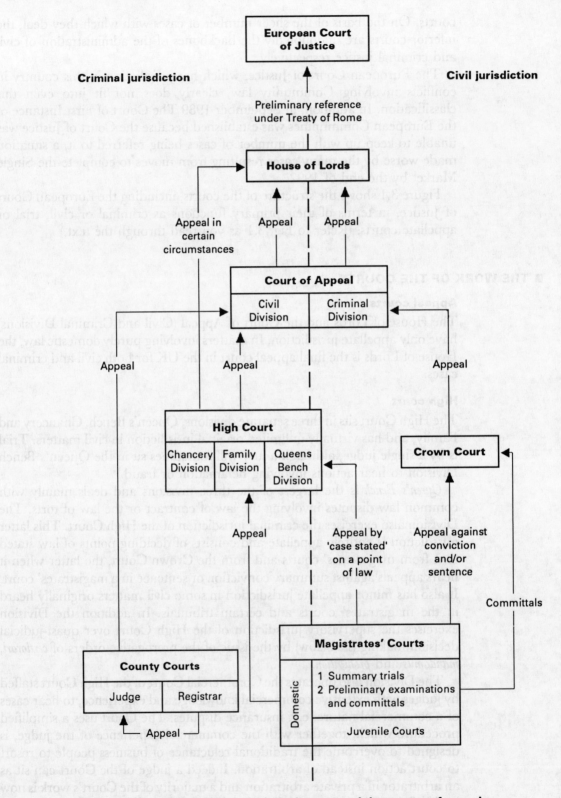

Criminal jurisdiction

Civil jurisdiction

Fig. 3.1 The principal civil and criminal courts and the system of appeals

The *Chancery Division* exercises original civil jurisdiction in matters which were originally heard in the Court of Chancery (abolished in 1875), e.g. over trusts, the redemption and foreclosure of mortgages, specific performance of contracts concerning land and partnership actions. The Division has statutory jurisdiction in company liquidation, bankruptcy, tax cases, town and country planning matters and probate disputes. It also has minor appellate jurisdiction, e.g. income tax appeals from the Commissioners of Inland Revenue.

The *Family Division* has exclusive original (trial) jurisdiction over matrimonial disputes and disputes involving children. It has limited appellate jurisdiction from the magistrates' courts and county courts in similar civil matters.

You can see from this outline of their jurisdiction that much of the work of the Queen's Bench and Chancery Divisions of the High Court is of direct relevance to banks.

Crown court

The Crown Court has exclusive original jurisdiction to try all indictable offences, i.e. offences, generally of a serious nature, where the trial must be by judge and jury, and jurisdiction to hear appeals against summary conviction or sentence from a magistrates' court. In addition, High Court judges may sit in the Crown Court to exercise the High Court's civil jurisdiction outside London.

County courts

The jurisdiction of the county courts is entirely civil and derived solely from statute. It is limited geographically, each court dealing with local disputes, and financial maxima are imposed by statute on the value of the disputed claims which they can hear. For example, at present the maximum claim in actions founded on contract and tort is £5,000 and in equity matters, such as trusts, £30,000. Although they may seem to operate as judicial debt-collecting agencies at times, they deal with a wide range of civil conflicts, including important socio-legal matters such as disputes between landlords and tenants and divorce petitions.

County court trials are by a single judge. The judge is assisted by a *registrar* who exercises both an administrative and a judicial function, the former of which is largely delegated to subordinates. Unless the parties object, a registrar may try actions where the claim does not exceed £500 or any other actions with their consent. Appeal lies from the decision of the registrar to the judge.

Claims involving £500 or less – 'small claims' – are automatically referred to *arbitration* in the county court by the registrar as soon as a defence to the claim has been received. Normally, the registrar will be the arbitrator but, if either of the parties ask, the dispute can be referred to the judge or to an outside arbitrator for arbitration.

County court arbitration hearings have the great advantages of informality, speed and cheapness. The strict rules of evidence (as used in the court) do not apply. In fact, the arbitrator is allowed to adopt any method of procedure which seems convenient and which will give each party a fair and equal opportunity to present their case. In particular, the arbitrator plays an active role in determining the relevant facts, testing the evidence and introducing relevant points of law – something of a compromise between the traditional adversarial procedure of English courts and an inquisitorial procedure (*see* below). Perhaps of most importance is the 'no-costs' rule. Neither side can recover the cost of solicitors' fees, although court fees, travelling expenses and other reasonable costs incurred in preparing the case can be awarded. In practice, the 'no-costs' rule tends to keep solicitors out of the arbitration procedure; their presence in it should be, almost by definition, unnecessary anyway.

Magistrates' courts

Magistrates' courts have both criminal and civil jurisdiction, although the importance of the former far outweighs that of the latter. Magistrates have jurisdiction to try *summary offences*, i.e. those which do not have to be tried by jury, certain hybrid offences which may be tried either by judge or jury in the Crown court or by summary procedure in a magistrates' court, and offences committed by children and young persons under the age of 17. In addition, they conduct *preliminary examinations* of indictable offences in order to establish whether or not the prosecution has sufficient evidence (a *prima facie* case) to justify the accused being committed on bail or in custody to stand trial before judge and jury in the Crown Court.

The civil jurisdiction of the magistrates' courts is very varied and includes the recovery of certain debts, e.g. unpaid income tax and business rates, and the renewal and revocation of licences. Of greatest importance is its domestic civil jurisdiction. For example, it can make orders that one spouse need no longer live with the other and that the defendant must pay a reasonable weekly sum to the complainant as maintenance.

ACTIVITY 3.1

Complete the table below. The first row of boxes is done for you.

Court	Civil jurisdiction?	Criminal jurisdiction?	Original jurisdiction?	Appellate jurisdiction?
House of Lords	Yes	Yes	No	Yes
Court of Appeal				
High Court				
Crown Court				
County Court				
Magistrates' Court				

ACTIVITY 3.2

Court cases are held in public and you have the right to attend them. If you have never done so, arrange a time when you can visit your local Magistrates' Court, perhaps with a friend or colleague. On the evening after your visit, record your observations about it.

■ ARBITRATION

Arbitration is a quasi-judicial process used in civil disputes where the parties involved agree to allow a third party to resolve the dispute between them. It is an alternative to the judicial process and not a replacement for it. Most arbitration agreements are in writing and the arbitration process is regulated either by one of a number of specific statutes, which provide for disputes arising out of their provisions to be settled by arbitration, or by the Arbitration Acts 1950 and 1979.

Referring disputes to arbitration

A dispute can be referred to arbitration under the provisions of a specific statute or in accordance with a term contained in the contract between the parties in dispute. Since the Middle Ages the courts have recognised such contractual terms and enforced the arbitration awards made. Today, provision for disputes to be referred to arbitration is frequently found in partnership agreements, insurance and building contracts and in industrial relations.

It is not possible for an arbitration agreement to prevent access to the courts because such an agreement would be void on the grounds of public policy. However, a suitably worded provision will generally prevent one of the parties proceeding with court action until the dispute has first been referred to arbitration.

Arbitration procedure

Normally one arbitrator is appointed (often selected by a trade association or professional body), but each party may have the right to appoint an arbitrator of their own choice. Where this is so, an umpire must be selected whose function is to decide the dispute should the arbitrators fail to agree. A judge of the Commercial Court may sometimes sit as a sole arbitrator providing the judge can be released from his judicial duties.

The arbitration follows normal judicial procedure but by agreement it is possible to relax strict procedural rules and, in particular, to dispense with the rules of evidence. For example, while witnesses are often cross-examined and can be ordered to attend (by subpoena) by the High Court, evidence is frequently submitted by affidavit (a written statement made on oath).

The arbitrator's decision is in the form of an award. This may include the payment of money or costs and an order to perform the contract (specific performance). The award prevents the parties taking the issues decided to court and unless the arbitration agreement provides for an appeal, e.g. to an appeal committee or tribunal, the arbitrator's decision on the facts is final.

The role of the court

The role of the court is to ensure that the arbitration process is conducted fairly, not to restrict its use. For example, it can revoke the authority of an arbitrator or umpire and can set aside the award for delay or improper conduct, stay proceedings by an injunction and enforce the arbitration award in the same way as its own judgments. But it cannot hear appeals against the award except where a judge of the Commercial Court sits as arbitrator. If this last rule were reversed, reference to arbitration would be pointless. However, the Arbitration Act 1979 provides that there may be an appeal to the High Court on a question of law providing both parties consent or the court gives permission. Where, however, the parties have entered into an agreement which excludes the right to appeal (as opposed to the right to take the dispute to court in the first place), this is binding upon them. In any event the court will give permission to appeal only if it considers that the determination of the question of law could substantially affect the rights of one or more of the parties.

This procedure means that business persons can ensure that their disputes are decided solely by the method of their choice, without any review by the courts on questions of law, and that costly and protracted delays by (unnecessary) references of points of law to the court are prevented.

Advantages and disadvantages of arbitration

The *advantages* of arbitration can in some ways be considered to be the opposites of the disadvantages inherent in the judicial process. To the business world in general these advantages are most attractive.

- *Privacy*: arbitration takes place in private and the arbitrator's award is published only to the parties to the dispute.
- *Flexibility*: although counsel may appear for the parties the rules of evidence can be relaxed and the process is relatively informal, indeed the procedure can be tailored to the requirements of the specific dispute. In consequence, it is argued that disputes can be decided in a less emotionally charged and tense situation – after all the parties might need or wish to continue doing business with each other after the dispute is settled.
- *Expertise*: the resolution of many commercial disputes requires expert knowledge and a major advantage of the process is that a person with the necessary expertise can be appointed as arbitrator. This means that the parties do not need to spend time educating a judge to the technical aspects involved in the dispute. In fact trade and professional bodies maintain lists of suitably qualified persons. Many commercial arbitration agreements also leave the appointment of an arbitrator to the relevant trade or professional body.
- *Finality*: except in very exceptional circumstances, the arbitrator's award is final and binding; in litigation there is an appeals procedure which, if invoked, is almost invariably very lengthy, expensive and likely to confirm any ill-will that the original court action caused.

Arbitration does have *disadvantages* however.

- It is not, however, necessarily cheaper nor quicker than a court action. Experienced arbitrators can command high fees and lawyers (if employed) will charge the same fees as for litigation in court. Delays can easily occur while an arbitrator is agreed upon by the parties and even then the arbitrator is unlikely to be free to resolve the dispute immediately.

● Legal Aid (*see* below) is unavailable. This can be unfair where there is a marked imbalance in the financial resources of the parties in dispute, particularly if the arbitration agreement is used to stop a claim being pursued in court where Legal Aid may have been available to the financially weaker party.

■ ADMINISTRATIVE TRIBUNALS

Since the end of the Second World War in 1945 there has been a significant increase in socio-legal problems, mainly associated with the expansion of social and welfare services, with which the ordinary courts are frequently ill-equipped to deal. To resolve the inevitable conflicts which arise in such matters, increasing use has been made of administrative tribunals.

Administrative tribunals fall outside the ordinary court system and yet they have extensive powers of decision making which directly affect individuals. In fact, the adjudication of civil disputes between the individual and the state by a court rather than by a tribunal is the exception rather than the rule and the use of tribunals to resolve disputes between individuals is becoming steadily more common. Although they will usually have a legally qualified chairperson, they are normally staffed by non-lawyers. They may have original or appellate jurisdiction.

Their functions and procedures are regulated by the Tribunals and Inquiries Act 1971. This makes provision for a statutory right of appeal on a point of law from a tribunal to the Queen's Bench Division of the High Court and provides for considerable uniformity in standards and procedures, e.g. chairpersons are selected by the appropriate government minister and appointed by the Lord Chancellor. It also has established the Council on Tribunals to oversee the constitution and functioning of the most important administrative tribunals, including the work of the Director General of Fair Trading. The Council makes an annual report to the Lord Chancellor.

The work of administrative tribunals

There are many individual tribunals; their only common element being that they are all statutory bodies which exercise functions laid down by particular acts of Parliament. For example, the lands tribunals deal with disputes over compensation paid to owners of land which has been compulsorily purchased by government departments or local authorities, and the Registered Designs Appeal Tribunal hears appeals from the Comptroller-General of Patents, Designs and Trade-marks. However, they play their most important roles in welfare and employment law. The national insurance tribunals decide disputed claims to unemployment and sickness benefits and appeals against the withdrawal of supplementary benefit are heard by the supplementary benefits appeals tribunals. Industrial tribunals deal with a wide range of disputes arising from employment.

Advantages and disadvantages of administrative tribunals

Administrative tribunals are generally considered to have the following *advantages*.

- They are usually staffed by expert lay-people and tribunals are able to consider policy criteria far better than judges.
- They are relatively cheap, legal representation is unnecessary and costs are not usually awarded.
- A decision is reached relatively quickly.
- They are flexible in that they are not bound by a doctrine of binding precedent, although they must be consistent in their decisions.
- They are relatively informal.
- Reasons for a decision are given if requested.

However, the increasing use of administrative tribunals has its own *disadvantages*.

- Arguably, there are too many kinds of tribunals and they often have overlapping jurisdictions.
- More fundamentally, they are said to infringe the *rule of law* (which aims to protect the individual from arbitrary government) in that they are run by government departments with an interest in the dispute.
- Though administrative tribunals are relatively informal when compared to the courts, most of the applicants to them tend to be very much out of their depth in any situation involving 'officialdom'. This being so, expert advice is often required in their applications but this is usually hard to obtain.

Control and supervision of tribunals

Unless granted by statute there is no right of appeal to the ordinary courts against the *decisions* of administrative tribunals, for such a right would nullify most of the advantages that they possess as a means of resolving conflicts. However, it is essential that administrative justice should exist within a framework of effective legal controls and safeguards.

Judicial control

Judicial control takes two main forms:

- the supervisory jurisdiction of the High Court; and
- any statutory rights of appeal which exist from a tribunal to the High Court.

Appeal must usually be on a point of law.

The supervisory jurisdiction of the High Court is exercised by a Divisional Court of the Queen's Bench Division through the issue of the prerogative orders of *certiorari*, *prohibition* and *mandamus*. They are issued following an *application for judicial review*, a procedure which encompasses a claim for damages. The leave of the High Court is required before an application for judicial review can be made.

Tribunals are kept within their jurisdiction by the orders of *certiorari* and *prohibition*. An order of *certiorari* brings a dispute, already resolved or still under the process of adjudication, before the High Court for the Court to consider whether the tribunal has acted in excess of its jurisdiction and whether the rules of natural justice have been broken. If such is found, the High Court will quash the decision made or remit the matter to the tribunal with a direction to reconsider and reach a decision in accordance with the findings of the court. It is also used to correct errors of law apparent on the record of the proceedings. It cannot be used to challenge the merits of the decision.

An order of *prohibition* is issued to prevent something from being done. It can be used to prevent inferior courts and tribunals exceeding their jurisdiction when exercising judicial or quasi-judicial powers.

Mandamus is an order to perform public duties or to exercise statutory powers. It may be issued against inferior courts and tribunals where they wrongfully refuse to deal with a dispute within their jurisdiction.

Administrative supervision

This is exercised by the *Council on Tribunals*. The Council was established in 1985 to review the constitution and working of tribunals and enquiries. It must be consulted about procedural rules relating to them and it can make recommendations on its own initiative to the Lord Chancellor. Although its investigations have rarely had any effect on decisions already made, substantiated complaints generally lead to improvements in procedure. This is, therefore, the main function of the Council.

■ LEGAL AID

Legal Aid is a scheme which pays or contributes to the cost of a litigant's legal fees. It is funded by the State and administered by the Legal Aid Board. The scheme is designed to enable a person unable to pay legal fees to obtain legal representation in court proceedings. To the parties involved it probably seems part and parcel of the judicial conflict-resolving process.

Legal Aid in both criminal and civil cases is governed by the Legal Aid Act 1988. The Act, as periodically amended, determines applicants' eligibility to Legal Aid and any contribution that they must make to the court costs – a means test system based on income and savings is used.

Legal Aid in civil court proceedings

Legal Aid will be granted if applicants fulfil two conditions:

- they must be in receipt of income support or satisfy a means test;
- the applicant must satisfy the Board that there are reasonable grounds for taking or defending the action.

Two main criticisms are made of the present scheme. First, with the exception of the Employment Appeal Tribunal and the Lands Tribunal, Legal Aid is not available in cases heard by administrative tribunals, even though the use of the tribunals in conflict resolving is steadily increasing. It is never available for arbitration hearings. Second, too many people are excluded from the scheme on financial grounds; in particular, the means test is unfair to the prudent saver.

Legal Aid in criminal court proceedings

An application for Legal Aid in criminal cases is made to the appropriate court and applicants must include a statement of means with their applications. Legal Aid in criminal cases differs in two further ways from the civil scheme.

- A criminal Legal Aid order is made before any possible contribution has been assessed. The need to expedite the trial of criminal cases explains this difference.
- Legal Aid is rarely refused, except on financial grounds, where the applicant is charged with a serious offence and it must be granted on a murder charge. The grant of civil Legal Aid is far more discretionary.

After the conclusion of the case, the court may order any assisted person to make a contribution to the costs according to their financial commitments and resources.

■ THE BANKING OMBUDSMAN

Disputes will invariably arise between banks and their customers. When they do it is normally in the interests of both sides to settle them amicably without involving outside parties, as we have explained. For example, a missing credit transfer can usually be found and an apology is usually sufficient. If a dispute cannot be resolved in this way, then resort to legal action is possible. However, this takes time, costs money and can cause bad publicity and distress. Indeed, in relation to the amounts involved and the increasing competitiveness of the financial marketplace, it is sometimes commercially far better for a bank to stand a small loss than fight – if the customer has the resources and determination to pursue the claim.

Nevertheless, the vast numbers of cheques and payment slips processed each day and the increasing use of ATMs and electronic funds transfer creates ever greater opportunity for fraud, greater risk of error and potential for maladministration. Mistakes will happen and disputes will ensue. Against this background the Office of the Banking Ombudsman was established in January 1986 to resolve disputes acting as a neutral arbiter between banks and customers and to investigate customer complaints. Nevertheless, the aim of the Banking Ombudsman scheme is conciliation and settlements by agreement are actively encouraged, in fact many referrals are settled at a very early stage.

The Banking Ombudsman is funded by the major banks – 20 at present, including the Abbey National, and covering at least 99 per cent of all people in GB with bank accounts. His services are free and he is independent of the banks, being responsible to an independent Ombudsman Council – consisting of five lay persons and three representatives of the banking industry – which also gives the Ombudsman general advice and guidance. Personal customers – individuals, sole traders, partnerships, clubs, trade unions and charities ('individuals' as defined by the Consumer Credit Act 1974) – may take a dispute to the Ombudsman but corporate customers, e.g. companies, cannot. Here we use 'customers' in a general sense because the complainant need not have an account with the bank, s/he must only have been provided with banking services (*see* below). (Credit card accounts are often operated for customers who do not have current accounts with the bank owning the credit card company.) The scheme covers bank employees and their spouses. However, a referral is very much the last resort. Customers must first try to resolve the dispute at branch level, asking the branch staff to refer it to a higher level if they are still dissatisfied. Only after the bank's own complaints procedures have been exhausted will the Banking Ombudsman become involved.

If the bank involved considers that the complaint involves a point which could have important consequences for the bank or banks generally, or involves an important or novel point of law, it may serve written notice to this effect on the Ombudsman. Having received such notice, the Ombudsman's investigation must be immediately stopped and the issue referred to the court. The bank involved, however, must undertake to pay all the legal costs incurred by the complainant.

The Banking Ombudsman's jurisdiction is restricted to complaints relating to the provision of banking services by a bank participating in the scheme. Included in the term 'banking services' are:

- credit card services;
- executor and trustee work;
- advice and services relating to taxation, investments and mortgages; as well as
- operation of accounts.

Estate and travel agency operations, finance house subsidiaries, and banking services provided abroad are not included.

However, there are limits on the Ombudsman's jurisdiction.

- Only alleged mistakes involving less than £100,000 can be dealt with.
- Complaints involving the commercial judgment of the bank, the rejection of a loan application for example, or involving the use of its discretion under a will or a trust are outside the terms of reference.

The Ombudsman can order a bank to rectify a mistake and can make an award to a maximum of £100,000. Banks participating in the scheme are bound to abide by decisions and awards of the Ombudsman but customers are not, they can still take the dispute to court.

In arriving at his decision, the Ombudsman is not bound by strict legal considerations. His function is to determine whether poor administration has caused inconvenience or loss or damage to the complainant and make a decision which is fair in the circumstances, it is not to assess whether the action complained of is or is not lawful. (In awarding compensation for 'inconvenience', the Ombudsman has wider powers than the courts.) His decision is based on existing standards of good banking practice as determined by consultation with the banking industry. In reaching his decision the Ombudsman takes into account the Code of Banking Practice produced jointly in 1991 by the Association for Payment Clearing Services (APACS), the British Bankers' Association (BBA) and the Building Societies Association (BSA) in response to the government's 1990 White Paper 'Banking Services Law and Practice'. This Code, among other things, sets out the standards of good banking practice which banks, building societies and card issuers will follow (*see* further Chapter 5). For example, it requires that banks will have their own individual procedures for handling their customers' complaints; that they will inform their customers of this procedure; that they should belong to the Banking Ombudsman Scheme if they subscribe to the Code; and that they will provide their customers with information about the Scheme.

The Ombudsman therefore monitors and promotes compliance with existing standards, it is *not* his function to determine what those standards should be. (Note that the Code of Banking Practice applies to building societies and that the Building Societies Ombudsman also takes it into account when making his decisions.)

To date, the most common complaints are disputed withdrawals from ATMs, closely followed by 'irregular conduct' of an account, for example, not supplying statements or not paying standing orders, and disputes about bank charges.

Both banks and customers stand to gain from the existence of the Banking Ombudsman. The office helps to maintain and improve public confidence in banks' operations while to customers the office offers a way to pursue effectively complaints without having to take on the might of a bank in court.

The Banking Ombudsman scheme is not part of the state system of courts and tribunals nor is it a conventional arbitration body. It uses neither a judicial nor quasi-judicial process to resolve disputes, even though the subject matter could form the substance of court action for breach of contract. Instead it uses an investigatory process to arrive at decisions. While the decisions bind the banks that are members of the scheme, they do not have the force of law and do not prevent the customer from taking subsequent court action. Nevertheless, as far as the banking industry is concerned, the scheme is very much part of conflict resolving.

ACTIVITY 3.3
Produce the draft of a short leaflet suitable for customers which concisely explains the role of the Banking Ombudsman. Set out his jurisdiction in the form of a table.

■ SUMMARY

1 Banks will consider a variety of factors besides their legal position before bringing or defending a court action.

2 A judicial process involves a judge making a reasoned decision according to known rules of law on the basis of the evidence available to both parties and offered to the court.

3 A quasi-judicial process is very similar but has less formal rules of procedure and evidence and is used in arbitration hearings and tribunals.

4 Courts can be classified according to:
- whether they deal with mainly criminal or civil disputes (most deal with both);
- whether they have solely or mainly original or appellate jurisdiction (some have both); or
- whether they are superior or inferior courts.

5 The most important courts in terms of level of function are the House of Lords and Court of Appeal. Both have solely appellate jurisdiction.

6 The Queen's Bench and Chancery Divisions of the High Court are those in which most disputes involving banks will be resolved.

7 In terms of volume of work, the county and magistrates' courts are the most important.

8 County court jurisdiction is limited financially and geographically. It has an arbitration procedure for small claims.

9 The main functions of the magistrates' courts are the summary trial of minor offences and the preliminary examination of indictable offences. They also have, however, important civil jurisdiction.

10 Arbitration is a quasi-judicial process used in civil disputes where the parties agree to allow a third party to resolve the dispute between them.

11 The business community has used arbitration to resolve disputes for many centuries.

12 Most disputes between the individual and the state are resolved by administrative tribunals.

13 The courts supervise administrative tribunals by the issue of prerogative orders. Administrative supervision is exercised by the Council on Tribunals.

14 Compared to courts, arbitration hearings and tribunals have the advantages of:
- flexibility;
- informality;
- lack of publicity;
- greater practical expertise in the subject matter.

They may also offer a quicker and cheaper method of resolving a dispute.

15 The Banking Ombudsman can deal with a wide range of complaints from personal customers to the value of £100,000 but only when a bank's own complaints procedure has been exhausted.

■ SELF-ASSESSMENT QUESTIONS

1 Explain why obtaining a definitive ruling was so important to the banks concerned in the *Boland* and *Tai Hing* cases.

2 What are the similarities and what are the differences between judicial and quasi-judicial processes?

3 Which courts are superior courts?

4 Name the courts which have either exclusively civil or exclusively criminal jurisdiction.

5 What is meant by original jurisdiction?

6 Name the two divisions of the High Court in which most actions involving banks will be heard. What is the name of the third division?

7 How is the jurisdiction of the county court limited?

8 Explain why the county court arbitration procedure facilitates the recovery of small claims.

9 Outline the jurisdiction of the magistrates' courts.

10 When is an umpire appointed in an arbitration?

11 In what circumstances can an appeal be made to the High Court from an arbitrator's decision?

12 Explain the advantages of an arbitration procedure to business people.

13 Explain the conflict resolving role of administrative tribunals.

14 By what processes are administrative tribunals controlled and supervised?

15 What is the jurisdiction of the Banking Ombudsman?

■ MULTIPLE-CHOICE QUESTIONS

1 In which of the following courts would a bank bring an action to recover an overdrawn balance of £10,000?
   A Magistrates' Court
   B County Court
   C High Court
   D Crown Court

2 Which of the following courts has exclusively civil or exclusively criminal jurisdiction?
   A House of Lords
   B High Court
   C County Court
   D Magistrates Court

3 If a bank wished to appeal against a first instance decision against it in an English court, which of the following courts could ultimately hear the appeal?

A the High Court
B the Crown Court
C the House of Lords
D the Judicial Committee of the Privy Council

4 Which of the following courts has exclusive original jurisdiction to try indictable offences?
A Magistrates Court
B Crown Court
C Queen's Bench Division of the High Court
D Court of Appeal (Criminal Division)

5 Which of the following bodies is the lowest in the hierarchy of those dealing with criminal cases?
A County court
B Magistrates court
C Administrative tribunal
D Crown court

6 Which of the following Acts of Parliament set up the Office of the Banking Ombudsman:
A The Banking Act 1979
B The Banking Act 1987
C Financial Services Act 1986
D None of these

4 Contract law and banking: the background

OBJECTIVES

After studying this chapter you should be able to:
1 Understand the role of contract law in the business of banking;
2 Explain why banks use standard form contracts wherever possible;
3 Discuss the nature and essential elements of a contract: agreement, bargain, and the intention to create legal relations;
4 Discuss the contractual requirements of form; capacity, reality of consent and legality;
5 Relate the principles of contract law to everyday banking transactions.

■ INTRODUCTION

This is the first of two chapters on contract law. It is a very important part of your studies because contract law is the basis of virtually all commercial law. This first chapter covers the general principles of contract law, the next, banker-customer contracts. At all times, however, it is important that you 'think banking'. Try to relate theory to practice, ask yourself how things are done in your own branch and why. Obtain copies of documents we mention and generally try to take the law from these pages and into your bank.

If this is the approach, why study the theory? Why not just concentrate on the practice? Such an approach is tempting in a vocationally oriented course and may appear more logical. However, it is probably safer to adopt a compromise between the two. There are four reasons for this. First, it is by studying the theory that we can best understand the practice. The practice would be too confusing for most of us to use as the starting point since it would need much case study to determine the principles involved. At a basic level most things can be understood using commonsense but commonsense soon ceases to be adequate as the complexities of human and organisational behaviour are encountered and the scale of activities increases. For example, buying a newspaper and lending £100m to a property developer are both contracts, yet they can hardly be considered as comparable arrangements.

Second, while most of us can get along fine without a great deal of theoretical knowledge while things are going well, an understanding of the theory becomes very useful when things do not go so well. There is no need to understand the technicalities of contract law when a contract is being performed according to its terms but an understanding may become all important if a dispute arises over their meaning or the contract's performance.

Third, in your work you deal with customers and colleagues. They may look to you for explanations of the theory behind the practice or expect you to be conversant with it when discussing a particular issue. You have your own needs every bit as much as the bank has its needs. Finally, of course, your studies are vocational education rather than training, as a till procedures course is for example. Thus, some theoretical study is perfectly proper and you will be expected to show an understanding of it in your examination answers.

■ SOME BASIC IDEAS

The need for contract law

Contract law is central to all aspects of modern banking. Besides the 'basic' banking contract with a customer covering the operation of an account, there are many other contracts that a bank enters into with various categories of customers. Obvious examples include overdrafts and loans, specific safe custody arrangements and contracts for insurance services. And besides customer contracts, there are all the contracts on the resource side of the business, for example, contracts with employees and suppliers. In short, a bank, indeed any business organisation, pursues its objectives by entering into voluntary agreements with other organisations and individuals. Resources are acquired and services sold by making agreements complying with a set of rules which must have the force of law to ensure the smooth operation of commercial activity. These rules constitute the law of contract.

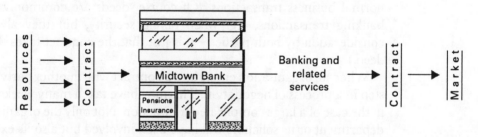

Fig 4.1 The role of contract law

Too often the law is viewed as a constraint upon a person's activities. Justifiably, this may be so in the case of the criminal law or the law of torts, where society prohibits particular activities or protects a certain rights, but the law of contract should be viewed as a *facilitating medium* enabling organisations to operate. It cannot be viewed realistically as a medium of constraint, automatically involving sanctions for anyone who becomes involved with it. However, unless society wishes to have a commercial world in which there are no rules and no protection for the weak, some constraints in the law of contract are clearly necessary, for example in employment and consumer contracts. We discussed the Consumer Credit Act 1974, an example of this, in Chapter 2.

Thus, contract law provides a framework, a more or less definitive foundation upon which a bank can build its activities and with which it can regularise its operations, both externally in its dealings with customers and other organisations and internally with its own employees and shareholders.

Before we start to look at what a contract is, it is important to realise that the vast majority of commercial transactions never result in any dispute or court action. Most run their course according to their contractual terms. Even where there has been a clear breach of these terms by one of the parties the other will frequently not take legal action, as we explained in Chapter 3. The breach of contract has to be seen in perspective. Legal action frequently loses a business goodwill, high costs are involved, with no certainty of recovering them, and at the very least time and trouble are involved. The advantages of taking legal action must be weighed against its disadvantages: a legal remedy versus financial and general business considerations.

What is a contract?

Contract law consists of *legal rules* governing the enforceability of obligations arising from voluntary agreements between individuals or organisations. A contract is simply an *agreement which the courts will enforce.* The law in this sphere reflects its commercial origins and an agreement will only be enforced if it is also a bargain that is intended to create legal relations between the parties. Each side must give something of value for what they receive from the other; a mere agreement where one party receives without giving anything in return is not enforceable. To this there is one exception – an agreement made by deed. This is a historical legacy which is extremely unlikely to be found in normal business transactions. (Of course, deeds are commonly executed in banking transactions, e.g. when taking security, but they always involve consideration by both parties – it is just that the contract takes the form of a deed.)

When an organisation enters into a contract with another party it is the final step in a process of negotiation. This may have taken many weeks to conclude in the case of a large complicated transaction. Not only the organisation's legal department or its solicitors will have been involved but also its executives and financial advisers, for such a contract may involve important questions of policy, procedure and financial planning. Alternatively, the contract may have been an ordinary retail sale or a contract for the provision of a simple service, in which case the customer and possibly the organisation's employees may have been only vaguely aware that they were entering into a legal relationship involving well-defined and important rights and duties.

ACTIVITY 4.1

Before you read any further, make a list of all the different agreements which you consider to be contracts that you have entered into for yourself or on behalf of your bank over the last week. As you work through this chapter, decide which were and which were not enforceable contracts by applying the rules of contract law to them. (Don't include more than one purchase of a newspaper or sale of foreign currency – try to list as many *types* as you can.)

Freedom to bargain

Whatever the exact nature of the contract, the parties are free to negotiate with each other and conclude a voluntary bargain, stipulating and agreeing the terms which they wish the contract to contain. The courts will uphold the bargain, good or bad, provided the essential elements required by the law exist.

However, in many cases this freedom to bargain is rather illusory. Sellers are often only willing to sell their goods or services on their own standard terms of business. In such a situation the buyer's only real freedom is to accept the seller's terms or to buy elsewhere. In this country it is difficult to imagine the parties bargaining in an ordinary retail sale. Bank mortgages or guarantees are very much 'take or leave it' contracts, although they are not presented, and probably never thought of, as such. The forms of contract used contain many standard terms making them lengthy and complicated documents. While the bank may want to lend to the customer every bit as much as the customer wants to borrow from the bank, it will never be prepared to negotiate the basic terms of the agreement.

ACTIVITY 4.2

Consider the list of agreements you made in the first activity. In which of them, if any, did you or, perhaps, the other party have any freedom to negotiate the terms?

Standard form contracts

These are contracts where the terms are predetermined, they are not subject to negotiation between the parties. Standard form contracts are not new, the standard terms found in policies of insurance and bills of lading evolved over a long period of time to best represent the commercial interests of all involved. Such standard form contracts, or at least the terms, are of *general application* in the particular area of economic activity.

Banks and many other business organisations, however, design and use their own standard form contracts so that they can trade on the terms they want. This, of course, invariably means the terms that are most advantageous to them, legally, commercially and administratively. For example, it enables procedures to be standardised, which means a time saving and fewer staff errors. Indeed, the use of standard form contracts is also to the advantage of the other parties in so far as they know in advance the terms, their rights and obligations, and can plan accordingly. The disadvantage, if any, will lie in the terms themselves. Such standard form contracts – known as *contracts of adhesion* – are of more modern origin and differ from the older type in that they have not been the subject of negotiation and evolution over the years.

Most standard form contracts are perfectly proper and unobjectionable. Those used by the major holiday tour operators, i.e. their booking forms, are models of clarity and show that legally binding agreements do not have to be couched in very formal and often difficult language. (No doubt the market has not only determined the nature of the holidays offered but also the format of the contract used to purchase them.)

Some standard form contracts take away rights the other party would have had but they only do what the law allows and are well within accepted standards of commercial morality. An example of such a contract is a bank guarantee. The common law favours a surety because the surety takes responsibility for someone else's debt. Under a bank's contract of guarantee the surety will, for example, accept postponement of their right of proof in the bankruptcy of the principal debtor until the bank has been paid in full, and accept the bank's statement of the extent of their liability as conclusive evidence of it. Similarly, s/he accepts that the bank can vary its arrangements with the principal debtor without their consent and, in the case of a guarantee by more than one surety (a joint and several guarantee), release any surety or release or vary any security it holds without prejudicing its position or affecting the liability of any other co-surety. In fact, the surety is left only with the right to rescind (set aside) the contract for misrepresentation.

The courts have always been aware of inequality in bargaining power and have to some extent redressed the balance by, for example, restricting the effect of exclusion and limitation clauses. In *Tai Hing* (1986), a modern banking example, (*see* p 22) the banks had included express terms in their contracts with their customers which sought to impose a duty on customers to check their statements and raise any queries within a specified period, at the end of which the statements would be deemed to be correct. Since the terms sought to exclude a right 'traditionally' enjoyed by customers (not to have to check bank statements) and to impose a specific duty, the Privy Council held that the terms would only be enforceable if their effect was made absolutely clear to the customers. On the facts, this had not been done and the terms were without legal effect.

Parliament, however, has only comparatively recently begun to play its role. Statutes such as the Consumer Credit Act 1974, the Supply of Goods and Services Act 1982 and the Unfair Contract Terms Act 1977 are examples of this statutory intervention. The last is particularly important in that it subjects most exclusion or limitation clauses to a judicial test of reasonableness if they are pleaded as a defence. It is therefore a significant restraint on the ability to use standard form contracts unfairly.

ACTIVITY 4.3

(a) Obtain copies of:
- a credit card agreement;
- a guarantee;
- a charge form;

and carefully study them. Identify the clauses in them which protect the interests of your bank. (You will probably need to ask the meaning and effect of some of the clauses but this will stand you in good stead later in your course.)

(b) Obtain a copy of a tour operator's booking form (contract), you may well have one in a holiday brochure at home. Compare it with the forms you obtained from your bank. What differences do you notice? Account for those differences.

An alternative view

Conventional contract law theory is based on the notion of *freedom to bargain*.

This assumes that the parties bargain from positions of equal strength and have complete freedom in their decision-making. But is any bargaining actually involved? Certainly not in the commercial sense in most consumer contracts. We have a system where the seller fixes the price and the terms of business and the buyer's freedom is essentially to accept or reject these. Often, of course, the buyer is not in a position to reject. The goods or services are needed and no suitable alternative source of supply may be available. If one is, as would be the case in banking, the buyer is likely to be presented with much the same terms of business. In banking specifically, the customer is a prisoner of a combination of market forces and structure, which fix the price of the service, and the law, which determines the terms of the contract. Here we are just stating fact, it is not some strange 'anti-bank' propaganda. Banks, as you know, will go out of their way to be helpful and are usually only too happy to lend people money – but on their terms.

Although you have yet to cover the basic principals of contract law bear in mind that there are some who argue that the whole emphasis of conventional contract law theory is wrong. How often, they ask, do business people analyse their contracts in terms of offer and acceptance – 'Not very often.' is the answer. They are concerned with concluding a mutually satisfactory *bargain* by negotiation, often over a considerable period of time, and protecting their interests if the other side does not keep its side of the bargain. On many occasions, a contract in the strictly *legal* sense is never concluded. The legal technicalities are often regarded as matters of little relevance to modern commercial practice and business and commercial exchanges frequently fail to conform to the conventional theoretical model of a contract. Where a formal contract is used in a commercial exchange, a business will always try to use a standard form – its own of course – wherever possible. A standard form contract provides a safe, simple, proven and economical way of doing business.

The position may become interesting from a theoretical perspective when both sides use standard forms in their negotiations, i.e. to use conventional legal terminology, the 'offer' contains standard terms and conditions and so does the 'acceptance' – different ones. This is referred to as a *battle of the forms* and it becomes difficult to determine which of the two sets of standard terms and conditions is the basis of the contract. How can the parties be said to have concluded the all important agreement? The practice is clearly at odds with the theory. Of course the parties have reached an 'agreement' if they are doing business with each other, the theoretical problems only surface on the relatively rare occasions when a dispute arises. Interestingly enough, theory finds it hard to cope with such situations. While the conduct of the parties clearly suggests an agreement was made, there is equally clearly no agreement on the terms and conditions. Perhaps arbitration by specialists rather than the judicial process is better equipped to resolve such disputes. Alternatively, business people may ignore all forms of formal conflict resolving and rely on informal arrangements or make provision for bad debts. Indeed, there are those that argue that business practice is non-contractual – the opposite of our introduction to this chapter.

The essentials of a valid contract

A valid contract has three essential features.

1 The *agreement*, consisting of one party making an offer which is accepted by the other.
2 The *bargain*; there must be an element of exchange, the law requiring what is called 'consideration'.
3 The *intention to create legal relations*.

These features are represented diagrammatically in Fig 4.2.

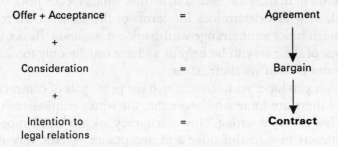

Fig 4.2 The essentials of a valid contract

In addition there are four other requirements which, although not essential features as such, will effect the validity or enforceability of the contract should it be defective in one or more of these respects (*see* below). To cite a specific example, by a very old statute, the Statute of Frauds 1677, a guarantee (a promise to answer for the debt of another) is only enforceable at law if there is *written evidence* of the guarantee – verbal evidence, no matter how conclusive, is not enough. Thus, even though there is a definite agreement, consideration (the granting of a loan to the principal debtor in return for the promise to answer for it if the principal debtor does not make payment), an intention to be legally bound by the arrangement, full contractual capacity in both parties, no evidence on which to question the genuineness of the agreement and no evidence of any form of illegality, the court will not enforce the promise merely because there is no written evidence of it.

These four further requirements are:

1 the *required form*, e.g. writing, although most contracts require no particular form;
2 *legal capacity* to make the contract, e.g. minors who, in particular, are subject to special rules;
3 *genuineness of consent* to the terms of contract, e.g. the terms may have been misrepresented by one of the parties or one party was unduly influenced by the other;
4 *legality*, e.g. the contract may be against public policy such as where an employment contract restricts employees' rights to freely accept other employment on leaving their current employer.

In the rest of this chapter we discuss each of these requirements in turn and cite a number cases. There are two reasons for citing these cases:

- they illustrate the situations we discuss; and, more importantly,
- most of contract law is derived from cases and any dispute arising from the contract would be resolved in court by reference to decisions in similar cases.

The cases we describe are all well-known and their principles apply to all fields of business. Remember, however, that such well-known cases either laid down a principle which to us now seems self-evident and/or were clear-cut and often extreme situations. Many contractual problems encountered today are, of course, often more involved although, ultimately, a simple rule of law will probably be applied to settle the dispute once the exact nature of the dispute has been determined and all the evidence and arguments have been heard.

Void, voidable and unenforceable

Agreements which fail on one of these four further requirements are either *void*, *voidable*, or *unenforceable*. We need to explain each of these terms.

A *void* contract is a contradiction in terms since it has never been a contract and is, therefore, without legal effect. Despite this, it is a useful term to describe a situation where the parties intended to enter into a contract, and apparently did so, but legally or physically the agreement can have no effect. In *Strickland v Turner* (1852), for example, an annuity was void because neither party to it knew that the person on whose life the annuity was taken out had already died!

A *voidable* contract can be rejected by the 'innocent' party but it is perfectly valid until it is rejected. For example, if your consent to the agreement was obtained by fraud, other misrepresentation or by the exercise of undue influence, you have the right to rescind (set aside) the contract when you realise this. However, because the contract is valid until avoided, subsequent events may prevent you rejecting. For example, in *Lewis v Averay* (1971) a rogue obtained a car from L by posing as a famous actor whose cheque book and studio pass he had stolen. The sale was clearly voidable for fraud. He then sold the car to A posing as L. In an action by L to recover the car from A, it was held that when A bought the car in good faith and for value from the rogue, A obtained good title to it. The contract of sale between L and the rogue had ceased to be voidable and L could not recover the car.

An *unenforceable* contract is perfectly valid and therefore property or money transferred under it cannot be recovered. However, it is not enforceable because the necessary legal evidence of it is missing. Thus, if you fail to fulfil your obligations, the other party cannot compel you to do so. We have already mentioned that a guarantee requires written evidence of its terms to be enforceable.

■ THE AGREEMENT

Offer

The law requires that one party must make a definite offer to the other, although it need not be express but may be made by implication. The presence of an automatic car park, for example, is an implied offer to any motorist that they may park inside in return for a specified payment.

Similarly, an offer does not have to be made to a specific person or group of people, it can be made to anyone – the world at large. In *Carlill v Carbolic Smoke Ball Co* (1892) the company offered to pay £100 to anybody who used their 'smoke-ball' in the way described and still caught influenza. When sued by Carlill, who had used the 'smoke-ball' and caught influenza, the company unsuccessfully pleaded, *inter alia* (among other things), that it could not be held to its promise as it had not made the offer directly to Carlill.

An offer must be distinguished from an *invitation to treat*. This is an invitation to enter into negotiations or to make an offer which may or may not result in the conclusion of an agreement. Most organisations advertise or display their products and while these may be interpreted by the man in the street as 'offers' to sell goods or provide services, at law no offer is made. Hence, in *Pharmaceutical Society of GB v Boots Cash Chemists (Southern), Ltd* (1952) a prosecution under the Pharmacy and Poisons Act 1933, which made it an offence to sell any listed poison '... unless the sale took place under the supervision of a registered pharmacist ...', failed because it was held that selection of an item from a self-service display did not amount to a sale. The display was an invitation to treat. The customer had made the offer by selecting the article, the defendants had accepted it and completed the sale when a pharmacist approved the transaction near the cash-desk. At law, therefore, the sale took place according to the provisions of the Act.

As you will see in later chapters, land is a complicated concept at law and considerable formality is attached to its sale and transfer as a consequence. A series of cases show that the courts are generally unwilling to acknowledge the existence of an offer to sell land unless the clearest evidence of this intention exists. In *Harvey v Facey* (1893) a telegraphed reply giving the lowest cash price at which the defendant was willing to sell his property was held not to amount to a definite offer to sell and in *Clifton v Palumbo* (1944) an 'offer' to sell a large estate for £600,000 was held to be merely a statement of price. However, in *Bigg v Boyd Gibbons Ltd* (1971) the Court of Appeal found that the parties had concluded a contract to sell the property in question, even though only the names of the parties, the property and the price were certain. These aspects, however, are the essential features of the agreement in a contract for the sale of land. This attitude towards land and its relative legal complexity accounts for the formality associated with taking mortgages over land.

ACTIVITY 4.4

Consider the following situation. The CIB Department Store is holding its annual sale and the star bargain is a top-of-range TV which is marked with the price of £50. You decide you want it and spend two reasonably uncomfortable days and nights queuing outside the shop to ensure that you are first in the queue. You are, and when the sale begins you rush to the TV department, thrust your £50 at the salesperson and say 'Where is it then?'. 'Where is what – Sir?' is the reply. After some increasingly heated exchanges it turns out that CIB never intended to sell the TV at that price at all: the promotion was designed to attract people like you to the sale.

You are not pleased and decide to take steps to recover damages for breach of contract by the CIB Department Store. Will you be able to do so? Give your reasons.

Termination of the offer

At any time after the offer has been made it can be revoked (withdrawn) by the offeror (the person who makes the offer) provided the revocation is communicated to the offeree (the person to whom the offer is made) before the latter has accepted the offer. Although the offeree incurs the responsibility of deciding whether the notice is reasonable, the decision in *Dickinson v Dodds* (1876) clearly shows that it is not necessary for the offeror to revoke personally. In that case, an offer to sell a house to the plaintiff was held to have been effectively revoked after the defendant sold it to a third party and the plaintiff was informed of this by a fourth. He had received sufficient notice of the defendant's revocation.

When the offer has been revoked it terminates through the positive act of one of the parties involved. This is also the case where the offeree accepts or rejects the offer that was made. However, an offer can terminate in other ways. The offeror may have specially stated that the offer was to remain open for a limited period and it will automatically terminate if not accepted within that time limit. If no time limit is stated, it is a question of fact whether the offer still exists after a given time has passed. Offers of mortgage and other loans from banks always state a period in which the customer must accept the offer. This, of course, is largely to enable the bank to monitor and control its projected lending.

Offers are sometimes made subject to a condition that must be fulfilled before any acceptance of the offer creates a binding agreement: a condition precedent. It is normal when buying a second-hand car to want a valid MOT certificate for the car and therefore X might say to Y: 'I offer to buy your car for £600 provided it passes its MOT test'. Should the car not pass, X's offer to buy terminates.

In *Financing Ltd v Stimson* (1962) a more difficult situation arose. The defendant alleged the existence of an implied condition. He had signed an 'agreement' to buy a car, which he had seen at a dealer's premises, from the plaintiff on hire-purchase terms. The 'agreement' stated that the plaintiff was only to be bound when the plaintiff signed it. The defendant paid the first instalment and took the car away but, being dissatisfied, returned it two days later. The car was then stolen from the dealer's premises and recovered badly damaged. In ignorance of all these events the plaintiff signed the 'agreement'. On discovering what had happened they sold the car and sued the defendant for breach of the 'agreement'. The Court of Appeal held that the 'agreement' was in fact an offer which had been made subject to an implied condition that, until it was accepted, the car would remain in substantially the same state as when the offer was made. The defendant's offer had therefore terminated before it was accepted by the plaintiffs.

Acceptance

The agreement is completed by the offeree accepting the offer which has been made. Just as the offer must be firm and certain, so too must the acceptance. No agreement results from 'I'll think about it' or 'I might buy that'. Legal obligations must be definite and only a complete acceptance of the offer will result in an enforceable agreement.

The same is true where the offeree wishes to have a second opinion before being committed to a contract. For example, when a second-hand car is offered for sale, a potential purchaser might say 'I'll buy it providing it passes a garage inspection'; this is not a definite acceptance. Such conditional acceptances are also common when the offeree does not wish to be legally bound until a formal contract is drafted. The phrase 'subject to contract', which solicitors invariably include in preliminary correspondence relating to the sale of land, operates as an express denial of any binding agreement.

Should the offeree wish to try to vary the terms of the offer it is a question of fact whether the proposals amount to a counter-offer and a rejection of the original offer or merely a request for original form. In *Hyde v Wrench* (1840) a reply to an offer, quoting a lower price for the land that the defendant wished to sell, was held to be a rejection of the original offer preventing the plaintiff subsequently accepting the offer at the original price.

In some agreements there is no express acceptance; the offeree does not say 'I accept' but the existence of a firm acceptance can be implied from the circumstances. In *Brogden v Metropolitan Rail Co* (1877), B had supplied coal to MR for a number of years without any formal agreement and at length the parties decided to put their dealings on a more formal footing. A draft agreement sent by MR was amended and approved by B and then returned. MR's agent did not complete the formalities required but both sides began to deal with each other according to the terms of the draft. B had not accepted the draft because he had added a new term by his amendment and it was up to MR to accept or reject this. However, the subsequent conduct of the parties could only be explained on the basis that the draft had been agreed by both sides. On the facts a binding contract existed. *Brogden's Case* is an old example of the theory that much business can be considered 'non-contractual' in the strict sense. It is also an early illustration of the theoretical problems posed by the parties exchanging forms without formally reaching agreement on them. Both points we discussed earlier.

Communication of acceptance

It is not enough merely to accept the offer, the acceptance must be communicated. Usually this is done verbally or by letter.

In this context it has long been established that remaining silent in response to an offer is not an acceptance of it. If the law were otherwise, contractual liability could be imposed on an unwilling person by merely stating that their silence was acceptance of the offer. However, in the offer the offeror may expressly or by implication waive the need to communicate acceptance. In *Carlill v Carbolic Smoke Ball Co* (1892), for example, the company argued that

Carlill had not communicated her acceptance but it was held that the nature of the offer implied that it was unnecessary to do so. Her conduct was her acceptance.

The postal rule The post is a basic form of communication in business and special rules relate to postal acceptance of offers. Normally an acceptance by post is complete as soon as it is posted, provided it is properly stamped and addressed. Once posted, the acceptance cannot be withdrawn but an offeror will be bound by a postal acceptance even if it is never delivered. In contrast, a postal revocation of an offer is only effective when actually brought to the offeror's attention.

The postal rule is an *exception* to the general rule that acceptance must be communicated and cannot apply where the terms of the offer specify actual communication within a time limit. In *Holwell Securities Ltd v Hughes* (1973), for example, the proper construction of an option to purchase property '... exercisable by notice in writing to intending vendor at any time within six months from the date thereof ...', was that the notice had to be delivered to him personally and a properly posted letter which never arrived did not amount to an exercise of the option.

Specifying the method The offer may itself specify the way in which it is to be accepted and the method then amounts to a term of the offer and must be accepted along with the rest of the terms. However, the courts allow flexibility and where the requirement is not obligatory they will accept another method equally as good. In *Yates Building Co Ltd v R J Pulleyn & Sons (York) Ltd* (1975), for example, a letter exercising an option was held to have been wrongly rejected even though it was sent neither by registered post nor recorded delivery as requested. On the facts the requirement was held not to be obligatory and the letter sent was equally effective. Where the offeror does not stipulate any particular method of communication, the effectiveness of the method chosen depends upon the facts of the case. An offer by telex or fax, for example, implies a similar method of acceptance.

ACTIVITY 4.5

On 1 January Jack writes to his hill-walking friend Jill offering to sell her his car for £2,500 knowing that she has been looking to buy such a car. He states that he must have an answer by 10 January at the latest because he needs the money to buy another car on the 11 January. Jill writes back, her letter arriving on the 3 January, saying that the price was rather more than she could afford to pay at once and would he accept payment in two equal monthly instalments. Jack does not reply to this letter and Jill fails to contact him by telephone because he is spending time with his new ballroom dancing partner Buster. Jill wants the car and manages to put together Jack's asking price. She writes accepting Jack's offer on 8 January, her letter arriving on 10 January. On 9 January Jack sells his car to Buster for £2,000 and informs Jill of this after her letter has arrived.

Jill is not pleased and wished to take action against Jack for breach of contract, maintaining that Jack was under an obligation to sell the car to her.

Consider the strength of her case.

Certainty in the agreement

There must be *certainty* in the agreement reached by the parties. The law will not enforce vague agreements. In *Loftus v Roberts* (1902), an agreement where an actress was engaged at '… a West End salary to be mutually arranged between us …' was held to be unenforceable because the salary, an important term in the agreement, was clearly too vague. Similarly, in *Scammel v Ousten* (1941) an agreement to buy a motor van on the 'usual hire-purchase terms' was too vague because at the time there were no usual hire-purchase terms which could have been implied into the contract.

The law recognises, however, that there are a number of ways in which vagueness can be rectified and it will enforce agreements that can be made certain. For example:

- terms may be implied into (included in) the agreement by acts of Parliament, the courts or by trade custom to give it certainty – the implied terms in the banker-customer contract are good examples of judicial implied terms;
- the parties to the agreement may have had dealings with each other before and it may be possible to remove any uncertainty in the agreement by referring to these previous dealings;
- the agreement itself may provide a way to remove the uncertainty. For example, a provision under which disputes on the contract are to be referred to arbitration. Partial inexactitude should not defeat the entire contract.

It is worth noting that it is usually only when things go wrong that disputes about the exact terms, or even the existence of the contract, arise because they offer a potential way to avoid liability. When things are going well, neither side is going to worry if lawyers would wring their hands in horror at regrettably incomplete or uncertain wording. Any contract entered into by a bank should be a model of clarity and completeness, of course, but you should think more like the business person while appreciating the lawyer's point of view.

Perhaps the best-known example of a term being implied into contracts is the condition found in s.14 of the Sale of Goods Act 1979 that all goods sold in the course of a business must be of 'merchantable quality'. But you will see below that the banker-customer contract depends almost entirely on *implied terms*.

The banker-customer agreement

How does this model of the contractual agreement relate to the banker-customer contract? The would-be customer makes the offer to the bank. This is done by completing a standard account opening form. The bank then accepts the application by agreeing to open an account in the applicant's name, or rejects the application. If references are required and the opening of the account is made specifically dependent upon satisfactory ones being received, no contract is concluded until they are, for here the bank's acceptance of the offer is conditional.

Although it marks the commencement of important rights and duties on both sides, between bank and would-be customer the exact point at which a contract is concluded probably matters little in practice unless the bank collects a cheque for that person. Should the person have no title to the cheque, the bank could only claim the protection of the Cheques Act 1957, s.4 if it acted *for a customer* – a person for whom it had agreed to open an account and with whom it therefore has a contract.

When an account is being opened, particularly a personal account, it is very doubtful that the bank would give, or the would-be personal customer would ask for, detailed explanations of all the implied terms of the banker-customer contract. As for *express terms*, the application form is unlikely to contain more than a short section of terms covering *joint accounts*. Under these the account holders accept joint and several liability for any overdraft, authorise the bank on the death of one of the account holders to deliver any credit balance, security or safe custody item against the signature of the survivor(s), and release the bank from its duty under the Customer Credit Act 1974 to provide duplicate statements of account to all the account holders. The rest of the terms are implied and we cover these in the next chapter. In all probability, most customers would have some difficulty understanding them and/or little interest in knowing.

An application to open a business account will involve rather more specific terms but these deal in the main with the opening and operation of the account, e.g. who has authority to sign cheques, and not with the more general rights and duties of banker and customer.

Some banks have produced leaflets explaining the terms of the contract and these are very helpful to any customer who wants to know – and you!

It is perhaps surprising that the contract contains no express term allowing the bank to charge the customer for its services – the customer is presumed to agree to this rather than actually agreeing, nothing about the appropriation of payments – the legendary (or infamous!) *Clayton's Case* covers this, and no express authorisation to disclose details of the customer's financial affairs in response to a status enquiry. All is implied from case law.

This, of course, is contrary to the practice in many other areas of business where standard form contracts are the norm. Indeed, very detailed standard contracts have been used by banks for many years to lend, particularly personal loans; to take security; and for all forms of automatic banking, cheque and credit card agreements contain very precise express terms. Here the banks do not rely on terms being implied by the law. The reasons are that the risks involved are higher and they wish to protect their position, and such transactions lend themselves to standard forms because of their standard nature.

ACTIVITY 4.6

(a) Obtain samples of the forms and leaflets we have mentioned above and read them carefully.

(b) Carefully study the printed conditions which apply to your own cheque or credit card. You will find that they are very specific on all important matters.

■ THE BARGAIN

A contract is a bargain and a bargain involves an element of exchange – each side must give and receive something of value to and from the other. Goods in exchange for cash is a simple but perfect example.

Therefore, the law will only enforce a promise when it has been bought by the person who wishes to enforce it. *Consideration is the price of the promise.* An agreement in which consideration is present is nearly always an enforceable bargain. More formal judicial definitions of consideration exist but they often serve merely to cloud the essential simplicity of the concept. Even so, over the years the law has evolved a series of requirements which must be fulfilled before the proposed consideration will be acceptable.

Consideration must move from the promise

The consideration must be provided by the person to whom the promise was made and who wishes to enforce the promise. In other words, only the parties to the contract can acquire rights and obligations under it. A third party cannot enforce a contract. This fundamental common law principle is known as *privity of contract.*

Consideration must not be past

The consideration must not precede the promise that it supports. In *Re McArdle* (1951), a father's will left his house jointly to his children. One of the children and his wife still lived with the mother and the wife made substantial improvements to the house. The other children subsequently agreed to contribute towards the cost. An action to enforce the agreement failed because the improvements preceded the promise to contribute towards them.

Exceptions

Previously requested services If one person asks another to do something for them in a way which raises the presumption that s/he will be paid, a subsequent promise to pay will be enforceable. In *Re Casey's Patents, Stewart v Casey* (1892), a promise to give a one-third share of the patent rights, in return for services which the plaintiff had already performed in promoting and selling the patents, was enforced. The services had been requested and it was clearly understood that they were to be paid for.

Bills of exchange A statutory exception exists in the Bills of Exchange Act 1882, s.27. This states that in relation to bills of exchange, '... an antecedent debt or liability ...', i.e. a previous or existing liability, is 'valuable consideration'. A bill of exchange contains a promise to pay a specific sum of money and many bills are accepted and cheques drawn (a cheque is the most common type of bill of exchange) to settle existing (past) debts. Thus, the consideration given for the promise contained in the bill is past, e.g. payment by cheque for goods delivered a week ago. In short, the consideration precedes the promise. Clearly, however, this exception is necessary in order for cheques and other bills of exchange to fulfil their function as a method of payment. It is also a good example of the needs of commerce, via the Law Merchant, affecting the rules of contract law. (If in *Re McArdle* (1951), for example, the other children had given the wife a cheque, she could have enforced the promise of payment contained in it. Similarly, if the wife had been asked to make the improvements and then the promise of payment was made, the promise would have been enforceable: *Re Casey* (1892).)

ACTIVITY 4.7

Kylie is going on holiday for a month and asks her neighbour Jason to look after her four pet Siamese cats while she is away. Jason is somewhat reluctant to do so because the previous month they had badly savaged his pit-bull terrier that he had been given the previous Christmas. Nevertheless he agrees, after explaining that it would mean he would have to cancel his planned annual fly-fishing weekend.

On Kylie's return Jason explains that the cats have been quite a handful and that she needs to collect her last two week's post from the local post office. Kylie is full of remorse and promises to pay Jason £100 for his time and trouble.

After six weeks she has still not paid him. Can Jason enforce her promise? Would it make any difference if Kylie had given Jason a cheque for £100 and then stopped it?

Consideration must be sufficient

The consideration must be of some legal value. It must be sufficient but it need not be commercially adequate. For example, a person could sell a car for £1.00 and the law would not question the bargain that the parties had struck, provided that the bargain was not defective in any other respect. It is up to the parties to reach their own bargain, the law does not question their commercial judgment. In *Chappel & Co Ltd v Nestlé & Co Ltd* (1960), for example, N offered for sale a record of 'Rockin Shoes' for 7.5p plus three wrappers from their chocolate bars. C owned the copyright in the tune and brought a successful action for breach of copyright when N paid the statutory 6.25 per cent royalty on the 7.5p received for each record. The court held that the wrappers, while being of little or no commercial value to N, were part of the consideration for the record and therefore royalties were payable on them as well! (It was a test case brought to protect the copyright.)

Insufficiency

Consideration is said to be *insufficient* where the person providing it is merely fulfilling an *existing legal duty*. This may be either a contractual duty or a public duty. In *Stilk v Myrick* (1809), two sailors deserted their ship and the master, unable to recruit replacements, promised the rest of the crew that they would share the wages of the deserters if they would complete the voyage home. This they did but they were held to be unable to enforce the master's promise. In *Collins v Godefroy* (1831), C was under a public duty to give evidence in court for G and accepted G's promise to pay him six guineas (£6.30) for doing so. C could not recover the sum because he had provided no consideration, he had merely fulfilled his public duty.

This principle was refined by the Court of Appeal in relation to contractual duties in *Williams v Roffey Bros & Nicholls (Contractors) Ltd* (1989). Here RB&N

were the main contractors for the refurbishment of a block of flats and had contracted W to do the carpentry work. RB&N became worried that W would not complete their work on time and offered W extra money to do so because their own contract contained a penalty clause. W sued for this extra payment and RB&N pleaded lack of consideration. It was held that W was entitled to payment. The principle behind the decision is that where a promisor obtains a benefit through the contractual performance, obtaining that benefit can amount to consideration for an extra payment provided the promise was not obtained by economic duress or fraud. (*Stilk v Myrick* (1809) still applies where no benefit is secured as a result of the promise.)

It follows that if you exceed your duty you provide consideration for a promise of payment. In *Glasbrook Brothers v Glamorgan CC* (1925), GB wanted to protect their mine during a strike. GCC, the police authority, were under a public duty to provide protection but had a discretion as to its exact form. GCC were prepared to offer only a mobile force but subsequently agreed to provide a permanent guard in return for £2,200. The payment was held to be enforceable because on the facts GCC had done more than the law obliged them to do. In *Hartley v Ponsonby* (1857) the scope of the contractual duty of a group of sailors was at issue. They had been offered extra wages to continue working a ship after the crew had become so depleted that continuing the voyage was dangerous. On the facts, their original contractual obligation had been discharged by the changed circumstances and they were free to enter into a new contract. The extra wages could therefore be recovered.

Part payment of a debt

A somewhat different problem arises where a person pays or promises to pay part of a debt in return for the creditor promising to forgo the balance. Here it is a question of avoiding an existing duty, not enforcing extra payment. It is not uncommon for a business organisation to be in a position where it has to forgo the balance of a debt to avoid liquidity problems. By the time the full debt is recovered a crisis could have arisen. This means that a firm might be forced, indeed even willing, to accept £5,000 in payment for a debt of £7,500 in order to pay its own overheads and thereby stay in business.

This economic truth, coupled with an almost traditional reluctance on the part of business people to resort to legal action, has resulted in a divergence of theory and practice. At law the balance can be recovered because the debtor has provided no consideration for the creditor's promise; they have not even fulfilled the legal obligation that the were already under. In *Foakes v Beer* (1884) the House of Lords confirmed the rule when Beer sued Foakes for the interest owed to her on a judgment debt. The House rejected Foakes' argument that, in return for his payment of a lump sum and the balance of the judgment debt in instalments, she had agreed to take no further action on the matter. Payment of the lump sum was no consideration for B's promise because F was already under a legal duty to make the payment.

To this rule a number of exceptions were laid down in *Pinnel's Case* as long ago as 1602. Payment of a lesser sum amounts to consideration where at the creditor's request it is paid at an earlier date or at a different place. The debt is similarly satisfied where the debtor gives or does something else, which may be worth more or less, with the creditor's consent. In each of these cases the debtor has introduced a new element into the transaction giving the creditor something other than that to which he was contractually entitled. The exceptions make commercial sense: an earlier payment of less might solve an acute cash-flow problem, while payment at a different place may be convenient (particularly so in olden days), and if the creditor wishes to take payment in kind, e.g. goods instead of money, a contract is after all a private bargain between two or more individuals.

Promissory estoppel A more modern exception exists where it would be unfair for the promisor who agrees to accept less to go back on his or her word. This exception emerged in the *High Trees Case* (1947) and is known as *promissory* or *equitable estoppel*. In 1939 the plaintiffs had leased a block of flats to the defendants. In January 1940 they agreed in writing, but without the defendants providing consideration, to accept only half of the rent due under the lease because the war had caused many of the flats to be unoccupied. From 1940 to 1945 the defendants paid the reduced rent. However, when the flats were again full in 1945 the plaintiffs brought an action claiming that they were entitled to the full rent not only for the future but also from 1940, thereby seeking to go back on the written agreement. To test their claim they sought payment of the full rent for the last six months of 1945. On the facts, the actual claim succeeded because the agreement was intended to be a temporary arrangement which would cease to operate when conditions changed, as they had by mid 1945. However, the judge was of the opinion that had the claim been pursued right back to 1940 the plaintiffs would have failed because they would have been *estopped* (prevented) from going back on their promise, even though the defendants had given nothing in return.

The application of the principle of *promissory estoppel*, to prevent the promisor going back on his word, is at the *discretion of the court* and later cases show that it can only be used as a *defence* against a person seeking to enforce their original contractual rights and never as the basis for a legal action. A promise can only be enforced where consideration has been given for it. It is unresolved whether promissory estoppel merely suspends the promisor's original rights or whether it extinguishes them entirely. If the former is the case, promisors can reassert their rights by giving adequate notice of their intention to do so. For example, if a buyer has waived a contractual delivery date they would subsequently be able to take back their promise and exercise their right to reject delivery after giving the seller a reasonable ultimatum.

Another situation where payment of less is full satisfaction for a greater sum owed is to be found in insolvency law. As part of *voluntary arrangement* made to avoid insolvency debtors may make compositions (as they are called) with their creditors under which their creditors each agree to take a proportion of what they are owed. The creditors are bound by the composition because any action to recover the balance would amount to fraud against their fellow creditors.

Banks and consideration

First of all you must remember that consideration is a two-way concept. If you buy a pair of jeans, the price paid is the consideration for the jeans and the jeans are the consideration for the price. The same is true of banker-customer contracts.

In terms of consideration, perhaps the more specific contracts are the simpler. For example, a customer pays a premium for foreign currency and pays interest on loans, receiving a service and the currency or the loan in exchange. In the basic banker-customer contract, i.e. for an account, the element of consideration is rather harder to identify. After all there is no charge, as such, for a current account and most banks offer some form of 'free banking', often if the customer merely stays in credit. Clearly, the customer receives the benefits of having a bank account but what does the bank receive in exchange? Where bank charges of various kinds are levied these form part of the consideration but where they are not, the bank obtains, again by an implied term in the contract, the right to dispose of the customer's money as it pleases – with the proviso that it must honour the customer's cheques. As you surely know, banks lend out their customers' funds at a profit so this right is of absolutely fundamental value to the whole business of banking.

■ THE INTENTION TO CREATE LEGAL RELATIONS

The existence of a definite bargain between the parties still does not mean that an enforceable contract exists. The law requires that the parties must have intended their bargain to be legally binding. In effect this requirement is more apparent than real, for every commercial agreement is presumed to be legally binding unless the contrary is proved by the person who disputes the presumption. In the event of a dispute the question is decided by considering the facts of the case. In *Carlill v Carbolic Smoke Ball Co* (1892), for example, the defendants had advertised that they had deposited £1,000 with their bankers as evidence of their good faith. This deposit was held to be sufficient indication that their promise was not intended to be only a 'mere puff' but a statement upon which they expected to incur legal liability.

It is possible, however, to expressly exclude legal liability in a commercial agreement by including a suitably worded clause – an honour clause – in which the parties declare that their agreement is not to be binding at law. In *Rose and Frank v Crompton* (1923), for example, C had given R rights to sell their carbon paper for three years with an option to extend the time. The agreement was subsequently extended but a year before it was to expire C terminated it without giving the specified notice and refused to execute orders which they had received before the termination. R sued for wrongful repudiation of the agreement and for non-delivery of the goods already ordered. There was an 'honourable pledge clause' in the original agreement. On these facts R succeeded in the action for non-delivery because it was held that each accepted order constituted a separate contract. R failed, however, in the claim for wrongful repudiation because the express declaration in the original agreement that it was not to impose legal consequences meant that C did not have to abide by the clause dealing with notice or, indeed, any other term of the agreement.

A specific banking example of a commercial agreement that is understood not to be legally enforceable is the *letter of comfort*. A letter of comfort is difficult to define but can perhaps be best described as a type of guarantee which may be accepted by a bank instead of a proper guarantee, even though it amounts to no more than a 'gentleman's agreement'. For example, one may be given by a parent company to 'secure' a loan to a subsidiary company, in which the parent company (typically) undertakes to maintain its holding in the subsidiary and declares that its policy is to ensure that the subsidiary will always be in a position to meet its liabilities to the bank. Such undertakings and declarations were held by the Court of Appeal in *Kleinwort Benson Ltd v Malaysia Mining Corporation Berhad* (1989) to amount merely to statements of fact and not to a contractual promise to meet the debts of the subsidiary company. (From a commercial point of view therefore, the value of a letter of comfort depends on the standing of the parent company in the commercial world.)

In contrast, social and domestic agreements are not presumed to be legally binding. If one of the parties wishes to enforce such an agreement, that party must prove the required intention. This is done by producing evidence to show that the social agreement is in reality a commercial arrangement or that the domestic relationship has ceased to exist. In *Merritt v Merritt* (1970), an agreement between a wife and her husband, by which he promised to pay £40 a month to her and to transfer the matrimonial home into her sole name in return for her paying the outstanding mortgage payments, was legally binding because the domestic relationship had ended when the husband had left his wife to live with another woman.

Needless to say, with the exception of relatively uncommon letters of comfort, all agreements made between banks and their customers, their employees, their suppliers; indeed every person or organisation with which they deal, will be commercial agreements and therefore legally binding. While banks may be very honourable organisations, they prefer to do business relying on legal rules rather than honour – so to speak!

ACTIVITY 4.8

Consider the following situation. You and a group of friends book a holiday together. The arrangements are fairly elaborate (how many bottles of *Sunblot* etc), you forgo the chance of a free holiday with your parents in Bognor (*opportunity cost* remember!) and book your leave, displeasing your manager in the process. Two months before the departure, two of the group change their minds about going and vow never to speak to you again after a bad row over nothing in particular. As far as you and the rest of the group are concerned, the holiday is now far less attractive; what's more the attractive group discount is no longer available.

Assuming that you wanted to, could you take legal action against the reneging pair for the extra expense and general time and trouble that you will incur. Give your reasons.

■ FURTHER REQUIREMENTS

The presence of an 'agreement', a 'bargain' and an 'intention to create legal relations' are the essential elements of a valid contract but four other factors have an important bearing on its validity and enforceability. These factors may be termed 'form', 'contractual capacity', 'reality of consent' and 'legality'. They can best be considered, as possible defects in the bargain the parties have struck. As you will see, the first three are of considerable relevance to banks while the fourth, hopefully, is not.

Form

It is a common and understandable misconception that contracts have to be written, or at least recorded in writing, for in a great many transactions one or both of the parties signs a written contract or receives a written receipt. This practice is seldom based on legal requirements but on the practical needs of administration. Within an organisation records must be kept, accounts filed and sent, stock turnover monitored and generally a whole host of internal functions either directly depend on, or are fuelled by, written records of the organisation's transactions.

Legal requirements as to form are comparatively few and the most formal document known to English law, the deed – a document that must be signed, witnessed and delivered (but no longer sealed: Law of Property (Miscellaneous Provisions) Act 1989) – is only commonly required in the law of contract where a legal estate in land is transferred or a legal mortgage over land is created.

More recently a requirement that certain contracts must be written has proved effective in consumer protection and all consumer credit agreements regulated by the Consumer Credit Act 1974 are required to be in writing. A regulated agreement which fails to satisfy the statutory requirements can only be enforced against the debtor on the order of the court. The Law of Property (Miscellaneous Provisions) Act 1989 now requires a contract for the sale of land to be in writing, something which was normal anyway. Other contracts which must be in writing include bills of exchange (including cheques), and contracts for the transfer of shares in a registered company.

Finally, under the Statute of Frauds 1677 a contract of guarantee (a promise to answer for the debt of another) must be evidenced in writing, i.e. the creditor must have documentary evidence of it although the guarantee itself can be given orally. In practice of course, commercial guarantees, such as those given by directors to their company's bank as security for a loan to their company, are invariably very formal *written* contracts.

All the contracts mentioned above affect banks.

Contractual capacity

Traditionally, the law took as its norm the sane, sober, solvent, adult human male and anyone or anything else either had to be protected from society or suffered disabilities within it. Today most of the disabilities have gone but special rules exist concerning the contractual capacity of minors.

Minors

A minor is a person under the age of eighteen: Family Law Reform Act 1969. Minors' contracts can be divided into *three* categories:

- Valid contracts;
- Voidable contracts;
- Unenforceable contracts.

Valid contracts Valid contracts are binding on the minor. There are two kinds.

1 *Contracts for necessaries* Necessaries are goods and services which a minor reasonably needs to exist. Such things as food, clothing and somewhere to live are definitely necessaries but other things can be necessaries in the particular circumstances, e.g. a motor bike or a car could be considered a necessary for a minor who has to travel a considerable distance to college or work and for whom public transport is unavailable. A bank account for a minor aged, say, 15–17 would almost certainly be considered a necessary although, providing the account was maintained in credit, the bank would only ever need to sue for its charges. (*See* p 142 for position in relation to loans.)

However, even if particular goods are capable of being necessaries, to enforce the contract against the minor the other party must show that:

- the goods were actually supplied to the minor, a contract for goods yet to be supplied is unenforceable;
- the minor required the goods both at the time of sale and at the time of delivery, i.e. s/he was not already sufficiently well provided with such goods;
- the goods were suitable to the minor's lifestyle. Thus, for example, while a wrist-watch could almost certainly be considered a necessary, an expensive *Cartier* or *Longines* wrist-watch would probably only be held to be a necessary when supplied to a very wealthy minor.

In short, two questions must be answered positively. First, was the item *capable* of being a necessary. Second, was the item *actually* a necessary in the circumstances. Even then, a minor is only liable to pay a reasonable price, this may not be the contractual price. The principles outlined above would presumably also apply to services supplied to the minor.

Three old cases can be usefully compared. In *Ryder v Wombwell* (1868) it was held that items of jewellery and an antique goblet could not be considered necessaries despite the minor's high income. In *Nash v Inman* (1908) a Saville Row Tailor supplied 11 fancy waistcoats to N, a Cambridge undergraduate. Although they were capable of being necessaries, it was established that N already had sufficient numbers of such waistcoats and they were therefore not necessaries in the actual circumstances. In *Chapple v Cooper* (1844), however, it was established that a minor is liable on a contract for the burial of his wife and children. Goods and services for a minor's family are considered on the same basis as for the minor himself.

A trading contract no matter of what kind and no matter how commercially advantageous is never binding on a minor.

2 *Beneficial contracts of service* These are contracts of employment that are to the

minor's benefit, e.g. contracts that provide for an element education and training or articles of apprenticeship. The court will look at the contract as a whole to decide whether it is for the minor's benefit and therefore binding. In *Doyle v White City Stadium Ltd* (1935), for example, a professional boxer entered into a contract which contained a clause that stated that he should lose his prize-money if he was disqualified during a fight. This occurred but he sought to recover the prize-money maintaining that since he was a minor and the clause was not to his benefit the contract was not binding on him. He was, however, held to be bound by it because taken as a whole it was to his benefit; in particular he received a licence to box and was able to gain expertise in his profession.

In *De Francesco v Barnum* (1890), F, a 14 year old girl, entered into an apprenticeship deed with B to be taught stage dancing. In the deed she agreed not to marry during the apprenticeship nor to accept professional work without B's permission. B did not undertake to find her work, nor to maintain her when she was not working; her rate of pay when she was working was very low. He was also able to terminate her apprenticeship if she proved unsuitable for stage dancing. On the facts the contract was held to be unreasonable – she was at the absolute disposal of the defendant – and she was not bound by it.

Voidable contracts These are contracts under which minors acquire an interest in subject matter of a *permanent nature* which involves *recurring obligations*, e.g. a lease, a partnership agreement or shares. Such contracts are binding on minors unless they avoid them during minority or within a reasonable time thereafter. It follows that they are liable on obligations arising before the repudiation but not on those arising after, e.g. rent under a lease.

Unenforceable contracts All other contracts entered into by minors (including contracts of loan, even loans to enable minors to purchase necessaries) are unenforceable against them but are enforceable by them against the other parties. Minors can, however, *ratify* contracts on attaining their majority and the contracts then become binding on them.

If a minor wishes to recover money or property transferred under an unenforceable contract, s/he must show a total failure of consideration, i.e. no benefit of any kind has been obtained under the contract. If, however, the minor has received property under an unenforceable contract, or s/he repudiates a voidable contract, under the Minors' Contracts Act 1987, s.3 the court '... may if it is just and equitable to do so, require the minor to transfer to the other party any property acquired by the minor under the contract, or any property representing it'. Thus, it may be possible to recover property transferred to the minor.

Other special cases

Partnerships Unlike a company, a partnership does not have a legal existence separate from its members; it is not a corporation. Thus, strictly speaking, a contract cannot be made with a partnership, it must be made with the individual members. In practice it is usual to make a contract with one or more members as agent(s) of the others and providing they have actual authority to enter into the contract or it is within the usual course of the firm's business, the other partners will be bound by the contract. (Actual authority can be either express, i.e. clearly stated authority, or implied, i.e. intended and understood between them but not actually spelt out in so many words. Acts within the firm's usual course of business give rise to apparent or ostensible authority – authority as it appears to others.) For practical reasons, it is, however, possible to take action against the partnership in its firm name (the name under which it carries on business) and such an action is deemed to be an action against every partner.

We discuss the implied authority of partners in the context of partnership accounts in the next chapter but note that a bank will not wish to rely on a partner's implied authority to bind the other partners when it is a simple matter to obtain their express consent to a transaction, e.g. a loan to the partnership.

Clubs and societies Most clubs and societies are not corporations and therefore do not have their own separate legal existence. They cannot, therefore, make their own contracts and cannot be sued. Legal action must be taken against the officers, and any other member, who authorised a contract on behalf of the club or society. (*See* p 145.)

We might note here two further points. First, the *ultra vires* rule (beyond the powers of) no longer applies to the transactions of a company. It was abolished by the Companies Act 1989. Although subject to extensive exceptions, a company's contractual capacity was formerly limited to acts which were within the objects clause of its memorandum of association. A company now has unlimited contractual capacity (*see* p 43). Second, local authorities are subject to the *ultra vires* rule in their contracts and although you are reasonably unlikely to become involved with a local authority in your career, *Hazell v Hammersmith and Fulham London Borough Council* (1991) is a spectacular illustration of the possible consequences of the rule (*see* p 46).

Reality of consent

An agreement where one of the parties did not or could not freely and fully consent to the terms will generally not be enforced.

Undue influence

Where one party to a contract is subject to the dominant position of the other, undue influence, an equitable principle, can arise. If it is proved, it renders the contract voidable at the option of the weaker party and the contract may be rescinded by the court. As you will see below, however, the relationship between the parties alone is not enough to avoid the contract.

In certain well-defined relationships, known as *fiduciary relationships*, this type of position is presumed to exist, for example, solicitor and client, doctor and patient and parent and child. In other relationships the dominant position must be established by the party wishing to avoid a contract for undue influence. The banker-customer relationship falls into this latter category:

Lloyds Bank Ltd v Bundy (1975). In this case the defendant, an elderly farmer of little business sense, twice mortgaged his home, his only asset, to the bank to secure the overdraft of his son's company. The bank knew that the company was in financial difficulties but did not explain this fully to the defendant, although it knew that he relied upon them totally for advice in such matters. The son's company became insolvent and the bank eventually sought possession of the house. The bank's action failed, the bank had been seeking a benefit from the defendant and there was a conflict of interest. The relationship between the bank and the defendant was one of trust and confidence which imposed a duty on the bank to ensure that the defendant received informed independent advice before entering into the commitment. The bank was in breach of that duty of care and could not be allowed to benefit from the transaction. While this 'special relationship' is unlikely to arise frequently, banks must be aware of the possibility.

Many of the leading cases on undue influence are old and somewhat amusing, for example, mother superiors taking financial advantage of novices (apprentice nuns) or gypsies threatening to turn people of feeble intellect into toads! These are of limited relevance to banking! However, the leading House of Lords' decision (the highest judicial body) is a banking case: *National Westminster Bank plc v Morgan* (1985). Mr and Mrs Morgan were joint owners of their home. They mortgaged it to the bank to secure the refinancing of a previous loan from a building society, on which they had fallen behind with the repayments when Mr Morgan's business got into difficulties. Mrs Morgan did not want the new mortgage to extend to advances for her husband's business activities and she was assured, wrongly but in good faith, by the bank manager that it did not. The bank sought possession of the house when the couple fell into arrears with the repayments. Mr Morgan died soon afterwards without any business debts to the bank and Mrs Morgan appealed against a possession order on the grounds that she had signed the legal charge (the mortgage) because of undue influence from the bank manager. The House dismissed her appeal and upheld the possession order.

The *ratio* of the case is that a contract will not be set aside for undue influence merely because a confidential relationship is proved to exist. It must be shown that the contract is wrongful and to the clear disadvantage of the party seeking relief. Relief is given to prevent *victimisation* of one party by the other, not merely because of their relationship. The mortgage Mrs Morgan has signed was not to her disadvantage because it had enabled her to remain in her home. Nor had the bank exploited its position, on the facts no special relationship had arisen. (Which way do you think *Bundy's Case* would be decided today?)

In addition to its relevance to taking mortgages, undue influence is of particular importance when a guarantee is taken as security (*see* Chapter 6).

Misrepresentation

Misrepresentation occurs where one party to a contract is misled by the other – fraudulently, negligently or innocently – as to the true facts of the situation with the result that they enter into the contract. Misrepresentation makes the contract voidable and always entitles the innocent party to rescind (set aside) the contract and, where made fraudulently or negligently, always to an action for damages. An action for damages is also available for innocent misrepresentation in certain circumstances under the Misrepresentation Act 1967.

It is reasonable to assume that only rarely over the years will a bank have deliberately misrepresented the truth to a customer or other contracting party. Professional standards should ensure that negligent misrepresentation (the bank should have known the statement were untrue) is also relatively uncommon. Innocent misrepresentation? Well human or system error means that this will happen. Banks may attempt to protect themselves with disclaimer clauses against possible liability but the Misrepresentation Act 1967 subjects any such disclaimer to a test of reasonableness – the forerunner of the test found in the Unfair Contract Terms Act 1977 (*see* Chapter 2).

Misrepresentation could affect any contract a bank enters into with any customer, from the opening of a current account to taking property into safe custody. In practice, however, it is most likely to be relevant when security is taken, the customer later arguing that the bank misled them as to the true facts or consequences. Remember, rescission for misrepresentation is the one right which the surety retains when entering a bank's contract of guarantee. The consequence of misrepresentation is, of course, a reason why banks will always insist on customers obtaining independent advice where there is a chance of the customer misunderstanding, or being prejudicially influenced into making, the contract.

Mistake

Occasionally, a contract will be void and a total nullity where one party or both parties makes a mistake. But most types of mistake have no effect at all. For example, the law will not assist customers if they underestimate their capacity to repay a loan or if a bank wishes to avoid a contract for the purchase of expensive computer equipment because it wrongly assessed its need for it.

Where, however, the mistake either prevents any agreement being reached at all, or where an agreement is reached which lacks any foundation because of the mistake, the contract will be *void*. Most such situations occur in contracts of sale. The former situation can arise where the seller mistakes the identity of the buyer or, more likely, where the buyer and seller are at cross-purposes as to the subject-matter of the contract, the seller wishing to sell X but the buyer wishing to buy Y.

In the latter situation the effect of a mistake is very limited. The contract will only be void if, without the knowledge of either the buyer or seller, the intended subject-matter of the contract has ceased to exist for the purposes of the contract before the agreement was concluded. This could happen where the seller's agent has already sold the goods to another buyer or where they have been physically destroyed. In *Galloway v Galloway* (1914), a separation deed was set aside because it was made on the mistaken assumption of both parties that they were in fact married to each other!

Clearly, these situations are of very little relevance at all to banking. One that is, theoretically at least, is known as *non est factum* – translated as 'it is not my deed' (not what I intended to do) but now carrying the more general meaning of a document mistakenly signed. Basically, where a party to a contract, e.g. a surety under a contract of guarantee, can prove that s/he thought the document that s/he signed was fundamentally different the court may set aside the contract for mistake. An example could perhaps be a person signing a guarantee in the mistaken belief that s/he was witnessing a will or where the guarantee was for a substantially greater amount. However, a plea of *non est factum* will not normally protect a literate person possessing full legal capacity and the person seeking to avoid the contract must establish that s/he acted without negligence. Thus, signing a document without reading it would defeat the plea. Continuing the example of guarantees, possible problems in this respect can easily be avoided by ensuring that a guarantee is signed and witnessed at the bank or attested (certified as valid after having been explained) by a solicitor. From what we have said above about legal theory and what you know about banking practice, you could reasonably conclude that *non est factum* is of more academic interest than practical importance.

Legality

All contracts must be within the law. Illegality is an umbrella term in the law of contract, covering contracts which involve actual criminal acts, e.g. an organisation allowing employees to include their tax liability in their expense accounts thereby defrauding the state, to contracts which merely offend public policy. A contract in which people restrict their future freedom to carry on their trade, business or profession as they please comes into this latter category. An example would be a contract of employment containing a term which prevents employees from working for a competitor of their employer for a certain period and/or within a certain area after leaving their jobs. Such a restriction will be upheld only if it can be proved to be reasonable and necessary for the protection of the employer's legitimate trade interests. A further example where such a restriction may be justified is where an established shop is sold with its goodwill and the vendor agrees not to open a similar shop within a certain area and/or time.

In all cases those aspects of the contract which are illegal or tainted with illegality are void but where the contract merely offends public policy the offending parts may be severed from the whole and the rest enforced. Employees whose contracts contain unlawful restraints of trade can still enforce the payment of wages owed to them although their employer cannot enforce the clauses in which the unreasonable restraint is contained.

■ BREACH OF CONTRACT

We made the point at the start of this chapter that of the many millions of contracts that are entered into each year it is only a very small minority that are not performed according to their terms. There is not a lot that can go wrong when you use a bus or a train or buy the weekly groceries, is there? What, however, happens when a contract is broken? You saw in Chapter 1 that the breach gives rise to *strict liability*. But what does this mean in practice? What remedies are available to the 'injured party'?

We start with the rule that any breach of contract, no matter how minor, entitles the injured party to *sue for damages*. The amount, or *quantum* of damages, is the financial loss incurred; the purpose of an award is to put the parties in the position they would have been in had the contract been performed according to its terms. For example, if a supplier fails to supply, the buyer's loss would be assessed in terms of any higher price paid for the materials elsewhere, the cost of the delay caused, e.g. loss of profit and operating costs, and general management and administrative expense. If a bank wrongly pays a cheque or fails to remit funds, the customer's loss would primarily be the financial consequences that were a foreseeable result of the bank's breach of contract. For example, the amount of the cheque plus any interest charges should the account have become overdrawn as a consequence, or the cost of lost present or future trade contracts through payment not being made as required.

Where there has been a breach of a major term, such as a failure to supply or a failure to meet quality specifications in a manufacturing contract (a *condition* as opposed to a *warranty*, to use the correct terminology) the injured party is entitled to *repudiate* (reject) the contract – that is, the obligations that they incur under it – instead of or in addition to bringing an action for damages. Most of the obligations incurred by a mortgagor under a bank mortgage are (legally) conditions entitling a bank to repudiate the mortgage *irrespective* of whether the bank has suffered any actual loss. Having the (legal) power to do this is one thing, whether it would be a sensible course of action is another. Professional and commercial judgment must be involved.

An award of damages is the usual remedy sought when a contract has been broken. Business is about money, a breach of contract usually causes financial loss and the purpose of the action is to compensate the party who has been caused such loss. Occasionally, however, money is an inadequate compensation; the subject matter of the contract may be unique and by definition financial compensation cannot provide a substitute. In such situations the court has the power to order *specific performance* of the contract, i.e. that the contract be performed according to its terms. A contract for the sale of land is the best example of where specific performance might be awarded if one of the parties failed to fulfil their obligations, i.e. failed to execute the conveyance transferring legal title. Another example is an equitable mortgage, the mortgagor's undertaking to execute a legal charge when requested to do so may be enforced by an order of specific performance (*see* p 201).

Figure 4.3 is a summary diagram of contact law. (A very effective study/ revision technique is to enlarge such a diagram or draw a series of diagrams, one for each central element. Many people respond well to a visual summary

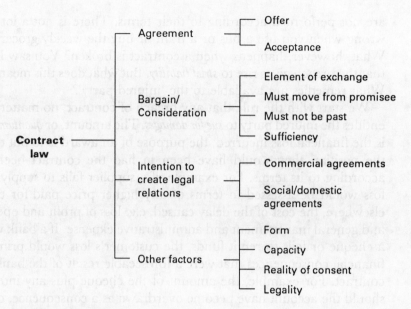

```
                              ┌─── Offer
              Agreement ──────┤
            ┌                 └─── Acceptance
            │
            │                 ┌─── Element of exchange
            │                 │
            │   Bargain/       ├─── Must move from promisee
            │   Consideration ─┤
            │                 ├─── Must not be past
Contract ───┤                 │
   law      │                 └─── Sufficiency
            │
            │   Intention to   ┌─── Commercial agreements
            ├── create legal ──┤
            │   relations      └─── Social/domestic
            │                        agreements
            │
            │                 ┌─── Form
            │                 │
            └── Other factors ─┤─── Capacity
                              ├─── Reality of consent
                              │
                              └─── Legality
```

Fig 4.3 Contract law

of a topic. Drawing such diagrams helps you to understand the structure of a subject and the completed diagrams provide at a glance an overview of the information and how each piece relates to the others.)

■ ANSWERING CONTRACT LAW QUESTIONS

'Explanation' questions

Questions asking you to explain the rules of contract law are usually very straightforward, and for this reason may be harder to score high marks on than the *apparently* more difficult problem questions.

In such questions the key to good marks is to think carefully about what the question asks, what sort of response is required, and then *plan* your answer accordingly before beginning to write out your answer. Believe it or not, if a question asks for a letter to be written, a surprising number of students will completely ignore the instruction and lose, perhaps, three marks straightaway.

Look out for very specific instructions. You are quite likely to be asked to illustrate the law in the context of the banker-customer contract. Failure to do so will obviously lose you marks. Provided you follow this guidance and, of course, know what you are talking about, you should have no problems with such questions. (You should know by now the importance of being able to refer to banking examples in this subject.)

'Problem' questions

These are generally unpopular because they are perceived to be difficult and are also often quite long. The fact is that they are usually quite easy once you have worked out what they are about. The Examiner expects you to spend more time thinking about the answer and less time writing. Therefore they can usually be answered in a couple of sides of paper – in other words you don't necessarily have to write that much in your answer.

The secret of answering these questions is to apply the '4Ps' formula – a tried and tested technique.

- *Problem*. What is the legal issue(s) involved in the question? It is not the question itself. In other words, it is not whether X's claim will succeed but the legal points on which the success or otherwise of X's claim will depend.
- *Principle*. Statements and explanations of the relevant law.
- *Precedent*. You must refer to 'Authority', that is relevant decided cases or, where statute law is involved, relevant legislation. Doing this is part of the discipline of the subject. As such it is similar to referring to experiments in science or extracts from poems in literature. You are substantiating the law you use.
- *Prognosis*. This is a fancy word for a conclusion (and it keeps the alliteration going).

Although it is best to start with a *statement of the problem* – which immediately tells the Examiner that you know exactly what the issue is and that you have thought about the question – and end with the prognosis, the four 'Ps' can be discussed in any order. You could start your answer by explaining a leading case or by stating the relevant legal principle. The point to remember is that your answer must cover all four 'Ps'.

So, your answer could begin:

In this question it must be decided whether ... The law requires that ... (Problem first)

or

In *X v Y* it was held that ... In this situation it must be decided whether this principle applies to ... (Precedent first)

or

Contract law requires that ... For example in *X v Y* it was held that ... but in *A v B* it was held that ... It must be decided in this question which case applies. (Principle first)

You will notice here that we have tended to combine principle and precedent. This is often going to be the case, the important thing is that you deal with each of the '4Ps'.

Let's apply this formula to the following question. On second thoughts, *you* try applying the formula to it and then compare your approach to ours. Don't worry if you find it difficult to do at first, once the 'penny drops' you will be able to tackle such questions with confidence. (You'll find our outline answer at the end of this chapter.)

Memorandum
To: Student
From: Manager

As you know, we agreed a personal loan of £5,000 to Ms Angelides yesterday to

107

enable her to buy a car. She came in today very annoyed because the car she wanted had been sold to somebody else. I certainly do not intend giving her any legal advice about this, but for my own peace of mind I would like you to remind me of the legal principles involved here. The facts are as follows.

Mr Jones of High Street Cars offered to sell her a car a week ago giving her until yesterday to raise the money. She was about to go to pay for it, courtesy of our loan, when she was phoned by a friend who said that she had just seen the car being driven out of the garage. Nevertheless she went to the garage and said she was accepting his offer to sell the car and where was it! Mr Jones apologised but said that 'business was business'.

Please let me know whether Ms Angelides had a contract and whether she would be able to claim damages or expenses. Are there any cases which cover this aspect of contract law.   [20]

■ SUMMARY

1 Banks, in common with all other business organisations, pursue their objectives by entering into voluntary agreements with other organisations and individuals.

2 Contract law provides a framework around which banks can build their activities and regularise their operations.

3 A contract is an agreement which the courts will enforce.

4 Standard form contracts enable banks to contract on the terms most favourable to them, as dictated by legal theory and practical experience, and to simplify contractual arrangements. They do, however, greatly reduce the ability of customers and others to freely negotiate the terms of contracts.

5 The essentials of a valid contract are:
   ● an agreement;
   ● an exchange of value – the bargain (known as consideration); and
   ● an intention by the parties that their bargain should be legally binding.

6 The agreement consists of one party making an offer which is accepted by the other.

7 An offer can be revoked at any time before it has been accepted provided the revocation is communicated to the offeree.

8 To be effective, an acceptance of an offer must be definite and, unless the requirement has been waived, communicated to the offeror.

9 *Prima facie*, a postal acceptance is complete as soon as it is posted and cannot be retracted afterwards.

10 There must be certainty as to the terms of the agreement, although this certainty can be provided from outside the contract itself, e.g. by terms being implied into the agreement. The banker-customer contract is an excellent example of a contract in which few terms are express but many are implied.

11 A contract is a bargain in which both parties give and receive something of value; this is known as consideration.

12 Cheques are an exception to the rule that past consideration is no consideration.

13 Consideration must be legally sufficient (of some value) but need not be commercially adequate.

14 To be legally enforceable, the parties to an agreement/bargain must have intended to create legal relations.

15 Few contracts are required to be in a particular form, although:
- contracts covered by the Consumer Credit Act 1974 must be in writing;
- contracts transferring legal estates in land or creating a legal mortgage over land must be by deed; and
- guarantees must be evidence by a note or memorandum in writing.

16 Minors have only limited contractual capacity, most contracts they enter into are voidable at their option or unenforceable against them.

17 A contract to which one of the parties did not freely and fully consent because of undue influence, misrepresentation or, possibly, mistake is liable to be set aside.

18 The problem of undue influence is particularly important in respect to guarantees and third party security.

19 A contract, or parts of it, tainted with 'illegality' will not be enforced.

20 A breach of contract entitles that innocent party to sue for damages. If the breach is of a major term (a condition), the innocent party may also repudiate the contract. In some circumstances, the court will order specific performance of the contract.

■ SELF-ASSESSMENT QUESTIONS

1 Why can the law of contract be considered a 'facilitating medium' in banking and business activity generally?

2 Define a contract.

3 To what extent does freedom to bargain exist between a bank and its customers?

4 What is meant by a standard form contract? Give banking examples of such contracts and examples of the terms they contain.

5 Why do some people argue that many commercial agreements are not contracts in the strict legal sense of the word?

6 State the three essentials of a valid contract and the four further requirements.

7 State the *rationes decidendes* (the plural) of the following cases: *Carlill's Case, Boots Cash Chemists, Dickinson v Dodds.*

8 What is the postal rule?

9 State the ways in which certainty can be given to an apparently uncertain agreement.

10 Why are cheques an exception to the rule that past consideration is no consideration?

11 Explain what is meant by consideration having to be legally sufficient but not commercially adequate.

12 Explain the *obiter* principle formulated in the *High Trees Case*.

13 Relate the principles of offer and acceptance and consideration to opening and operating a bank account.

14 Name two contracts that must be evidenced in writing in order to be enforceable.

15 In what ways does the contractual capacity of minors differ from that of adults?

16 What is meant by undue influence?

17 What is the *ratio* of *National Westminster Bank Plc v Morgan* (1985)?

18 What remedy is available for all types of misrepresentation?

19 What is a plea of *non est factum*?

20 In an action for breach of contract, how is the amount of damages calculated?

■ MULTIPLE-CHOICE QUESTIONS

1 In which of the following relationships is undue influence presumed to exist in contract law?
A parent and child
B husband and wife
C banker and customer
D employer and employee

2 To which of the following rules of contract law is a cheque an exception?
A each party to a contract must give and receive something of value
B consideration must be of some value
C past consideration is no consideration
D consideration must be provided by the party seeking to enforce a promise made directly to him

3 In which of the following situations does the rule that 'past consideration is no consideration' *not* apply?
A in an action against the bank by the payee of a 'stopped' cheque
B in an action against the drawer by the payee of a 'stopped' cheque
C when a 'guarantee' is taken to secure a loan to a minor
D when a mortgage is taken to secure unauthorised borrowing

4 If a contractual offer can be accepted by post, the acceptance is effective when:
  A it is posted
  B it is delivered
  C it comes to the offeror's attention
  D the offeror acts upon it

5 Ordinary members of a non-trading partnership incur:
  A unlimited liability for all debts of the firm
  B limited liability for all debts of the firm
  C liability only for debts on contracts they personally authorised
  D liability as laid down in the articles of partnership

6 A public limited company's legal capacity to enter into a particular contract is determined by its:
  A certificate of incorporation
  B memorandum of Association
  C articles of Association
  D None of these

7 Which of the following is definitely not a regulated agreement under the Consumer Credit Act 1974?
  A a loan to a partnership
  B an overdraft
  C a loan to a private limited company
  D a 'Gold Card' credit card agreement

8 An enforceable regulated agreement under the Consumer Credit Act 1974:
  A can be made verbally
  B can be made verbally provided there is a sufficient written memorandum of the agreement
  C must be made in writing
  D must be written and in the form of a deed

9 Which of the following contracts must by law be in writing?
  A a guarantee
  B an agreement covered by the Consumer Credit Act 1974
  C a legal mortgage
  D an agreement to open and operate a joint account

10 If one party to a contract misrepresented the facts to the other, that other party is always able to:
  A rescind the contract
  B repudiate the contract
  C claim damages
  D seek amendment and specific performance of the contract

11 In which of the following situations could the contract be void?
  A Shahid guarantees his wife's business borrowing after she has exerted pressure on him to do so
  B Sam buys a car from Banger Motors after the salesperson mistakenly told Sam that the recorded mileage was genuine
  C Charles orders radios from Ho, a manufacturer based in Hong Kong, but

when they are delivered Charles and Ho find that they misunderstood each other as to the radios' specifications

D Assia, a minor, obtains a loan from Midtown Bank

■ OUTLINE ANSWER TO CONTRACT LAW QUESTION

The two *problems* involved are (a) Mr Jones can be held to his promise to hold the offer open; and (b) Has he effectively revoked his offer to sell and has Ms Angelides had sufficient notice of this? Possibly three marks for making these points.

The *principles* involved are (a) a promise, i.e. that of Mr Jones, is only enforceable if supported by consideration; (b) an offer can be revoked at any time before it is accepted provided that the revocation is communicate to the offeree; and (c) revocation can be communicated by a third party. Probably ten marks were available for all these points.

The one *precedent* that was expected was *Dickinson v Dodds*, authority for the rule that communication of revocation can be by a third party. Say two marks for the case which means that it is not worth writing more than a short paragraph/ couple of sentences on it.

Prognosis/conclusion – no evidence of consideration for Mr Jones's promise therefore he cannot be held to it.

Debatable whether Ms Angelides had sufficient notice. If she had, Mr Jones's offer is no longer available to her; if she had not, her acceptance results in a contract and J is liable to her. Say seven marks for making these points. (Not so difficult was it.)

5 The banker-customer contract

OBJECTIVES

After studying this chapter you should be able to:
1 Define the terms banker and customer and explain the importance of the definitions;
2 Describe the various aspects of the banker-customer relationship;
3 State a bank's legal rights and duties;
4 Outline the procedures for opening, operating and closing accounts;
5 Outline the circumstances in which a bank's authority to make payments from its customer's account is terminated;
6 Explain how legal considerations affect the opening, operation of, and the lending on different types of accounts.

■ THE CONTEXT

Banking is a rapidly changing industry. The distinctions between banks and other financial institutions, particularly building societies, are becoming increasingly blurred. While the 'traditional' account operating activities of banks are still most important, banks offer an ever wider range of services to their customers. The concept of a bank as a 'financial supermarket' is with us. Thus, while this chapter takes as its basic subject the 'traditional' banker-customer contract – basically opening, operating and lending on a current account – you must remember that banks also enter into a wide range of more specific contracts. Most of these are with customers as legally defined and many are, of course, associated with the basic contract, but some are with individuals and organisations who have no account with the bank. For example, bank-owned credit card companies do not insist that cardholders have accounts with the parent bank, and anyone can avail themselves of a bank's foreign exchange, trustee or insurance services.

ACTIVITY 5.1

Before you read further, spend five minutes noting down as many different services offered by your bank as you can. All these services are sold by making contracts with the 'customer'.

■ DEFINITIONS

We must begin by defining the terms 'banker' and 'customer'. You may, at first, consider this rather unnecessary – after all everyone knows what a bank is, and presumably a banker is someone who works in one. Similarly, a customer is clearly someone who uses the services of a bank. Well, we must be rather more precise because your relationship with your customers gives rise to important legal rights and duties quite apart from any commercial considerations. So, we must ask two preliminary questions:

- who is a banker; and
- who is a customer?

Who is a banker?

If you look for an answer in the Banking Act 1987, you will be disappointed. As you saw in Chapter 2, the Act's purpose is the regulation of deposit-taking and it only deals specifically with 'banks' in so far as the use of the name 'bank' is restricted by the Bank of England to larger authorised institutions. Even then, overseas banks are exempt from this restriction. The Act tells us very little about the role and characteristics of a banker. Unfortunately, the same is true of other relevant statutes. For example, according to the Bills of Exchange Act 1882, s.2, the term '... includes a body of persons whether incorporated or not who carry on the business of banking.'

Our most profitable line of enquiry is to consider the phrase *business of banking*, for here we will see that the common law has considered the activities inherent in this business as being the criteria for determining who is and who is not a banker. In *United Dominions Trust v Kirkwood* (1966), it had to be decided whether UDT were moneylenders within the meaning of the Moneylenders Act 1900 or, as they maintained, bankers and therefore exempt from registration under the Act. The Court of Appeal identified the performance of three activities as definitive characteristics of bankers:

- bankers accept money from, and collect cheques for their customers and place them to their credit;
- bankers honour cheques or orders drawn on them by their customers when presented for payment and debit their customers accounts accordingly;
- bankers keep current accounts, or something of that nature, in their books in which the credits and debits are entered.

In addition, the court stressed that the definition was not static and would always depend on current practice. Indeed, the majority of the court accepted a secondary test of the reputation of the organisation in question with other bankers as a means of determining whether the organisation could be regarded at law as a bank. On the facts, UDT, while not a conventional bank, were held to satisfy both tests.

Who is a customer?

If you thought that statute would define a customer, you would again be mistaken. Once more we must look to the common law. Decided cases show that a customer of a bank is a person who has entered into a contract with the bank for the opening of an account in his or her name. Strictly speaking, the account must be a current account but it is submitted that a contract to open a deposit account or a credit card account should also make a person a customer since the same or very similar activities are performed for the 'customer'. There is no modern authority on this point. (In defining 'customer' in this way we are using the term in a strict legal sense. In the more usual sense, a customer is anyone who makes a contract for any of a bank's services, e.g. foreign currency or travel insurance, even though they may not have an account with the bank.)

It is not essential for a course of dealings to be maintained over a period of time, the relationship is contractual and therefore arises when the customer's offer is accepted by the bank. The existence of an account or a contractual agreement to open one is essential however. No matter how many transactions have taken place between a bank and an individual, such as cashing uncrossed cheques payable to the individual, that person will not be a customer unless and until their application to open an account has been made and accepted, i.e. a contractual relationship established. To cite authority, in *Ladbroke v Todd* (1914), it was said that '... a person becomes a customer of a bank when he goes to the bank with money or a cheque and asks to have an account opened in his name, and the bank accepts the money or cheque and is prepared to open an account in the name of that person ...'; and in *Commissioners of Taxation v English, Scottish & Australian Bank* (1920), '... the word 'customer' signifies a relationship in which duration is not of the essence.'

Nevertheless, a banker may owe duties to another person before an account is opened, and even if an account is never opened. In *Woods v Martins Bank Ltd* (1959), a bank manager who negligently gave bad investment advice to a person lacking any business experience who intended to become a customer, and who did so shortly afterwards, was held to owe him the same contractual duty of care as he would have done if the person had already been a customer.

The importance of the definitions

The definitions are of far more than academic interest although, no doubt, they are called into question only rarely. We saw in *United Dominions Trust v Kirkwood* (1966) that the definition was central to the case but the best illustrations are found in the rights and duties owed under the banker-customer contract, particularly the bank's duty of confidentiality to its customer (*see* below) and in the statutory protection afforded to banks when they collect and pay cheques.

Under the Cheques Act 1957, s.4, a collecting bank is protected against an action for conversion by a cheque's true owner if it collects it on behalf of a *customer* and the Bills of Exchange Act 1882, s.60 similarly protects a *bank* if it pays a cheque bearing a forged or unauthorised endorsement. (*See* generally Chapter 8.) An account may be opened with a stolen cheque, for example, and quite apart from the matter of taking references, if a course of business was necessary to establish a person as a 'customer', collection of this first cheque would not be protected under s.4.

This protection, which depends on these basic definitions, is perhaps taken for granted but you must remember that without it retail banking would very probably grind to a halt in a matter of weeks.

ACTIVITY 5.2

It is always a good idea to learn definitions that are likely to be asked in the examination paper. The definitions of 'banker' and 'customer' are two such definitions. Learn them and also make sure you can explain and illustrate why the definition is of practical importance.

■ THE BANKER-CUSTOMER RELATIONSHIP

The relationship between banks and their customers is contractual, primarily that of debtor (the bank) and creditor (the customer) with the roles reversed where the customer is indebted to the bank. This was established in *Foley v Hill* (1848). The decision also established that contrary to the usual debtor-creditor relationship, where the debtor is obliged to seek out their creditor to make repayment, the customer (the creditor) must come to the debtor for repayment. If it were otherwise, a bank would have to try to persuade customers to withdraw their balances every time they visited the bank! The customer must demand repayment from the bank.

Various categories of rules govern the workings of this relationship.

General rules of contract law

In the previous chapter we discussed the basic principles of contract law and saw, in broad terms, how they apply in a banking context. This whole chapter considers this in more detail.

Perhaps the most remarkable fact about the banker-customer contract is its informality and the importance of implied and not express terms as the basis of the contract. (We commented on this in Chapter 4.) It is made without written agreement but by oral discussion, completion of largely administrative forms, the sending of brief letters and on the basis of banking custom and practice. How many customers are aware (or made aware at present) of the rights and duties which are implied into the contract? (*See* below.)

However, the position may possibly change. At least one major bank has produced customer leaflets explaining in everyday language the main terms of the banker-customer contract. Credit card agreements – excellent examples of standard form contracts – already detail the terms of issue and the responsibilities of the cardholder and the increasing use of electronic banking is likely to continue this trend, particularly in relation to a customer's obligations with respect to the use and care of cash or credit cards and any associated PIN (personal identification number).

The Code of Banking Practice published in 1991 (*see* page 74) is likely to accelerate such a trend. While not seeking to regulate the relationship between banks and their customers, the Code does require that customers have clear information about their relationship with their bank. Where banks (and building societies) express the terms and conditions of a banking service in writing they must do so in plain language with the aim of providing a fair and balanced view. More specifically, they must explain how any variation of the terms and conditions will be notified and they must give customers reasonable notice before any variation takes effect.

Under the Code, banks are also required to provide customers with details of charges payable in connection with the normal operation of their accounts and the basis of interest payments on borrowing. You have already seen in Chapter 3 that customers must be given information on the bank's complaints procedure.

As we saw in Chapter 2, one feature of British case law is its evolutionary nature. The Law Merchant was absorbed into the common law by the judges – and important parts of it were subsequently codified into statutes. A similar thing happened with the customs and practices of banking, they became 'codified' by case law into what is referred to as the *implied contract* between banker and customer. While *Foley v Hill* (1848) established the true basis of the relationship, in *Joachimson v Swiss Bank Corporation* (1921) the Court of Appeal laid down the basic implied terms in the contract and emphasised the single, indivisible nature of the contract although there might be separate additional contracts entered into for specific purposes, e.g. a contract of loan. (Today a contract for a credit card would be another example.) Among other terms recognised in *Joachimson* is that a bank undertakes to receive money and collect cheques for its customer's account; that it will comply with its customer's written orders, e.g. cheques, addressed to the customer's branch to repay any part of the funds deposited; and that it will give its customer reasonable notice before closing the account if it is in credit. The case also established that the bank is not obliged to pay the customer the full amount of his or her balance until the customer makes a formal demand for the balance to the branch at which the current account is kept. The legal rights and duties of a bank which we discuss below are in large part derived from the 'codification' of judicially implied terms in *Joachimson*.

You will no doubt recall that in the *Tai Hing Case* (1986) the Privy Council reviewed some of the more important aspects of this implied contract.

One specific rule established by case law which is particularly important to banks and which we can conveniently discuss here, comes from the decision in *Devaynes v Noble* (1816), always referred to as the *Rule in Clayton's Case* (1816). You will immediately see why. The *Rule* states that in a current account payments in are appropriated to the debit items in date order, unless the customer or the bank, if the customer does not, takes steps to appropriate particular credits against particular debits. An example will show you how the *Rule* works. Look at Fig 5.1 and the commentary on it.

X, Y and Z were in partnership. At the date of X's retirement on 1 June – which determines X's liability – the firm's overdraft was £5,000. The account is continued unbroken. The credit of £2,000 on 3 June reduces the debit balance and X's liability for it to £3,000, and the credit on 5 June further reduces both to £1,000. The debit on 7 June increases the overdraft to £5,000 but X's liability *remains* at £1,000, as it does on 9 June when a debit increases

Date	Debits	Credits	Balance
1 June			c/f 5,000 Dr
3 June		2,000	3,000 Dr
5 June		2,000	1,000 Dr
7 June	4,000		5,000 Dr
9 June	2,000		7,000 Dr
11 June		1,000	6,000 Dr

Fig 5.1 Account of XYZ

the overdraft to £7,000. The credit on 11 June then reduces the overdraft to £6,000 but, through the operation of the *Rule*, also cancels X's remaining liability on the account. This is so even though the overdraft has actually increased and only Y and Z are now be liable on it. For this reason, banks will invariably take steps to avoid the *Rule* operating to their disadvantage wherever possible – most commonly by simply breaking the account.

Rules of agency

In important respects a bank acts as its customer's agent, e.g. in collecting and paying cheques for its customer or in, say, buying and selling shares. Where is does act as an agent, a bank owes a duty of care to its principal – its customer.

Trust principles

A bank may expressly act as a trustee for its customers through, for example, its trust department or subsidiaries. Where it does, the law of trusts imposes upon it duties and liabilities with respect to the care and use of the trust property. Indeed, if a bank holds itself out as having particular expertise as a trustee – which will presumably always be the case – it owes a greater duty of care than an ordinary individual who assumes a role as trustee, e.g. under a will or a family property settlement. However, a bank does *not* hold its customer's deposits on trust for the customer. If this were the case, the bank would be unable to use the funds (the trust property) for its own commercial purposes. (For the same reason a bank does not act as its customer's agent in relation to the customer's deposits.)

In practice the duties and liabilities incurred by a trustee are more likely to affect you in relation to *constructive trusts*, i.e. situations where a person becomes involved in the affairs of a trust, and therefore incurs duties in relation to the trust property, without being appointed as a trustee. For example, a bank would be liable as constructive trustee to the beneficiaries if it knowingly allowed a trustee to wrongfully appropriate trust funds held in an account for the trustee's own benefit. A simple example would be to knowingly allow a solicitor to draw cheques on a client account for the solicitor's own purposes. In all cases of possible liability as constructive trustee it is a question of whether the bank has 'knowingly' facilitated the breach of trust. (*See* further page 144.)

Rules of bailment

A bailment arises where one person (the bailor) deposits goods with another (the *bailee*) for a specific purpose on terms that the goods will ultimately be redelivered to the bailor or otherwise dealt with according to the bailor's instructions. While the bailee obtains possession of the property, ownership remains with the bailor.

The use of a bank's safe deposit (safe custody) facilities by its customer gives rise to a bailment agreement. Under such an agreement the bank (as bailee) incurs a duty of care and acquires a right to be paid, if a fee is to be charged, and a (contractual) 'lien' over the property if payment is not made. (Note that the 'lien' – in fact it is not strictly a lien at all (*see* p 194) – only applies to unpaid safe custody charges; it does not apply to borrowing on any account.) Property held in safe custody would typically include jewellery, deeds and other documents, and, increasingly, computer discs.

The law draws a distinction between a gratuitous (unpaid) bailee and a bailee for reward (a paid bailee). Both may be liable in *tort* for loss or damage to the property bailed but the former is only expected to take the same care of the property as a reasonably careful person would take of similar property of their own. The latter, however, owes an additional *contractual duty* to the bailor under which they are judged against the highest professional standards.

Modern safe custody facilities and procedures mean that a bank is unlikely to be liable for the tort of *negligence* in relation to safe custody deposits although this is always a possibility should property held in safe custody be destroyed by fire or otherwise lost or stolen. Remember too that the Unfair Contract Terms Act 1977 subjects any term or notice excluding or limiting possible liability for negligence in relation to goods, in this case as bailee, to a test of reasonableness.

A bank is perhaps more likely to incur liability in relation to a safe custody deposit in the tort of *conversion*. Conversion can be committed in many ways but most commonly by wrongfully taking possession of goods; wrongfully damaging or destroying them; wrongfully disposing of them or by refusing to part with them when possession is demanded by someone entitled to possession.

The essence of the tort is that the defendant's conduct amounts to a denial of the plaintiff's *right to possession and control* of the property, usually by denying the plaintiff's title in some way. You can see that the last two examples above are relevant in relation to safe custody deposits. A bank would for example commit conversion by refusing to hand over the property held in safe custody when the depositor (bailor) demands it or by delivering the property to an unauthorised person. Liability in conversion is *strict*, that is the breach of the legal duty resulting in the infringement of the individual's legal right is enough, proof of intention or negligence is unnecessary. This means that a bank would still be liable in conversion even if it should wrongfully deliver property held in safe custody by pure mistake or against the most skilfully forged authority: in both instances it would still have infringed the bailor's rights in the property bailed.

Note, however, that merely being in possession without title is not conversion. There must be an intention to keep the property in defiance of the owner's rights. This situation would arise if the property held in safe custody did not belong to the bailor. In the event of the ownership being disputed in such a situation, the bank would have to make it clear that it was prepared to deliver the property to whoever was proved to be its true owner.

The distinction between a paid and a gratuitous bailee is, in theory, relevant in banking in so far as some customers are offered safe custody facilities without specific payment for them (an apparently gratuitous bailment) while a specific charge is made in other cases (a bailment for reward). The better view today, however, is that a bank that accepts property for safe custody can nearly always be regarded as a bailee for reward. In other words, the bailment is considered to be part and parcel of the wider contract with the customer, whether or not specific payment is made for the facility. In any case, the same high standard of care is always taken of property deposited for safe custody whatever the exact nature of the bailment agreement.

Rules of banking practice

All trades and industries develop their own commercial customs (rules) and banks are no exception.

Such rules may have evolved over a considerable period of time and usually reflect the commercial environment of which banking is itself part. The rules contained in the Bills of Exchange Act 1882, and the judicial interpretation of them, for example, are largely the codified practices of merchants developed over the previous 100 years or so. Even where such rules have not been codified into statute law, they are largely recognised and enforced by the courts and may acquire the force of mercantile custom at common law if they are universally accepted.

A full survey of the rules of banking practice is out of place in this book but one example will illustrate the relationship between banking practice and the law. In *Baines v National Provincial Bank Ltd* (1927), it was held that a bank is allowed a reasonable period of time to complete its business after its advertised closing time. Thus, in the case the bank was allowed to debit its customer's account with a cheque (for £200) cashed five minutes after closing time and a countermand of it the following morning was ineffective. The decision is important in itself but let us consider it in relation to s.60 of the Bills of Exchange Act 1882. This section, as we saw earlier, protects a banker who pays a cheque which bears a forged or unauthorised endorsement against liability to its true owner (its holder) provided the banker pays it in good faith and in the *ordinary course of business*. Relying on the decision in *Baines* which, remember, is a judicial recognition of banking practice, we can safely say that (uncrossed) cheques paid in a busy branch within ten minutes or so of the advertised closing time would still be considered as paid in the ordinary course of business. It follows that the protection of s.60, if required, would still apply.

Special relationships

We saw in the previous chapter that there exists a number of specific *fiduciary relationships* where one party is presumed to be in a position of dominance over the other and which can render voidable any contract made between them, e.g. solicitor and client and parent and child. You learnt that the banker-customer relationship is *not* one of these specific relationships but that a very similar *special relationship* can arise on the facts: *Lloyds Bank v Bundy* (1975). The point to note here is that if such a special relationship is proved the bank's position is no longer governed merely by the terms, express and implied, of the original contract. The bank will owe its customer a separate and strict duty of good faith, particularly where the possibility of a conflict of interests arises, and the concept of undue influence assumes greater importance. Note that *Woods v Martins Bank Ltd* (1959) (*see* above) can be considered an earlier example of a special relationship existing between a bank and a customer (in the wider sense of the term).

ACTIVITY 5.3

If the Bundy facts were to recur today, would the bank's charge be set aside for undue influence?

Another form of *special relationship* was essential to the principle in *Hedley Byrne v Heller & Partners Ltd* (1963). (Note, however, that this special relationship is *not contractual* and has nothing to do with the banker-customer contract. We cover it here because it is convenient to do so.) The case established that liability in the tort of negligence for negligent statements causing purely financial loss can arise, in the absence of an express disclaimer, where the circumstances show that the skill and judgment of the person making the statement is being relied on by the person to whom the statement is made (the special relationship). (We have mentioned the case already in previous chapters but it warrants further discussion.)

The facts were that the plaintiffs, advertising agents, asked their bank to inquire into the credit worthiness of a potential client Easipower Ltd through the latter's bank Heller & partners Ltd. Satisfactory replies were given to two such enquiries on the strength of which the plaintiffs incurred substantial expenses on Easipower's behalf. Easipower subsequently went into liquidation and HB sought to recover the losses they had incurred from Heller & Partners Ltd on the grounds that the replies had been made negligently. As you will recall from our earlier references to the case HB's action failed, but not because the House of Lords did not think that Heller & Partners Ltd owed them a duty of care when making the statement, but because of the disclaimer – 'For your private use and without responsibility on the part of the bank or its officials.'

Note that the *Hedley Byrne* principle was reviewed and refined by the House of Lords in *Caparo Industries v Dickman* (1990), where it was held that auditors of a company's accounts did not owe a duty of care to shareholders or members of the public who purchased shares in reliance on the audited accounts. The purpose of the audit was to enable shareholders to make corporate decisions not for individuals to make personal decisions about whether or not to deal in a company's shares. The House of Lords emphasised that the duty of care will only arise where sufficient *proximity* existed between the plaintiff and defendant, i.e. where:

- a special relationship exists between the maker of the statement and the person acting on it, the special relationship being based on the statement having been directed towards specific persons in the knowledge that it will be relied on;
- the person making the statement has expertise in the matter; and
- it is reasonable to impose a duty of care.

ACTIVITY 5.4

What information does your bank give to would-be customers about the terms of the banker/customer contract? Do you have any leaflets or information sheets? Do they ever ask? What happens if they do ask? How does your bank compare with others in this respect?

■ A BANK'S LEGAL RIGHTS AND DUTIES

Arising from the banker-customer contract are a number of legal rights and duties. Although these are almost all *implied* and not express terms of the contract, they are crucial to the operation of accounts. Having said this, there is no rule of law which actually prevents a bank including *express* terms in the contract which will vary, replace or exclude those implied by the courts. But the ability to do this is subject to two important limitations. First, the courts are very unwilling to accept and enforce express terms that vary established practice, particularly if the effect of them is to take away rights the other party would have enjoyed, unless there is the clearest evidence that the other party was made aware of them, understood them and accepted them. Second, any term which attempts to exclude the liability of one of the parties is subject to the Unfair Contract Terms Act 1977 (*see* page 38) and will only be enforceable if the court considers that the term is reasonable.

Rights

1 To *charge its customers reasonable commission* for services rendered to them, and to *charge interest* on loans made to them.

2 To *repayment on demand* from its customers of any overdrawn balance on a current account. In *Williams and Glyn's Bank v Barnes* (1980), however, it was held that a reasonable period of notice must be given where the terms and circumstances of the contract of lending clearly *imply* such notice.

3 To be *indemnified* by its customers for expenses and liabilities incurred while acting for them.

4 To *exercise a lien* over any of its customers' securities that are in its possession, other than those deposited for safe custody, for any money owing to it. (A lien, pronounced le-en, is a right to retain possession of the property of another in lieu of payment due from that person.)

5 To *dispose of its customers' money as it pleases* provided it honours its customers' valid cheques. This right – which has been vital to the development of commercial banking as we know it – derives from the decision in *Foley v Hill* (1848) (*see* page 116).

6 To *combine* or set-off accounts. Where a customer has more than one account with a bank, the bank is entitled to settle an overdrawn balance on one account by transferring money from the credit balance on another. The right would arise, for example, where the bank receives notice of the death or mental incapacity of its customer or where its customer has a bankruptcy order made against them or, in the case of corporate customer, goes into liquidation.

The final two legal rights of a bank are probably better termed *duties of the customer*.

7 A customer is under a duty *to exercise due care in drawing cheques* in order not to facilitate fraud. This right was established in *London Joint Stock Bank Ltd v Macmillan and Arthur* (1918), where a partner in the defendant firm signed a cheque payable to the payee or to bearer made out by a clerk for the sum of £2. The amount payable was shown in figures only. The clerk fraudulently altered the figures to read £120, wrote this amount on the cheque and obtained payment from the plaintiff, the firm's bank. The court held that the bank was entitled to debit the firm's account with the value of the cheque as altered because the firm had broken its duty as a customer. The rule in *Macmillan and Arthur* by analogy also applies to standing orders.

8 A customer is under a duty to inform his or her bank of any known forgeries on the account. This was established in *Greenwood v Martins Bank Ltd* (1932) where G's wife held the chequebook for G's account at MB and over a period of time drew a number of cheques on the account by forging G's signature. G eventually discovered the forgeries but did not inform MB. His wife committed suicide some eight months later and G sought to recover from MB the amount of the forged cheques. Normally, of course, a forgery of the drawer's signature is 'wholly inoperative' (Bills of Exchange Act 1882, s.24), i.e. has no legal effect, and does not entitle a bank to debit the account. Here, however, the bank was entitled to debit G's account with the value of the cheques because G was estopped (prevented) from denying the genuineness of the signatures by his failure to inform MB of the forgeries after he discovered them.

You will recall from Chapter 2 (*see* page 22) that the duties imposed by *Macmillan & Arthur* and *Greenwood* were confirmed in the *Tai Hing Case* (1986) but that the Privy Council refused to accept the banks' argument that customers owe wider duties to take reasonable precautions in managing their affairs in order to prevent their cheques being forged and to check bank statements for unauthorised debit items. Interestingly enough, the three banks involved in the case had included express terms in the contracts with their customer which basically sought to impose on the company a duty to examine its bank statements and query them within a given time, after which they would be considered to be accurate. The Privy Council refused to give effect to these express terms for the reasons we discussed above.

Duties

1 To *abide by any express mandate from its customer*, such as a standing order.

2 To *honour its customer's cheques*. This duty is subject to a number of provisos, for example:

(a) the cheque must be properly drawn and not stale – a cheque is stale when it has been in circulation for a considerable period of time, usually more than six months; (A cheque is overdue when it has been in circulation for an unreasonable length of time, a question of fact but possibly where it is not presented within ten days of its issue – there are no decisions on this point.)

(b) a sufficient credit balance or an agreed overdraft facility exists;

(c) there is no legal bar to payment, such as a garnishee order or an injunction;

(d) the customer has not countermanded payment;

(e) the bank has no notice that its customer has died, become mentally incapable of managing their affairs or had an insolvency petition presented against them;

(f) there has not been an insolvency order made against them.

By analogy this duty also applies to the payment of standing orders.

3 *Not to disclose information about its customer's affairs*. In *Tournier v National Provincial and Union Bank of England* (1924), it was held that this duty of secrecy is not absolute but *qualified* and disclosure is justified in four situations.

(a) Where the bank is compelled by law to do so. For example:

- by a court order under the Bankers' Books Evidence Act 1879 or the Drug Trafficking Offences Act 1986 (*see* Chapter 2) or a witness order;

- following an official request by the Department of Trade and Industry acting under powers contained in the Companies Act 1985 or by the Inland Revenue acting under the Taxes Management Act 1970 and the Income and Corporation Taxes Act 1988; or

- where although there is no compulsion to disclose information, a failure to do so may constitute a criminal act and disclosure has statutory protection. Here the disclosure will not be an actionable breach of contract. For example, protected by the Drug Trafficking Offences Act 1986 and by the Prevention of Terrorism (Temporary Provisions) Act 1989 are disclosure on suspicion or belief of the location of funds which might be used for possible offences under these Acts. The Criminal Justice Act 1988 protects a disclosure to the police of a suspicion or a belief that property has been obtained as a result of an indictable offence (a serious offence, one triable in the Crown Court by judge and jury).

(Note that these are just important *examples* of a bank disclosing information under compulsion of law. The complete list is extensive.)

(b) Where the bank has a duty to the public to do so. The extent of this exception is uncertain and certainly seldom invoked. It would probably apply in wartime if the bank discloses that one of its customers is trading with the enemy.

(c) Where the bank's own interests require disclosure, for example, where legal proceedings are required to enforce repayment of an overdraft, or where a surety asks to be told the extent to which his guarantee is being relied upon.

(d) Where the bank has the express or implied consent of its customer to do so, e.g. where it supplies a reference for its customer or where it replies to a status enquiry about its customer from another bank.

A quite different duty of confidentiality is imposed on banks by the Data Protection Act 1984 (*see* page 39).

4 To *render statements of account* to its customer periodically or upon request. (Note that customers do not owe a duty to check their statements: *Tai Hing Case* (1965).)

5 To *collect cheques and other normal banking instruments* for its customer and to credit the amounts collected to their account.

6 *To exercise proper care and skill* in carrying out any business it has agreed to transact for its customer. By a term implied into contracts of service under the Supply of Goods and Services Act 1982 s.13, any person who supplies a service in the course of business must carry out the service with reasonable care and skill. Banking operations are therefore covered by this section. Furthermore, any purported exclusion of this implied term is subject to the 'reasonableness test' imposed by the Unfair Contract terms Act 1977. Even without this statutory provision, a similar duty arises at common law when a bank acts as agent for its customer.

This duty of care and skill is evident in relation to any activity or transaction carried out or entered into on behalf of a customer, including safe deposit facilities (*see* above), but it is of most practical importance in relation to the collection and payment of cheques. Everyday, bankers pay and collect many thousands of cheques on behalf of their customers. Each payment and collection must be properly made in accordance with legal rules and banking practice if a banker is to enjoy the necessary protection afforded by the Bills of Exchange Act 1882 and the Cheques Act 1957, and the decisions of judges. Before we leave this particular duty, it is worth noting that the duty of care and skill can extend beyond the scope of traditional branch banking; it can for example, cover investment advice: *Woods v Martins Banks Ltd* (1959) (*see* above).

7 To *give reasonable notice before closing a credit account.* There are two reasons behind this duty. First, it gives the customer time to make other arrangements. Second, it means that the bank does not have to return cheques already issued by the customer. This saves administrative effort and prevents an allegation that the bank damaged its customer's reputation by returning the cheques unpaid.

ACTIVITY 5.5

(a) Produce a leaflet suitable for customers which sets out simply but comprehensively the terms of the banker-customer contract. You should pay attention to the presentation of the information because the visual appeal of leaflets produced by banks is important to their image and therefore their competitive ability. (Remember that 'simple' does not necessarily mean non-technical. Using correct terminology (perhaps with a short explanation of particular terms) is fine, but the use of jargon for its own sake is not.

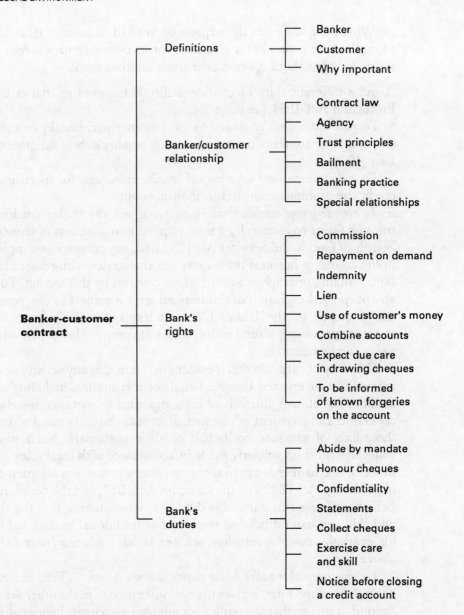

Fig 5.1 Summary of the banker-customer contract

(b) Produce diagrams similar to Fig 5.1 to summarise in more detail each of the four main topics shown on Fig 5.1.

■ OPENING AND OPERATING A BANK ACCOUNT

Introduction

Banks largely make their profits by lending out the money which customers have deposited with them. Therefore they compete for customers. The various inducements to open accounts offered to students are excellent examples – the student of today being, at least in theory, the worthwhile customer of the future. However, the legal framework governing banking operations requires that they take certain precautions before opening an account. A particularly important case in point is the protection afforded to a collecting bank by s.4 of the Cheques Act (1957) (*see* above). Clearly, if the bank collects a cheque for a customer who is not entitled to receive payment – the customer may have stolen the cheque or be in possession under a forged endorsement – and the bank did not take up its customer's references before opening the account, the protection of s.4 would not be available. The bank would not have acted 'without negligence' as required. This, however, is the strict *legal* position. Banking practice varies, as we explain below.

Opening an account

Before opening either a current or a deposit account, a bank must be satisfied as to the character and standing of the applicant and know their employer's name and nature of the employment. This information can be obtained either:

- by a *personal introduction* from an existing customer or another branch or bank; or
- by *taking references*, usually two, one of which should be from the applicant's employer.

In the latter case, if the referee is unknown to the bank, the authenticity of the reference should be checked, for example, through the referee's own bank.

Taking references should avoid opening what may become an unsatisfactory account and usually secures the protection of s.4. Indeed, as the law stands at present, a bank *must* obtain satisfactory references before opening an account if it wishes to benefit from the statutory protection available. However, although some banks insist on references in certain higher risk situations, the trend has been for few references to be taken and fewer to be checked. Accounts are frequently opened on production of satisfactory identification, e.g. a driving licence or passport, certainly identification is the single most important thing to check, and either a satisfactory enquiry through a credit reference agency or satisfactory internal credit scoring. At law this is clearly a dangerous practice – it has yet to be considered judicially, references are required as the law stands – but commercially it has made good sense on the basis that the time and expense involved in taking and checking references outweighs the risk of not doing so. In addition, a fiercely competitive environment demands that opening an account should be as easy as possible. The situation perhaps nicely illustrates the possible conflict between traditional banking virtues and attitudes, arguably embodied in the law, and the more market oriented approach dictated by change in the financial services industry.

Opening formalities

Banks differ as to the exact procedures and formalities involved in opening an account. You should obtain your own bank's account application form and ensure that you are familiar with the specific opening procedures. However, the following are the standard opening formalities.

1 *Specimen signatures* of all parties to the account must be obtained.

2 A *mandate covering all operations* on the account must be obtained if it is other than a sole account.

3 A *cheque book* should only be issued when a satisfactory introduction or references have been obtained and checked and any cheque opening the account cleared.

4 A *cheque guarantee card* should only be issued after the bank has established that the account will apparently be run in a regular and responsible manner, or where there is no doubt about the person's integrity and responsibility as an account holder.

5 If possible, *commission and interest charges should be agreed* when the account is opened in order to avoid having to rely on a banker's implied right to recover reasonable charges and commission. Most banks do, in fact, have standard tariffs for charges and commission.

ACTIVITY 5.6

How do the account opening formalities differ in your bank/branch? Why? Are you familiar with your account opening form and do you understand the purpose of everything on it? If you do not, ask a more experienced colleague.

Operation of an account by an agent

What is agency?

First, who is an agent? An *agent* is a person who acts on another's behalf, the other person being known as the *principal*. The essential feature of the relationship created is that the agent is able to alter the principal's legal position in relation to third parties by making contracts with them. Since agents contract on their principals' behalf, it follows that agents generally incur neither rights nor liabilities on any contract that they make.

A bank will often have to deal with people who are agents, such as directors of companies, partners in firms and occasionally a person who holds a power of attorney, and it is important for a bank to ascertain and understand the scope and extent of the agent's authority before dealing with the agent. Remember also that an important aspect of the banker-customer relationship is a bank's role as agent in collecting cheques. In addition, a bank may also act as an agent in dealing with securities on its customer's behalf, and in connection with the numerous other services that a bank can provide or arrange for its customers.

Some basic points

You should note the following points about customers delegating their authority to agents in connection with bank accounts.

1 Delegation by the principal is not always permitted by law. Trustees, for example, have very limited powers to delegate.

2 If there are two or more parties to the account, all parties must authorise

the delegation. For example, where A and B operate a joint account, both must authorise C to sign cheques in place of B.

3 Since agents act on behalf of their principals, agents need not themselves have contractual capacity, a minor, for example, can act as an agent. (It would, of course, be unusual to deal with an agent who was under some form of legal disability.)

4 The power to sign on an account does not include the power to draw, accept or endorse bills of exchange on behalf of the principal, nor to overdraw or charge the principal's property as security unless such powers are expressed in the mandate.

5 When a customer wishes to appoint an agent to operate an account on their behalf, a written mandate must be taken from the customer; standard mandate forms exist for this purpose. The mandate will stipulate that the bank has authority to act on the agent's signature and that the bank will continue to act on the agent's instructions until a written revocation of authority is received from the account holder.

6 A specimen of the agent's signature is required.

7 The agent must sign on the account in a way that avoids personal liability. The usual way is to sign 'Per pro' or 'For and on behalf of' followed by the signature. (But note the position in relation to company cheques, *see* p 137.)

Unauthorised acts by an agent

The general position. What is the position where agents act in excess of their authority? The agents are personally liable because by their actions they have warranted that they have authority which in truth they have not. The agents are, therefore, liable for *breach of warranty of authority*. This, however, may be of little use to a bank that has acted on an agent's instructions, for the sums involved may be great while the personal resources of the agent may be small. A bank, in these circumstances, would wish to make the principal liable if at all possible. Leaving aside the possibility that the principal may accept liability to preserve their reputation and banking facilities – technically the principal is said to *ratify* the agent's unauthorised act – in what circumstances can the principal be made liable at law?

Most agency situations arise as a result of a contract in which the express terms of the agency are spelt out. If a bank has knowledge of them it must, of course, adhere to them. However, in addition to the actual authority (express or implied) given by contract, agents will also at law have apparent (or ostensible) authority to undertake acts which are reasonably necessary for the completion of their authorised tasks. For example, an agent employed to sell land has apparent authority to sign a written contract as required by the Law of Property (Miscellaneous Provisions) Act 1989.

Agency can also be created by *estoppel* where one person allows another to appear to third parties to be their agent. Where a third party relies on this appearance and deals with that person as an agent, the 'principal' is *estopped* (prevented) from denying that person's authority. Such agency results from the principal's words or conduct, not from an agreement between the agent and principal. A simple banking example of agency by estoppel would be where a customer has regularly sent an employee to collect bank statements. If the employee was dismissed but still came to collect a statement as usual, but for his or her own purposes, and the bank provided it, estoppel would arise because the customer would be prevented from denying to the bank that the ex-employee was still their agent for that specific purpose. Once notice to the contrary was given, the estoppel would cease to operate.

The problem of an agent's unauthorised acts affecting a bank arises mainly in two areas: first, unauthorised *borrowing* and second, wrongfully *handling cheques*.

Unauthorised borrowing. If an agent borrows money from a bank without authority, the debt cannot be enforced against the principal unless the principal either ratifies the loan or is estopped from denying the agent's lack of authority. (Since the Companies Act 1989 abolished the *ultra vires* rule, this is no longer a problem in relation to companies: *see* page 43.)

Wrongfully handling cheques. Whenever an agent handles cheques for the principal, the possibility arises that the agent may be exceeding his or her authority. For example, the agent may draw cheques on the principal's account payable to him/herself without authority or s/he may endorse cheques payable to his or her principal and pay them into his or her own account. A bank would be liable to the true owner of the cheque if its negligence allowed the agent to act in this way. In *Midland Bank Ltd v Reckitt* (1933), for example, the bank was held to have acted negligently, and was therefore liable to its customer, when it collected for the personal account of a solicitor cheques drawn by him on the account of the customer for whom he held power of attorney. The power of attorney did not remove the need to make enquiries before paying the cheques.

Termination of bank's authority to pay

A bank's authority to make payments from its customer's account ends in the following main circumstances. (We cover this topic in more detail in Chapter 8, this is just an introduction.)

- *Countermand of payment*: only the drawer can countermand payment and the countermand must be in unequivocal terms, to the branch on which the cheque was drawn and must give complete details of the cheque.
- *Death or mental incapacity*. It is *notice* of the death or incapacity which terminates the authority, not the actual event.
- *Notice of an insolvency petition*: this is a bankruptcy petition in the case of an individual or a partnership, a winding-up petition in the case of a company.
- *Winding-up or bankruptcy order*: it is the making of the order, not notice of it, that terminates the authority.
- *Legal bar* to payment: this may be either a garnishee order or an injunction.
- *Third party rights*: the bank must know or have good reason to suspect that the account is being operated fraudulently.

ACTIVITY 5.7

Exactly what are your bank's standing instructions on telephone countermands? What happens if a written confirmation never arrives?

Closing an account

As you have already seen, a bank must give reasonable notice before closing an account in *credit*. What is reasonable is a question of fact in the circumstances. A bank will usually close an unsatisfactory account by requesting the customer to withdraw the balance and return any unused cheques. A formal notice in writing is necessary if the customer does not comply with the request. A credit account would be regarded as unsatisfactory where cheques exceeding the available balance on the account are frequently drawn or where the customer otherwise inconveniences the bank.

Since an overdraft is normally repayable on demand, a bank has no difficulty in closing an unsatisfactory *account in debit* which has been operated beyond the agreed limit. Where an agreed limit is not exceeded, a threat to close the account should be made unless the way the account is conducted improves. In the case of a *loan account*, there must be a breach of the loan agreement, for example, failure to make repayments as prescribed, before the account can be closed because the loan agreement will have been entered into for a fixed period. A loan is not repayable on demand.

Bank statements

A bank owes a duty to its customers to keep accurate records of transactions on their accounts. Customers have no obligation to check bank statements and inform the bank of an inaccuracy in them. Furthermore, if a customer does check the statements, the customer is not estopped (prevented) from subsequently challenging their accuracy: *Chatterton v London & County Bank* (1890), reaffirmed by the Privy Council in *Tai Hing* (1985) (*see* Chapter 2).

Overcrediting the account

If you overcredit a customer's account, the excess credit may not be recoverable. However, to defeat a claim for repayment, the customer must fulfil three conditions, as illustrated in *United Overseas Bank v Jiwani* (1976):

- the state of the account must have been misrepresented to the customer by the bank;
- the customer must have been misled by the misrepresentation; and
- as a result of the reliance, the customer must have changed their position in a way which would make it inequitable (unfair) to require them to repay the money.

Let us consider the case itself. The amount of $11,000 was credited by telex to the defendant's Swiss bank account making a total balance in the account of $21,000. The defendant issued a cheque for $20,000 in connection with the purchase of a hotel. Subsequently, written confirmation of the telex was received but the bank mistakenly treated this as a second credit and advised the defendant accordingly. The defendant then issued a second cheque, for $11,000, towards the hotel purchase. The bank sought to recover this amount from him. The court allowed the claim. On the facts the defendant had alternative funds which he would have used for the purchase, irrespective of the mistaken credit. Thus, while the first two conditions were, on the facts, satisfied, the defendant failed to satisfy the third.

Quite clearly an argument such as 'I wondered where the extra £25,000 shown on my statement came from – so I bought a BMW.' is not going to impress anybody!

Incorrectly debiting the account

Whatever the reason for the incorrect debit, a bank is obliged to refund the amount. Quite simply, it has no mandate for the debit. If, as a result of incorrect debits, cheques are dishonoured for apparent lack of funds, a bank is liable for the wrongful dishonour of the cheques and must compensate the customer for the injury to the customer's credit and reputation. This may even result in an action in tort for defamation. By analogy, the position is the same where there is an incorrect debit of a standing order.

Power of attorney
Definition

A power of attorney is a *deed* giving a person(s) (the donee or attorney) power to act on behalf of the person giving the power (the donor). The power of attorney may be either *specific* – for a particular purpose, or *general* – general authority for a particular period of time. It is usually encountered where the donor is going abroad or ill, or where a trustee or personal representative wishes to delegate their power for up to one year.

A general power granted in the form prescribed by the Powers of Attorney Act 1971 and expressed to be made under the Act, gives the donee authority to do on behalf of the donor anything that the donor can lawfully do by an attorney. However, since it is uncertain whether even this general (unlimited) power gives an attorney authority to borrow or charge assets as security, a bank will prefer to have specific clauses inserted dealing with these acts.

Banking practice in relation to powers of attorney

You must examine the power of attorney carefully to ascertain its exact nature and extent. It is usual for the donor's bank account to be specifically mentioned and authority given to the attorney to operate the account. Since a general power to operate a bank account does not usually include authority to do so, specific clauses must be included if the attorney is to collect, draw and endorse bills of exchange; borrow money; charge the donor's property as security and withdraw safe custody items. More generally, a bank must also ensure that:

- the attorney's identity is verified;
- the power is still in force;
- it is properly executed as a deed (*see* p 43); and
- the power is operated strictly according to its terms.

You will see later (Chapter 6) that banks are sometimes given power of attorney when they take an equitable mortgage over land, for this enables them to realise the security far more easily if repayment of the advance is not made.

Revocation of a power of attorney

There are five ways in which a power of attorney may be revoked:

1 By the donor *expressly revoking* the power, unless the power is expressed to be irrevocable.

2 By the *death, mental incapacity or bankruptcy* of the donor or donee. However, under the Enduring Powers of Attorney Act 1985, a power of attorney can be created which is not automatically revoked when the donor becomes mentally incapacitated. Such a power facilitates the administration of the donor's affairs without interruption just when the ability to do so is probably most needed.

3 When the *purpose for which it was given is fulfilled.*

4 When the *period for which it was given expires.*

5 By *implication*, for example, where a new power is executed or where the donor again begins to operate the account personally. Good banking practice demands that such implied revocation be checked and confirmed with the donor.

Standing orders and direct debits

A *standing order* is a standing instruction given by a customer to make a regular periodic payment from their account to the account of a customer of the same or other bank. Each order must be signed by the customer in accordance with the mandate for the account and it can only be cancelled on the written instructions of the customer.

The purpose of a *direct debit* is the same as a standing order. It differs in that the beneficiary's (the person receiving payment) bank raises the entries receiving the debits through the clearing system or by computer entries. Written authority must be given by the payer to their bank enabling it to debit the account, and the beneficiary must agree to *indemnify* the paying bank against all claims which may arise before the beneficiary can operate the system.

Both standing orders and direct debits are used to make regular payments, such as mortgage, insurance and subscription payments, from an account. The greater flexibility of the direct debit has resulted in an increase in its use and a corresponding decrease in the use of the standing order.

■ DIFFERENT TYPES OF ACCOUNTS

While you may provide a similar range of services and facilities for the vast majority of your customers, they are far from being an homogeneous body. Different groups exist and different legal rules may apply to them. It follows that different banking considerations may also apply.

Joint accounts

A *joint account* is any account opened in the names of two or more persons, other than an account of a partnership, personal representatives or trustees. The typical joint account is that of a husband and wife.

The mandate

The mandate, signed by all the parties to the account, must include the following:

- a clear indication as to *who can make withdrawals* from the account, e.g. 'either to sign' or 'all to sign';
- admission of *joint and several liability* for any overdraft (*see* below); and
- a *survivorship clause*, i.e. a statement that the bank may pay the entire balance on the account to the survivor(s) on the death of one of the joint account holders.

Without the last clause the bank would have to get instruction from the deceased's personal representative as to how to deal with the deceased's share of the funds.

Points to note

You should note five further points about joint accounts.

- The bankruptcy or mental incapacity of any one party *cancels the mandate*.
- The mandate will expressly provide that payments from the account can be made notwithstanding the *death* of one of signatories. But for this express term in the contract, at common law the death would cancel the mandate. Incorporating this term enables the account to be continued.
- Any one party can *countermand* payment of a cheque.
- If an *agent* is to sign on the account, all the parties must sign the authority for the agent to do so.
- If one party opens an account in the joint names of him/herself and another *without the latter's authority*, the authority of both parties is still necessary to authorise a release of funds.

Joint and joint and several liability

The distinction between these two forms of liability is important to a bank. If you study the consequences of the distinction carefully you will see why a bank will always insist upon joint and several liability being admitted on all joint accounts as well as on the accounts of partnerships, executors and trustees.

Joint liability is shared liability for a debt or other obligation. It gives the bank, or any other creditor, a joint right of action against all those liable on the contract. This can be exercised by suing one debtor, a combination of them or all of them, if need be in successive actions. (Originally, joint liability gave only one right of action, i.e. once judgment was obtained, the joint right of action was exhausted – no subsequent actions could be brought against any joint debtor not sued in the original action.)

Joint and several liability is shared and individual liability. It therefore gives a right of action against the debtors severally (individually), i.e. each debtor is individually liable for the whole (joint) debt, in addition to a combined joint right of action against all parties liable. (This individual liability always meant that individual actions could be brought against the debtors until the debt was cumulatively satisfied.)

Given that the original main distinction between the two forms of liability is now part of legal history, joint and several liability is today imposed for three reasons.

1 Joint and several liability gives a *right of combination* (*see* page 123) between private accounts in credit and an overdrawn joint account when the mandate on the joint account is determined or as otherwise agreed. This is because each party is separately liable for the joint debts. No such right of set-off exists where only joint liability is accepted.
2 The death of one joint account holder completely releases the deceased's estate from liability for debts on the account; this is *not* so with joint and several liability.
3 Joint and several liability enables a bank to claim for money owing on the joint account against the estate of a bankrupt joint account holder while retaining its rights against the solvent parties. This is probably not so where only joint liability is admitted.

You will recall that earlier in this chapter we explained and stressed the importance of the *Rule in Clayton's Case* (1816). While joint and several liability strengthens a banker's position where a joint-account holder dies or becomes bankrupt, in both cases the joint account must be *stopped* and a new account opened (to prevent the *Rule* operating), thereby preserving the liability of the deceased or bankrupt joint-account holder for any debit balance. In fact, the mandate may expressly exclude the operation of the *Rule*, in which case such action is not legally necessary – although a bank will almost invariably still stop the account.

Registered companies

A thorough discussion of the legal framework relating to companies is outside the scope of this book. You will, perhaps, have covered companies as organisations in your previous studies. If so, bear that in mind when you read this section. Here we will just cover a few particularly important points and then concentrate on companies from the banker-customer perspective.

What is a company

A company can be defined as an organisation of individuals who contribute finance to a common stock which is to be used for business activities and who share the profit or loss arising. The common stock is the company's financial capital and the contributors of it are its members, the shareholders. A *limited company* is one where the liability of its members to contribute towards the payment of its debts is limited to either their investment in the company, that is, a company limited by shares, or to the amount that they have undertaken to contribute should the company be wound up through insolvency, that is, a company limited by guarantee. Most limited companies are limited by shares and companies limited by guarantee are usually non-profit maximising organisations, e.g. Polytechnics and some other large colleges. Under the Companies Act 1985, a newly registered *public* company must be limited by shares.

A company is a *corporation*, in other words an artificial legal person recognised by the law as having an existence, rights and duties quite separate and distinct from the individuals who are its members. This concept is fundamental to the relationship between a bank and its company customers, as it is to the framework of company law and, indeed, commercial activity generally.

The vast majority of companies are incorporated by registering certain documents with the Registrar of Companies in accordance with the Companies Acts. These documents are:

- the memorandum of association;
- the articles of association;
- a statement of the names of the intended first director(s) and the first secretary, together with their written consents to act as such, and the intended address of the company's registered office;
- a statutory declaration of compliance with the Companies Act 1985 regarding registration; and
- a statement of the company's capital, unless it is to have no share capital.

Memorandum and articles of association

Of these documents, the memorandum of association and the articles of association are the most important. The *memorandum of association* applies to the external activities of the company, while the *articles of association* regulates its internal administration, the relationship between the company and its members and the relationship among the members themselves. The contract between the company and its members is made on the basis of these documents.

You saw in Chapter 2 that the Companies Act 1989 abolished the *ultra vires* rule in relation to the dealings of the company with third parties, a company therefore has unlimited contractual capacity irrespective of what the objects clause in its memorandum might state. However, the rule still exists in so far as a shareholder can take action to stop the company making contracts which are outside the objects clause. The 1989 Act also allows a company to state in its objects clause that it is a 'general commercial company', a statement that permits the company to carry on any trade or business and gives it power to do all things incidental to such activities.

It is possible that these apparently important changes will result in far less change than might be imagined – and partly because of the attitudes of banks. Banks are notoriously and rightfully careful when lending and taking security to ensure that nothing should prejudice their ability to recover the advance. It is likely, therefore, that banks will want to see the objects of the company clearly stated in its memorandum of association and will not be satisfied with the general commercial company statement. This would be to ensure that there cannot possibly be any argument with the company or its shareholders that the company had power to act as it did, e.g. to give a guarantee. It could also be considered bad banking practice to lend to a company for purpose XYZ where the objects clause stated its activities to be ABC.

Company bank accounts

A company can pursue its business activities in much the same way as a sole trader or partnership and this includes operating a bank account. Nevertheless, as a consequence of a company's corporate status and the very comprehensive legal framework regulating the operation of companies, special care must be taken before opening a company bank account. Before doing so, a bank must ensure that:

- the company has been properly incorporated, for which sight of the certificate of incorporation is required;
- in the case of a public company, that the company has received a trading certificate from the Registrar of Companies; (The trading certificate confirms that the share capital requirements of public company have been met.)
- it obtains or inspects a copy of the company's memorandum and articles of association and makes sure that they are up to date, if need be by making a search at Companies House; (Note that doing this is of far less importance since the Companies Act 1989 abolished the *ultra vires* rule.)
- it receives a certified copy of the resolution appointing the first directors, if they are not named in the articles (and afterwards that it is notified when a director retires or a new director joins the board); and
- the bank's mandate form is signed by the chairman and secretary of the company after the resolutions that they contain have been passed by a meeting of the board of directors.

Company cheques. A person signing a cheque becomes a party to it and thereby incurs liability on it if it is not paid by the drawee bank. It therefore follows that if a signatory wishes to avoid this liability they must make it absolutely clear that they sign in a representative capacity. Traditionally this is done by using words such as 'per pro', or 'for and on behalf of', followed by the full name of the company, the signature and the signatory's capacity within the company, for example, director or secretary. If the representative capacity is not made clear, the signatory incurs personal liability on the cheque.

The position differs in relation to company cheques because the Court of Appeal held in *Bondina Ltd v Rollaway Shower Blinds Ltd* (1986) that providing a cheque is printed with the company's name and account number, the company and not the person signing is liable on the cheque even if the representative nature of the signature is not stated. The reason is that it is clear that the drawer of the cheque is the company and not the person signing it.

The principle above does not affect the rule that failure to state the company's name accurately and in full means that the person signing the cheque or other bill incurs personal liability if it is not paid by the company: Companies Act 1985, s.349. This provision is applied strictly. In *British Airways Board v Parish* (1979), omission of the word 'Ltd'. Was held to be a breach of s.349 and sufficient to render the person who had signed a cheque personally liable on it. Another example: in *Maxform SpA v Mariani and Goodville Ltd* (1979), Goodville Ltd traded under its business name of 'Italdesign' and its sole director accepted bills drawn on the company in that name. Three bills were dishonoured by the company when they were presented for payment. The court held that the director was personally liable on them. Use of the business name was insufficient to avoid liability under s.349, the director should have accepted in the form in which the company's cheques were signed – 'Goodville Ltd trading as Italdesign'. Such decisions are clearly to the advantage of a bank or the holder of a bill of exchange.

Misuse of the account. In operating a company's account you must always be aware of the possibility that one or more of the directors could be using the account for their own purposes. This is most likely to occur in the case of small companies and 'one-man' companies in particular, perhaps innocently through ignorance of a director's duties and the requirements of company legislation. If such misuse occurs and a reasonably aware business person would have realised that it was happening, a bank will be liable to the company for the loss incurred.

Company borrowing

It is usual for borrowing powers to be vested in the directors but occasionally borrowing must be sanctioned by the company in a general meeting. Any limitation on borrowing powers in the memorandum can be ignored but the articles frequently limit those of its directors. If the directors act *ultra vires* when making the contract of loan, the loan and any security given in support of it can only be enforced if it can be shown that the lender acted in good faith. The Companies Act 1985 provides that knowledge that the transaction is *ultra vires* the directors (such knowledge the bank would almost invariably have) is not of itself bad faith but since the meaning of 'good faith' is not clear a bank could still be presented with a problem in enforcing repayment or the security. (*See* also p 219.)

If the loan and therefore the security proves unenforceable against the company, the bank could sue the directors who entered into it personally. However, more profitable courses of action would be to ask the company either to *ratify* the transaction at a general meeting or to *alter the articles retrospectively* at a general meeting to increase or to abolish the limit on its directors' borrowing powers.

Partnerships

'Partnership is the relation which subsists between persons carrying on a business in common with a view of profit': Partnership Act 1890, s.1. A full discussion of partnership law is outside the scope of this book but we can usefully add a few important points relevant to banking to what you will probably have already learnt about partnership in your other studies.

Partners as agents

Agency is the foundation of partnership law relating to a firm's dealings with outsiders. Apart from actual authority (express or implied) given by the other partners, each *general partner* has apparent or ostensible authority (authority as it appears to others) to bind fellow partners when acting in the usual course of the firm's business, unless the outsider either knew that the partner had no authority in the matter, or knew or believed that s/he was not a partner. Thus, an outsider dealing with general partners is not affected by any secret limitation on their authority. (This is a basic principle of agency.) For example, in *Mercantile Credit Ltd v Garrod* (1962), A and B had entered into partnership to let garages and to repair motor cars. The partnership deed expressly excluded the buying and selling of cars. A, without B's knowledge, purported to sell a car, to which he had no title, to the plaintiff. The proceeds were paid into the partnership bank account. In an action against B it was held that B was accountable for the proceeds since the buying and selling of cars *appeared* to be within the firm's normal course of business. The limitation in the partnership deed was no defence.

A partner in *either type of partnership* has implied (actual) authority to bind the firm by:

- buying and selling goods in the course of the firm's business;
- receiving payment of debts due to the firm, and giving receipts for such payment;
- engaging employees for the firm; and
- drawing cheques.

In a *trading partnership* (one whose business consists mainly of buying and selling) a partner's implied authority also includes:

- borrowing money on the firm's credit; (It follows that a loan to a non-trading partnership must be expressly authorised by all partners. In practice a bank will require express authorisation of the loan from all partners in either type of partnership.)
- pledging (*see* page 192) the firm's goods or securities, including deeds of the firm's premises, to secure such borrowing; and
- signing bills of exchange on the firm's behalf.

In *neither* type of partnership does a partner have an implied authority to execute deeds or to give a guarantee in the firm's name – both limitations are relevant to banking.

Liability of partners

For debts and other obligations, the liability of the partners is *joint*; for torts authorised by the firm or committed in the ordinary course of the firm's business liability is *joint and several*. You have already seen the difference between joint and joint and several liability. It has always been standard banking practice to insist on each partner accepting joint and several liability in dealings between a bank and a partnership.

The partnership account

Rarely, if ever will a bank have to verify the existence of a partnership but it must ensure that the names of all the partners are known. The easiest way to do this would appear to be by inspecting the articles or deed of partnership because the members would be named in it. However, a bank does not normally ask to see or obtain a copy of the firm's articles or deed of partnership because if it did it would be deemed to have knowledge of any limitation on a partner's authority. This could be to a bank's disadvantage in its dealings with the firm. However, under the Business Names Act 1985, the names of persons using a business name must be legibly stated on all business letters and written demands for payment. These must give an address where court documents can be served and accepted. In addition, a notice giving the names and addresses of the partners using the business name must be displayed prominently in any place where business is carried on and to which customers have access. A bank should therefore note the names on the firm's business stationery. (The same applies to the name and address of a sole trader or a registered company using a business name.)

The importance of *verifying the names* of all the partners lies, once again, in the statutory protection of s.4 of the Cheques Act 1957. We can illustrate this with an example. In *Smith and Baldwin v Barclays Bank Ltd* (1944), the defendant bank collected cheques payable to a firm for the private account of its customer after he had produced a certificate of registration (under the Registration of Business Names Act 1916 – now repealed) showing him to be its registered proprietor. The customer, however, was a partner in a firm, not a sole trader, and had been able to obtain the certificate because the partners collectively had not registered the firm name. On these facts, the bank was held not to have collected the cheques negligently, it was entitled to rely on the certificate produced by its dishonest customer. By analogy, a bank who checks that the statutory requirements under the Business Names Act 1985 have been fulfilled would probably be considered to have acted without negligence unless there are circumstances which a reasonable bank (not a detective) would consider warranted further investigation.

References should be taken to ensure the firm's suitability as a customer, although this requirement may be waived where one or more of the partners is already known to the bank. The account must be operated in the names of all the partners and the mandate, showing how and by whom the account is to be operated, must be signed by all the partners. However, the mandate may be cancelled by any one partner and any one partner can countermand payment of a cheque, irrespective of whether or not that partner signed it.

You have seen above that the partners will be required to admit *joint and several liability* in the mandate. In relation to partnerships, there are three specific reasons for this:

- a credit balance on a partner's private account may be set-off against a debit balance on the firm account;
- the bank will rank equally with separate creditors should a partner die or become bankrupt; (Normally, separate estate pays separate creditors and joint estate joint creditors, any balance remaining on one going to augment the other estate.)
- should the partnership itself become bankrupt, the bank has a double right of proof; it may prove against both the joint estate of the firm and the separate estate of each partner, including any security the partners have deposited to secure personal borrowing.

If a partner *retires* or dies and the firm continues in business, new mandate forms must be signed by the remaining partners and any incoming partner. New security forms must also be completed unless those held remain effective despite changes in the constitution of the firm. If the firm's account is in *credit*, it may be continued unbroken, although cheques drawn by the retiring partner should be confirmed by the remaining partners. A retiring partner or a deceased partner's estate remains liable for the firm's *debts*. However, the account must be broken (although a clause in the security forms may make this unnecessary *at law*) and further entries passed through a new account, in order to preserve the liability and the bank's rights over any security deposited by the partner personally to secure the account. This procedure is dictated by the *Rule in Clayton's Case* (1816), which we have already explained.

Partnership borrowing

A partner in a *trading partnership* has implied authority to borrow money for use in the firm's business and to charge the firm's assets to secure such borrowing. The mandate will, however, usually contain the express undertaking of all the partners to be liable for any advance made to the firm. (Why should a bank rely on implied authority to enforce a loan and security against the other partners when it is a very simple matter to ensure that they expressly accept liability.) Express power must be given to partners in a *non-trading partnership* to borrow money or to give securities on behalf of the firm. It is, in fact, usual for a bank to insist on all the partners executing the necessary documents where the firm's property is pledged or mortgaged as security for an advance whatever the type of partnership involved.

Minors

In the previous chapter we saw that a minor has only limited contractual capacity. (Revise that section now if you need to.) In particular, contracts of loan made with a minor are *unenforceable* although after the age of 18 a minor can *ratify* the loan. A cheque, or other bill of exchange, is also unenforceable against a minor in any capacity (drawer, acceptor (of a bill of exchange), or endorser) but the cheque, or other bill, can be enforced against other parties to it. For example, a person who took a cheque in payment from a minor and then endorsed it to a third party is liable on the cheque to that third party if the cheque is not paid, but the minor is not.

Minors' bank accounts

Up to the age of seven, a minor's credit account will normally be treated as a *trust* account (*see* below), the parent(s) being the trustee. After that age the minor is usually allowed to operate the account personally. If 'unusually' frequent or large withdrawals are made, a bank would probably inform the parent(s) although technically, at least, this would constitute a breach of the bank's duty of secrecy.

A minor should generally not be permitted to overdraw an account or be granted a loan because the debt created is not enforceable against the minor. This is so even if the advance was intended to be used to buy necessaries. If, however, part or all of an advance is spent on necessaries, that sum can be recovered from the minor on the basis that the supplier of the necessaries would have been able to enforce payment. For the same reason a cheque representing the loan drawn in payment for necessaries can be debited to the minor's account. (Neither of these rights alters the fact that the loan is unenforceable, recovery is based on a different legal principle, technically known as *subrogation*.)

However, under the Act the court can order the minor to repay any money lent or hand over any property bought with it if it considers it just and equitable to do so. The former is far less likely to be possible than the latter because the funds advanced are likely to have been mixed with other funds, e.g. in an account, and are therefore not identifiable. Should cash have been provided, and paid into an account, only the actual notes and coins advanced can be recovered. Proving that notes and coins are the ones that were advanced is somewhat difficult!

Finally, and of considerable practical importance, the Minors' Contracts Act 1987 provides that a guarantee of a loan to a minor is enforceable even though the loan itself is not. Thus, we can conclude from the discussion above that whether or not to make a loan to a minor is more a question of policy and judgment than law since a bank can adequately protect its position.

The practice of allowing minors cheque guarantee cards is clearly a risk because of the unenforceability of any overdraft created. Although, in theory the bank could seek recovery of property bought with the money under the Minors' Contracts Act 1987, in practice the bank's only remedies are procedural, taking back the card or closing the account. However, the risk is calculated to be small and more than justified in terms of marketing and customer goodwill.

Personal representatives

When somebody dies, the persons appointed to wind up and distribute the estate are called personal representatives. If appointed by a will they are known as *executors*; if appointed by the court they are known as *administrators*, for example, where the deceased dies intestate (without leaving a will).

Before an executor can deal with the deceased's account and securities their appointment and authority must be confirmed by *probate*. This is a process where the will is exhibited and proved in court, the original being deposited in the court registry and a copy, called the *probate copy* made out under the court's seal and delivered to the executor, together with a certificate of its having been proved. *Letters of administration* is the official document from the court empowering the administrator to administer the deceased's estate.

The deceased's account

The account will be stopped on reliable notice of the death. The probate certificate or letters of administration must be presented to the bank and recorded before the balance on any credit account can be withdrawn. The same applies to securities and safe custody items deposited by the deceased. The personal representatives will be informed of the liability on any account and if securities are held for any borrowing, the personal representatives must decide whether to pay off the amount, and thereby obtain the release of the securities, or have them sold to realise and pay off the amount owed.

Any credits received after the death can be credited to the account or held in a suspense account until the personal representatives obtain authority to act, provided that you do not have notice that the payments have ceased to be due on the death. This would be the position, for example, in relation to an annuity payable during life.

The personal representative's account

An *executor's account* can be opened immediately on the death of the testator (the person making the will). An *administrator's account* is not usually opened until letters of administration are produced. In either case, reference should be sought if the individuals are unknown to the bank.

The *mandate* for the account will normally provide that any one representative can sign for and bind all in connection with estate affairs and that all admit *joint and several liability*. The latter gives a right to set-off credit balances in the personal representative's personal accounts against a debit balance in the executor's/administrator's account. Any one representative can countermand a cheque drawn on the personal representative's account.

Borrowing

Personal representatives may wish to borrow for one of three reasons, to:

- facilitate the administration of the estate;
- continue the deceased's personal business; or
- pay inheritance tax.

Joint and several liability ensures that they incur personal liability on the loan, although they are entitled to be *indemnified* out of the estate. The bank is *subrogated* to their position for the moneys it has advanced. If the bank requires *security* for the advances, specific assets can be charged and/or the personal representatives can charge their own personal property.

Executors/trustees

When the estate is wound up, an executor automatically becomes a trustee in relation to any property remaining which the will directs must be held in trust for beneficiaries. An administrator may be placed in the same position by the court. When this position is reached, the account must be operated as a trust account.

Trustees

A trust is an arrangement whereby legal title to property is given by one person to another (trustee), with the latter promising to use the property for the benefit of a third person (the beneficiary).

A trust account is not necessarily opened as such, in fact it is any account which to the bank's actual or constructive knowledge is being operated by trustees, or persons acting in some other fiduciary capacity. Sometimes the account may be opened as 'Trustee of ...' in which case the bank has actual notice that it is a trust account, and sometimes as, say, 'A N Other, Squash Club Account', or as a 'client account' by a firm of solicitors, in which case the bank has constructive notice. Alternatively the trust account may arise by operation of law, for example where personal representatives become trustees if a trust arises out of the deceased's estate (*see* above).

To open a trust account a mandate signed by all the trustees must be obtained. Since trustees cannot normally delegate their authority among themselves, all trustees are required to sign on an account unless the trust instrument or law permits delegation. The Trustee Act 1925, as amended by the Powers of Attorney Act 1971, for example, allows a trustee to delegate his duties by power of attorney for a period of up to one year.

A very strict duty of good faith is imposed on trustees and if they, even innocently, misapply trust property they commit a breach of trust for which they are liable to the beneficiary. What is more, the law also allows an action against a bank or (other person) that intentionally or, more likely, negligently facilitates any such breach. Whether or not a bank is liable when a breach of trust occurs is always a question of fact in the circumstances. Mere suspicion, or an accusation by a beneficiary of trust funds being misapplied would not of itself justify dishonouring a trust cheque but allowing a trustee to draw a cheque on the trust account to reduce a personal overdraft, particularly if the bank had been pressing for repayment, would almost certainly mean that the bank had knowledge of the breach of trust and intentionally or negligently facilitated it.

Trustees have no *implied power* to borrow or charge trust property as security, such powers must be expressly given by the trust deed. If borrowing takes place, the trustees must accept joint and several liability for this enables the bank to set off a credit balance on a trustee's personal account against a debit balance on the trust account.

Clubs and societies

The first point for you to remember here is that unincorporated clubs and societies have no legal existence separate from their members and therefore cannot be sued in their own name. Furthermore, members are not liable for borrowing on the association's behalf by its officers unless they have individually assented to it although appointed officers are probably liable for borrowing authorised by the management committee. You can see, therefore, that such account holders present, at least in theory, rather more problems than you might imagine. A minority of clubs and societies will be registered companies, possibly limited by guarantee rather than by shares, and these clubs and societies must be treated in the same way as other registered companies.

The mandate must be in accordance with the rules and constitution of the association, a copy of which may be lodged with the bank, and confirm that at a meeting of the association it was resolved to open an account and to authorise the persons named to operate the account. The chairman and secretary should certify the mandate.

ACTIVITY 5.8

(a) Produce draft check lists/briefing notes covering the following:

- opening an account;
- agents and bank accounts;
- termination of authority to pay;
- powers of attorney;
- joint accounts, including joint and several liability;
- company accounts.

Pay particular attention to the way you present the information. You could, for example, produce summary or flow charts rather than text. Remember that what you produce must be suitable for use by colleagues who may not have had the benefit of the Banking Certificate course. Therefore it should not only state what must be done/what the legal position is but also explain the law where necessary. If actions have to be recorded, make sure that your check lists/briefing notes include a facility for doing this. (You may well have similar check lists/briefing notes at work and, if so, you could use these for ideas on how best to develop your own.)

(b) Produce diagrams similar to Fig 5.2 to summarise in more detail each of the five main topics shown on Fig 5.2.

■ SUMMARY

1 A bank is a corporate business organisation that accepts money, collects and honours cheques for its customers and keeps current accounts.

2 A customer is a person who has entered into a contract with a bank for a current account to be opened in his or her name.

3 The banker-customer relationship is essentially the contractual relationship of debtor-creditor.

4 Other rules clarify the relationship; those of agency, bailment, banking practice and, in some cases, particular requirements of good faith.

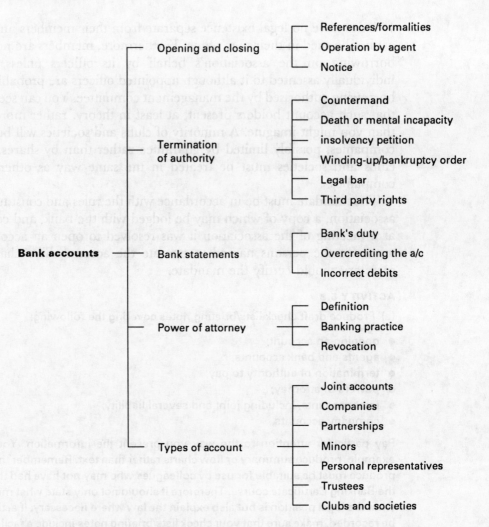

Fig 5.2 Customers and their accounts

5 Although the banker-customer contract is usually made very informally and with few express terms, implied into it are a number of well established terms dictating a bank's rights and duties.

6 Among other duties owed to customers, a bank must:
- abide by its customers' mandates;
- honour its customers' cheques; and
- maintain confidentiality about its customers' affairs.

7 Customers owe two legal duties to their banks:
- to draw cheques with reasonable care in order not to facilitate fraud (*London Joint Stock Bank v Macmillan & Arthur* (1918); and
- to inform their banks of known forgeries on their account (*Greenwood v Martins Bank Ltd* (1933)).

8 When an account is opened, certain formalities must be observed, in particu-

lar, references should be taken and checked. An agent's proposed operation of the account requires particular care.

9 A bank's authority to pay its customer's cheques is terminated in one of six ways, most commonly by the customer countermanding payment.

10 A bank is usually able to recover an incorrect credit to an account but is always obliged to refund an incorrect debit.

11 All joint account holders must accept joint and several liability. Among other things this gives a bank a right to combine accounts and, should one account holder die, preserves the liability of the estate.

12 A company is a corporation and exists at law independently from its members. It has unlimited contractual capacity.

13 Partners incur joint and several liability for debts incurred during the ordinary course of the firm's business. Joint and several liability is specifically accepted in the account mandate.

14 Members of a trading partnership have implied authority to borrow but it is usual for all partners to expressly authorise borrowing.

15 Minors have limited contractual capacity. In particular, a loan cannot be enforced against a minor even if it was made to finance the purchase of necessaries, although the minor can ratify it after attaining majority. The Minors' Contracts Act 1987 provides that a guarantee of a loan to a minor is enforceable.

16 A personal representative appointed by will is known as an executor; one appointed by the court, as an administrator.

17 Personal representatives must accept joint and several liability for any borrowing in connection with the administration of the estate.

18 A bank is liable to the beneficiaries of a trust if it knowingly or negligently facilitates a breach of the trust.

19 Trustees have no implied power to borrow or charge trust property as security.

20 Members of an unincorporated club or society are not liable for borrowing on the association's account unless they have individually assented to it.

■ **SELF-ASSESSMENT QUESTIONS**

1 Define the terms *banker* and *customer* and explain why the definitions are important.

2 State the *Rule in Clayton's Case*.

3 How could a bank commit conversion with respect to property held in safe custody?

4 List the rights and duties of a bank.

5 State the two duties of a customer.

6 At law, precisely why is it important to take the check references before opening an account?

7 Explain how agency can arise by estoppel.

8 List the circumstances in which a bank's authority to make payments from its customer's account is terminated.

9 In what circumstances is a bank unlikely to be able to recover moneys wrongly credited to an account?

10 What is a power of attorney?

11 Distinguish between joint and joint and several liability. What are the advantages of joint and several liability?

12 What must a bank check before opening an account for a registered company?

13 What is the position if a bank enters into a contract with a company which is outside the actual or apparent authority of the company's directors?

14 What is the extent of the implied authority of a member of a trading partnership?

15 In the context of a partnership account, what are the specific advantages of the partners accepting joint and several liability?

16 What are the main provisions of the Minors' Contracts Act 1987?

17 What is the term for a personal representative appointed by will?

18 State the circumstances in which a personal representative may wish to borrow on the account.

19 Give an example where a bank would have indirect notice that an account must be operated as a trust account.

20 What legal problem arises when an unincorporated club or association wishes to borrow?

■ MULTIPLE-CHOICE QUESTIONS

1 Which of the following relationships is the essence of most banker/customer contracts?
A agent-principal
B bailee-bailor
C debtor-creditor
D creditor-debtor

2 *London Joint Stock Bank v Macmillan & Arthur* (1918)/*Baines v National Provincial Bank Ltd* (1927)/*Greenwood v Martins Bank Ltd* (1933) (match the case with the appropriate statement) established that:
A a customer owes a duty to his bank to complete a bill of exchange drawn on the bank with reasonable care

B a customer owes a duty to his bank to draw cheques with reasonable care

C a bank is allowed a reasonable period of time to complete its business after its advertised closing time

D a customer can in certain circumstances be prevented from denying the genuineness of a forged signature on a cheque

3 *Ladbroke v Todd* (1914) established that:

A a person becomes a customer of a bank when the bank accepts money from that person and agrees to open an account in that person's name

B a course of dealings is necessary to establish a person as a customer of a bank

C a bank can owe legal duties to a person before that person becomes a customer

D a customer can only countermand a cheque in writing

4 The actual decision in *Hedley Byrne & Co v. Heller and Partners Ltd* (1963) established that:

A a special relationship exists between a bank and its customers

B a bank can owe a duty of care to a person to whom it supplies a reference on one of its customers

C when providing a reference, a bank can avoid possible liability for negligence by including a suitable disclaimer in the reference

D the Unfair Contract Terms Act 1977 may prevent a bank relying on any disclaimer it has included in a reference

5 The Business Names Act 1985 applies to:

A all business organisations

B all non-corporate business organisations

C companies only

D sole traders only

6 When opening an account for a private company, which of the following would you definitely *not* need to see?

A the certificate of incorporation

B a trading certificate issued under s.117 of the Companies Act 1985

C the company's memorandum and articles of association

D a copy of the resolution appointing the first directors

7 If a bank wrongfully dishonours a cheque and returns it marked 'Refer to drawer', it could be sued for:

A libel

B slander

C libel and slander

D libel or slander

8 A joint account mandate will impose joint and several liability on the account holders in order to:

A avoid the *Rule in Clayton's Case* (1816) operating to the bank's detriment

B conform to the rules of The Committee of London and Scottish Clearing Bankers

C avoid the mandate being cancelled by the death of one of the parties

D avoid the death of one of the parties releasing his or her estate from liability for any overdrawn balance on the account

9 A partner in a non-trading partnership does *not* have implied authority to:

A buy and sell goods in the course of the firm's business

B give receipts for payment of debts due to the firm

C draw cheques on the partnership account

D borrow money on behalf of the partnership

10 When a banker gives an inaccurate opinion or reference about a customer:

A he may be liable to his customer for breach of contract

B he may be liable to the person requesting the opinion or reference for breach of contract

C he may be liable in tort

D he can invariably exclude all his possible liability by including a suitable disclaimer

11 A personal representative appointed by will is known as:

A an executor

B an attorney

C a notary

D an administrator

6 Property

OBJECTIVES

After studying this chapter you should be able to:
1 Distinguish between real and personal property and between ownership and possession;
2 Define land and the terms freehold and leasehold;
3 Explain and distinguish between estates and interests in land;
4 Explain the various types of ownership of land.
5 Distinguish between registered and unregistered land;
6 Outline the system of land registration;
7 Outline how title to different types of property is proved and transferred;
8 Relate the above to banking operations.

■ INTRODUCTION

Many banking operations directly involve property; cheques, land, guarantees, stocks and shares and life policies are all types of property. Specifically, you will be most concerned with taking property as security.

In this chapter we cover the types of property involved in usual banking operations but we pay particular attention to land because this is more complicated and probably the most common form of security taken. Before we look at specific types of property, however, we must discuss the basic classification of property and the concepts of ownership and possession.

Real and personal property

Our legal system classifies property into 'real' and 'personal', the former comprising *only* freehold interests in land and the latter everything else, including leasehold interests in land. (We explain these terms below.) In fact, freehold and leasehold interests in land are treated in much the same way and it is usual to refer to leaseholds as 'chattels real' when classifying property to distinguish them from 'chattels personal', that is other forms of personal property. Look carefully at the categories shown in Fig 6.1. We will explain some of the terms used.

The word 'chattel' is a linguistic corruption of 'cattle', the ownership of which is still regarded as a measure of wealth in a few societies. A 'chose in action' is property which does not physically exist and which consequently cannot be effectively protected by physical means, only by court action. Consequently, it is often referred to as intangible property. Examples include rights in negotiable instruments (such as cheques), patents, copyrights and the

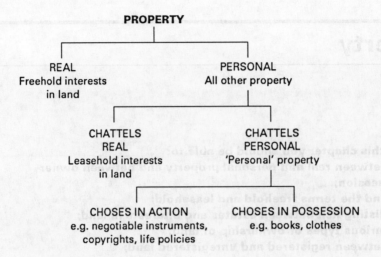

Fig 6.1 Types of property

goodwill of a business. You will see later on that apart from land, banks nearly always take charges over choses in action as security for loans, life policies and shares being obvious examples. 'Chose', by the way, is an old French legal term for 'thing'. 'Choses in possession' are property with a physical existence, such property can therefore be physically possessed and protected, this book or your clothes for example.

The historical background

These somewhat strange-sounding categories are a legacy of the very rigid procedural rules which the common law courts (the Royal Courts) developed early in our legal history. If a man's freehold land (a woman could not own land at that time) was wrongfully taken from him, and this happened quite frequently in a society where might was largely right, he could recover the actual land by bringing a *real* action (technically an action *in rem*, Latin for 'against the thing') in the common law courts. If, however, he was dispossessed of anything else he could not recover the actual property and was only entitled to bring a *personal action* (technically an action *in personam*, Latin for 'against the person) for money compensation against the person who had taken it. So where do leaseholds fit in? The answer is simple, the concept of the leasehold interest, essentially a commercial creation, developed rather later than the freehold, by which time legal procedure had become so rigid that the real action available to the freeholder could not be adapted to a leaseholder's claim. In time, however, a remedy developed which enabled a leaseholder to recover his land if he had been wrongfully dispossessed.

Already you can see that a knowledge of legal history can be helpful in fully understanding our system of property classification. Indeed, the concept of ownership as applied to land is still based on ideas dating back to William the Conqueror and the Normans' own particular form of feudalism. Fortunately, the present system can be described and explained in general terms without more than a few passing references to the past. Nevertheless, it is a quite remarkable fact that it was not until the Law of Property Act 1925 that our system of land law made any real concessions to the increasingly complex urban society that it served. Even today, land law may be criticised for being old-fashioned and unnecessarily complex in both principle and practice.

Banks and personal property

Before we begin to look at ownership and transfer of title to property, we must identify the types of personal property with which we shall be dealing and define the term 'land'; as you will see it has an extensive meaning. Much of the law concerning personal property, its title and transfer, is to do with the sale of goods and is regulated by the Sale of Goods Act 1979. This, however, is of limited relevance to banks since banks will avoid taking goods, valuables for example, as security unless they must. Therefore, we are going to restrict our discussion to those forms of personal property which are usually taken as security for an advance: stocks and shares, life policies, guarantees and debentures.

It should not have escaped you that all these types of property are choses in action as far as the rights they confer are concerned – you cannot physically enforce your rights under any of them – but the certificates or other documents evidencing or conferring those rights are choses in possession and someone who wrongfully takes or deals with them is committing the tort of conversion against their true owners (quite apart from committing the crime of theft). Remember, we discussed this in Chapter 5 in the context of a bank wrongfully delivering property held in safe custody.

Ownership and possession

Ownership

Ownership is difficult to define but it can be said to be the right of a person to *enjoy property as fully as the law permits*. For example, the owner may sell his or her property, give it away or leave it to a friend by will. The holder in due course of a cheque (*see* page 240) – its owner – can enforce the promise of payment embodied in the cheque against any person who signed it and thus became a party to it before it was negotiated to the holder in due course, the right to enforce the cheque is absolute.

If you own a car, however, although you may drive it on a public highway, the law requires it to be taxed and insured and you to have a valid driving licence. This is a simple example of a limitation on an owner's ability to do with their property exactly what they wish. Often the owner has the right to destroy the property although the law does impose limits on this right in various ways! Try destroying your middle-of-a-terrace house for example. The state has also imposed various restrictions on the rights of ownership, of land in particular, by statute. Letting property, for example, is regulated by the Rent Acts and the Town and Country Planning Acts regulate the use of land.

Possession

While possession is often evidence of ownership, it means *exclusive use and control*

153

of an item of property, not rights over or title to it. This requires a possessor to have:

- continuing physical control over the item, temporarily leaving property does not fail this requirement but losing it does; and
- an intention to exclude others from controlling it.

A possessor is not necessarily the owner. Safe custody, for example, gives the bank possession of the article bailed, the bank fulfils the requirements above, but ownership remains with the customer. Thieves may well be the possessors of property they have stolen but they are clearly not its owners! The thief of a bearer cheque is an unusual case. The thief is clearly not its owner but, by the Bills of Exchange Act 1882, possession makes the thief the *holder* of the cheque. As such a person taking a transfer of the cheque from the thief can gain a perfect title to it (*see* page 238).

Ownership and possession compared

In comparison with possession, ownership is an abstract legal concept. If you lend this book to a friend, for example, you lose possession but you still own it. Possession is legally simpler, usually being denoted by physical possession. But ownership is the superior concept. If X owns the freehold of Whiteacre, X may lease it to Y for, say, 50 years, thereby giving up possession to Y who then enjoys some of the rights of ownership. However, the ultimate right of ownership and eventual possession remains with X or X's successors in title. Similarly, if X were to mortgage Whiteacre to a bank to secure a loan, the bank would acquire a right in Whiteacre but ownership would remain with X unless X defaulted on the repayments and the bank exercised its power of sale.

ACTIVITY 6.1

(a) To what extent do you think it is possible to enjoy absolute ownership of the following property?
- A freehold house.
- A car.
- A cheque.

(b) Give an example of a bank possessing property but not being the owner of it.

◼ LAND

Definition

At law the term 'land' covers not only the visible surface of the earth but also, in theory, everything above and below the surface and rights over land. When the term is used in Acts of Parliament it is defined by the Interpretation Act 1978 as including '... buildings and other structures, land covered with water, and any estate, interest, servitude or right over land.' (We explain these terms later.) Hence, we can say that land includes minerals, buildings, fixtures in buildings, reasonable rights in the airspace above the surface and rights over another's land such as a right of way.

As a banker you should not think of land in purely legal terms. Economists, for example, view land as a *resource*, a space in which to undertake economic activity and are therefore interested in its utility. Lawyers, on the other hand, are primarily concerned with its *ownership*, the *transfer* of that ownership, restrictions *upon its use* and the *legal obligations* arising from its occupancy. Banks are primarily interested in the *value and suitability of land as security*. However, if you reflect on this for a moment you will see that as a banker you are really interested in both the other perspectives. On the one hand you are concerned to ensure that your interest is legally recognised and protected, and enforceable, on the other you are interested in the commercial value and the ease with which the security can be realised. This concern is really based on the economist's perspective.

Earlier on we used the term 'fixture'; this requires explanation. Fixtures are items which *at law* have become part of the land or building to which they are attached. In deciding whether an object is a fixture, the law looks at the degree to which it is attached to the building (the greater the degree of annexation, the more likely it is to be a fixture) and, more importantly, the purpose of the annexation. If the intention was to permanently improve the building, and not merely to enjoy the object itself, it is a fixture. For example, fitted cupboards in a house and permanent installations in a factory are fixtures, while pictures hung on walls and moveable machinery are not.

Since what is in a building can be very valuable, whether or not an item is a fixture or a fitting could effect the value of a bank's security. This is particularly true of industrial and commercial property, fixed plant and machinery for example.

Some more history

Since the Norman Conquest in 1066 all land in England has been theoretically owned by the Crown alone and the same has been true of the rest of Great Britain for many centuries. The most that anyone else can own is one of two legal *estates* which now exist: a freehold estate or a leasehold estate, an estate being a measure of a person's interest in a particular piece of land in terms of time. In feudal days an estate was held on a certain *tenure*, originally the provision of goods or services of some kind, and later the payment of a sum of money. We still have tenancies and rents of course, but these are very different from the original feudal ideas of tenure which have now almost entirely disappeared.

As new demands from a changing society were made upon it, the system of land law was altered and added to but not reformulated. By the early twentieth century it had become completely archaic and as a result was extremely complicated. Change came in 1925, the Property Legislation of that year completely reforming the system of land law and conveyancing (the transfer of estates and interests in land). Specifically it:

- reduced all remaining feudal tenures to one common form – 'common socage' – which may now be regarded as identical to the term 'freehold';

- removed outdated concepts, in particular feudal rights;
- introduced a system of registration and transfer of title to land based on that used for shares;
- reduced the number of *legal estates* to two and the number of *legal interests* to five with the aim, in conjunction with the previous reform, of simplifying conveyancing.

We cover those aspects of these reforms relevant to you later in the chapter.

Legal estates

A legal estate is a right to the land itself, i.e. the right to possession or the right to receive rents arising from the possession of the property by another person. Originally an estate was held on a certain *tenure*. You may remember from your history lessons that various services had to be performed in return for a grant of land under the feudal system. You may also remember that these feudal services gradually became replaced by the payment of money and that with inflation these payments became worth so little that they were not worth enforcing.

A fundamental point before we go any further: a legal estate is a concept and is quite separate from the physical land to which it relates, the Crown owns the land itself. Thus, an estate can be bought and sold, transferred by gift or by will, without affecting the land itself or the possession of it. This is basic to your concern with land as a banker; the abstract nature of estates and interests makes it very simple to use land as security. A legal mortgage over land, for example, while conferring rights sufficient to ensure its adequacy as security, does not affect the *use* of the land or the rights of occupation until and unless the terms of the mortgage are breached, normally by non-payment. Another, and more basic example, is that it is possible to buy the freehold of a large block of flats without in any way affecting the rights of occupation of the many tenants in the flats.

The Law of Property Act 1925 reduced the number of possible legal estates to two: freehold and leasehold.

Freehold land

All land in this country is held on freehold tenure – free as opposed to unfree in feudal days. For all practical purposes this amounts to absolute ownership. Freeholders may, for example, dispose of their estates to anyone they please. Nevertheless there are important restrictions upon their power to do as they like with their land. The common law prevents them from using their land in a way which would cause an actionable nuisance to their neighbours, and their right to develop land is restricted by the Town and Country Planning Acts. They are also subject to compulsory purchase powers.

Before 1925 there were a variety of freehold estates which the common law recognised but since the 1925 property legislation only the *fee simple absolute in possession* is recognised as a *legal* estate. (You will see the significance of the term 'legal' as you progress through this chapter.) This is not to say, however, that the former estates have disappeared as such, but they can now exist only as *equitable interests* in land in conjunction with a trust.

The words used in the term *fee simple absolute in possession* have the following meanings.

- *Fee*: an estate of inheritance, that is, one that may be inherited or which may pass by will.
- *Simple*: the inheritance is not limited to a particular class of the freeholder's heirs, such as males only, or the children of a particular marriage. (An estate where the inheritance was so limited was known as a *fee tail* (*tailé*: cut down); this can now exist only as an equitable entailed interest).
- *Absolute*: not subject to any conditions, as a *life estate* (now only possible as a *life interest*) would be.
- In *possession*: takes effect immediately, and not, say, from 1 January 2000. The words include not only the right to immediate physical possession but also the immediate right to receive rent and profits where the land is leased and therefore subject to another's right of occupation (*see* below).

Leasehold land

As you have seen, all land in this country is held on freehold tenure but the estate owner may create from the freehold an estate of *limited duration*: a leasehold. This can be illustrated diagrammatically; look at Fig 6.2. The *freehold* of Whiteacre is owned by A. A leases it to B for 99 years (the head lease) for £5000 a year. B in turn leases most of it to C for 90 years at, say, £4500 a year and so on down the chain until a small part is let to F. Alternatively, the *whole* of Whiteacre could be sublet a number to times, often at a profit, leaving F as the last sub-lessee and the present occupier. Yet again, B could transfer (assign) the lease to C who transfers it to D etc. Here there only ever exists the one lease. In all three cases, the right to occupy the land normally reverts back to A (the freeholder) when the (head) lease expires, i.e. at the end of 99 years. The points to note from this are, first, that leaseholders are usually able to sublet their land and, second, provided each successive sub-lease is for a shorter period, a number of legal estates can exist at any one time over the same piece of land.

Confusing? Or is it? Your own bank may lease its premises and may possibly sublet accommodation in excess of its needs. The lease was invented centuries ago for commercial reasons (land was then virtually the sole source of wealth and money could be raised by selling its use for a given period) and it still very much fulfils commercial functions. Land as an economic resource is frequently acquired by buying a lease and high rents in return are a profitable source of income.

Technically a leasehold estate is a *term of years absolute*, and it is the only other legal estate in land which can exist under the provisions of the Law of Property Act 1925. The words 'term of years' include not only leases for a specific number of years but also those of less than a year or from year to year, although short leases are commonly referred to as tenancies. 'Absolute' means that the estate is not subject to any conditions.

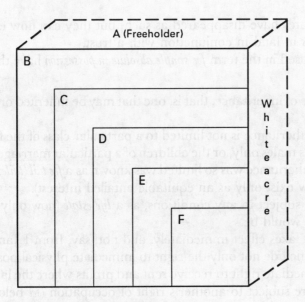

Fig 6.2 Creation of leases

To create a *legal estate* the Law of Property Act 1925 requires a lease for more than three years to be created by deed, a formal written document which declares itself to be a deed and which must be signed, witnessed and delivered. However, a legal estate for a term not exceeding three years may be created orally or in writing provided it takes effect in possession (immediately) and at the best rent that can reasonably be obtained. To transfer a lease (an assignment) requires a deed to be executed, no matter how short the term assigned.

The essential features of a leasehold estate are that:

- it gives the right to *exclusive possession*;
- it is for a *definite term*, i.e. the start of the term and its duration are fixed or can be determined;
- it creates the relationship of landlord and tenant.

The fact that a leasehold is for a limited term is the essential distinction from a freehold estate, for the latter is of unlimited duration.

At common law the land leased reverts back absolutely to the freeholder at the end of the lease. This position can no longer be regarded as acceptable either socially or commercially and a number of statutes now significantly vary this common law position. The Leasehold Reform Act 1967 gives leaseholders of houses, originally let for twenty-one years or more at a low rent and held for at least five years, the right to enforce a sale to them of the freehold on payment of the value of the freehold interest in the site. Alternatively they may ask for a fifty-year extension of the lease. These rights are known as leasehold *enfranchisement*.

The Landlord and Tenant Act 1954 protects tenants of flats under long tenancies (twenty-one years or more) at low rents and many other tenancies of both furnished and unfurnished property are protected by the Rent Acts.

However, under these Acts the *statutory tenancy* that the tenant is given only protects the tenant's personal right of occupation, a much lesser right than that acquired under the Leasehold Reform Act 1967. Statutory tenants cannot, for example, pass their tenancies on to others, either during their lifetimes or by will.

The Housing Act 1985 covers dwelling houses let to an individual or individuals jointly by local authorities for occupation as dwellings. Under the Act *secure tenants* have their position protected and acquire various rights, for example, the right to take in lodgers without the landlord's consent and the right to sublet part of the dwelling house with the landlord's permission. Above all, perhaps, a secure (council) tenant of at least two years' standing has the right to acquire the freehold (of the house) or a long lease (of the flat).

A tenant of business premises is given protection by Part II of the Landlord and Tenant Act 1954. The Act applies to all property occupied by a tenant for the purpose of any trade, profession or employment. The basic aim of the legislation is to allow tenants to conduct their businesses in premises indefinitely, subject to the landlord's legitimate rights when the tenancies expire or a tenant abuses the terms of the tenancy. If a tenant does not wish to give up possession and applies to the court in the proper way, the court is *bound* to grant a new tenancy unless the landlord objects on one of seven grounds specified in the Act, for example, failure to repair the premises or persistent delay in paying rent. A new tenancy granted by the court will be for a maximum of fourteen years but no limit is placed on the number of applications that a tenant can make under the Act.

ACTIVITY 6.2

If the property you live in is leasehold, try to find a copy of the lease and read through its terms carefully. What restrictions does it contain as to use of the property? What rights does the landlord have?

Interests in land

An interest in land is a right to a claim against the land of another less than a claim to possession. As you read above, an estate is a right to the land itself, that is, it gives possession or the right to receive rents. Interests in land can be either legal or equitable.

Legal interests

These are rights against the land itself – often referred to as rights *in rem* – and are therefore enforceable against all other persons. Thus, whoever acquires the land is bound by any legal interest which exists over it, whether or not they had knowledge of it before the acquisition. Banks must therefore be aware of possible legal interests when a mortgage of land is taken as security because the bank's right to realise the security will be affected by any existing legal interests.

Since 1925, a legal interest must be held in fee simple absolute in possession, or for a term of years absolute. Under the Law of Property Act 1925 (as amended) there are five types of legal interests.

1 *Easements, rights or privileges.* This may be bare rights over the land of another (an easement), for example rights of way; or rights to take something of value from the land of another (a profit *à prendre*), such as fishing or shooting rights. Sometimes easements can be quite amusing. For example, in places where houses were built with backyards rather than gardens a right to hang washing over another's land is not uncommon and even, would you believe, a right to use another's outside toilet – a legally enforceable convenience, you may say!

These examples may seem amusing but remember they were, and in some cases still are, very important to the everyday lives of the people involved. Remember, too, that these rights are legally enforceable so even the largest organisation would not build across a right of way without purchasing it from the owner first. Such interests can also be very valuable. For example, fishing and shooting rights can be worth fortunes.

2 *Rentcharges.* A rentcharge charges a piece of land, quite independently of any lease or mortgage, with the payment of a periodic sum of money to the owner of the rentcharge. Rentcharges are found only in one or two areas of the country, notably Greater Manchester, and they were created as a way of retaining a perpetual source of income from the land after it was sold for housing development. Under the Rentcharges Act 1977, however, no new rentcharges may be created and existing ones will eventually be extinguished.

3 *Charges by way of legal mortgages.* As a banker these are the legal interests with which you are most concerned. (Creating a mortgage by a legal charge was introduced by the Law of Property Act 1925.)

4 *Charges on land imposed by law.* Such charges are of little practical importance and you are most unlikely to encounter one as a banker.

5 *Rights of entry.* These must be in respect of a legal term of years absolute or attached to a legal rentcharge. A landlord usually has the right to re-enter if the tenant fails to pay rent or comply with obligations (covenants) in the lease.

Equitable interests

An equitable interest in land originally only gave a right against the person who granted it (a right in *personam*), but was finally established as being enforceable against anyone except a purchaser who bought the legal estate in good faith and for value (gave 'consideration' for it) without notice of the interest. This is important and you should make sure that you have understood this point. As you will see, the requirement of 'notice' or, more correctly, the substitution of *a system of registration in lieu of notice*, is particularly important.

The Property Legislation of 1925 provided that all estates, interests and charges in or over land, both legal and equitable, other than the fee simple absolute in possession, the term of years absolute and the five legal interests listed above would subsequently take effect as *equitable interests*. For example, a life estate became a life interest, a fee tail became an entailed interest and a future fee simple (that is, one not in possession) became a future interest. With the four important exceptions listed below, all these, as you have read, must now be created behind a *trust*. The exceptions are:

1 *Restrictive covenants.* These are agreements whereby one person promises to restrict the use of their land for the benefit of another's adjoining land, for example, an agreement preventing the land from being used for the purposes of trade (quite often the sale of alcohol).

2 *The equity of redemption.* The right of a mortgagor to redeem the mortgaged property upon payment of the outstanding principal and interest. (This is clearly important to you and we cover it more fully below.)

3 *Equitable charges.* These are interests in land given as security for the payment of a sum of money. The person in whose favour a charge was made is entitled to take legal action for the sale of the land if payment is not made. (Again this is relevant to practical banking and we cover it later on.)

4 *Estate contracts.* A little more technical and of less relevance to banking, these arise where the freeholder or leaseholder contracts to convey the estate to the other party involved, or to create a term of years (lease) in the other's favour. Until the actual deed has been executed no legal estate is transferred but the contract to execute the deed gives rise to an equitable interest which the courts will enforce, i.e. equity will very probably order specific performance of the contract, that is execution of the deed. An exchange of contracts for the purchase of a house is an example of an estate contract.

Types of ownership

This section would appear better placed if we included it below under 'Title to property and its transfer'. We have chosen not to do so because you need to be familiar with some of the concepts and terms covered in this section in order to be able to understand easily other parts of this chapter.

Legal and equitable ownership

There is both legal and equitable ownership of a legal estate in land. Legal ownership gives legal title to the estate and the equitable (or beneficial) interest in it gives the right to benefit from the estate. Usually the two forms of ownership are exactly combined and here the distinction is irrelevant. Where they are not a trust arises, specifically a 'trust for sale', the legal title being owned by the trustee(s) and the equitable interest by the beneficiary(ies).

An equitable interest distinct from legal title would arise where someone other than the legal owner paid part or all of the purchase price for the land, or where under a family arrangement the land must be used for the benefit of various family members, often children (who are unable to hold legal title themselves). The former situation is an example of an implied trust for sale (as arose in *Boland*), the latter an example of an express trust for sale (as arose in *Flegg*). (We discuss these cases on pages 166–7.)

Only a maximum of four joint owners can share legal title to land and where there are more joint owners, a maximum of four must hold on trust for all. An example of this is where (up to four) partners hold legal title to partnership property for the benefit of all the partners, including themselves.

The legal owner can transfer title free from the beneficial interest (unless it is also an overriding interest – *see* below), the beneficial owners being entitled to the appropriate share of the proceeds of the sale. Such a transfer may, of course, be a breach of the trust and therefore give the beneficiaries a right of action against the trustee.

Shared ownership

Shared ownership can take the form of a joint tenancy or a tenancy in common. If property is owned by X and Y under a *joint tenancy*, on Y's death X automatically becomes the sole legal owner of the property. This is known as the 'right of survivorship'. (We have already mentioned this in the context of joint accounts and the 'survivorship clause'.) If, however, the property is owned under a *tenancy in common*, Y's share would pass according to the terms of Y's will or, if Y had not made one, according to the rules of intestacy.

Although legal and equitable ownership and shared ownership are normally associated and encountered in relation to land, both concepts can apply to any type of property.

Registration and protection of interests in unregistered land

From a banking operations perspective this is more important to you than a knowledge of the interests themselves. This is because it dictates the procedure used when taking a charge on land as security and the value of that security when charged.

Before and after 1925

With the considerable number of *legal* estates and interests existing *before* 1925, the purchasers of land took the risk of there being an estate or an interest in existence of which they were completely ignorant at the time of purchase and which would affect their possession after the purchase. On the other hand, the position of the holder of an equitable estate or interest was even worse. Their position was secure *only* if the purchaser had notice of their estate or interest; their equity (as it was and is known) would be lost if the legal estate was purchased in good faith and for value without notice of the equity. (Look back at our definition of an equitable interest.)

After 1925 the position of a purchaser of land was greatly improved, the number of legal estates and interests had been reduced. But this in turn meant that many more equitable interests would now exist and the *doctrine of notice* was no longer adequate protection for them. The Land Charges Act 1925 (now consolidated with later amendments in the Land Charges Act 1972) introduced a state system of registering interests over *unregistered land* and this is the key to their protection. A registrable right is void against a purchaser ('purchaser' includes a mortgagee) of the legal estate *unless it is registered*, even if the purchaser had notice of the interest.

A short but important digression at this point. Our discussion so far has concerned only *unregistered land*; in fact most urban land in the country is now registered and in due course all will be. Where title to land is *registered*, such interests (called *minor interests* under the registration scheme) must be protected by an entry on the *Charges Register* and not under the Land Charges Act. The effect is the same, however, and the old rules on notice similarly do not supply.

Land charges registers

Under the Land Charges Act 1925 there are five registers of registrable interests, the *register of land charges* being the most important. This, in turn, is divided into six classes: A to F. Of these, class C is most important to you because under this class are included puisne mortgages and equitable charges. (A legal or equitable mortgage (of unregistered land) supported by a deposit of the title deeds with the mortgagee and the rights of beneficiaries under a trust for sale are not registrable.)

In addition to the national registration system, there are registers of local land charges kept at the registering local authority. These record charges acquired by the local authority under statutory authority, such as charges for making up roads or laying drains, and intended compulsory purchase orders.

Puisne mortgages

The system of registering interests in land applies mainly to equitable interests for these are the more vulnerable. However, some important legal interests are also registrable, in particular a *puisne mortgage* – pronounced 'puny'. A puisne mortgage is a legal mortgage of unregistered land which is not supported by a deposit of the title deeds with the mortgagee. It is a common security taken by banks to secure overdrafts. Normally you would take a deposit of the title deeds as security but with a second, or any subsequent, mortgage the deeds will already be in the possession of the first mortgagee (for example, a building society or another bank) and therefore unavailable. (Note that a second mortgage and a puisne mortgage are not the same thing, a second mortgage is just by far the most common example of a puisne mortgage. There are other circumstances in which the title deeds are not available for deposit.)

Overreaching

On the sale or mortgage of unregistered land equitable interests incapable of registration in the Land Charges Registry can be *overreached* under the Law of Property Act 1925. This means that a purchaser or mortgagee (such as a bank) of the legal estate takes free from the interests *whether or not the purchaser or mortgagee is aware of them.* The interests overreached now attach to the proceeds of the sale and can be enforced against the trustees; they can no longer be enforced against the land itself. In other words, the interests still exist but are represented by different rights, while title to the land can be freely and safely transferred because it is uncluttered by interests which could frustrate this.

Trusts for sale are not land charges and therefore the equitable interests arising under them cannot be registered. Thus, if land subject to a trust for sale is sold or mortgaged by at least *two trustees* (overreaching requires there to be at least two trustees or a trust corporation to be involved) the interests of the beneficiaries (the equitable owners) are overreached, even if the beneficiaries are in occupation, and even if the purchaser or mortgagee knew of the interest. In short, it is quite safe for a bank to take a mortgage from two joint owners (the trustees) of unregistered land.

A sale or mortgage by a *single trustee* does not overreach the equitable interest but in this case a purchaser or mortgagee without *actual or constructive notice* of the interest still takes free from it at common law. This principle would affect a bank where, say, A and B are married and A has an equitable interest in property of which B is the legal owner and B, without A's knowledge, gives a mortgage over it to the bank to secure personal borrowing. A's equitable interest is not overreached and the position depends on whether or not the bank has *actual or constructive knowledge* of the interest. If the bank has, its mortgage is subject to the interest; if it has not, it takes free of the interest. However, if A and B were joint legal owners and a parent who lived with them had an equitable interest in the property by virtue of having contributed to the purchase price, a mortgage by both A and B would overreach the interest of the parent because the mortgage would be taken from two trustees. As you saw above, this would be so even if the mortgagee knew of the interest. (The parent's interest would still exist, of course, but would be an interest in the proceeds of the sale of the property and not in the property itself.)

Actual notice is straightforward but constructive notice (where notice should have been gained from the circumstances) is more complicated. For example, if the legal owner is not in actual occupation, a purchaser or mortgagee is deemed to have constructive notice of the interests of persons who do occupy the land if enquiries are not made of them.

ACTIVITY 6.3

Midtown Bank took a legal mortgage over Mr Smith's property 'Wilmton Villa'. The property, title to which is unregistered, includes a large paddock at the bottom of which is a track along which Miss Jones, the owner of the neighbouring property, has a right to walk to a field owned by her on the other side of the paddock. The Bank did not inspect the property when the charge was taken but the searches (investigation of the registers at the Land Charges Registry) did not reveal anything adverse to the security. Mr Smith has defaulted on the mortgage and the Bank wishes to sell the property. Are its rights as mortgagee subject to Miss Jones's right to walk across the property? Give reasons for your answer.

Registration of title to land

You have probably heard of and might even have seen bundles of deeds which somehow or other prove a person's title to a piece of land. Great mystique attaches to them and they are often attractive and interesting documents. In reality, however, they are an incredibly inefficient way of proving title to anything in an age of electronic databanks. In particular, each time title is transferred there has to be a fresh investigation of the deeds to establish that the transferor's title is good.

Deeds are used to prove title to *unregistered land* and what we have said so far in this chapter relates to unregistered land. However, we did make the point that title to all land in this country will eventually be registered at one of a number of district land registries.

The registration system

This is governed by the Land Registration Act 1925, as amended. Basically, the system replaces title deeds as proof of title to unregistered land and the separate investigation of title necessary on every conveyance of unregistered land with a title investigated and guaranteed by the state and proved by a state maintained register. Many charges and encumbrances affecting the land are also shown on the register. However, whether title to land is registered or not, charges acquired by statute by any local authority must still be registered in the Local Land Charges Registers and charges on land given by companies must be registered on the Companies Register to be valid.

It is worth repeating before we move on that if title to land is registered, the system of registering land charges in the Land Charges Register *does not apply*.

Registered interests

Only the two estates – freehold and leasehold – can be registered, but restrictions exist on the registration of the latter (*see* below).

Overriding interests

Overriding interests bind the purchaser or a mortgagee of registered land even though the purchaser has no notice of them and they are not mentioned on the register. So what are overriding interests, which appear to run contrary to the whole idea of registering interests?

Overriding interests are those interests which could be discovered from enquiries of the occupier or by an inspection of the land itself and not, if title to the land was unregistered, from the title deeds and documents relating to the land. Examples include:

- legal easements and profits à prendre;
- rights of a person in actual occupation;
- leases for terms of 21 years or less.

If you think for a moment you will appreciate that all three examples would be discovered by enquiry and/or inspection. Not included are spouses' statutory rights of occupation under the Matrimonial Homes Act 1983, these must be protected by an entry on the register.

Quite simply, the effect of overriding interests means that it is imperative for any would-be purchaser or mortgagee, a bank for example, to make enquiries or undertake an actual investigation of the land and its occupancy, through a solicitor or surveyor perhaps, to ensure that no overriding interest exists. Note that the overriding interest *must exist at the time of the purchase or mortgage* to affect the purchaser's or mortgagee's rights. Thus, a bank taking a mortgage is not affected by any rights that may arise subsequently.

Persons in actual occupation We can illustrate the need for care by considering the rights of a person in actual occupation, i.e. occupation which has a degree of permanency, a situation which is commonly encountered when taking land as security. This can be summarised as follows. A person who contributes to the purchase price acquires an equitable interest in that property and if that person is also in actual occupation of the property, that person has an overriding interest in it. This cannot be overreached (*see* above) on a subsequent sale or mortgage by a *sole registered owner* (sole trustee) and a possession order will not be granted against the occupier: *Williams & Glyn's Bank v Boland* (1980). If, in the same circumstance, title to registered land is registered in joint names, i.e. *two trustees*, then a purchase or a mortgage from the trustees overreaches even the overriding interest of the beneficiary: *City of London Building Society v Flegg* (1987).

Flegg and Boland Let us look at these two cases in detail. In *Williams & Glyn's Bank v Boland* (1980), Mr and Mrs Boland had bought a house with their joint earnings, although it was conveyed (title was transferred) to Mr Boland alone and he appeared as the sole registered proprietor on the Land Registry register. Mr Boland's company borrowed money from the bank and he gave his personal guarantee as security. Without telling his wife he also mortgaged the house to the bank under a registered charge to support the guarantee (an unsupported guarantee is worth 'only the paper it is written on'). The bank did not ask either of the Bolands whether Mrs Boland had an interest in the house. Subsequently Mr Boland's company ran into difficulties and the bank called upon Mr Boland to pay under his guarantee. When he could not do so it sought possession of the house with the intention of selling it to recover the money owed. Mrs Boland resisted the bank's claim. The House of Lords held that the Bank's action for possession must fail. Her financial contribution to the purchase of the house gave her an equitable interest in the property and, because she was in actual occupation when the bank took the legal charge from her husband, her interest was an overriding interest under the Land Registration Act 1925, s.70. The bank's rights under the mortgage were therefore subject to Mrs Boland's right of occupation.

The decision is of great importance in land law, and of direct significance to banks. Furthermore, the decision goes far beyond the actual facts. It applies to all forms of registered property, not just to matrimonial homes and other dwelling houses, and it protects *any person* with a financial stake in the property who is in actual occupation at the time the mortgage is executed or the legal estate transferred. Lord Wilberforce in the House of Lords expressed its scope in the following words, it covered '... a man living with his mistress or ... a man and a woman, or two persons of the same sex, living in a house in separate or partially shared rooms'. Some wit even suggested at the time that it might cover an adopted cat which came with a legacy which was used to build a conservatory in which the cat lived!

In *City of London Building Society v Flegg* (1987), Mr and Mrs Flegg bought a house with their daughter and son-in-law, the Maxwell-Browns, but the property was conveyed into the sole names of the Maxwell-Browns on an express trust for sale for themselves as joint tenants. The Maxwell-Browns mortgaged the property to the plaintiff and subsequently defaulted on the repayments. The plaintiff commenced proceedings to enforce the mortgage against both the Maxwell-Browns and the Fleggs. The former conceded defeat and the issue was whether the mortgage bound the Fleggs. The House of Lords held that it did and a possession order was granted against them. The crucial distinction with *Boland* was that in *Flegg* title to the property had been registered in joint names. (Note, however, that the Fleggs' interest was not ignored by the law. But it was an interest in the proceeds of the sale of the land, not an interest enforceable against the land itself.)

When decided, *Boland* alarmed banks because of its apparently wide application; the *Flegg* decision clearly shows that the overriding interest arising under *Boland* is an exception to the general principle that a beneficiary's interest under a trust for sale is overreached on a sale or mortgage of the property. Nevertheless, *Boland* is established law and it gives a clear warning. When you intend to take a charge over land from a sole registered proprietor you must identify all occupiers, ascertain their financial stake, if any, in the property and secure their agreement to the owner's mortgage. This agreement usually takes the form of a *deed of postponement* under which these other occupiers declare that the bank's interest in the property as mortgagee shall rank above whatever interest they have in the property. Alternatively, the bank could ask a single trustee (the sole registered proprietor) to appoint a co-trustee.

ACTIVITY 6.4

The *Boland* and *Flegg* decisions are worth a little work on your part. Revise the two cases and complete the following tasks.

- Briefly summarise the facts of the cases. (A useful exercise is you are asked in the examination for examples of *rationes decidendes* or cases relevant to banking. On either occasion a short summary of the facts will probably be worth one or two marks.)
- State the *ratio decidendi* of each case.
- On what ground(s) can the cases be distinguished?

Minor interests

These consist of all interests in registered land other than registrable interests (freehold and leasehold) and registrable charges (e.g. legal mortgages), and overriding interests. Examples include the rights of a spouse to occupy residential property under the Matrimonial Homes Act 1983, equitable mortgages, the rights of a beneficiary under a trust, and the rights of creditors when a bankruptcy petition has been presented against the registered proprietor. A registrable interest or charge which is not registered within two months of its creation also takes affect as a minor interest, e.g. failure to register a legal mortgage on the charges register within the two months means that it only takes effect as an equitable mortgage (*see* page 199).

Broadly speaking, minor interests – which can only be equitable interests – correspond to those charges registrable under the Land Charges Act 1972 in the case of unregistered land. Minor interests require protection by an entry on the register and, as with registrable interests in unregistered land, knowledge of the interest is completely immaterial because registration has completely superseded the doctrine of notice. However, even when registered some interests can still be *overreached* by a purchaser or mortgagee. One such interest is that of a beneficiary under a trust for sale.

Overreaching

The principle of overreaching applies to equitable interests in both registered and unregistered land. From the perspective of a bank as a mortgagee the position in regard to a beneficiary's interest under a trust for sale is as follows.

1 If the beneficiary's interest is not registered – and most are not – the bank is unaffected by it, *unless* the interest proves to be an overriding interest which cannot be overreached because the mortgage is taken from only one trustee as in the *Boland* situation.

2 If a mortgage is taken from at least two trustees or a trust corporation, even an overriding interest is overreached, as in the *Flegg* situation.

3 If the interest is protected by an entry on the register (the form of which need not concern you here), it is still overreached, and the bank's mortgage is unaffected by it, provided again that the mortgage was taken from at least two trustees or a trust corporation.

Once again, the beneficiary's interest is converted into an interest in the proceeds of the notional sale of the property, it is no longer an interest in the land itself.

The Register

Look at Fig 6.3 which reproduces a typical register from the Land Registry. You will see that it is divided into three parts.

1 *The Property Register.* This describes the land and the estate for which it is held, refers to a map or plan showing the land (also given in Fig 6.3) and notes any interest held for the benefit of the land, such as easements or restrictive covenants.

In Fig 6.3 you can see that there are two easements referred to. The first is a right of way over a shared driveway granted when the land was first registered. The second relates to drainage rights through pipes running under the land, presumably sold for development, mentioned in Note 1 in this register as having been removed from the registered title.

2 *The Proprietorship Register.* This gives the nature of the title and the name, address and occupation of the registered proprietor. It sets out any restrictions affecting the proprietor's right to deal with the land.

In the case of the register reproduced the proprietor has *title absolute* – a state guaranteed perfect title – and there is a restriction preventing the registration of a transfer of title by the survivor of the joint registered proprietors without a court order.

3 *The Charges Register.* This contains entries relating to certain rights against the land, such as legal mortgages and restrictive covenants and notices

H.M. LAND REGISTRY

TITLE NUMBER   SO19834

Edition 1

opened 14.8.1965

This register consists of 2 pages

A. PROPERTY REGISTER

containing the description of the registered land and the estate comprised in the Title

ADMINISTRATIVE AREA	PARISH OR PLACE
(County, County Borough, etc)	
SOUTHUMBERLAND	OLDCASTLE

The Freehold land shown and edged with red on the filed plan of the above title registered on 14 August 1965 known as 97 Acacia Gardens, together with a right of way over the part of the driveway at the side not included in the title.

NOTE 1:-The land edged and numbered in green on the filed plan has been removed from this title and registered under the title number or numbers shown in green on the said plan.

NOTE 2:-There is appurtenant to the land in this title the following right reserved by the Transfer dated 12 March 1971 referred to in Entry No.4 of the Charges Register:-

"EXCEPT AND RESERVING to the Transferor for the benefit of the Transferors' retained land the full and free right to the uninterrupted passage and running of water and soil through the drains and sewers now existing or within 21 years hereafter to be constructed in or under the land hereby transferred."   (15.4.1971)

The land is now in the County of Southumbria, Oldcastle District. (15.1.1979)

B. PROPRIETORSHIP REGISTER

stating nature of the Title, name, address and description of the proprietor of the land and any entries affecting the right of disposing thereof

TITLE ABSOLUTE

Entry number	Proprietor, etc.	Remarks
1.	~~PERCY BYSSHE SHELLEY of 97 Acacia Gardens, Oldcastle, Southumberland, Steel Erector, registered on 14 August 1965.~~	~~Price paid £4250~~
2.	ROBERT BROWNING, Sales Representative, and ELIZABETH BARRETT BROWNING, his wife, both of 97 Acacia Gardens, Oldcastle, Southumbria, OL3 5PJ., registered on 15 January 1979.	
3.	RESTRICTION registered on 15 January 1979:-No disposition by one proprietor of the land (being the survivor of joint proprietors and not being a trust corporation) under which capital money arises is to be registered except under an Order of the registrar or of the Court.	

Any entries struck through are no longer subsisting

R 22

Demand No. 189442 42,000 30.12.74 W.G. & F.M.Ltd.

TITLE NUMBER SO19834  SPECIMEN

C. CHARGES REGISTER

Page 2

containing charges, incumbrances, etc., adversely affecting the land and registered dealings therewith

Entry number	The date at the beginning of each entry is the date on which the entry was made on this edition of the register.	Remarks
1.	14 August 1965-The part of the driveway at the side included in the title is subject to rights of way.	
~~2.~~	~~14 August 1965-CHARGE dated 12 July 1965 registered on~~ 14 August 1965 to secure the moneys including the further advances therein mentioned. *15·1·1979*	
~~3.~~	~~PROPRIETOR-HIGH STREET BANK LIMITED of 44 High Street, Oldcastle, Southumberland, registered on 14 August 1965.~~	*H.M. LAND REGISTRY WD1*
4.	15 April 1971-A Transfer of the land edged and numbered SO22463 in green on the filed plan dated 12 March 1971 by Percy Bysshe Shelley to John Keats contains the following covenant by the transferor:- "The Transferor hereby covenants with the Transferee and his successors and assigns as owners for the time being of the land hereby transferred that he the Transferor will not at any time use the land remaining in title number SO19834 or permit the same to be used for any purpose other than as the site for a single private dwellinghouse with the usual garages outbuildings and appurtenances."	*H.M. LAND WD7 REGISTRY*
5.	15 January 1979-CHARGE dated 18 December 1978 registered on 15 January 1979 to secure the moneys including the further advances therein mentioned.	
6.	PROPRIETOR-WEYFORD BUILDING SOCIETY of Society House, The Avenue, Weyford, Blankshire, registered on 15 January 1979.	*H.M. LAND WD8 REGISTRY*

Any entries struck through are no longer subsisting

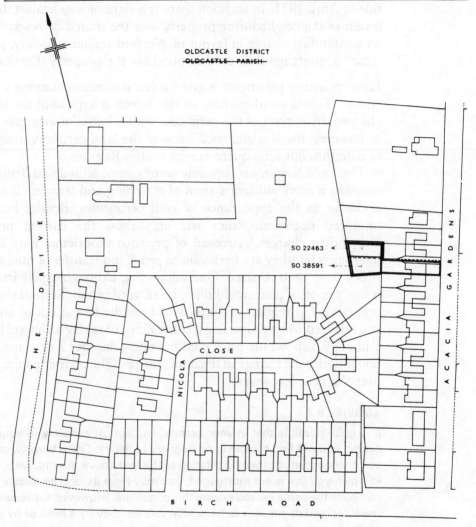

H.M. LAND REGISTRY		TITLE NUMBER	
		SO 19834	
ORDNANCE SURVEY PLAN REFERENCE	TZ 3367	SECTION G	Scale 1/1250
COUNTY ~~SOUTHUMBERLAND~~ SOUTHUMBRIA		© Crown copyright 1963	

OLDCASTLE DISTRICT
~~OLDCASTLE PARISH~~

SO 22463

SO 38591

THE DRIVE

NICOLA CLOSE

ACACIA GARDENS

BIRCH ROAD

Fig 6.3 A Land Registry register

protecting rights over the land, for example, those of creditors when a bankruptcy petition has been presented against the proprietor or a spouse's right to occupy a house owned by the other spouse. A purchaser or mortgagee is bound by the entries in the Charges Register.

Read the Charges Register through in Fig 6.3. Entry number 4 recites a covenant entered into in favour of the transferee of one of the two parcels of land at the rear of the property when they were removed from the registered title in April 1971. In addition there is a right of way against the property in favour of the neighbouring property over the shared driveway (Entry 1), and an outstanding charge in favour of Weyford Building Society, presumably to secure a mortgage loan used to purchase the property (Entries 5 and 6).

Each registered proprietor is given a *land certificate* containing a copy of these entries. This is the document of title which is kept until the land is sold or charged, by deposit of the certificate with a bank for example. Proof of title is, however, the Register itself because the land certificate may become out of date through subsequent entries on the Register.

The Land Registry is currently being computerised and besides, hopefully, meaning a more efficient system of searching and transfers it will also mean a change in the appearance of land certificates. Besides being computer produced documents, they will only show the current proprietor and outstanding charges. A record of previous proprietors may be historically interesting but they are irrelevant to proof and transfer of title, as are charges which have been released. One interesting, although legally irrelevant point, is that the price paid would often be entered in the 'Remarks' column of the proprietorship register and this would usually be cut out of any photo-copy you received when processing a conveyance or taking a charge. Entry number 1 in Fig 6.3 shows the price paid but entry number 2 does not. (You will no doubt notice the change in the appearance of the register copies you deal with over the next few years.)

ACTIVITY 6.5

It is quite possible that in your branch, and almost certainly in your local training centre, you will find sample Land Registry registers. Try to borrow, or at least ask to see, them and study them in relation to the text above. Alternatively, if the property in which you live is not mortgaged, you may have its land certificate at home. If so, complete the same exercise using this certificate. (However, for security reasons it is usual for land certificates to be held in safe custody by a bank or by a solicitor even when the property is not mortgaged.)

Registration

This is still not compulsory in all areas of the country. Even in a compulsory registration area, registration is only necessary on a conveyance on sale of a freehold or the creation or assignment on sale of certain leases. In other words, if a property has been owned by the same person for many years, even though it may be situated in a compulsory registration area, the title will not be registered. It will have to be registered, however, as soon as the property is sold.

A consequence for you is that for the foreseeable future you have to have an understanding of both registered and unregistered land until, with the passing of time, all property in compulsory registration areas is sold and the remaining areas become subject to compulsory registration and the same process takes place there.

We mentioned the registration of leases a little earlier. Registration of a lease is only compulsory where it is granted for a term of 21 years or more, or a lease with 21 or more years to run is assigned on sale in a compulsory registration area.

■ TITLE TO PROPERTY AND ITS TRANSFER

Here we deal with all the types of property that are commonly taken as security for bankers' advances and which we mentioned at the start of this chapter. Once again, however, much of the text will be devoted to land, both because it is more complicated to prove and transfer title to land than other forms of property, and because land is the best and usually preferred form of security for banks to take. However, we have already said much about the title to land in the previous section (in order to give coherence to our discussion of land) and therefore you will be beginning this section with a good introduction.

Land

The method by which title to land is transferred depends primarily upon whether the title is registered or unregistered. Unfortunately, we have to spend more time on unregistered land, because the methods are more complicated, even though most urban land is now registered. Simplification of the system was, you will remember, the main reason for introducing the system of land registration.

Unregistered land

Freehold. The freehold title to unregistered land is proved by a collection of deeds and documents which together must show a chain of title concluding with that of the vendor. They are known as the *title deeds*.

Transfer of title is effected in a two stage transaction. The first stage is the *contract*; this binds vendor and purchaser to complete the transfer, it does not transfer title. It is usual to use the Law Society's standard contract for sale which contains two closely printed A4 pages of general conditions and a further page of proforma (fill in the missing words type) special conditions which vary the general conditions where necessary. The second stage is the *conveyance*, which transfers title to the legal estate to the purchaser (*see* Fig 6.4).

Under the Law of Property (Miscellaneous Provisions) Act 1989, s.2 a *contract* for the sale of land must:

- be made in writing;
- incorporate in one contract all the terms the parties have expressly agreed;
- be signed by each party.

173

In practice the method adopted is usually an 'exchange of contracts' in which case all the terms must be contained in both parts. By the Law of Property Act 1925, s.52(1), the *conveyance* must be by deed. (Note that the conveyance reproduced in Fig 6.4 bears a seal. This is because it pre-dates the Law of Property (Miscellaneous Provisions) Act 1989 which abolished the requirement that deeds executed by individuals must be sealed.)

Under the contract of sale the vendor must produce for the purchaser's inspection an *abstract of title* showing evidence of title going back at least 15 years to a good root of title. The root of title may be:

- a *conveyance* which transferred the legal estate to the vendor;
- a *mortgage*; or
- an *assent*, a signed document transferring the legal estate in land from the personal representatives of a deceased holder to the person who inherits the land under the will or intestacy.

Following the exchange of contracts, the purchaser (usually their solicitor) examines the deeds, making such enquiries as they consider to be necessary. Arrangements are then made for completion, at which the conveyance executed by both parties is handed over with the title deeds (of which the conveyance now forms part) in exchange for the balance of the purchase price, usually in the form of a bank draft.

Leasehold. A leaseholder can transfer the legal estate by *assigning* to another person the whole of the remaining term unless prohibited from doing so by the terms of his lease. (An *assignment* is a deed transferring the legal estate in leasehold land. It is similar to the conveyance used to transfer unregistered freehold land.) Subject to the same proviso, a leaseholder may grant a *sub-lease* for a term shorter than that which the leaseholder holds.

Title is also evidenced by a collection of *title deeds*, although the actual lease to be assigned may be the only document. Completion is also similar to completion on sale of freehold land, the lease or an assignment of the original lease being delivered against a bank draft for the balance of the purchase price or payment of the rent. A copy of the lease or the assignment will be placed with the other title deeds.

Registered land

Title to registered land is proved by the registers at the Land Registry. Transfer of title is effected by a short, simple form of registered transfer (*see* Fig 6.5). This replaces the conveyance or assignment necessary to transfer title to unregistered land.

At completion, the vendor hands to the purchaser the land certificate and a signed registered transfer against payment of the balance of the purchase price. The land certificate and completed transfer are sent to the Land Registry where the new proprietor (the purchaser) is entered on the register and on the land certificate. The land certificate is then returned to the new proprietor as evidence of title.

Date   *15 December* 1982

MRS N M KEATS

- to -

MRS H PALFREMAN AND

MR D PALFREMAN

C O N V E Y A N C E

- of -

freehold plot of land situated and known

as No. 52 Lambton Road Chorlton-cum-Hardy

in the City of Manchester

THIS CONVEYANCE is made the *fifteenth* day of *December* One thousand nine hundred and eighty two between NORAH MARIAN KEATS of 52 Lambton Road chorlton-cum-Hard in the City of Manchester (hereinafter called the 'Vendor') of the one part and HELEN PALFREMAN and DAVID PALFREMAN of 15 Zetland Road Chorlton-cum-Hardy aforesaid (hereinafter called the 'Purchasers') of the other part

WHEREAS the Vendor is the owner in fee simple in possession of the property hereinafter described and intended to be conveyed subject as hereinafter mentioned but otherwise free from encumbrances at the price of Twenty two thousand pounds (£22,000)

NOW THIS DEED WITNESSETH as follows:

IN pursuance of the said agreement and in consideration of the sum of Twenty two thousand pounds now paid by the Purchasers to the vendor (the receipt whereof the Vendor hereby acknowledges) the Vendor as Beneficial Owner hereby conveys unto the Purchasers ALL THAT plot of land situate in Chorlton-cum-Hardy aforesaid containing in the whole Four hundred and thirty square yards or thereabouts and more particularly delineated and described in the plan annexed to the conveyance (hereinafter called the 'Conveyance') made the Seventeenth day of September One thousand nine hundred and twenty five between J Lane & sons Limited of the one part and Jabez Whitehead of the other part and thereon edged red AND ALSO the dwellinghouse erected thereon and numbered 52 Lambton Road Chorlton-cum-Hard aforesaid TOGETHER with the rights easements and appurtenances thereto belonging and the rights of way and drainage granted by the Conveyance EXCEPT and RESERVED like rights of way drainage and otherwise as more particularly mentioned to be excepted and reserved in and by the Conveyance AND ALSO EXCEPT and RESERVED as mentioned to be excepted and reserved in and by a Conveyance made the twenty fourth day of November One thousand nine hundred and twenty four between the Right Honourable Maurice Baron Egerton of Tatton of the first part Montague Ellis and Robert Henry Grenville Tatton of the second part and the said J Lane & Sons Limited of the third part and Ernest Lane and Clifford Lane of the fourth part TO HOLD the same unto the

Purchasers in fee simple as joint tenants in law and equity <u>SUBJECT</u> henceforth to the payment of the yearly rent charge of Five pounds limited in use and made payable by and to the observance and performance of the covenants on the part of the Grantee and the conditions contained or referred to in the Conveyance

<u>IT IS HEREBY CERTIFIED</u> that the transaction hereby effected does not form part of a larger transaction or of a series of transactions in respect of which the amount or value or the aggregate amount or value of the consideration exceeds Twenty five thousand pounds

<u>IN WITNESS</u> whereof the parties hereto have hereunto set their hands and seals the day and year before written.

<u>SIGNED SEALED</u> and <u>DELIVERED</u> by the said Norah Marian Keats in the presence of:

N M Keats

> *B S Wordsworth*
> *Dove Cottage*
> *Egerton Road*
> *Chorlton, Manchester*
>
> *Manager*

<u>SIGNED SEALED</u> and <u>DELIVERED</u> by the said Helen Palfreman and David Palfreman in the presence of:

Helen Palfreman

David Palfreman

> *Jill Barber*
> *50 Malvern Road*
> *Akrington*
> *Middleton*
> *Manchester*
>
> *Secretary*

Fig 6.4 A conveyance of unregistered land

If a purchaser created a mortgage over the land to secure a loan to purchase it, the mortgage is entered on the charges register and a charge certificate (not the land certificate) is sent to the mortgagee.

Stocks and shares

Stocks and shares can be classified in two ways: according to the organisation which issued them, for example, a registered company or the government (we are not concerned only with shares in companies); or according to the method by which title to them is established and transferred. As a banker you are concerned with both classifications but here it is appropriate for us to adopt the latter.

Under this classification, stocks and shares are classified as registered or bearer securities.

Registered securities

Title. The company or other organisation issuing the securities will maintain a register in which the holders' names and addresses and the amount of their holdings are recorded. The register is the proof of title but a registered holder receives a certificate in their name as *prima facie* evidence of title.

Every company maintains its own register of shareholders and stockholders. The holders of British government stock and national savings securities are registered on either the National Savings Stock Register, and receive a certificate issued by the Director of Savings, or in books kept at the Bank of England and receive a certificate issued by the Bank.

Transfer of title. Transfer of the legal title is effected by sending the appropriate transfer form signed by the transferor, and sometimes the transferee, and the relevant certificate to the organisation which issued the securities for details of the new ownership to be entered on the register. A new certificate is then issued in favour of the transferee.

The form of transfer used is nearly always the simplified *stock transfer form*. This contains details of the price paid for the shares, the name of the issuing organisation, the number and value of the securities held, details of the transferor and transferee and the former's signature. It is not signed by the transferee. To meet the needs of the Stock Exchange's computerised accounting system, shares in public companies are transferred using the Talisman transfer form. This is a variant of the stock transfer form. The transferee is always SEPON Ltd. In a few cases the transfer must be by *deed* or by a *common form of transfer*.

Units in *unit trusts* can be transferred by any method approved by the trustee but most commonly they are transferred by a stock transfer form. Usually, however, holders realise their investments by selling the units back to the managers of the trust. This requires completion of the *form of renunciation* on the back of the certificates.

In mid-1992 the International Stock Exchange plans to introduce Taurus (transfer and automatic registration of uncertificated securities). The objective

Transfer of Whole to Joint Proprietors (1)

HM Land Registry

Form 19(JP)

(Rules 98 or 115, Land Registration Rules, 1925)

Stamp pursuant to section 28 of the Finance Act 1931 to be impressed here.	When the transfer attracts Inland Revenue Duty, the stamps should be impressed here before lodging the transfer for registration.

(1) For a transfer to a sole proprietor use printed form 19.

County and district (or London borough) ....

Title number(s) ....

Property ....

Date .... 19 In consideration of ....

....

pounds (£ ....) *the receipt of which is hereby acknowledged* (2)

(2) Delete the words in italics if not required.

I/We (3) ....

(3) In BLOCK LETTERS enter the full name(s), postal address(es) (including postcode) and occupation(s) of the proprietor(s) of the land.

....

....

.... *as beneficial owner(s) hereby transfer to* (4)

(4) If desired or otherwise as the case may be (see rules 76 and 77).

(5)

(5) In BLOCK LETTERS enter the full name(s), postal address(es) (including postcode) and occupation(s) of the transferee(s) for entry in the register.

the land comprised in the title(s) above mentioned (6) (7)

(6) Enter any special clause here.

(7) A transfer for charitable purposes should follow form 36 in the schedule to the Land Registration Rules, 1925 (see rules 121 and 122).

(continued overleaf)

(8) Delete the inappropriate alternative.

The transferees declare that the survivor of them (^{8}) $\frac{can}{cannot}$ give a valid receipt for capital money arising on a disposition of the land.

(9) If a certificate of value for the purposes of the Stamp Act 1891 and amending Acts is not required delete this paragraph.

(^{9}) It is hereby certified that the transaction hereby effected does not form part of a larger transaction or series of transactions in respect of which the amount or value or aggregate amount or value of the consideration exceeds £...................................

(10) This transfer must be executed by the transferee(s) as well as the transferor(s).

(^{10}) Signed as a deed by

....

in the presence of

Name ....   Signature of witness ....

Address ....

Occupation ....

(^{10}) Signed as a deed by

....

in the presence of

Name ....   Signature of witness ....

Address ....

Occupation ....

(^{10}) Signed as a deed by

....

in the presence of

Name ....   Signature of witness ....

Address ....

Occupation ....

(^{10}) Signed as a deed by

....

in the presence of

Name ....   Signature of witness ....

Address ....

Occupation ....

Fig 6.5 A registered transfer form

of Taurus is to dispense with paper share certificates for shares listed on the Exchange (listed public companies) replacing them with computer entries. Company registers will be linked to the Taurus computer. While the company register will remain proof of title, any transfer will be effected through a simple book entry in the Taurus computer, no collection and exchange of paper share certificates will be necessary. The collection and exchange of certificates is a major bottleneck in the clearing and settlement process and this 'dematerialisation' of share certificates should remove it. If, however, the owner wants a physical certificate, the shares can be withdrawn from Taurus and a new certificate issued by the company registrar. (Note that 'dematerialisation' will mean the loss of safe custody income by banks since there will be fewer shares to hold in safe custody.)

Some registered securities are not transferable at all, e.g. national savings securities and the shares in some building societies. This has obvious implications should they be offered to you as security.

Bearer securities

The main types of bearer securities are bearer bonds, scrip certificates or letters allotment, share warrants to bearer and bearer debentures. All are *negotiable instruments*. This means that whoever is in possession of them, even a thief, is their *holder*, i.e. the holder is not necessarily the true owner. As the holder, that person can transfer a perfect title by mere delivery provided the transferee (the person to whom the security is transferred) takes in good faith, for value and without notice of any defect in the transferor's title. Technically the transferee becomes a *holder in due course*. (*See* generally Chapter 8.) This attribute makes bearer securities excellent for security purposes; unless there are circumstances which warrant investigation, taking bearer securities as security for a loan gives a bank a perfect title to them.

Life policies

A life policy is a contract between the policy-holder and the life assurance company whereby the company in return for regular premiums agrees to pay the policy-holder (or his or her estate) a specified sum on the death of the life assured or on a certain date, whichever is the sooner. Title to a life policy is vested in the policy-holder and the policy is evidence of title.

Insurable interest

The policy-holder may or may not be the person whose life is assured because it is possible to insure lives other than your own. What is required is an *insurable interest*.

Except where a person insures his or her own or spouse's life, an insurable interest is a *pecuniary* interest; in other words the financial loss which would be suffered by the proposer on the death of the assured. For example, creditors can insure the life of their debtors to the amount of the debts and guarantors can insure the lives of the principal debtors to the amount of the guarantee.

Assigning a life policy

Perhaps you have never considered the idea of *transferring title* to a life policy but this can be done by *assigning* (transferring) the interest (the right to claim under the policy) to a third person. The transferee does not have to have an insurable interest in the life assured. (*Assured* rather than *insured* is the correct term because death is certain at some time.) The ability to assign a life policy is important to a bank not only for the purpose of taking a life policy as security but also because sale of the policy may be a more profitable alternative to surrender if the policy holder wishes, or is compelled, to realise the value of the policy before its maturity. (Companies exist which buy life policies as medium to long-term investments.)

By the Policies of Assurance Act 1867, s.5, an *assignment* of a life policy must be either by an endorsement on the policy itself or by a separate document of assignment. Both must be signed and witnessed. A deed is often used by banks but this is not a legal requirement.

After a policy has been assigned the assignee may sue, if necessary, for the policy moneys in their own name although this right is subject to two conditions. First, the assignee takes the policy subject to any prior defects in title or personal defences available against the assignor. An example would be invalidation of the policy for non-disclosure of material facts, even if the information is not asked for by the proposal form – it is a contract *uberrimae fidei* (of the utmost good faith) e.g. that the assignor had suffered from a serious illness or that s/he was a regular smoker or a hang-glider enthusiast. In other words, any defence which would have been available against the policy-holder (the assignor) is available against the assignee. (Compare negotiation – a life policy is not a negotiable instrument: *see* generally Chapter 8.)

Second, notice in writing must be given to the company which issued the policy. This notice is necessary to vest legal title to the policy in the assignee. (Again, compare negotiation.) Sometimes a policy will be assigned a number of times. Where there are second or subsequent assignments, priority of interests between the assignees is determined by the date on which notice of assignment was received by the issuing company.

A life policy will state where notices of assignment are to be given; usually this will be the company's principal place of business. The company is bound by the 1867 Act to give written acknowledgement of the notice if requested in writing to do so by the assignee. The usual practice is send the notice in duplicate, the company receipting and returning one copy. A small fee is payable for this although it is often waived.

Guarantees

Definition

A guarantee is 'A promise to answer for the debt, default or miscarriage of another' if that other person fails to meet their obligation(s): Statute of Frauds 1677, s.4. The rather formal language of this old statute means that the guarantor undertakes to make a payment if someone else, who should make it, does not.

Guarantees and indemnities

At this point it is useful to distinguish a guarantee from an indemnity. Under a guarantee, the *surety* (guarantor) incurs only *secondary liability*; under an indemnity, the *indemnifier* incurs *primary liability*. For example, if when Mr Smith asks you for a loan, Ms Brown says 'Lend him the money he wants, if he doesn't pay you back, I will.', Ms Brown is offering to guarantee the loan and would incur only secondary liability. If, however, Ms Brown says, 'Lend him the money, I will see that you are repaid.', she has offered to indemnify the bank and would incur primary liability. Put another way, liability under a guarantee is conditional, it only arises *if* the principal debtor does not pay. Liability under an indemnity is not conditional. It is, of course, a question of construction should a dispute arise as to the nature of the undertaking, although banks' standard form guarantees avoid this problem arising. The distinction between a guarantee and an indemnity is of practical importance in so far as a guarantee must be supported by written evidence – such as one or more letters which confirm the oral evidence of the contractual terms – to be enforceable in court while an indemnity need not. Bank guarantee forms are clearly written evidence and problems will not arise in this context.

Ultra vires clause

Bank guarantee forms usually include an *ultra vires* clause just in case the loan proves to be unenforceable against the customer through any legal limitation or lack of contractual capacity. This could happen, for example, where the loan is made to an unincorporated club or association. Under such a clause the surety undertakes to accept primary liability as principal debtor for any sums which cannot be recovered from the customer. The contract thereby becomes an indemnity as well as a guarantee. A typical clause might read:

> The Guarantor's(s') liability shall not be affected by the irregular exercise of borrowing powers of the Principal of a corporation or by the Principal(s) being under any disability or by an association or other unincorporated body not having a legal existence being named as principal or by any other act or circumstances (whether known or not to the Bank and the Guarantor(s) or either/any of them) as the result of which any indebtedness or liability incurred or purported to be incurred by the Principal(s) is void or unenforceable by the Bank against the Principal(s) the Guarantor(s) in any such case to be liable to the Bank as principal debtor and by way of indemnity for the same amount as that for which the Guarantor(s) would have been liable by way of guarantee had a valid and enforceable indebtedness or liability as between the Principal(s) or the association or body named as principal and the Bank been created.

Such a clause is an excellent example of banks using the law, standard form contracts in particular, quite legitimately to their own advantage.

ACTIVITY 6.6

Obtain a copy of your bank's guarantee form and identify its *ultra vires* clause. (A copy of the form will be useful to you in the next chapter.)

Title to a guarantee

The question of title to a guarantee or transfer of that title does not really arise. The guarantee itself is proof of the lender's right to enforce payment against the guarantor according to the terms of the guarantee and this right is never in practice transferred. However, bank guarantees are usually expressed to be in favour of the bank, 'its successors and assigns'. This means that if there is any change to the constitution of the bank, or if it merges or is amalgamated with another bank the guarantee is not invalidated.

Note that it is also possible for a person to specifically charge an asset, such as a house, to secure another's borrowing. This is known as third party security. In effect, third party security *amounts* to a guarantee but it cuts out the actual contract of guarantee.

Debentures

Debentures are documents issued by companies acknowledging loans and charges securing them. Only companies can issue debentures and by them companies raise much of their finance. Debentures are of four main types.

Secured and unsecured

The former grants a mortgage or charge over the property of the company; the latter is given without security, it merely acknowledges the debt.

Single or series

A single debenture is issued to cover a single debt, for example to a bank to secure an overdraft. More usually debentures are issued in series to several or many holders as a way of raising money. These rank *pari passu* (equally) among themselves.

Registered or bearer

Most debentures are registered in the names of the various holders in the same way as shares; their transfer is similarly registered. Bearer debentures are negotiable instruments transferable by delivery. They are not registered but Treasury consent is required for their issue.

Perpetual or redeemable

The former are only repaid when the company is wound up, the latter are repayable on or before a specified date.

Title and its transfer

Once again, it is not usual to talk about 'title' to a debenture since the debenture itself is proof of entitlement to the rights it confers. Debentures are transferred, however; a fixed-sum debenture quoted on a stock exchange being transferable in the same way as stocks and shares. A bearer debenture can be transferred by mere delivery.

Banks' debentures are usually transferable, but one bank that accepts a transfer of a debenture from another or from any other organisation will seldom rely on the wording of the original debenture. Each bank has its own practices and procedures, albeit similar, and each drafts its own debentures to cover all foreseeable contingencies in conformity with those practices and procedures and its own experience. Thus, it is standard practice to take a new debenture in its own form and have the original debenture discharged.

Type	Proof of title	Transfer of title
Registered land	Register/land certificate	Land certificate and signed registered transfer sent to Land Registry where registers are amended and certificate sent to new proprietor
Unregistered land		
Freehold	Title deeds	Contract/conveyance
Leasehold	Title deeds	Contract/assignment
Life policies	Policy	Assignment
Stocks and shares	Register of shareholders/certificate	Signed transfer form and certificates sent to the issuer of the securities.
Bearer securities	Possession of the securities	New details entered on the register. Delivery of the certificates – negotiable instruments

Fig 6.6 Proof of title to property

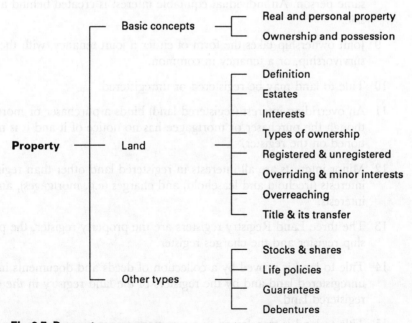

Fig 6.7 Property: a summary

ACTIVITY 6.7

Using Fig 6.7 as the basis, draw other, more detailed diagrams of 'property'.

■ SUMMARY

1 Property is classified as either 'real' property, freehold estates and interests in land; or 'personal' property, everything else.

2 Ownership is the right of a person to enjoy property as fully as the law permits. Possession is the exclusive use and control of property.

3 'Land' includes not only the surface of the earth but buildings and fixtures in buildings, certain rights above and below the surface, and rights over another's land.

4 An estate in land is a right to the land itself – possession; an interest in land is a right to a claim against the land of another less than a claim to possession.

5 Two legal estates exist: the fee simple absolute in possession (freehold) and the term of years absolute (leasehold).

6 A freehold estate or interest takes effect immediately and has an unlimited duration, a leasehold estate or interest is for a limited duration.

7 Interests in land can be legal or equitable.
  • A legal interest (a right *in rem*) is enforceable against all other persons.
  • An equitable interest (a right *in personam*) is usually only enforceable against a purchaser or mortgagor if it is registered.

8 Legal and equitable ownership of land may or may not both be vested in the same person. An individual equitable interest is created behind a trust for sale.

9 Joint ownership takes the form of either a joint tenancy, with the right of survivorship, or a tenancy in common.

10 Title to land may be registered or unregistered.

11 An overriding interest (registered land) binds a purchaser or mortgagee even though the purchaser or mortgagee has no notice of it and it is not mentioned on the register.

12 Minor interests are all interests in registered land other than registrable interests (freehold and leasehold) and charges (e.g. mortgages), and overriding interests.

13 The three Land Registry registers are the property register, the proprietorship register and the charges register.

14 Title to land is proved by a collection of deeds and documents in the case of unregistered land and by the registers of the land registry in the case of registered land.

15 Title to land is transferred in a two stage transaction: first, a contract of sale between buyer and seller and, second, the conveyance (freehold) or assignment (leasehold) in the case of unregistered land, or by the completion of a form of registered transfer in the case of registered land. In both cases, the transfer takes the form of a deed.

16 In the context of their use as security, stocks and shares are usefully classified into registered and bearer securities. Title to registered securities is transferred by details of the new owner being entered on the register of holders; title to bearer securities is transferred by their delivery.

17 A valid life assurance policy requires the original policy-holder to have an insurable interest in the life assured.

18 Title to a life policy is transferred by assignment. The assignee need not have an insurable interest in the life assured.

19 A guarantee is a promise to repay the debt of another if that other person does not make repayment. To be enforceable, a guarantee must be supported by written evidence.

20 Debentures are documents issued by companies acknowledging loans and charges securing them.

■ SELF-ASSESSMENT QUESTIONS

1 Distinguish between real and personal property.

2 Explain, with the aid of a banking example, how ownership and possession can be distinguished.

3 What is the technical terminology for freehold and leasehold estates?

4 Distinguish between an estate and an interest in land and between a legal and an equitable interest.

5 Why is it important to register equitable and some legal interests in land?

6 Why are overriding interests in land important to banks?

7 Why are the *Boland* and *Flegg* decisions important?

8 What are minor interests?

9 Name the three Land Registry registers.

10 Distinguish between a joint tenancy and a tenancy in common.

11 Distinguish between legal and equitable ownership of land.

12 What is meant when we say that title to land is transferred in a two stage transaction? What is the importance of the first stage?

13 How is a lease of unregistered land transferred?

14 How is title to registered securities established?

15 Why is title to bearer securities transferred by delivery?

16 What is an insurable interest in the context of a life policy?

17 How is title to a life policy transferred?

18 Define a guarantee.

19 Why are *ultra vires* clauses included in bank guarantees?

20 What is a debenture?

■ MULTIPLE-CHOICE QUESTIONS

1 Title to registered land/unregistered land (match the type of land with the appropriate) is proved by:
A searching the Land Charges Registry
B a collection of deeds and documents unreg
C the Land Registry registers
D an abstract of title

2 Which of the following statements is *not* a characteristic of a term of years absolute for more than three years?
A it must give the right to exclusive possession
B it must be for a definite period of time
C it must give the right to immediate possession
D it must be created by deed

3 Which of the following is *not* an essential characteristic of a leasehold estate?
A it must always be created and transferred by deed
B it gives the right to exclusive possession
C it is for a definite period
D it creates the relationship of landlord and tenant

4 *Williams & Glyn's Bank Ltd v Boland* (1980)/*Cuckmere Brick Co Ltd v Mutual Finance Ltd* (1971) (match the case with the appropriate) established that:
A a legal mortgagee is under a duty to take reasonable care to obtain the true value of property if he exercises his right of sale
B a legal mortgagee must act in good faith in making arrangements for the sale of property held as security
C a legal mortgage gives a bank an overriding interest in the property mortgaged
D a legal mortgagee may be prevented from exercising his power of sale if a third party is in actual occupation of the property mortgaged

5 The right of the owner of Blackacre to cross Whiteacre is:
A a restrictive covenant
B a profit à prendre
C an easement
D a right of entry

6 An overriding interest:
A must be registered at the Land Charges Registry
B can be registered at the Land Registry
C must be registered where there is a single registered proprietor
D cannot be registered

7 Property as security

OBJECTIVES

OBJECTIVES

After studying this chapter you should be able to:
1 Explain the nature and function of security;
2 Identify and distinguish between different types of security arrangements;
3 Define the terms 'mortgage', 'pledge', 'lien' and 'charge';
4 Distinguish between legal and equitable mortgages;
5 Outline how charges are taken over land, stocks and shares, and life policies;
6 Explain the use of guarantees and debentures as security;
7 State and compare the attributes of different types of securities;
8 Appreciate a bank's position as holder of security.

■ WHAT IS SECURITY?

By the term 'security' we mean the acquisition of rights over property taken to support a borrower's personal undertaking to repay which can be exercised if the borrower (debtor) does not. An example is a power of sale.

Security for bankers' advances can take many forms, in extreme cases where borrowing is unauthorised, banks have been known to end up with a bizarre collection of items in their strongrooms including, we have been assured over the years, numerous bottles of vintage port and at least one Lamborghini carburettor! While it is usual to think of security in terms of, say, a mortgage of land or a life policy, you must remember that each individual form of security has the same basic function and effect.

■ WHAT IS THE FUNCTION OF SECURITY?

Loans should not be made on the strength of the security offered; quite the reverse in fact. You should have decided that you want to make the loan before you even look at the security available. If the proposition does not seem viable in *its own right* then it is quite wrong to lend against good security knowing that it will probably have to be relied on as the source or repayment.

What then is the function of security? The answer is that it is *insurance* against unforeseen and unforeseeable circumstances. The bank acquires some right over and above the basic contractual right to sue the customer if repayment is not made according to the terms of the contract. (This is a right *in personam* and does not do you much good if your customer has disposed of their assets!)

This is not to underrate the importance of security in the lending decision, however, the provision of suitable security is a major factor. Indeed, customers frequently do not fully appreciate its importance, even its basic function and, in particular, the full ramifications of having given it.

Two specific reasons

So far we have talked in general terms about the function of security but we can be more precise about the *reasons*. First, should the customer become insolvent, the bank avoids the *full consequences of the customer's bankruptcy* (if an individual or a partnership) or *liquidation* (if a limited company). Provided suitable securities have been taken the whole debt can be recovered by their realisation, with any surplus being paid over to augment the assets available to other creditors. If the advance was unsecured, the bank would only be able to prove for the amount owed in competition with the other unsecured creditors receiving, perhaps, just a very small percentage (so many pence in the pound) of the debt after the total assets available for distribution have been divided by the total liabilities.

The second reason concerns the customer's *willingness* rather than capacity to repay. It is neither good banking practice nor kindness to your customer to allow the bank to be thought of as an easy source of money, to be repaid when the *customer* wants to repay. More importantly, it is fundamentally important that bank advances should be 'turning-over' continually. Thus, while it is virtually inconceivable that a major UK bank would ever find itself in this position, delay in repayment of a substantial loan could damage its cashflow position. Taking suitable security avoids this possible problem – it can be sold to effect repayment – and also avoids the expense and general hassle involved in litigation.

■ TYPES OF SECURITY ARRANGEMENT

Besides classifying and discussing securities by physical type, such as land, life policies, etc., we can classify them according to the nature of the arrangement entered into and then go on to give some specific definitions. These, as you will see, are to some extent independent of the nature of the actual property taken as security.

Whole ownership

The customer (the debtor) can transfer the whole ownership of the property to the bank (the creditor) under a contract in which the bank agrees to retransfer it to the customer if the debt is repaid on the due date. A legal mortgage of shares and an assignment of a life policy take this form.

Possession

The customer can give the bank mere possession, not ownership, of the property. Clearly this stops the customer disposing of it but it does not directly assist the bank unless it also acquires the right to sell it. Pledges and liens (*see* below) take this form.

Documents of title

Documents of title, such as title deeds to land or share certificates, can be deposited by the customer with the bank. This gives the bank the right to retain the documents until repayment is made. This is sometimes referred to as giving the bank a 'lien' on them but this is incorrect because here the right to retain the documents is given by an express agreement whereas a lien arises by operation of law (*see* page 192).

The effect of the deposit is that the property represented by the documents cannot be dealt with without them and therefore provides the customer with a strong inducement to make repayment. In addition, a bank will normally give itself direct rights against the property in a contractual memorandum of deposit, primarily the right to sell the property, if repayment is not made.

Rights over property

Without giving any rights of ownership, possession or documents of title, the customer may give the bank certain rights over property. The right to apply to the court for an order for sale if the loan is not repaid is the essence of this type of security. Such a transaction is known as a *charge* (*see* below).

We must cover two other security arrangements. The first, a floating charge, is peculiar to companies and the second, a guarantee, involves a personal obligation and not rights over specific property.

Floating charge

A floating charge is an equitable charge which covers the fluctuating assets of a company, such as its stocks, without attaching to specific assets until crystallisation, i.e. until it becomes *fixed*. Crystallisation occurs:

- under the terms of the charge if the company commits a specified breach of the agreement such as failure to repay the capital sum on demand, or by the bank giving notice;
- automatically if the bank appoints a receiver;
- if the company commences winding up, even if it is not in default; and
- if the company ceases business.

Until crystallisation, a floating charge allows the company to freely dispose of the assets covered by the charge, their place being taken by others acquired in the general course of business.

A *fixed charge* given by a company is a legal or equitable mortgage of specific property.

Guarantee

A guarantee is a personal undertaking to repay a debt if another person who should make repayment does not. (We covered the nature of a guarantee as a type of property in Chapter 6.)

■ DEFINITIONS

Having explained the different legal arrangements that are possible when security is taken, we can now define the most common security transactions entered into by banks.

Mortgage

A mortgage is *the creation or transfer of an interest in property* as security for the payment of a debt or the discharge of some other obligation. The mortgage will include a provision for redemption, i.e. that on repayment or discharge of the obligation it will become void or the interest reconveyed. Possession of the property remains with the *mortgagor* (the borrower/customer), while the *mortgagee* (the lender/bank) obtains some or all of the rights of ownership, or the right to obtain ownership if the borrower defaults in repayment. In other words, if repayment is not made, the bank (or other lender) can take action against the property, directly or indirectly depending on the type of mortgage, to recover what is owed.

The term 'mortgage' is used very loosely. For example, legally a customer *gives* a mortgage to the bank and does not get one from the bank; it is also frequently taken to mean the money lent. Also remember that legal mortgages of *land* are almost invariably created by legal charge under the Law of Property Act 1925 and not, since 1925, by creating a lease. The legal charge does not give the mortgagee an estate in the land mortgaged as a lease would but does confer the same protection, powers and remedies.

Land is the form of property most usually mortgaged but choses in action, such as life assurance policies, can be mortgaged by assignment and goods by a conditional bill of sale, both subject to a condition that on repayment the property will be reassigned to the mortgagor. A mortgagor of goods is rare.

A mortgage may be either legal or equitable. A *legal mortgage* creates rights against the property itself whereas an *equitable mortgage* creates only personal rights against the mortgagor. A legal mortgagee is therefore in a stronger position than an equitable mortgagee. (Legal and equitable mortgages are discussed later.)

Pledge

A pledge is a *deposit of goods*, or documents of title to them, or *negotiable instruments* with a lender as security for a debt. It confers the power of sale if repayment is not made. (Pawnbroking is an example of utilising a pledge as security.) It differs from a mortgage in that the lender obtains possession of the property while the borrower retains ownership.

Lien

A lien is a right to *retain property* belonging to another until a debt is paid by that person. It differs from a mortgage or pledge in that it arises by operation of law from certain situations. For example, a garage would be entitled to a lien over its customer's car until a bill for repairs was paid. Mortgages and pledges are both the result of express agreements between borrowers and lenders.

A lien may be either particular or general. A *particular lien* gives the right to retain possession only to secure payment of money owing in respect of the particular property over which the lien is exercised. A *general lien* gives the right to retain possession until any amount outstanding is repaid.

Normally, a lien only confers the right to retain possession of property but by mercantile custom a *banker's lien* is a general lien which confers the right of sale and recoupment. You can exercise such a lien over any of your customer's documents in your possession other than those deposited with you for safe custody. In practice, this means that the lien can be exercised over cheques paid in to be collected and credited to the customer's account if the account is overdrawn, although the lien is lost when they are presented for payment. Other documents, such as life policies and share certificates, are likely to be held under a specific agreement – either for safe custody or as security – and therefore a lien cannot arise over them while they are so held. However, if a life policy, say, was originally held as security but the debt has been discharged by repayment without the customer asking for the return of the life policy, a lien could arise over the policy in respect of subsequent borrowing.

In Chapter 5 we saw that *safe custody* facilities give rise to a contract of bailment. We must emphasise that a bailment agreement is wholly inconsistent with a lien which can therefore never arise over articles held in safe custody. (Having said that, a safe custody agreement may provide that the items held may be retained until charges incurred have been paid – but this is not a true lien.) We also mentioned earlier in this chapter that taking possession of documents of title under a security arrangement gives rise to the right to retain them until repayment is made. This is sometimes referred to as 'contractual lien' but because such a 'lien' does not arise by operation of law but by agreement, this is not a true lien in the legal sense.

Charge

A charge is usually regarded as a type of mortgage. However, a mortgage creates or conveys an interest in the property mortgaged subject to a right of redemption whereas a charge merely gives certain rights over the property charged as security, for example the right to ask the court for an order for sale of the property. (NB A *legal charge* under the Law of Property Act 1925 does create an interest in land and to avoid confusion is better considered in practice as a mortgage, and not as a charge, because it creates the same rights in the land.)

Assignment

Assignment is the transfer of title to choses in action (intangible property). A legal mortgage of a life policy is taken by assignment. The assignment has to be in writing and written notice must be given to the life assurance company.

■ TAKING SECURITY FROM INDIVIDUALS

In Chapter 4 we covered the issue of 'reality of consent' − undue influence, misrepresentation and mistake − in making contracts generally and indicated its importance when taking security for advances, particularly guarantees. Look back at our coverage to refresh your memory on the issue and the leading cases and then study the section below.

Undue influence

You will recall that undue influence renders a contract voidable at the option of the weaker party provided that that person can show:

- they were subject to the other's dominance; and
- they suffered a real and obvious disadvantage as a result.

In some cases the dominance is exercised by the bank but more likely it is exercised by someone who is considered to be acting as agent for the bank, e.g. a debtor who persuades, say, a relative to guarantee their proposed borrowing from the bank, or one joint owner of a house who persuades the other joint owner − typically a husband persuading his wife − to execute a mortgage deed over it.

In *Avon Finance Co Ltd v Bridger* (1985) Mr and Mrs B bought a retirement home partly with a mortgage and partly with money from their son. What they did not know was that their son had raised a loan from AV to help him provide his contribution. This loan was secured by a second charge on the property and the son persuaded his parents to execute the charge at the office of AV's solicitor by misleading them as to its nature and by exerting influence over them. The son later defaulted on the loan and AV sought possession of the house. This was refused because AV had used the son as its agent to obtain the Bs' signatures on the charge. Clearly, the Bs had also suffered a real disadvantage as a result of the transaction.

However, in *Bank of Credit and Commerce International SA v Abody* (1989) the court took a different view. Here the matrimonial home was in Mrs A's sole name and Mr A persuaded her to charge it to secure a loan to a company controlled by Mr A of which Mrs A was an officer. In fact Mrs A never took an active part in any business affairs and signed any document her husband put in front of her. The company defaulted on the loan and BCCI sought a possession order. This was granted. Although Mrs A had acted under her husband's dominance and he in turn was acting as agent for the Bank, Mrs A could not show that she had suffered any real disadvantage. On the contrary, she had benefited from the support the loan had given to the company's business.

Misrepresentation

The essence of misrepresentation as discussed in Chapter 4 is that one party is misled by the other − fraudulently, negligently or innocently − and as a result is induced to enter into a contract when they would not otherwise have done so. The contract is voidable at the option of the party misled.

An unusual example of this occurred in *Lloyds Bank plc v Waterhouse* (1990) where W guaranteed a loan to his son from L to enable his son to buy a farm. The guarantee was in the bank's standard form and contained an 'all monies' clause which meant that it covered not only the borrowing to buy the farm but also any other borrowing the son might make. The son borrowed far more than was necessary to buy the farm and eventually W was called upon to pay on his guarantee. At this point W disclosed that while he may have appeared to be familiar with business matters and, indeed, was reasonably successful himself, he was illiterate and had no idea what terms the guarantee contained although he realised what it was. On the facts W was able to avoid the guarantee because he had asked about its terms and the bank had merely told him that it was intended to provide security for the loan to his son to buy the farm. W was able to establish that he would not have signed the guarantee if he had known that it contained the 'all monies' clause. In short, the bank had negligently misrepresented the terms of the guarantee.

Note here that where a security contract is not voidable for misrepresentation – because the misrepresentation was not the cause of the contract being entered into – damages may be recoverable in the tort of negligence under the *Hedley Byrne* principle (*see* page 121) for the loss that results from a negligent misrepresentation, e.g. a misrepresentation as to purpose or scope of the security.

ACTIVITY 7.1

You have been approached by one of your customers, Mr Tompkins, for a loan to Tompco Ltd, a company in which Mr Tompkins is the only major shareholder. The security that Mr Tompkins offers is a charge by his wife over her separate property. Mrs Tompkins has her own bank account at your branch. In terms of value etc. the security is acceptable but the rules of your bank require that all persons offering 'third party security' receive independent legal advice before charging their property.

Your manager has asked you to write to Mrs Tompkins, with a copy to her husband, informing her of the bank's rule and also explaining why the rule exists. It is probably a situation where a little tact is needed!

■ TYPES OF SECURITY

Introduction: basic principles

Although this book is written for a 'law' course, law should not be considered in a vacuum. It would be quite possible to cover different types of security – how they are taken, protected, etc. – from a purely legal perspective but this would paint a somewhat incomplete picture of the role of security in the business of banking. Bankers have wider perspectives. For this reason we are going to begin this section with a brief consideration of the basic principles of taking security. You should treat this as an introduction but be prepared to explain the attributes of different types of security in an examination since these arise partly from legal principles and procedures and partly from the wider commercial world which the law regulates.

The attributes of good security

1 *Value.* Security should have a value which is stable and easy to check. The value should be at least that of the advance but usually a sufficient margin is required, especially where the value can fluctuate, as is the case with shares. Checking the value can involve merely consulting a table in the schedule of a life policy or an analysis of financial statements when shares in a private company are offered as security.

2 *Checking title and charging the security.* This should not be too costly or complicated, it is no good being offered excellent security for an urgent loan if you cannot check title and charge the security before the repayment date! The possible complexity of a charge over unregistered land can be compared with the simplicity of a charge over bearer securities – they are negotiable instruments and therefore title passes by delivery – in this respect.

3 *Protecting the security.* How easy is protection effected and how effective is it? A mortgage of land can be protected absolutely, for example, but protection is relatively complicated. Conversely, protection of a legal mortgage of a life policy is simple but not total. Your customer could develop a sudden fascination with some bizarrely dangerous activity and possibly invalidate the policy by killing him or herself.

4 *Realisation.* The security should command a ready market and be easy to realise. This is of the essence from a commercial point of view. It is commercial nonsense to lend over a two-year term and then have to rely on a security which takes three years to realise. Besides the attributes of individual types of security, you will see that property over which a legal mortgage is taken is easier to realise than that covered by an equitable mortgage.

A final point of general application and one based on basic legal principles is that it can be better to take security for a loan to Mr X from Ms Y or Mr Z rather than from Mr X himself. Technically this is known as taking *third party* security. The advantage is that you have completely separate rights against the debtor and, in effect, the guarantor. If the debtor will not pay, you can sue the debtor and threaten insolvency proceedings. If the debtor cannot, you can prove for your debt in the insolvency proceedings receiving whatever dividend is finally paid. The important point, however, is that your action against the debtor does not affect your rights against the security taken from the third party. These are still available to you. Thus, you are able to recover your money from two sources, independently or in combination.

ACTIVITY 7.2

Customers who wish to borrow usually realise that they will be asked to provide security for the borrowing. However, many of them are not aware of the attributes a bank looks for in the security offered. Write an explanatory letter to a customer who has enquired about this very point. Apart from the information above, research what other information or leaflets are available in your branch/bank which you could include with/utilise in your letter. Remember that you are writing to a customer on behalf of your bank. Thus, you must adopt a suitable style and tone, and comply with the accepted formalities of letter-writing and, of course, not use bank jargon.

Land

You already know that security is taken over land by executing a *mortgage*, that this creates an interest in the land mortgaged and that this interest can be legal or equitable. Thus, mortgages or land may be either legal or equitable. (The same is true for most other types of property taken as security.)

A *legal mortgagee* acquires *rights against the property itself* in addition to the personal action available against the mortgagor for the principal and interest due. An *equitable mortgage* gives no rights against the property, only *personal rights* against the borrower; principally a right to share in the proceeds of sale of the property when sold and a right to seek the court's aid in enforcing this right. Together with the different procedures used, the wider and more effective remedies given by a legal mortgage are today the main practical distinction between legal and equitable mortgages.

Legal mortgage

A legal mortgage is nearly always effected by a charge by deed expressed to be by way of legal mortgage. This legal charge was a creation of the Law of Property Act 1925. Before then, and very occasionally today, a mortgage of land was a form of lease.

In the case of *unregistered land*, the mortgage will be retained by a bank with the other title deeds. These will have previously been obtained from the prospective borrower. In the case of *registered land*, the mortgage (charge form) must be sent with a duplicate and the land certificate to the Land Registry. The Registrar will retain the land certificate and issue to the bank in its place a charge certificate which includes one sewn-in copy of the mortgage. The legal charge will be entered on the Charges Register. (*See* Fig 7.1.)

ACTIVITY 7.3

Study fig 7.1; this is a typical legal charge form used by banks. Work through this form (or one of your own bank's charge forms – it will use different forms for different situations) and discover the purpose and effect of the clauses. In particular discover the reasons for including clauses 1 and 7.2.

To do this you will need to refer to more advanced books on banking law, or bank security manuals or, on a suitable occasion, ask a colleague experienced in security work.

(In asking you to do this activity we realise that, strictly, we are going beyond the requirements of the syllabus. However, you will be acquiring relevant knowledge and this can only enhance your professional expertise.)

Equitable mortgage

A bank can create an equitable mortgage in one of two ways.

1 By taking a *deposit* of the *title deeds* or *land certificate* together with *a written memorandum of deposit (contract)* incorporating all the terms of the mortgage and signed by the bank and the mortgagor. (Before the Law of Property (Miscellaneous Provisions) Act 1989 changed the law by requiring all contracts relating to land to be in writing, a deposit of the land certificate alone created an equitable mortgage.)

197

**The Royal Bank
of Scotland plc**

Legal Charge

Secs 3 (Personal)

THIS IS AN IMPORTANT DOCUMENT. SIGN ONLY IF YOU WANT TO BE LEGALLY BOUND. YOU ARE RECOMMENDED TO TAKE INDEPENDENT LEGAL ADVICE BEFORE SIGNING.

Date: 19

Definitions

Mortgagor:

Bank: The Royal Bank of Scotland plc

Interest: Interest at the rate(s) charged to the Mortgagor by the Bank from time to time

Property:

(Land Registry Title No:)

Mortgagor's Obligations: All the Mortgagor's liabilities to the Bank of any kind (whether present or future actual or contingent and whether incurred alone or jointly with another) including banking charges and commission

Expenses: All expenses (on a full indemnity basis) incurred by the Bank or any Receiver at any time in connection with the Property or the Mortgagor's Obligations or in taking or perfecting this deed or in preserving defending or enforcing the security constituted by this deed or in exercising any power under this deed or otherwise with Interest from the date they are incurred

Charge

1   The Mortgagor covenants to discharge on demand the Mortgagor's Obligations together with Interest to the date of discharge and Expenses and as a continuing security for such discharge and as beneficial owner:–

1.1   Charges the Property to the Bank (to the full extent of the Mortgagor's interest in the Property or its proceeds of sale) by way of legal mortgage of all legal interests and otherwise by way of specific equitable charge

1.2   Assigns to the Bank the benefit of all covenants and rights affecting or concerning the Property subject to re-assignment on redemption

Repair Alteration and Insurance

2.1   The Mortgagor will keep the Property in good condition and comprehensively insured to the Bank's reasonable satisfaction for its full reinstatement cost and in default the Bank (without becoming liable to account as mortgagee in possession) may enter and repair or insure the Property. The Mortgagor will deposit with the Bank the insurance policy or where the Bank agrees a copy of it

Fig 7.1 A legal charge

2.2   The Mortgagor will not make any alteration to the Property without the prior written consent of the Bank

2.3   The Mortgagor will hold in trust for the Bank all money received under any insurance of the Property and at the Bank's option will apply the same in making good the relevant loss or damage or in or towards discharge of the Mortgagor's Obligations Interest and Expenses

Restrictions on Charging Leasing Disposing and Parting with possession

3   The Mortgagor will not without the Bank's prior written consent:–

3.1   Create or permit to arise any mortgage charge or lien on the Property and the Mortgagor requests the Chief Land Registrar to enter a restriction on the Register of any Registered Land that except under an order of the Registrar no disposition by the proprietor(s) of the land is to be registered without the consent of the registered proprietor of this deed

3.2   Grant or accept a surrender of any lease or licence of the Property

3.3   Dispose of or part with or share possession or occupation of the Property

Powers of the Bank

4.1   The Bank may without restriction grant or accept surrenders of leases of the Property

4.2   Section 103 of the Law of Property Act 1925 shall not apply and the Bank may exercise its power of sale and other powers under that or any other Act or this deed at any time after the date of this deed

4.3   The Bank may under the hand of any official or manager or by deed appoint or remove a Receiver or Receivers of the Property and may fix and pay the fees of a Receiver but any Receiver shall be deemed to be the agent of the Mortgagor and the Mortgagor shall be solely responsible for the Receiver's acts defaults and remuneration

4.4   All or any of the powers conferred on a Receiver by Clause 5 may be exercised by the Bank without first appointing a Receiver or notwithstanding any appointment

4.5   The Bank will not be liable to account to the Mortgagor as mortgagee in possession for any money not actually received by the Bank

4.6   Section 93(1) of the Law of Property Act 1925 shall not apply to this deed

Receivers

5.1   A Receiver shall (in addition to all powers conferred on him by law) have full power to carry out work at or sell lease charge deal with dispose of and manage the Property and do anything which he considers conducive or incidental to managing and realising the Property or the income from the Property and he may borrow any money he requires for those purposes

5.2   A Receiver shall have power to remove store and dispose of any furniture or goods found in the Property which the Mortgagor shall refuse or omit to remove and the Receiver will account to the Mortgagor for the proceeds of any sale after deducting all Expenses incurred under this sub-clause

5.3   In the case of Joint Receivers any power may be exercised jointly or severally

5.4   A Receiver shall apply all money he receives first in repayment of all money borrowed by him and his expenses and liabilities and in payment of his fees and secondly towards the remaining matters specified in Section 109(8) of the Law of Property Act 1925

Power of Attorney

6   The Mortgagor hereby irrevocably appoints the Bank and any Receiver severally to be the Attorney of the Mortgagor (with full power of substitution and delegation) in the Mortgagor's name and on the Mortgagor's behalf and as the Mortgagor's act and deed to sign or execute all deeds instruments and documents which may be required by the Bank or any Receiver pursuant to this deed or the exercise of any of their powers

Appropriation

7.1   Subject to Clause 7.2 the Bank may appropriate all payments received for the account of the Mortgagor in reduction of any part of the Mortgagor's Obligations Interest and Expenses as the Bank decides

7.2   The Bank may open a new account or accounts upon the Bank receiving actual or constructive notice of any charge or interest affecting the Property and whether or not the Bank opens any such account no payment received by the Bank for the account of the Mortgagor after receiving such notice shall (if followed by any payment out of or debit to the Mortgagor's account) be appropriated towards or have the effect of discharging any part of the Mortgagor's Obligations outstanding at the time of receiving such notice

Preservation of other Security and Rights and Further Assurance

8.1   This deed is in addition to any other security present or future held by the Bank for the Mortgagor's Obligations and shall not merge with or prejudice such other security or any contractual or legal rights of the Bank

8.2   The Mortgagor will at the Mortgagor's own cost at the Bank's request execute any deed or document and take any action required by the Bank to perfect this security or further to secure on the Property the Mortgagor's Obligations

Notices

9.1   Any notice or demand by the Bank may be sent by post or telex or delivered to the Mortgagor at the above address or the Mortgagor's address last known to the Bank

9.2   A notice or demand by the Bank by post shall be deemed served on the day after posting

9.3   A notice or demand by the Bank by telex shall be deemed served at the time of sending

Governing Law

10   This deed shall be governed by and construed in accordance with the laws of England

Interpretation

11.1   The expressions 'Mortgagor' and 'Bank' where the context admits include their respective successors in title and assigns

11.2   If two or more persons are included in the expression 'Mortgagor' then the use in this deed of the word 'Mortgagor' shall be deemed to refer to such persons both together and separately and the Mortgagor's Obligations shall be their joint and several obligations and each of them shall be primarily liable by way of indemnity for the liabilities to the Bank of the other or others of them

11.3   References to the 'Property' include any part of it

11.4   Interest will be calculated both before and after demand or judgment on a daily basis and compounded quarterly on such days as the Bank may select but after a demand Interest will also be calculated on the Mortgagor's Obligations together with accrued Interest as at the date of the demand

In Witness whereof this deed has been duly executed

Signed and **Delivered** as a deed
by the first named Mortgagor
in the presence of:–

                          _____

Witness' name in full

_____

_____

Signature

_____

Address

_____

Occupation

Signed and **Delivered** as a deed
by the second named Mortgagor
in the presence of:–

                          _____

Witness' name in full

_____

_____

Signature

_____

Address

_____

Occupation

2 By taking an *equitable charge*. Such a charge is unusual since it would be unaccompanied by the title deeds but it can be created by any written memorandum (contract) signed by the parties in which the terms of the agreement including the security arrangements are detailed. As you should remember, the charge creates no actual interest in the property, but the bank can seek the court's sanction for the sale of the property if repayment is not made.

Since an equitable mortgage does not convey a legal interest in the property to the mortgagee, the mortgage cannot be enforced without the consent of the court. In other words, an equitable mortgagee (unless the mortgage was taken by deed, *see* below) cannot sell the property without the court's permission while a legal mortgagee can. It is for this reason that the bank's standard *memorandum of deposit* includes an undertaking to execute a legal mortgage as and when called upon to do so by the bank (*see* Fig 7.2).

ACTIVITY 7.4

(a) Identify the clause in the memorandum of deposit reproduced in fig 7.2 which imposes on the borrower the undertaking to execute a legal mortgage when called upon to do so by the bank.

(b) Repeat activity 7.3 for fig 7.2, this time concentrating on clauses 3.3, 5 and 11.2.

Second mortgages

It is possible for any number of mortgages, legal or equitable, to exist at the same time over one piece of land. A bank may be prepared to accept a second mortgage as security for an advance if the value of the property is sufficient to repay both the first mortgage and the proposed second mortgage, i.e. there is sufficient *equity* in the property.

The main disadvantage of a second mortgage is that the first mortgagee may exercise their legal remedies (*see* below) without reference to, and therefore to the possible detriment of, the second mortgagee.

A second legal mortgage is usually created by a legal charge and a second equitable mortgage by a general equitable charge. No deposit of title deeds or land certificate is possible. The former will be in the possession of the first mortgagee and the latter will be in the possession of the Land Registry.

Procedure on taking a mortgage over land

In due course you may attend a securities course on which you will learn the procedure for taking a mortgage over land and other types of property in detail. Here we give you just an outline. (Remember that in your examination you will be tested on the legal aspects of the process and not on the wider banking operation aspects.)

1 *Title.* The first step is to *investigate the customer's title* to the land. This may be done by an experienced member of staff or by a solicitor. A search must be made of:

- the Land Charges Register (unregistered land), or the Land Registry

The Royal Bank of Scotland plc

Memorandum of Deposit of Securities (with Transfers)
Secs 19

THIS IS AN IMPORTANT DOCUMENT. SIGN ONLY IF YOU WANT TO BE LEGALLY BOUND. YOU ARE RECOMMENDED TO TAKE INDEPENDENT LEGAL ADVICE BEFORE SIGNING.

Date: 19

Definitions

Mortgagor:

Bank: The Royal Bank of Scotland plc

Interest: Interest at the rate(s) charged to the Mortgagor by the Bank from time to time

Securities:

Together with all other stocks shares bonds or other securities at any time deposited with or transferred to the Bank or its nominee by the Mortgagor

Mortgagor's Obligations: All the Mortgagor's liabilities to the Bank of any kind (whether present or future actual or contingent and whether incurred alone or jointly with another) including banking charges and commission

Expenses: All expenses (on a full indemnity basis) incurred by the Bank at any time in connection with the Securities or the Mortgagor's Obligations or in taking or perfecting this deed or in preserving defending or enforcing the security constituted by this deed or in exercising any power under this deed or otherwise with Interest from the date they are incurred

Charge

1   The Mortgagor covenants to discharge on demand the Mortgagor's Obligations together with Interest to the date of discharge and Expenses and as a continuing security for such discharge and as beneficial owner charges to the Bank the Securities and all income derived from the Securities and all rights attaching to the Securities

Fig 7.2 Memorandum of deposit

Undertakings by the Mortgagor

2.1 The Mortgagor undertakes to deposit with the Bank all documents relating to any bonus or rights or other issue of stock or shares in respect of the Securities

2.2 The Mortgagor undertakes to pay all calls or other payments due from time to time in respect of the Securities

Powers of the Bank

3.1 Section 103 of the Law of Property Act 1925 shall not apply and the Bank shall have the power to sell the Securities in whole or in part at any time after the date of this deed

3.2 The Bank may at its discretion pay any calls or other payments due from time to time in respect of the Securities or payable in respect of any rights attaching to the Securities

3.3 Section 93(1) of the Law of Property Act 1925 shall not apply to this deed

Restrictions on Charging

4 The Mortgagor will not without the Bank's prior written consent create or permit to arise any mortgage charge or lien on the Securities

Power of Attorney

5 The Mortgagor hereby irrevocably appoints the Bank to be the Attorney of the Mortgagor (with full power of substitution and delegation) in the Mortgagor's name and on the Mortgagor's behalf and as the Mortgagor's act and deed to sign or execute all deeds instruments and documents which may be required by the Bank pursuant to this deed or the exercise of any of its powers

Return of Similar Securities on Discharge

6 On discharge of this deed the Mortgagor will accept in place of all or any of the Securities delivery of other securities of the same class and denomination

Appropriation

7.1 Subject to Clause 7.2 the Bank may appropriate all payments received for the account of the Mortgagor in reduction of any part of the Mortgagor's Obligations Interest and Expenses as the Bank decides

7.2 The Bank may open a new account or accounts upon the Bank receiving actual or constructive notice of any charge or interest affecting the Securities and whether or not the Bank opens any such account no payment received by the Bank for the account of the Mortgagor after receiving such notice shall (if followed by any payment out of or debit to the Mortgagor's account) be appropriated towards or have the effect of discharging any part of the Mortgagor's Obligations outstanding at the time of receiving such notice

Preservation of other Security and Rights and Further Assurance

8.1 This security is in addition to any other security present or future held by the Bank for the Mortgagor's Obligations and shall not merge with or prejudice such other security or any contractual or legal rights of the Bank

8.2 The Mortgagor will at the Mortgagor's own cost at the Bank's request execute any deed or document and take any action required by the Bank to perfect this security or further to secure on the Securities the Mortgagor's Obligations

Notices

9.1 Any notice or demand by the Bank may be sent by post or telex or delivered to the Mortgagor at the above address or the Mortgagor's address last known to the Bank or if the Mortgagor is a company may be served personally on any director or the secretary of the Mortgagor

9.2 A notice or demand by the Bank by post shall be deemed served on the day after posting

9.3 A notice or demand by the Bank by telex shall be deemed served at the time of sending

Governing Law

10 This deed shall be governed by and construed in accordance with the laws of England

Interpretation

11.1 The expressions 'Mortgagor' and 'Bank' where the context admits include their respective successors in title and assigns

11.2 If two or more persons are included in the expression 'Mortgagor' then the use in this deed of the word 'Mortgagor' shall be deemed to refer to such persons both together and separately and the Mortgagor's Obligations shall be their joint and several obligations and each of them shall be primarily liable by way of indemnity for the liabilities to the Bank of the other or others of them

11.3 Interest will be calculated both before and after demand or judgment on a daily basis and compounded quarterly on such days as the Bank may select but after a demand Interest will also be calculated on the Mortgagor's Obligations together with accrued Interest as at the date of the demand

In Witness whereof this deed has been duly executed

Signed and Delivered as a deed by the Mortgagor
acting by a director and its secretary or two directors

)
)
)
)
)
)

_____
Director

_____
Secretary/Director

Signed and Delivered as a deed
by the first named Mortgagor
in the presence of:–

Witness' name in full _____

_____

Signature _____

Address _____

_____

Occupation _____

Signed and Delivered as a deed
by the second named Mortgagor
in the presence of:–

Witness' name in full _____

_____

Signature _____

Address _____

_____

Occupation _____

Registers (registered land);
● the Local Land Charges Register.

Where a company mortgages its land a search must also be made of the Registrar of Companies Register of Charges .

The searches are made to ensure that the proposed security and the customer's title to it are not subject to unacceptable adverse claims.

The decision in *Williams and Glyn's Bank Ltd v Boland and Another* (1980) highlighted the need to identify all occupiers of registered land and secure their agreement to the owner's mortgage in order to avoid an *overriding interest* prejudicing the right to realise the security and therefore its value.

2 *Valuation.* The next step is to *value the property*. Obviously the value must be sufficient to cover the advance. If a second mortgage is proposed there must be sufficient equity in the property after the first mortgage has been repaid in full. The valuation may be carried out by branch staff or by a professional surveyor, particularly when business property is offered as security.

3 *Insurance.* Insurance cover must then be checked and approved. Notice of the bank's interest must be given to the company concerned.

4 *Execution.* Having completed or checked these things the mortgage is then *executed.* On a *mortgage of unregistered land* the mortgagor must sign the bank's appropriate mortgage forms and acknowledge receipt of the advance in writing. The title deeds to the land, if available, must be deposited with the bank.

On a *mortgage of registered land* the mortgagor must execute the appropriate charge and stamp it. The charge must be registered at the Land Registry.

5 *Protection.* Lastly, the bank's position as mortgagee must be *protected by registration* where necessary. A mortgage of unregistered land, whether legal or equitable, *accompanied* by a deposit of the title deeds cannot be registered. An exception exists where the mortgage is given by a company. In this case, it must be registered in accordance with s.395 of the Companies Act 1985. This is done by lodging particulars of the charge (not the charge itself) accompanied by the appropriate form with the Registrar of Companies within 21 days of executing the mortgage.

Any mortgage which is *unaccompanied* by a deposit of the title deeds requires registration as a Class C charge at the Land Charges Registry. If legal it is registered as a puisne mortgage, if equitable as a general equitable charge. (Most such mortgages are second mortgages.) If the mortgage is a *floating charge* created by a company, it can only be registered with the Registrar of Companies.

A *legal* mortgage of registered land must be protected by sending to the Land Registry the land certificate, the original charge certificate and a duplicate, an application form and the Land Registry fee. The Registrar will register the charge, retain the duplicate and the cover of the land certificate and return the charge certificate to the bank.

As you have seen, an *equitable* mortgage of registered land is usually created by a deposit of the land certificate with the bank together with a memorandum of deposit (contract) signed by both the bank and the mortgagor. By doing this the bank acquires a (contractual) 'lien' on the land certificate which takes effect subject to overriding interests, registered interests and any existing entries on the register. The mortgage must be protected by sending a notice of deposit of a land certificate to the Land Registry signed by the mortgagor. The land certificate should also be sent so it can be endorsed with the notice of deposit. After endorsement, it will be returned to the bank. A bank is often prepared to have a legal charge form executed but hold it unregistered to save its customer and Land Registry fees. Such an arrangement creates only an equitable mortgage, however, and must be protected by a notice of deposit of a land certificate. The legal charge can, nevertheless, be registered at any time. This would be done, for example, if the bank thought it might have to rely on the mortgage in the near future and wished to strengthen its legal position.

ACTIVITY 7.5

Design and draw a flow-chart, suitable for use by junior staff or useful as information to customers, to show the steps involved in taking a mortgage over land. Do not forget to distinguish between legal and equitable mortgages. (A source of ideas may be your own bank's checklist for taking a charge or its security manual.)

For examination purposes make sure that you can distinguish between the *legal* and *procedural* steps involved in taking a mortgage. You will be sitting an examination in the *law* of banking, not its practice, and questions on this topic invariably emphasise the *legal* steps involved.

The mortgagee's (bank's) remedies

We explained in Chapter 4 how banks in common with all other business organisations always endeavour to use the law to their advantage. Standard form mortgages are an excellent example of this. Few customers are in a position to negotiate the basic terms of a mortgage and it is doubtful whether any customer would succeed in varying the standard terms relating to the bank's remedies for non-payment. While the loan may be of the utmost commercial advantage to the customer, legally a bank ensures that it has the advantage; all possible remedies will be available should the security have to be realised.

Another important preliminary point to make is that the distinction between legal and equitable mortgages really becomes important (at least in theory) when a security needs to be realised. A *legal mortgagee's* rights are superior to those of an equitable mortgagee. This is because an equitable mortgage only gives a right of action against the borrower personally while a legal mortgage gives rights to action against the property mortgaged in addition. Thus, an equitable mortgagee is unable to take action against the property mortgaged without the court's sanction and help. We say that an equitable mortgagee has a right *in personam* (against the person) while a legal mortgagee also has rights *in rem* (against the property). (But *see* equitable mortgages by deed below.)

Legal mortgagee. A legal mortgagee has five remedies. These may be used in any combination at the same time to ensure that the full debt is recovered.

1 *An action for the debt.* This is a personal action against the borrower for breach of the covenant to repay taken to recover the capital sum and any interest owed. It avoids the delay and effort involved in realising the security but it is only suitable where non-payment is the result of unwillingness rather than inability. This remedy is, of course, a general remedy and it is available to an unsecured creditor.

2 *Sale of the property.* Every mortgage *by deed* (legal or equitable) confers on the mortgagee the power to sell the mortgaged property. However, as you might expect, this power can only be exercised if one of certain conditions is fulfilled, specifically, under the Law of Property Act 1925, s.103:

- a demand for repayment has been made and the borrower has been in default for three months; or
- interest under the mortgage is two or more months in arrears; or
- the mortgagor has broken some other term of the mortgage.

In practice, the bank mortgage forms exclude the operation of s.103, and enable banks to exercise the power of sale immediately a demand for repayment of capital and/or interest is not met.

If the property is *occupied*, fulfilling one of these conditions is still not enough however. The bank must apply to the court for a possession order followed by an application for eviction if the borrower refuses to do the decent thing and go quietly! To avoid such an unpleasant process, a bank will usually give the borrower every reasonable opportunity to sell voluntarily. Particular protection is given to a spouse who has registered his or her right of occupation under the Matrimonial Homes Act 1983 of a house solely owned by the other spouse. Remember also the overriding interest that can arise in registered land under the *Boland* principle (*see* page 166).

A bank forced to exercise its power of sale is under a duty to take reasonable care to obtain the true value of the property. For example, in *Cuckmere Brick Co Ltd v Mutual Finance Ltd* (1971), the plaintiff company borrowed £50,000 from the defendant, mortgaging a building site with planning permission for 100 flats as security. Subsequently, with the defendant's permission, they obtained alternative planning permission for thirty-three houses. Some five years later the advance was called in and the site advertised for sale without any building having been started. Despite the plaintiff's protest, no mention of the planning permission was made in the advertisements for the property, which was eventually sold. The plaintiffs were able to establish that a much higher price would have been obtained for the land if the advertisements had mentioned the planning permission. The defendants were held liable for the difference between the two values.

3 *Appointment of a receiver.* A bank would appoint a receiver (of rent) where:

- a sale is impractical, for example, if the property is let; or
- where the property market is depressed and a sale would be unlikely to realise sufficient to repay the advance.

The power to appoint a receiver arises when the mortgagee becomes entitled to exercise the power of sale.

The money collected must be applied in the following order:

(a) in payment of outgoings such as rates and taxes;

(b) in payment of interest on prior charges, if any;

(c) in payment of insurances required by law or by the mortgage, and of the receiver's commission;

(d) in payment of interest due to the bank; and

(e) towards repayment of the principal debt due.

4 *Foreclosure.* This is an extreme remedy and requires the court's consent. Stated simply, foreclosure deprives the mortgagor (borrower) of the equitable right to redeem the mortgaged property (*see* below) and the property becomes the mortgagee's absolutely. It makes no difference if the value of the property greatly exceeds the debt outstanding.

In practice, this remedy is no longer used. While the term 'foreclosure' is sometimes encountered, it invariably means that the mortgagee has entered into possession and exercised their statutory power of sale. In the late 1980s and early 1990s a fall in property values and an economic recession saw an increase in the number of mortgagors either unable to meet their repayments or with properties worth less than their mortgage debt or both. Sometimes properties were simply abandoned. It is probably to these cases that the term 'foreclosure' is most commonly applied.

5 *Taking possession of the property.* Originally, a mortgagee could exercise this right even if there has not been a breach of the mortgage! It is usual for the mortgage to provide, however, that this right shall not be exercised unless the mortgagor defaults in repayment. A bank will seldom take possession of mortgaged property because appointing a receiver achieves the same results without the expense and accountability involved in taking possession.

Equitable mortgagee. It makes a difference whether the mortgage was merely *in writing* (under hand) or contained in *a deed*. If the former (under hand, as it is known), the bank (the mortgagee) only has a right (*in personam*) against the mortgagor. Thus, a bank holding an equitable mortgage under hand cannot take direct action against the property mortgaged by its customer, it must obtain the court's sanction and aid to realise the security.

A bank's remedies available will include:

1 *an action for the money due*;

2 *an action for specific performance* of the borrower's undertaking to execute a legal mortgage when requested to do so by the bank;

3 *an action for the sale of the property*;

4 the right to apply to the court for the *appointment of a receiver*;

5 *an action for foreclosure* (never sought);

6 if expressly given by the mortgage, a *right to take possession*.

If the mortgage was *by deed*, the bank, for practical purposes, is in the same position as if a legal mortgage had been executed. This is because an equitable mortgage by deed gives a statutory power of sale and, if included in the deed, the power to appoint a receiver, the two most useful remedies to a bank.

Redemption of mortgages

A mortgage is redeemed by the mortgagor repaying the advance. Once the mortgagee acknowledges receipt of the money the mortgage automatically terminates.

A mortgagor has a legal (contractual) right to redeem the property on the date stipulated in the mortgage. After this the contractual right to take back the property is lost. A moment's reflection will tell you that if enforced rigidly, this 'legal' right to redeem would be extremely inflexible and potentially unfair. In fact, several centuries ago it was not unknown for mortgagees to hide or generally make themselves unavailable on the contractual redemption date. They would then take possession of the land and bring an action for the debt a few days later, on the grounds that the debt had not been repaid according to the terms of the contract – which of course it had not. Quite an amazing state of affairs (to us) but, at the time, quite legal and enforced by the courts.

Gradually, however, equity began to take the view that a mortgage was given only as a security and that it was never intended to transfer title to the land to the mortgagee unless the mortgagor had no reasonable chance of repaying the loan – 'Equity looks to intent not to form.' is a general principle of equity. Thus, equity allowed a mortgagor to redeem property after the legal redemption date was passed provided:

- reasonable notice was given; and
- the principal and interest, and the mortgagor's expenses were paid.

This became known as the *equity of redemption*. Today, any term of a mortgage which attempts to prevent the borrower eventually redeeming the mortgaged property is void.

In relation to bank mortgages the equity of redemption is of more academic than practical interest because bank mortgages are repayable on demand, not on a specific date. However, the principle still applies and the mortgagor must be given the opportunity to repay.

Attributes as security

Advantages 1 A mortgage of land has one overriding advantage: *land never completely loses its value.* Indeed, a first legal mortgage of freehold land is the surest security that a bank can take.
2 Land has historically always *appreciated in value.*

Disadvantages 1 Land is sometimes *difficult to value* for security purposes; for example, where the value depends heavily on planning consent, the possibility of this lapsing must be considered.
2 Greater *difficulty and formality* attach to a mortgage of land than to other forms of security.

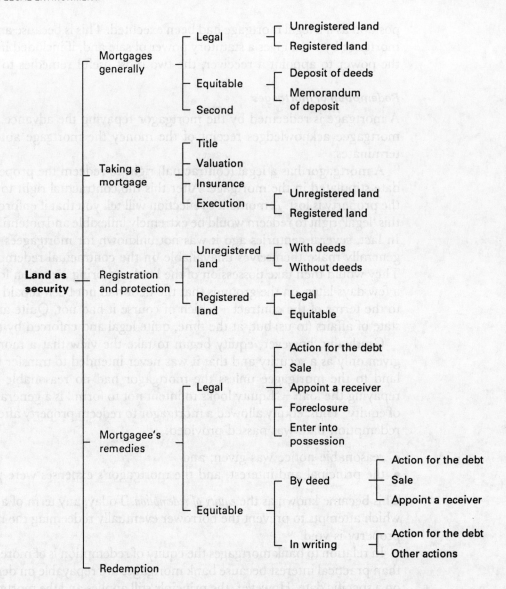

Fig 7.3 Land as security

3 Land is *not an easily realisable security*. In addition, realisation of the security could possibly lead to bad publicity, although a bank would never sell mortgaged property, particularly a dwelling house, unless all other practical possibilities for repayment had been explored without success.

4 A *second mortgagee* is subject to the rights of the first mortgagee.

5 Unless the mortgage is taken by deed, an equitable mortgagee must seek the *court's sanction* in any action for realisation of the security.

Stocks and shares

Of the two types of stocks and shares (registered and bearer) which we described in the previous chapter, it is registered stocks and shares, stock exchange securities in particular, that are usually taken as security.

Registered stocks and shares

Legal mortgage. A legal mortgage is effected by transferring legal title to the shares to the bank or, more usually, to its nominee company. In practice, most banks will prefer not to go this far in order to avoid the administrative cost which would follow from being registered as the holder of the shares and therefore receiving all communications from the company to its shareholders. An equitable mortgage, including a blank transfer (*see* below), is usually preferred.

Equitable mortgage. An equitable mortgage is created by merely depositing the share certificates. It is, however, standard practice to take a memorandum of deposit which expressly sets out the terms of the arrangement. In addition a bank will often take a *blank transfer* to strengthen its position. This is an incomplete transfer form, usually omitting the transferee's name but bearing details of the securities and the mortgagor's signature as transferor. This enables a bank to transfer legal ownership of the securities to its nominee company by inserting its name as transferee (thereby completing the document) and registering the transfer whenever it considers it necessary to do so. Alternatively, the transfer may be completed in favour of a purchaser if the bank exercises its power of sale under the mortgage.

A bank holding an equitable mortgage without a blank transfer would have to obtain a court order for the sale of the securities if its customer was uncooperative.

The introduction of Taurus (see Chapter 6) will not affect taking legal mortgages over shares in private companies at all and probably have little affect on the procedure for taking legal mortgages over shares in listed public companies. However, the method by which equitable mortgages over shares in listed public companies is taken must change unless the shares are withdrawn from Taurus. It is likely to be possible to register some form of 'caution' against the owner of the shares on the company's register and make appropriate amendments to the memorandum taken as evidence of the mortgage. Equitable mortgages over shares in private or unlisted public companies, as well as those withdrawn from Taurus, will presumably be taken in exactly the same way as at present. (When Taurus is introduced, discover how it affects your bank's policy and procedures for taking mortgages over shares in the Taurus system.)

Realising the securities. Should this be necessary, we again are concerned with the practical effects of the distinction between legal and equitable mortgages. A *legal mortgage* gives a bank the right to sell the securities on default in repayment. The advance is usually repayable on demand. If a blank transfer was taken with an *equitable mortgage*, this may be completed and the shares sold. If it was not, the borrower's consent and cooperation or a court order is required for the sale of the securities.

Bearer securities

Bearer securities are negotiable instruments and legal title to them is transferred by delivery. This means that they can be mortgaged just by depositing them with the bank. Provided that the securities are taken in good faith, for value (consideration is given for them) and without notice of any defect in the customer's title, the bank obtains a perfect legal title to them. It is usual, however, to take a memorandum of deposit in support of the deposit. This will specify the purpose of the deposit and confer on the bank an express power of sale if the overdraft is not repaid on demand.

If you think about it, equitable mortgages of bearer securities do not arise because a legal mortgage is obtained by their mere deposit.

Unit trusts

Trusts give rise to equitable interests in the trust property and therefore the holder of the units only has an equitable interest in them. This, in turn, means that only an *equitable mortgage* of unit trust certificates is possible.

The mortgage can be created in two ways:

- by transferring the units into the name of the bank's nominee company and taking a memorandum of deposit, or
- by depositing the certificates, which remain in the customer's name, with a memorandum of deposit.

In the latter case the form of renunciation on the back of the certificate may be signed by the mortgagor because this will enable the bank to send the certificates to the managers of the trust and obtain repayment. Alternatively, a blank stock transfer form may be taken which enables a later transfer into the name of the bank's nominee company to be made. Notice of the charge should be sent to the managers who will acknowledge and record it.

Attributes as security

Advantages 1 The customer's *title* to the securities can easily be established.
2 The *current value* of quoted stocks and shares can be ascertained easily and fairly precisely.
3 The security can be taken with *little difficulty*, formality or expense.
4 A legal mortgage can *easily and effectively be protected* by registering the mortgagee as holder of the shares in the books of the company.
5 Long-term *stability in value*, despite periodical set-backs; a mixed portfolio of shares as security enhances this advantage.
6 The security can *easily be realised* by selling on a stock exchange if a legal mortgage is held or a blank transfer was taken with an equitable mortgage.
7 *Release* of the security is easy.
8 *Bearer securities* have additional advantages, in particular:

- as negotiable instruments, title to them passes by mere delivery and a mortgagee acquires a perfect title despite any defect in or even non-existence of the mortgagor's title;

- the mortgage requires no formalities;
- the securities can be sold without reference to the mortgagor or to the court.

Disadvantages Certain disadvantages attach to certain types of stocks and shares and there is one general disadvantage − 1 below:

1 Fluctuations in *market value*: at best a forced sale in a depressed market would be to your customer's disadvantage and at worst would realise insufficient funds to repay the advance.
2 Shares are sometimes issued *partly paid* and these are occasionally encountered as security. When a call is made for the balance due on the shares, they are forfeited if the call is not paid. If held as security the bank may have to pay the call for its customer in order to retain its security. If a legal mortgage was taken over them, the bank, as their registered holder, is directly liable to pay. In addition, such shares are less marketable than fully paid-up shares.
3 *Unquoted shares*: these are normally associated with private companies but unquoted shares in public companies may sometimes be offered as security. They are both difficult to value and to realise. Under the terms of the company's articles, the shares may first have to be offered to existing company members who can to some extent, therefore, fix the selling price. Thus, the true value of the shares may not be realised and a mortgage of such shares is often considered as little more than evidence of a customer's financial status.
4 Shares in *private companies*: in addition to being difficult to value because they are unquoted, the company's articles of association will often affect their value as security. The articles may:

- prevent their use as security altogether;
- prevent another registered company, that is, the bank's nominee company holding them (only an equitable mortgage is possible in such a case); and/or
- restrict their transfer, thereby affecting their realisability.

Life policies

A bank will normally take a *legal mortgage* of a life policy by an *assignment by deed* of the mortgagor's rights to the policy moneys. (A deed is not actually required.) Written notice of the assignment *must* be given to the issuing company.

An *equitable mortgage* is taken by the policy being deposited with the bank, usually supported by a memorandum of deposit which sets out the purpose of the deposit (for security and not for safe custody), the terms of the mortgage and the rights of the bank as mortgagee. Equitable mortgages of life policies are comparatively rare because a legal mortgage is a much better security and is easily effected.

Attributes as security

Advantages 1 The *value* of a life policy can be easily determined, most do not fluctuate with market forces and most steadily increase in value.
2 *Title* to the policy can be easily checked.
3 *Realisation* of the security by a legal mortgagee is quick and simple.

Disadvantages 1 The mortgagor's *possible inability to pay the premiums*. If this happens the bank is put in the position of having to pay them in order to keep the policy alive if the advance has been allowed to exceed the current surrender value of the policy.

2 Some life policies are linked to unit trust investments and these can and do *fluctuate in value* in line with the general level of stock market investment. Thus, their surrender values can be reduced if stock market values are particularly depressed.

3 Possible *invalidation of the policy*, and hence the loss of the security, through the customer's breach of the *uberrimae fidei* obligation, or of the conditions in the policy. An insurance contract is one of the utmost good faith (*uberrimae fidei*) and the proposer (and the insurer) is under a duty of disclose all material facts, i.e. facts which would influence the judgment of a prudent insurer in fixing the premium or in deciding whether or not to accept the proposal. Failure by one party to do so makes the contract voidable at the option of the other. This rule applies however innocent the failure to disclose may be, e.g. no question was included on the proposal form relating to the specific information or, more likely, the answer 'No' was given in reply to a question such as 'Are there any other facts relevant to the proposal?'.

In practice, it is the proposer who is most affected by the rule since the proposer alone is in a position to know all the facts which might influence the insurer. An example of the rule working in the other direction would be where the insurer fails to disclose knowledge of previous dubious conduct by the broker with whom the proposer has dealt.

A life policy is likely to include an exclusion of cover if the policy holder indulges in inherently dangerous activities and death during such an activity renders the policy valueless to both the policy holder and the bank.

ACTIVITY 7.6

(a) Obtain a life policy proposal form; it is quite likely that your bank has them. Study it and identify the clause/question which embodies the *uberrimae fidei* obligation.

(b) If you have taken out life assurance find your policy and identify any exclusions that it contains. (If you have not taken out life assurance, ask to see the policy on the life of a member of your family or a friend.) Does any clause deal specifically with the assignment of the policy? (You may conceivably find a clause distinguishing between committing suicide while sane and while insane and the consequential rights of an assignee!)

Guarantees

In contrast to the other types of property we have covered, a guarantee involves a *personal obligation* and not the acquisition of rights over specific property. We are not, therefore, concerned with, say, legal or equitable mortgages, registration and protection, as we have been so far. Nevertheless, it is usual to take collateral security from the guarantor, for example, a deposit of title deeds or land certificate, to back up the personal undertaking unless there is absolutely no doubt about the guarantor's present and future ability and willingness to pay if called upon to do so. Where collateral security is taken, a bank must protect its position, according to the security taken, in the ways we have described above.

You should not understand from the above that taking a guarantee involves nothing more than obtaining a signature on a standard form. There are procedures to follow and pitfalls to avoid analogous to making searches and valuations in respect of land.

Legal capacity

The first step is to check the legal capacity of the principal debtor and the proposed guarantor. Regarding the former, you have already seen the potential problems posed by the lack of contractual capacity of clubs and societies. However, a loan can be safely made provided a suitable indemnity clause is included in the guarantee.

In relation to the legal capacity of the guarantor, certain special cases warrant a specific mention. If a bank takes a guarantee from two or more co-sureties they must accept *joint and several liability* so that if one of them dies the estate of the deceased remains liable on the guarantee; that surety may, for example, be the one with most funds.

A simple but important rule which must be rigidly adhered to is that a joint guarantee must be signed by all the guarantors. If it is not, it is not enforceable against any of them. In *National Provincial Bank v Brackenbury* (1906), for example, three out of four guarantors signed the guarantee and the bank advanced money in anticipation of the remaining signature. The fourth guarantor died without signing. In an action to enforce the guarantee, the failure to obtain the fourth guarantor's signature was held to discharge the liability of the other three.

Should one co-surety repay the whole debt, that surety has a right to compensation from the others in proportion to their respective liabilities under the guarantee.

Partnerships also require special care. A partner has no *implied* authority to give a guarantee in the firm name unless giving guarantees is part of the firm's usual course of business. You must, therefore, ensure that any guarantee given by a partnership is signed by all the partners in the firm.

A guarantee by a *registered company* must be accompanied by a certified copy of the board's resolution authorising it. To avoid any problems, banks provide draft resolutions for this purpose. Various statutory restrictions are imposed on a company's power to give a guarantee. For example, the Companies Act 1985, prohibits, with exceptions, a company from giving a guarantee which enables a person to purchase or subscribe for its own shares, or for those of its holding company; or guaranteeing a loan by a third person to one of its directors or a director of its holding company.

Reality of consent

A guarantee is a serious obligation to incur. In the final analysis a surety is inevitably at the mercy of the principal debtor's conduct and the law demands that the surety is in a position to make a free and independent decision whether or not to incur the obligation. Thus, a *misrepresentation of fact* by the creditor, in our case the bank, which misleads the surety will entitle the surety to avoid liability under the guarantee. (This is why security clerks are invariably told not to attempt to explain guarantees and security forms to customers just in case they misrepresent the effect of a clause. Customers should be told to consult a legal adviser of their own choice if they want any explanations.)

More subtle is the problem of *undue influence* which, if proved, again enables the surety to avoid the guarantee. Undue influence can take many forms but they all have the effect of preventing the person influenced from making a free and independent judgment. In some relationships, for example, solicitor and client, parent and child, a position of dominance is presumed to exist, in others it must be proved by the person seeking to avoid the guarantee. Where the party in the dominant position then victimises the weaker so that a contract between them is clearly to the advantage of the dominant party and to the disadvantage of the weaker party, then the weaker party can set the contract aside in equity (rescind) for undue influence. This is the ratio of *National Westminster Bank v Morgan* (1985) which we discussed in Chapter 4.

Occasionally a bank may be held to be in a position of dominance over a particular customer. Where this is so and a guarantee is offered by that customer, then the bank owes a very strict duty of care to the customer: *Lloyds Bank Ltd v Bundy* (1975), again discussed in Chapter 4. It should be pointed out, however, that this case arose more through bad banking practice than through anything else.

More commonly the potential for undue influence arises between the principal debtor and guarantor. Here the bank could be adversely affected where two conditions are satisfied.

- The dominant party acts at the bank's request and in effect as its agent to make the guarantee arrangements.
- The bank knows of the potential undue influence.

To avoid possible problems of undue influence a bank must ensure that a prospective guarantor receives independent legal advice before signing the guarantee whenever the bank considers it or the principal debtor is in a potential position of dominance over the prospective guarantor. A free will clause is consequently often included in the guarantee form to the effect that the surety understands the nature of the document and the liability incurred under it. Such a clause should be witnessed by the guarantor's own solicitor, or a similar professional adviser, who should sign the accompanying 'attestation clause'. This states that the nature of the guarantee and the obligations incurred under it have been explained to the guarantor.

No presumption of undue influence arises between husband and wife, although experience has shown that most problems concerning undue influence and guarantees occur when wives guarantee loans to their husbands. Remember in this context that any special treatment of a woman guarantor, such as including a 'free will' clause in her guarantee, must be based upon inability to understand or appreciate the arrangement, and not upon the grounds of sex: Sex Discrimination Act 1975. The usual practice is therefore to treat (quite rightly) all guarantors – be they male or female, married or single – in the exactly the same way. Indeed, your bank may adopt a policy of not taking a guarantee from anybody unless independent advice is first given.

Conceivably, a surety might subsequently maintain that they thought the guarantee that they signed was a completely different document; that he made a *mistake as to its nature*. A surety might maintain, for example, that they thought they were witnessing a conveyance or a will. Unlikely though this might seem, such a plea, known technically as a plea of *non est factum* (*see* page 104), could theoretically succeed. However, negligence on the surety's part, for example signing the guarantee without reading it, will defeat the plea.

The possible complication with *non est factum* can easily be avoided by ensuring that the guarantee is signed and witnessed at the bank or attested by a solicitor. In addition, this simple precaution would subsequently prevent the guarantor from successfully pleading that their signature had been forged.

Disclosure of information

A guarantee is not a contract *uberrimae fidei* (of the utmost good faith) as, for example, is a contract of insurance. This means that a bank is not under a duty to disclose to the guarantor all the facts known to it that may be relevant. Guarantors must obtain all the information they require. For example, in *Cooper v National Provincial Bank* (1945), the bank was held to be under no obligation to disclose to the guarantor of a wife's account that:

- her husband was an undischarged bankrupt;
- he had authority to draw on the account; and
- that the account had previously been operated in an improper and irregular fashion.

Nevertheless, a bank must obviously not mislead a prospective surety and it must ensure that any information volunteered is complete and true; and that it corrects an entire misunderstanding of the facts on the surety's part.

You will recall from Chapter 5 that a bank owes a duty of secrecy to its customer. A guarantee poses a conflict with this basic rule. Thus, it is either necessary to obtain the customer's authority to disclose relevant information to the prospective surety or to arrange a meeting with both parties to discuss any difficult situation.

With one exception (*see* below) a surety is not entitled to have or to inspect copies of the principal debtor's account but is entitled to know the extent of the liability under the guarantee. Care must be taken, however, because of the potential conflict with the bank's duty of confidentiality (*see* Chapter 5). The accepted practice is that where the debt does not exceed the guarantee, the surety can be told the actual amount of the guaranteed debt; where it does exceed the guarantee, merely that the guarantee is being fully relied upon. The exception to this practice of limited disclosure is where the guarantee is regulated by the Consumer Credit Act 1974 . Under the Act the surety has a statutory right (on payment of a small fee) to a statement of the principal debtor's account (whether it is in credit or debit), as well as to copies of the security document and the loan agreement.

If there is any material change in the principal debtor's circumstances, the bank is under no legal duty to advise the surety of this. Nevertheless, good banking practice normally demands that something should be done in order to avoid the guarantor being unfairly prejudiced by the debtor's action or situation. A meeting with the customer and surety can be arranged and, if need be, pressure exerted on the customer by a threat to demand repayment if the customer's co-operation is not forthcoming.

Attributes as security

Advantages 1 A guarantee is very *simple to take*: no registration is involved and no complications concerning proof of title arise. (Remember, of course, that it is usual to take other security in support of the guarantee and registration may be required and complications *may* arise here.)

2 A guarantee can *easily and immediately be enforced* by court action.

3 Since several parties can guarantee a loan, it is a useful security where a customer is unable to provide security but offers a viable business loan proposition.

Disadvantages 1 Unless supported by a cash deposit or collateral security, a guarantee is always of an *uncertain value* as a security; a guarantor's financial position can change very quickly. You should only accept an unsupported guarantee after careful investigation into the proposed guarantor's financial standing.

2 Court action may be necessary to *realise* the security, and a technicality may possibly defeat the bank's claim. For example, special rules apply to guarantees taken from partnerships and companies, although a defeat of the bank's claim would almost certainly be the result of carelessness when taking the security.

3 Many bankers hold the view that a guarantee is the easiest security to take but the hardest to enforce, in so far as liability to pay on a guarantee will often be contested.

ACTIVITY 7.7

(a) Obtain a copy of your bank's guarantee form (guarantee from an individual) and read it through carefully. Identify the *ultra vires* clause and ask a more senior colleague with experience of securities work to explain the other clauses it contains. Alternatively, you could do some research in more advanced text books on banking law and/or study your bank's securities manual. (You are not required to know the clauses and their effect for the examination but, as we said earlier, you have everything to gain if you make the effort to extend your knowledge and understanding.)

(b) Familiarise yourself with your bank's rules and procedures for disclosing information about the principal debtor's account to a surety when the guarantee is regulated by the Consumer Credit Act 1974.

Debentures

In common with guarantees, debentures do not themselves give rise to any rights over property, merely a right *in personam* against the issuing company. They are, remember, documents which merely acknowledge a loan. However, a bank will seldom take an unsecured debenture and (as with a supported guarantee) you must take the appropriate steps to register (if applicable) or otherwise protect the interest the bank acquires in the property charged to secure the debt.

A bank will almost invariably take a debenture on its standard terms, securing all moneys owing on any account held by the company at any time. Provided the bank has a free hand and there are no prior changes on the company's property, the debenture would normally be secured by a fixed charge on the goodwill of the business, book debts and any uncalled capital; a charge on any freehold or leasehold properties, including all fixtures and fixed plant and machinery from time to time in the properties; and a floating charge on all the other assets of the company. What you might call comprehensive security!

Registration of charges

In addition to any registration required by virtue of the nature of the property charged, the Companies Act 1985, s.395, requires that any charge (among others) to secure an issue of debentures be registered with the Registrar of Companies. This is done by sending details of the charge accompanied by Companies Form 395 to the Registrar of Companies.

By s.395, the registration must take place within *21 days* of the *creation of the charge*, i.e. the date it was executed, which is not necessarily the date it bears, and not within 21 days of the money being advanced.

The importance of making sure that a charge is registered in accordance with s.395 is that an unregistered charge is void against a liquidator or a subsequent registered mortgagee, even though the subsequent mortgagee has express notice of the prior unregistered charge. This does not, however, affect the actual loan acknowledged by the debenture, it becomes immediately repayable because of the other charge having been registered, and the bank's rights are reduced to those of an unsecured creditor. This means that if the company goes into liquidation, the bank's claim is postponed to those of secured creditors and preferential creditors such as the Inland Revenue (for unpaid PAYE) and employees (for unpaid salaries and wages). This must be borne in mind if you are ever asked to hold unregistered a charge from a company.

Remedies of the bank

A bank's debenture will protect its position by specifying in detail the circumstances in which it can intervene to enforce its security. Merely intervening strengthens its position in so far as it *crystallises* any floating charge contained in the debenture, i.e. the floating charge fixes on the property at that time covered.

If the bank holds an *unsecured debenture*, two remedies are available, it may:

1 sue for the principal and interest due; and

2 petition for the winding-up of the company on the grounds that it is unable to pay its debts.

If it holds a *secured debenture*, it may in addition:

3 exercise any of the powers conferred by the debenture, such as:

- appoint a receiver;
- sell the assets charged;
- take possession of the assets and carry on the business.

A bank's debenture form will contain the power to appoint a receiver on the company's failure to repay. This is the remedy usually chosen by banks.

A bank's debenture will provide that a receiver is the agent of the company in order that the company and not the bank is liable for the receiver's acts and remuneration. A receiver is under a duty to the company to use reasonable care to obtain the best possible price when selling the company's assets to make repayment. In *Standard Chartered Bank Ltd v Walker and Another* (1982), this duty was held to extend to a guarantor of the company's liability under the debenture because a guarantor is liable only to the same extent as the company – the more the overdraft is reduced, the better it is for the guarantor.

The facts were that the bank made a loan to a company secured by a debenture which gave the bank a floating charge on the company's assets and power to appoint a receiver. Subsequently, the directors of the company guaranteed the loan. The company's business declined and the bank eventually appointed a receiver, instructing him to realise the assets as soon as possible. He in turn instructed auctioneers to sell the company's machinery. This was expected to realise £90,000. The auction was a disaster and realised only £42,800 because it was held at the wrong time of year and was poorly advertised. This amount only just covered the costs of the realisation and, after payment of preferential creditors, nothing remained to pay off the bank's overdraft. The bank's action to enforce its guarantee was successfully defeated on the grounds of the incompetent conduct of the auction sale which the bank had authorised indirectly through its instruction to the receiver.

While the case is primarily concerned with the duties of a receiver (a receiver owes a duty to guarantors of a company's debts to get the best price when disposing of the assets), the Court of Appeal stated that a bank as mortgagee, despite what its debenture might say, is liable to the company and a guarantor of its indebtedness for the receiver's actions to the extent that it gives the receiver directions or interferes with the receiver's conduct, for example, giving specific instructions regarding a sale.

Attributes as security

Fixed charges. A fixed charge in a debenture – a legal or equitable mortgage of specific property, usually the company's premises – has the same general advantages and disadvantages as any charge over that particular type of property. In comparison with a floating charge it is to the *bank's advantage* in that specific property is always available as security for the advance, but to its disadvantage in that the property charged may depreciate in value. To a company, the disadvantage of a fixed charge is that it cannot dispose of the property charged without the bank's consent.

Floating charges. A floating charge is an equitable charge over the fluctuating assets of the company, for example its stock, which does not attach to any specific assets until it becomes fixed (crystallises). Until this happens (*see* page 191), the company can freely dispose of its assets; clearly an advantage to the company. A bank obtains the *advantage* of a range of assets as security under such a charge but the *disadvantages* of a floating charge are such that you should not take one by itself unless no other security can be offered.

It is beyond the scope of this book to look in any detail at the defects of a floating charge because they involve fairly difficult points of law. However, we will outline the main disadvantages.

1 There is a danger that the *assets of the company may be run down.* Since a company can freely dispose of the assets charged, your position depends to a certain extent upon the conduct of the company. It could, for example, realise the assets to repay other creditors. You should therefore ensure that the assets charged are maintained at a satisfactory level, although this is still no protection against a sudden depletion of the assets or a sudden and unforeseen fall in their value.

2 A *subsequent fixed charge on the company's assets takes priority* over an existing floating charge *unless* the person taking the subsequent fixed charge had notice of a clause in the floating charge preventing the company from creating a charge which would rank before or equally with the floating charge.

Such a clause is known as a 'negative pledge' clause and (since mid-1991) requires registration with the Registrar of Companies to be effective. Such registration is deemed to be notice to the world whether or not the subsequent chargeholder actually knew about the clause. In practice, such clauses will almost certainly be registered and therefore the floating chargeholder will gain protection against subsequent fixed charges. Thus, this disadvantage is more apparent than real.

3 The rights of a holder of a floating charge are subject to a variety of other *postponements*, principally to the rights of preferential creditors after crystallisation of the charge and to the rights of unpaid suppliers protected by a 'Romalpa clause' in their contract of sale. Both of these require a little explanation.

In a bankruptcy or liquidation there are certain categories of creditors. As the name suggests, *preferential creditors* are accorded a certain degree of preference. While they rank after creditors secured by a fixed charge, they rank before creditors secured by a floating charge and unsecured creditors. Examples of preferential claims include the Inland Revenue for PAYE income tax due for any one financial year and employees' wages and salaries due for the four months prior to the bankruptcy or liquidation subject to a maximum of £800 for each claimant.

The inclusion of '*Romalpa clauses*' in contracts for the sale of goods in now common. In essence they mean that the supplier retains the title to the goods supplied until payment for them is received. If the buyer subsequently becomes bankrupt or goes into liquidation, the supplier ranks before both preferential creditors and those secured by floating charges. This is fair enough, but it puts a bank offered a floating charge over a company's assets or security in a difficult position. The security may prove illusory but unless the bank is actually told about the arrangement it has no way of knowing about it. A Romalpa clause can, of course, also seriously affect the apparent strength of the company's balance sheet – a factor to be taken into account when the lending decision is being made. (The clause takes its name from the decision in *Aluminium Industries Vassen BV v Romalpa Aluminium Ltd* (1976), more generally it is referred to as a retention of title clause.)

Finally, a floating charge will be *invalidated* by s.245 of the Insolvency Act 1986 if the company goes into liquidation within two years (if the charge is in favour of a person closely connected with the company) or twelve months (if in favour of any other person) of having created the charge *except* for money paid in consideration for the charge at the time it is taken or subsequently, *unless*, in the case of a charge in favour of unconnected persons only, it is proved that the company was solvent immediately after the charge was created.

This is not quite so complicated as it might seem the first time you read it. It has a simple purpose. It prevents insolvent companies creating floating charges to secure past debts to the prejudice of their other unsecured creditors. This again illustrates the importance of a careful analysis of the company's financial position before the decision to make the advance is made.

ACTIVITY 7.8

Draw diagrams similar to fig 7.3 to summarise the use of stocks and shares, life policies, guarantees and debentures as security.

■ SUMMARY

1 The term 'security' means the acquisition of rights over property in support of a customer's personal undertaking to repay. It is taken as a form of insurance.

2 Various types of security arrangements are possible:
 - whole ownership;
 - possession;
 - documents of title;
 - rights over property; plus
 - a floating charge; and
 - a guarantee.

3 A mortgage is the creation or transfer of an interest in property as security for the payment of a debt.

4 A pledge is a deposit of goods, documents of title or negotiable instruments with a lender as security for a debt.

5 A lien is a right to retain property belonging to another until a debt is paid by that person.

6 A charge is a right over property.

7 When assessing the acceptability of security you are concerned with:
- its value;
- checking title and charging the security;
- protecting your interest; and
- realising the security.

8 Security is taken over land by executing a mortgage.
- A legal mortgage gives rights against the property itself.
- An equitable mortgage (unless taken by deed) gives only personal rights against the mortgagor (borrower).

9 A legal mortgage of land is almost always taken by a charge by deed under the Law of Property Act 1925. An equitable mortgage of land is taken by a deposit of the title deeds or land certificate together with a memorandum of deposit signed by the bank and the mortgagor and containing the terms of the mortgage.

10 A legal mortgagee's remedies are superior to those of an equitable mortgagee.

11 A legal mortgagee's remedies are:
- an action for the debt;
- sale of the property;
- appointment of a receiver;
- foreclosure; and
- taking possession.

An equitable mortgage by deed gives the mortgagee the right of sale and the right to appoint a receiver.

12 A mortgage is redeemed by the mortgagor repaying the advance. The equity of redemption enables a mortgagor to redeem the mortgage at any time.

13 A legal mortgage of registered stocks and shares is taken by transferring legal title to the mortgagee. An equitable mortgage is taken by a deposit of the share certificates. The deposit is usually supported by a 'blank transfer'.

14 Bearer securities are negotiable instruments and are charged by depositing them with the mortgagee, although a memorandum of deposit is usually taken.

15 A bank usually takes a legal mortgage of a life policy by an assignment by deed of the mortgagor's rights under the policy. Notice in writing must be given to the issuing company. An equitable mortgage, which is unusual, is taken by deposit of the policy.

16 A guarantee is a personal obligation, it does not involve acquiring rights over property, although a separate security may be taken in support of the guarantee.

17 When taking a guarantee, the following aspects are important:

- the legal capacity of both debtor and guarantor;
- the possible problem of misrepresentation or undue influence; and
- the rules regarding disclosure of information.

18 A debenture is a document issued by a company acknowledging a loan to it. Specific property will be charged as security to support the debenture.

19 A fixed charge is a legal or equitable mortgage of specific property. A floating charge is an equitable charge over the fluctuating assets of a company.

20 Details of any charge taken to secure a debenture must be registered with the Registrar of Companies in addition to any other registration that may be required.

■ SELF-ASSESSMENT QUESTIONS

1 What is the function of security? Give two specific reasons why it is taken?

2 Define and distinguish between a mortgage, a pledge and a lien.

3 List the attributes of good security.

4 What is the main practical difference between a legal and an equitable mortgage?

5 When investigating a customer's title to land, what searches are necessary?

6 What is the importance of Williams and *Glyn's Bank Ltd v Boland* (1980) in the context of taking land as security?

7 How does a bank protect its interest as mortgagee of land?

8 List the remedies of a legal mortgagee of land.

9 How do an equitable mortgagee's remedies differ from those of a legal mortgagee?

10 What is meant by the 'equity of redemption'?

11 What are the attributes of land as security?

12 Why is a legal mortgage of bearer securities obtained by their deposit alone?

13 What are the attributes of stocks and shares as security?

14 By what method is a legal mortgage of a life policy effected?

15 What is the meaning and importance of the term *uberrimae fidei*?

16 What are the attributes of life policies as security?

17 In what way does a guarantee differ from, say, a mortgage or a lien?

18 Explain why it is important to check on the legal capacity of the borrower and the prospective surety when a guarantee is offered as security.

19 Why does a bank guarantee impose joint and several liable on co-sureties?

20 What is the importance of *National Westminster Bank v Morgan* (1985) and *Lloyds Bank Ltd v Bundy* (1975) in the context of guarantees?

21 What are the attributes of guarantees as security?

22 Why is it important to register details of a charge contained in a debenture in accordance with the Companies Act 1985, s.395?

23 What is the principal remedy given in a bank debenture?

24 Distinguish between a fixed and a floating charge in a debenture.

25 List the possible defects of a floating charge.

■ **MULTIPLE-CHOICE QUESTIONS**

1 A bank will take a legal mortgage/equitable mortgage (match the type of mortgage with the appropriate option) of a life policy by:
A a deposit of the policy
B a deposit of the policy together with a memorandum of deposit
C exercising a lien over a policy already held in safe custody
D a separate deed of assignment

2 To be enforceable at law, a guarantee for a sum in excess of £25,000 must be:
A evidenced in writing
B in writing
C made by deed
D in the form prescribed by the Consumer Credit Act 1974

3 In relation to a guarantee accepted as security by a bank, which of the following statements is *incorrect*?
A the guarantor incurs primary liability
B If the debt secured proves to be legally unenforceable, the surety nevertheless remains liable
C If there is more than one surety, all must sign the guarantee before it is enforceable against any of them
D a 'free will' clause would be included where a wife guarantees a loan to a company in which her husband is the majority shareholder

4 Which of the following remedies is always available to both legal and equitable mortgagees of land without recourse to the court?
A an action for the debt
B sale of the property
C appointment of a receiver
D foreclosure

5 Which of the following statements is true about a mortgage?
A the mortgagee retains possession of the mortgaged property
B the mortgagor retains possession of the mortgaged property
C the lender acquires the right to retain the mortgaged property until the mortgage debt is repaid
D it can only be created by deed

6 Consider the following remedies that can be available to a bank holding a mortgage over land.
   i   an action for the debt
   ii sale of the property
   iii foreclosure
   iv taking possession of the property

When a bank holds an equitable mortgage made by deed, which of the following represents the extent of its remedies?
A   i
B   i & ii
C   i & iii
D   i & iv

7 A charge/lien/mortgage/pledge (match the word with the options below) is best defined as:
A   a conveyance of an interest in property as security for the payment of a debt
B   a deposit of goods, or documents of title to them, with a lender as security for a debt
C   a right to retain another's property until that person has paid a debt
D   an agreement giving a lender specified rights over property used to secure borrowing

8 A charge taken from a company to secure an issue of debentures must be registered with the Registrar of Companies within:
A   7 days
B   14 days
C   21 days
D   28 days

9 What minimum action is required by law to create an equitable mortgage over stocks and shares in favour of a bank?
A   their deposit with the bank
B   their deposit with the bank supported by a memorandum of deposit
C   their deposit with the bank supported by a blank transfer form
D   their deposit with the bank supported by a memorandum of deposit and a blank transfer form

8 Cheques and other means of payment

OBJECTIVES

OBJECTIVES

After studying this chapter you should be able to:

1 Understand the nature and functions of cheques and other bills of exchange, cheque cards and credit cards;
2 Explain a bank's position with regard to their use and misuse;
3 Explain the concept of negotiability as applied to cheques;
4 Explain the function and effect of crossings on cheques;
5 Define a holder in due course of a cheque and the rights possessed by such a holder;
6 Explain the possible liability of a bank in collecting and paying cheques;
7 State and explain the application of a bank's statutory protection when collecting and paying of cheques;
8 Explain the position of cardholders and card issuer in relation to the use and misuse of cheque guarantee cards and credit cards.
9 Appreciate how methods of payment and the law relating to them may change in response to the development and application of electronic technology.

■ INTRODUCTION

If there is one aspect of day-to-day banking with which you are thoroughly familiar, it must be handling cheques. Literally hundreds of thousands are issued, collected and paid every day. Despite the growth in electronic settlement between accounts, the cheque remains a very common method of settling both commercial and personal debts. Paying large sums of money in cash is both inconvenient and risky, despite the boost to your ego that might result! In this last chapter we want to build a supporting framework of theory behind your existing practical knowledge. We shall consider cheques from a legal perspective, in particular what can go wrong when a bank collects or pays a cheque and what is the legal position when something does go wrong.

To study cheques we must consider the legal concept of *negotiability*. A cheque, at law, is a negotiable instrument although, as you will read later, the 1990 White Paper 'Banking Services: Law and Practice' proposes that a crossed cheque should cease to be so. Negotiability is not new to you however. In Chapters 6 and 7 we mentioned it in the context of bearer securities and saw how title to a bearer security passes merely by delivery, a legal attribute of a bearer negotiable instrument. We have also mentioned a mysterious person known as the *holder in due course* and seen how such a person can obtain a better title than that held by the person who transferred the negotiable instrument to him or her! All this and more will be explained in this chapter.

A final point – we are taking cheques as the topic in this chapter, not bills of exchange and negotiability generally, for cheques are what you need to know about. Thus, this chapter is not intended as a 'what you've always wanted to know about bills of exchange' epic. Unless you work in the City of London, a specialist section of your bank, or in a branch with many customers involved in the import/export business, you will seldom see a bill of exchange other than a cheque.

■ WHAT IS A CHEQUE?

In general terms, a cheque is a written promise by the drawer that the bank on which it is drawn will pay the payee on demand the amount stated. More formally, the Bills of Exchange Act 1882, s.73 defines a cheque as '... a bill of exchange drawn on a banker payable on demand'. A definition you should learn.

Clearly, this implies that you should know what a bill of exchange is. However, although you may well wish to find out, for the purposes of your present studies you do not actually need to know! There is a simple reason for this. The definition (in s.3(1) of the Bills of Exchange Act 1882) lays down criteria for determining what is and what is not a bill of exchange. In practice, this question does not need answering in relation to cheques. While you occasionally may have to cope with a negotiable cow (seriously, it happened), cheques to the Inland Revenue written on shirts, protest cheques on eggs and oversize charity cheques (when your bank will probably enter into the spirit of things), cheques are written on standard cheque forms which, when properly completed, almost by definition satisfy ss.3 and 73. Cheques are cheques.

Having said that, what of cheques made out to 'cash' or to 'wages'? While they may look like cheques and, indeed, be treated as such by your bank, at law they are not. A cheque (bill of exchange) must be made payable to a specified person or to bearer; such 'cheques' are payable to neither. Nevertheless, they are valid orders to the bank from the customer to pay the stated amount from the customer's account. In addition to being a negotiable instrument, a cheque is a mandate from the customer authorising and directing his or her bank, according to the terms of the banker-customer contract, to pay the holder (the person entitled to payment). Needless to say, instruments made out to 'cash' or 'wages' are not negotiable.

For a different reason, a banker's draft is not a cheque. Here it is because the draft is not an order by one person addressed to another, as required by the Bills of Exchange Act 1882; it is addressed by the bank to itself, all branches of the bank being part of one legal entity (a corporation).

Parties to the transaction

Initially, three parties are involved:

- the drawer – the person who makes out the cheque;
- the drawee – the person to whom the order is addressed; and
- the payee – the person to whom the cheque is made payable.

If the cheque is transferred (negotiated), another person becomes a party to the transaction.

A couple of important points to mention here. First, the drawee of a cheque is always, by definition, a bank. Second, a bill of exchange other than a cheque must be accepted by the drawee to make it of commercial value, who thereby becomes the acceptor. A bill is accepted by the drawee signing it. By so doing, the drawee/acceptor becomes the person primarily liable on it, with the drawer and other persons who have signed (endorsed) it becoming sureties for the acceptor's payment. In other words, the person entitled to payment (the holder) must look first to the acceptor for payment but if the acceptor does not pay, the holder may look to the drawer (after all, the drawer was the person who drew the bill to pay a debt) or any person who subsequently incurred liability on it by signing it. In the case of a cheque, the drawer remains the party primarily liable – a cheque is not accepted remember – and any endorsers are sureties for the drawer's payment.

Above we have used the term 'party to the transaction' to mean anyone who was in some way connected with a cheque. However, the term 'party' has a stricter meaning at law: a party to a cheque (or other bill of exchange) is a person who has *signed* it and by so doing incurred liability on it. Thus, it covers the drawer (the customer) and any endorser. In the case of other bills it also covers, of course, the drawee/acceptor. Remember, a bank never accepts a cheque and therefore *never* becomes a party to it and therefore never incurs liability to the holder (most likely the original payee). Even if the bank wrongfully returns a cheque, the holder has rights of action against only the drawer and any endorsers. It is the drawer who has a right of action against the bank, for breach of contract, e.g. wrongfully debiting the account or wrongfully dishonouring the cheque.

Negotiation and endorsement

We have used both these terms a number of times already and it is important that you are absolutely sure what they mean.

Negotiation

Negotiation takes place when a cheque or other bill is transferred in such a way as to make the transferee the holder of it. A bearer cheque is negotiated by delivery, an order cheque by endorsement of the holder completed by delivery. (Delivery meaning the transfer of the instrument in such a way that the transferee is intended to become the holder of it.)

We must distinguish between *transfer* and *negotiation* at this point. The key to the distinction is to remember that the term 'negotiation' is a term unique to bills of exchange and other negotiable instruments and relates to the special attributes of negotiable instruments when title is transferred. (Technically a negotiable instrument is transferred by *assignment* – *see* page 193.) In the sense of physically transferring a cheque from one person to another, the terms tend to be used interchangeably but *negotiation* requires the transfer to be in accordance with the Bills of Exchange Act 1882, usually the need for a valid endorsement, as we explained above.

The more important point is the consequence of a negotiation to a holder in due course (*see* page 240). Taking a negotiation of a cheque as a holder in due course means that the transferee (holder) takes it free from any defects of title which affected the cheque while it was in the hands of the transferor or any other prior parties, and also free from any personal claims between prior parties. Examples of personal claims are a right to claim damages for breach of contract and the right to set-off a debt owed by the drawer to the payee against a claim on the cheque by the payee against the drawer. (We refer to these prior defects and claims as 'equities'.)

If the transferee does not take a transfer of the cheque as a holder in due course, we tend to use the term transfer in relation to the passing of title because although the cheque has been negotiated, the transferee, not being a holder in due course, does not enjoy the full benefits of negotiability, i.e. the ability to take free from prior equities. In a very general sense, therefore, you can think of negotiation as being an enhanced form of transfer. (More correctly negotiation is an enhanced form of assignment.)

Endorsement

Endorsement is the signature of the endorser on the cheque or other bill, i.e. that of the payee or a subsequent holder. The signature indicates the holder's intention to transfer his or her rights in the cheque.

Validity of an endorsement. To be valid, an endorsement must satisfy the following criteria.

1 It must be *written on the back* of the cheque.
2 It must be of the *entire cheque* and not part.
3 If there are two or more payees all must endorse, unless one is authorised to endorse for the others, such as a partner.
4 It should *correspond exactly* with the drawing or the previous endorsement. For example, if the payee's name is misspelt, the payee should endorse it with the same spelling, adding his or her proper signature if s/he wishes. Nevertheless, an endorsement which does not correspond exactly with the previous designation on the cheques is not invalid, but any *irregularity*, a question of fact, will prevent a transferee from becoming a holder in due course (see below). It is usual banking practice to refuse to pay cheques on which the endorsement does not correspond exactly with the name of the payee or previous endorsee. For example, an endorsement on a cheque 'John Smith' when the payee was designated 'J Smith' would be an irregular endorsement.

Types of endorsement. There are three types.

1 An *endorsement in blank* is where the holder merely signs the cheque on its back. The cheque becomes payable to bearer.

2 A *special endorsement* is where the holder adds a direction to pay a particular person. The cheque becomes payable to, or to the order of, the person specified, e.g. 'Pay X Signed Y'.

3 A *restrictive endorsement* is where the endorsement prohibits further transfer of the cheque, i.e. the holder cannot transfer their right to payment. An example of a restrictive endorsement would be 'Pay X only. Signed Y.'.

Points to note. An important point to remember is that any endorsement on a bearer cheque drawn as a bearer cheque is irrelevant and of no effect in this context. It can be ignored. Thus, a cheque drawn as a *bearer cheque* remains as such, it cannot be converted into an order cheque by a special endorsement. Conversely, a cheque drawn as an order cheque and converted to a bearer cheque by an endorsement in blank can be converted back to an order cheque by any holder writing an order to pay a specific person above the signature of the endorser.

The rule relating to bearer cheques drawn as bearer cheques can be important where an endorsement has been forged for example. On an order cheque the forgery prevents the transferee obtaining the right to payment, i.e. becoming the holder. On a bearer cheque you can have as many forged endorsements as you like; they do not affect the bearer's title, the bearer is still the holder and is entitled to payment.

Note, however, that a person who does endorse a bearer cheque becomes a party to it and incurs liability on it.

Cheques distinguished from other bills

The provisions of the Bills of Exchange Act 1882 relating to bills of exchange payable on demand generally apply equally to cheques; remember a cheque is a bill of exchange drawn on demand but specifically it is drawn on a bank. So, what are the distinctions?

Acceptance

The person on whom a bill of exchange is drawn (the drawee) is not liable on it until that person has accepted it, as we saw above.

A cheque is never accepted by the bank on which it is drawn. Hence, the rules relating to acceptance of bills of exchange – acceptance is fundamental to the law and commercial use of bills – do not apply to cheques. More importantly this means that a bank is never liable to the holder (owner) of a cheque if it does not pay it, for example where the drawer has countermanded payment. The only course of action open to the holder (usually the payee) is to sue the drawer and any endorser.

Negotiation

Relative to the number drawn, few cheques are negotiated – one estimate is less than 3 per cent – the vast majority being paid straight into the payee's account. In practice, therefore, the rules relating to negotiation are of limited relevance to cheques. Having said that, 3 per cent still represents a great many cheques!

Indeed, there has for a long time been a school of thought that argues that cheques should cease to be negotiable instruments altogether. The argument is that because so few are ever issued to be later negotiated the attribute of negotiability is completely unnecessary. It could even lead to unforeseen and awkward consequences. For example, you pay for a CD player by cheque, it will not work, you stop the cheque and think that is that. But you do not know that the seller has negotiated the cheque to a supplier in payment of a debt. Title to the cheque has passed to the supplier and the supplier can enforce the cheque against you; stopping the cheque is irrelevant to the supplier's claim. Granted, this is unlikely to happen in practice and crossing a cheque 'Not negotiable' prevents the situation arising in the first place. The latter position is so because the supplier would then take the cheque subject to any defect in the seller's title to it or subject to any counterclaim you had against the seller – in this case the fact that you were sold a CD player that did not work. In other words a cheque can be deprived of its negotiability very simply in any case. All the more reason, it is argued, why they should cease to be negotiable.

This argument has been adopted in the 1990 White Paper 'Banking Services: Law and Practice'. This proposes that a *crossed* cheque shall cease to be negotiable and that a cheque marked 'account payee' shall cease to be transferable (*see* page 237).

The use of the phrase 'not negotiable' on bills of exchange other than cheques prevents them from being *transferred*.

Crossings

The rules relating to crossings are confined to cheques (and certain other instruments); other bills cannot be crossed.

Forged and unauthorised endorsements

In certain circumstances, an order cheque bearing a forged or an unauthorised endorsement is discharged by the bank on which it is drawn making payment; in addition the bank is not liable for making the payment: s.60, Bills of Exchange Act 1882. Payment by the acceptor of a bill under similar conditions does not discharge it, rights and liabilities still exist on it.

Banker-customer contract

The collection and payment of cheques is part of the wider banker-customer contract. Such a relationship does not exist between the drawer and drawee of a bill although, of course, a bill of exchange can be drawn on a bank.

Legal characteristics of cheques as negotiable instruments

A cheque as a negotiable instrument has four legal characteristics.

1 *Title* is transferable by delivery or, in the case of cheque payable to order (the majority), by endorsement completed by delivery.

2 A person taking a transfer of the cheque in good faith and for value (a holder in due course) is unaffected by any defects in the title of prior parties as well as by mere personal defences, such as counterclaims, available among them.

Thus, the transferee *can acquire a better title* than that held by the transferor. For example, a person who acquired the instrument by fraud has only a voidable title to it, but a bona fide transferee for value from that person acquires a perfect title. What is important in practice is that a holder in due course acquires an absolute right to payment of the full amount of the cheque and can enforce this right against all parties to the cheque if the cheque is not paid by the drawee bank.

3 The holder *can sue in their own name.* As such, this is an important exception to the doctrine of privity of contract, i.e. that a contract can only be enforced by the parties to it (*see* page 92).

4 The holder *need not give notice of the transfer to prior parties* to establish their title.

The law relating to negotiable instruments developed from the practices of merchants, and these distinctive legal characteristics can all be explained by their commercial origins. For example, merchants would be unlikely to accept negotiated bills of exchange instead of cash if they knew that their rights to obtain payment of them could always be prejudiced by some defect in the title of prior parties to the bills or a counterclaim of which they were completely ignorant. Again, it would be a ludicrous situation if each time a £5 note (a type of negotiable instrument) changed hands notice and details of the transfer had to be given to the Bank of England!

As such negotiable instruments are an extension of the concept of assignment: the transfer of a right or interest in intangible property (a *chose in action*) to another person. You will recall that legal title to life policies is transferred by assignment, that written notice of the assignment has to be given to the issuing company and that, most importantly, any defect in the assignor's title, e.g. that it is voidable for failure to disclose a material fact, is also transferred, similarly any counterclaim for unpaid premiums. If a bank takes an equitable mortgage (assignment) then, additionally, it is unable to enforce its rights in its own name. (Thus, even when it has a legal mortgage, a bank which has taken a life policy as security can never be absolutely certain that its security is enforceable.)

Cheques as a means of payment

In your other studies you will have learnt that the UK banking system began with goldsmiths accepting deposits of gold and silver for safekeeping, leading to the emergence of private banks. Where does the use of cheques fit into this evolution?

Customers of these early banks soon realised that it was often inconvenient and sometimes dangerous to go personally to their bank to withdraw money each time they needed cash. Thus, the practice developed of customers giving written instructions to their bank to pay the bearer (a messenger) of the note the sum of money specified in it by withdrawal from their account. These written instructions or notes were the first cheques. Once this practice became generally recognised and accepted, it evolved further and such notes began to be used to make payments in settlement of debts. This was done by making the notes out to whoever required payment, instead of to bearer, and this person paid the note or order (the cheque) into their own account. Alternatively, the payee could endorse the note and thereby make it payable to someone to whom they in turn owed money and that person could then either endorse it again or pay it into their account. If you consider the modern use of cheques, it is in essence still the same.

The early banks were keen to promote the use of cheques and they began to provide special cheque forms to assist their customers. The use of cheques was to their advantage because withdrawals by cheque which were then paid into the payee's account meant that notes and coins did not change hands, merely the ownership of bank deposits. The position was the same if the payee banked with another bank provided the banks kept accounts with each other or at a central bank and had some means of clearing the cheques.

This process meant that only a small part of each fresh deposit needed to be kept in cash and also that any loan to a customer could be made through an overdraft, against, which cheques could be drawn, instead of handing over actual cash. Thus, what began as a practice for the convenience of customers became central to the process of credit creation.

■ CROSSINGS

Virtually all cheques bear two bold parallel lines across their face. This is the crossing. But why is it there, what is its origin, and what variants are possible on the basic or general crossing? First of all, a general statement of its legal meaning and effect.

A crossing is a direction to the *paying bank* that the money proceeds of the cheque should be paid only to another bank as agent of the payee and not directly to the payee in cash. A crossing therefore *restricts payment* of a cheque.

You may be thinking that there is one common situation where this rule is not applied. Banks will allow their own customers, or their known agents, to cash crossed cheques over the counter. Sometimes the customer is required to open the crossing by writing 'Please pay cash' and signing (not initialling) the opening, but more usually an opening is not requested. The practice, although technically incorrect at law; is convenient and promotes goodwill, while the risk involved is slight. The problem is avoided altogether if the customer makes out the 'cheque' to cash when withdrawing money. As you have seen, the 'cheque' is then not really a cheque at all because it is not made out to the order of a 'specified person, or to bearer' as required by the Bills of Exchange Act 1882, s.3(1). Legally, however, it operates as a demand for repayment which the bank is contractually bound to honour provided sufficient funds or an agreed overdraft facility exist. The crossing which the 'cheque' bears is therefore irrelevant in this situation.

Origin of crossings

Crossings are the result of banking practice, specifically the practice of the Clearing House in the 18th century. Clerks of different banks would meet to exchange cheques drawn on their respective banks, settling any outstanding balance in cash. In time the cheques were left in each bank's 'drawer' in the Clearing House instead of being given personally to the bank's clerk. So that each could make their accounts up properly and to enable them to return any cheque for lack of funds, the clerk of, say, bank X would write bank X's name between parallel lines on cheques which were left in, say, bank Y's drawer.

As this internal practice became known outside, customers began adding crossings to their cheques themselves because making cheques payable only through another bank account reduced the chance of a third party fraudulently obtaining payment. (Bear in mind that there were comparatively few bank accounts at that time and that banks were therefore better placed than they are today to detect possible fraud.) Customers crossed cheques adding the words 'and Company' (or 'and Co') between the parallel lines or the name of the payee's bank when they knew it. The latter crossing meant that if any person other than the payee tried to obtain payment of the cheque that person would have to do so at the payee's own bank and any attempted fraud would most likely come to light.

In the second half of the 19th century crossings were legally recognised as a material (integral) part of a cheque. By s.78 of the Bills of Exchange Act 1882, any unauthorised alteration of a crossing will discharge (end) the liabilities of the parties to the cheque.

The purpose of crossings today

More efficient methods of clearing have long since taken over the original reason for crossings and today they are used to minimise the chances of persons fraudulently obtaining payment of a cheque.

The best way to appreciate this is to consider the position with an uncrossed, or 'open', cheque. An uncrossed cheque does not have to be paid through a bank account, payment can be made over the counter. Thus, a person finding or stealing an uncrossed cheque would be able to obtain payment over the counter at the designated branch of the drawee bank provided that person had reasonable identification as the payee and provided the payee was not personally known to the bank. The first proviso certainly would not be difficult for a determined rogue to satisfy, and the second is most unlikely to apply.

Contrast the position with a crossed cheque. This, as you know, can be paid only through another bank account and therefore assumes that the rogue has one or can persuade someone with a bank account to pay in the cheque suitably endorsed by the rogue and obtain the proceeds on the rogue's behalf. In itself, although a deterrent to a would-be rogue, it is not that great a protection against fraud because a determined attempt to open an account in a fictitious name using bogus referees if need be will often succeed. Taken with other factors, however, it without doubt makes it considerably more difficult for a fraudulent person to obtain the proceeds of a cheque. In particular, the consequences of a crossing increase the time available for discovering the fraudulent activity and gives the drawer more time to stop payment of any stolen cheque.

235

Furthermore, even if payment has been made before the loss or fraud is discovered, it can almost always be recovered from the person for whom it was collected since that person would have to have an account at the collecting bank (*see* page 245). The exceptions would be where the rogue had opened an account in a fictitious name and could not be traced, or where a bearer cheque had been lost or stolen and the customer for whom it was collected had given value (something in return) for it to the finder or thief without knowledge of the circumstances. The customer would then be its true owner (its holder in due course) and entitled to the proceeds.

Having considered the purpose of crossings we must now look at the various types. The two primary categories of crossings are 'general' and 'special'.

General crossing

A general crossing consists of two transverse parallel lines across the face of the cheque, with or without the words 'not negotiable'. The words 'and Company' (or '& Co') may be added between the lines although they are purely a traditional addition and have no legal effect.

Where the words 'not negotiable' are added to the crossing they deprive the cheque of its negotiability. This means that the person taking the cheque does not receive and cannot give a better title than that of the person transferring it. (The ability to do so is, as you will see, the very essence of negotiability.) The words do not mean that the cheque cannot be *transferred*, however; a crossed cheque is just as transferable bearing these words as without them, the person to whom it is transferred is just in a far weaker position if the transferor's title proves to be defective (*see* below).

The effect of the words on an uncrossed cheque is uncertain, there is no statutory rule; they may merely deprive it of its negotiability, as on a crossed cheque, or prevent its transfer altogether, as they do on bills of exchange other than cheques. However, the point is relatively academic since uncrossed cheques are very unusual and uncrossed cheques bearing these words therefore extremely unusual.

Sometimes the words 'account payee' appear within the crossing. These words are, strictly speaking, not part of any crossing since they are a direction to the *collecting* bank as to how the money must be dealt with after its receipt. While they have no statutory significance, the courts recognise them as a warning to the collecting bank that collection of the cheque for a person other than the named payee without enquiry and sufficient explanation is *prima facie* proof of negligence. (You will see the relevance of this later in this chapter.) The words do not affect the negotiability of the cheque.

From what we have said, you have probably worked out that unless you are absolutely certain that a cheque you draw is going to be paid straight into the payee's account, crossing it 'Not negotiable, account payee' should ensure that you will not have an unknown third party seeking to enforce the cheque against you if the cheque is lost by or stolen from the payee, or later countermanded by you for whatever reason; advice which may prove useful to a customer.

Figure 8.1 shows the possible forms of general crossings.

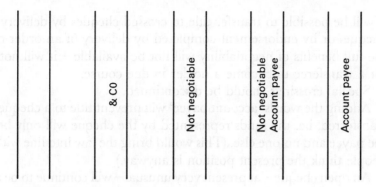

Fig 8.1 Types of general crossing

ACTIVITY 8.1

(a) A customer shows a cheque to you which has had the words 'Not transferable' added to the crossing and asks you what effect the words have. What would be your reply?

(b) Do the words 'Not negotiable' in a crossing prevent ownership of a cheque from being transferred?

Special crossings

A special crossing consists of the name of a *particular bank* and often a *particular branch* to which payment must be made. The name is itself the crossing and, while they would usually be present, two transverse lines (the essence of a general crossing) are unnecessary. The words 'not negotiable' and 'account payee' can be added to the crossing and they then have the same effect as on a cheque crossed generally. Figure 8.2 shows the forms of special crossings.

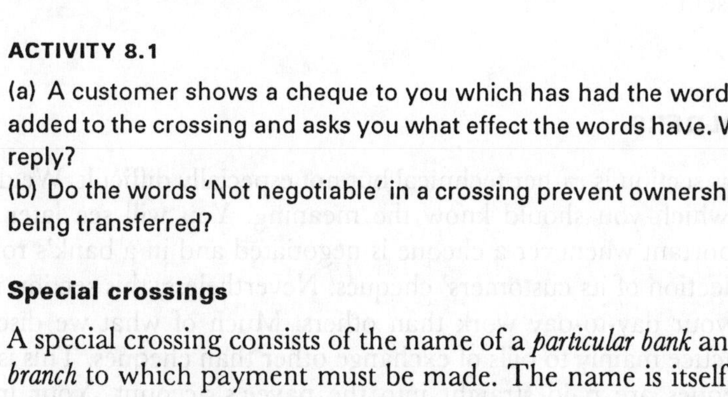

Fig 8.2 Types of special crossing

Proposed changes

The 1990 White Paper 'Banking Services: Law and Practice' proposes a number of important changes to crossings on cheques.

1 A crossed cheque should cease to be a negotiable instrument, whether or not the words 'not negotiable' are written on it. Note that this still means that

it will be possible to transfer title to crossed cheques by delivery (if a bearer cheque) or by endorsement completed by delivery (if an order cheque), but the full benefits of negotiability will not be available – it will not be possible for a transferee to become a holder in due course.

2 Special crossings should be discontinued.

3 Adding the words 'account payee' will prevent title to a cheque from being transferred, i.e. the funds represented by the cheque will only be payable to the payee and no-one else. (This would bring the law into line with what most people think the present position is anyway.)

4 An open cheque – at present very unusual – will continue to be a negotiable instrument presentable for cash (or payable through the clearing system) as at present.

■ TYPES OF HOLDERS

This section is rather technical but not especially difficult. We deal with terms of which you should know the meaning. You will see later that they are important whenever a cheque is negotiated and in a bank's role as agent for collection of its customers' cheques. Nevertheless, this section is less relevant to your day-to-day work than others. Much of what we discuss applies in practice mainly to bills of exchange other than cheques. This is because most cheques are paid straight into the payee's account. Your interest here is primarily that of understanding the theory so that you can understand and explain the practice when called upon to do so. Needless to say, this section is very important to your studies.

We have already seen that there are three primary parties to the transaction: the drawer, the drawee and the payee. (Be sure you can define them before reading on.) The holder is in a way another party to the transaction. But, instead of being identifiable as an individual in the way the drawer, drawee and the payee are, the holder is identifiable by applying *legal criteria to a particular person's possession of a cheque.*

The holder

The Bills of Exchange Act 1882, s.2, defines a holder as: 'The payee or endorsee of a bill who is in possession of it, or the bearer thereof'. To proceed further we need to consider the terminology – the legal criteria we referred to above – used in s.2.

Endorsee

We know the meaning of 'payee' so let us consider the term 'endorsee'. If a person wishes to negotiate (transfer) a cheque which is made out to them by name, for example 'Pay J Smith' or 'Pay J Smith or order', the cheque is an *order* cheque and can only be negotiated by J Smith first signing the cheque on the back. This is known as endorsing the cheque. J Smith may wish to negotiate the cheque to a specific person, say, P Brown, in which case the endorsement must read 'Pay P Brown' followed by J Smith's signature. P Brown is now the endorsee and, therefore, the holder of the cheque. Note that to be the holder the endorsee must be in possession of the cheque.

If J Smith merely signs the back of the cheque and does not specify to whom he intends to negotiate it, the endorsement is an *endorsement in blank* and the cheque becomes payable to bearer, that is, payable to whoever has possession of it at any particular time, that person being its holder. (Remember that an order cheque converted into a bearer cheque by an endorsement in blank can be converted back to an order cheque: *see* above.)

Bearer

A bearer as defined by the Bills of Exchange Act 1882, s.2, means someone in possession of a bearer cheque (bill). Essentially this is the opposite of an order cheque; a bearer cheque is payable to anyone in possession of it. Specifically, a cheque is payable to bearer if it is:

- drawn payable to bearer;
- endorsed in blank; or
- drawn payable to someone the drawer never intended to receive payment – technically a fictitious or non-existing payee – and usually associated with fraudulent activity.

A bearer cheque is negotiated by delivery alone.

Further points

It is worth exploring the term 'holder' a little more fully. You should note the following four points.

1 The term includes an *unlawful* holder, that is someone to whom the cheque is expressed to be payable but whose possession of it is unlawful. Examples include the finder or thief of a bearer cheque and the person who obtained the cheque's issue or transfer to themselves by fraud.

2 It follows from 1 above that anyone in possession of a bearer cheque is its holder. This includes a finder or a thief, although such a holder obtains *no rights* against the parties to the cheque and a claim brought by the finder/thief on the cheque will fail on proof of their defective title. The finder/thief can, however, transfer a good title to a holder in due course (*see* below).

3 The term does *not* include a *wrongful possessor*, for example, a person who has stolen an order cheque or a person holding under a forged endorsement – a forged signature is entirely inoperative, at law title has not been transferred.

4 Is the holder of a cheque its owner? It would be helpful if this was invariably the case but unfortunately this is not so. Tying together the points we have made above, you can see that a thief of a bearer cheque is its holder but clearly not its owner. In addition, a holder's title can be defective as, for example, where it was acquired by fraud. If this all sounds strange, think about the commercial origin of bill of exchange – it is all about the acceptability and transferability of written promises of payment.

Legal attributes of a holder

A holder has three main attributes.

1 A holder can enforce payment of a cheque in their own name against prior parties, although an action by the thief of a bearer cheque will obviously fail on proof of the theft.

2 Only a holder can transfer – by negotiation – the right to enforce the promise of payment against prior parties and to transfer that right to another party free from defects in title.

3 Payment to the holder discharges the cheque and therefore the obligations of the parties liable on it.

These attributes are also explained by reference to a cheque's commercial origins.

Holder for value

A holder for value is a holder of a cheque for which value (consideration as it is known in contract law) has at some time being given. The value need not have been given by the holder personally. For example, if a cheque is issued in payment for goods, value is given for it. If the cheque is then transferred by the payee as a gift, the transferee (the holder) is a holder for value.

A holder for value can enforce payment of the cheque against all persons who became parties to the cheque *prior to the value being given*. For example, A draws a cheque in favour of B as a gift, B endorses it to C, also as a gift, and C endorses it to D as payment for painting his house. D in turn endorses it to his daughter E as her pocket money. Let us consider the legal position. (Please remember that this series of transactions would be most unlikely to happen in practice. We have used it purely to make you think about the legal position. We have also assumed that each time the cheque is transferred it has been specially endorsed.)

A incurs no legal liability to either B or C, and B incurs no legal liability to C, because of the lack of consideration between the parties. D, however, gave consideration and can enforce payment of the cheque against A, B or C because A, B and C became parties to the cheque before D gave value for it. Similarly, E, the current holder for value, can enforce payment A, B or C – the value given by D makes her holder for value – but she *cannot* enforce it against D because she gave D no value (consideration) for the cheque. (As between the immediate parties to a cheque, consideration is always required to make the cheque enforceable.)

Unless it can be proved otherwise, any holder is a holder for value but as such obtains no better title than that possessed by the transferor, a holder for value does not take free from defects in title of prior parties. Thus, a holder for value does not enjoy the full benefits of negotiability as does a holder in due course.

ACTIVITY 8.2

A draws a cheque in favour of B. B endorses the cheque to C for value and C gives it to D as a gift.

(a) Is D a holder for value?

(b) Assuming that there are no defects in D's title, which party(ies) can D enforce the cheque against, if D can enforce it at all?

(c) Can D enforce the cheque against A's bank?

(d) Would it have made any difference to D's rights of enforcement if she had given value to C for the cheque.

Holder in due course
Definition

Section 29(1) of the 1882 Act defines a holder in due course as:

> ... a holder who has taken a bill, complete and regular on the face of it, under the following circumstances, namely (a) that he became the holder of it before it was overdue, and without notice that it had been previously dishonoured, if such was the fact; (b) that he took the bill in good faith and for value, and that at the time the bill was negotiated to him he had no notice of any defect in title of the person who negotiated it.

Since the rights of a holder in due course are in many ways what negotiability is all about, it is well worth spending time considering what must be fulfilled for a holder to be a holder in due course.

Requirements

1 *Complete and regular.* The cheque must be *complete and regular* on the face of it, i.e. technically correct. The rights of a holder in due course are such that the cheque must be above suspicion when it is taken in payment. This requirement can be explained by remembering that cheques are a substitute for cash payment. You surely would not be prepared to take a £20 in payment if a third of it was missing, or it had been torn into a number of pieces and stuck back together, or (apart from its obvious rarity value) if it lacked a serial number. The same thinking lies behind taking a cheque in payment.

An *incomplete* cheque is either undated, or does not state an amount, or lacks a required signature, such as an endorsement. *Irregularity* usually applies to endorsements and would arise where there is a clear and serious difference between the name of the payee or endorsee and their endorsement. The discrepancy must be such that it raises doubts about the genuineness of the endorsement.

Since an endorsement can account for an irregularity in the cheque, this must mean that the face of the cheque includes the back! For example, in *Arab Bank v Ross* (1952), the bank held two promissory notes (a type of negotiable instrument) drawn in favour of a firm 'Fathi and Faysal Nabulsy Company'. One partner had discounted them to the bank, endorsing them 'Fathi and Faysal Nabulsy'. It was held that omitting 'Company' from the endorsement made the notes irregular. The bank, therefore, was not a holder in due course of the notes, only a holder for value.

A cheque would also be irregular if it had been stuck back together after being torn up – but not if accidentally torn, a question of fact.

2 *Not overdue.* The holder must have taken the cheque *before it was overdue.* For

example, a bill payable on 30 June is overdue on 1 July and thereafter. A bill payable on demand is overdue when it appears to have been in circulation for an unreasonable length of time. Thus, the holder of a cheque (a bill payable on demand) may find that they are not a holder in due course if they do not present it for payment within a reasonable time of its issue. What is a 'reasonable time' is a question of fact to be determined by the individual circumstances of each case; there is no modern decision on the point. If a cheque is held to be overdue this does not mean, of course, that the cheque will not be paid, merely that the transferee does not take from prior defects in title.

Note that an overdue cheque is quite different from a 'stale' cheque, i.e. one which by banking custom and practice is more than six months old. 'Overdue' relates to the negotiability of the cheque, 'stale' relates to a bank's refusal to pay. It is usual for a bank to refuse to pay a cheque which is stale, instead it would be returned marked 'Out-of-date'.

3 *No notice of any previous dishonour.* The holder must have had *no notice of any previous dishonour.* A bank marking a cheque with a reason for dishonour would clearly prevent subsequent parties from becoming holders in due course, although a transfer of such a cheque is unlikely to take place for obvious reasons.

4 *Good faith.* The holder must have taken the cheque in *good faith.* Negligence alone is not lack of good faith, the transferee must know or suspect that all is not as it should be concerning the cheque.

In *Raphael and Another v Bank of England* (1885), for example, the numbers of some stolen notes were circulated to bankers and exchange dealers, including the plaintiffs, to whom they were likely to be presented. One such note was changed by the plaintiff without consulting the file of notices of lost and stolen notes, he merely asked to see the presenter's passport and obtained his signature and address on the note. On the facts, although he had been negligent, the plaintiff had taken in good faith and was therefore entitled to its value.

5 *Value.* The holder *must have given value for the cheque personally,* it is not enough that value at some time has been given.

6 *Negotiation.* The cheque must be negotiated to the holder. This means that the *payee* of a cheque, whilst its holder, cannot be its holder in due course. A cheque is issued to a payee not negotiated.

7 *No notice of defective title.* At the time of the cheque's negotiation to him/her, the holder must have *no notice of any defect in title* of the person who negotiated it. Notice means actual notice, or knowledge of suspicious circumstances coupled with a deliberate omission to investigate them. Put another way, actual knowledge of a defect in title or a suspicion of one followed by a deliberate failure to make reasonable enquiries, prevents a transferee from becoming a holder in due course.

What, however, does 'defective title' mean? By s.29(2) of the Act, the title of the person negotiating the cheque is defective if that person obtained the cheque by, among other things, fraud, coercion or other unlawful means. For our present purposes, misrepresentation and undue influence are good examples. (You should remember from Chapter 4 that both entitle the injured party to set aside (rescind) a contract.)

Points to note

Since you are going to be concerned with holders in due course in any further studies in banking law or banking practice, we are going to list a number of important points about them. The relevance and importance of some of them may well become more obvious during these further studies.

1 Every holder is *presumed* to be a holder in due course until fraud or illegality is admitted or proved in the issue or negotiation of the cheque. The holder must then prove that value in good faith has subsequently been given for the cheque.

2 A person who takes a transfer of a *bearer cheque* from a thief can be a holder in due course.

3 A person who took an order cheque bearing a *forged endorsement* cannot be a holder and therefore cannot be a holder in due course; that person is merely a *wrongful possessor*. This is because a forged signature is entirely inoperative (s.24) and therefore the cheque at law has not been endorsed at all. Thus, the person taking the cheque cannot be an endorsee and, remembering the definition of a holder, therefore not a holder.

4 Section 55(2) of the 1882 Act states that an endorser of a cheque is precluded (prevented) from denying to a holder in due course the genuineness and regularity of their signature and all previous endorsements. Now, a moment's reflection will tell you that there is something wrong here. You have just seen that a person taking under a forged endorsement is not a holder and therefore cannot be a holder in due course. And yet s.55(2) clearly implies that a person can be a holder in due course when a cheque bears a forged endorsement, otherwise there would be no point in being precluded, or estopped, from denying it.

From what we have said, it follows that in these circumstances the term 'holder in due course' in s.55(2) must have a special meaning. It in fact means a person who would have been a holder in due course *but for the forgery*. In short such a person has the *rights* but not the status of a holder in due course against *certain parties* to the cheque . Specifically, when a question of liability arises in this situation, persons signing the cheque *after* the forgery are prevented from denying the genuineness of what is actually a forgery and are therefore liable to the person in possession of the cheque. Hence estoppel will render the cheque valid and enforceable between the parties *subsequent to the forgery*. This means that the ultimate possessor will usually be able to obtain payment from the person who transferred the cheque to them and they in turn will be able to claim from the person who negotiated the cheque to them and so on. The loss will eventually lie with the person who first took the cheque when it bore a forged endorsement unless that person can trace and recover from the forger. This, of course, is unlikely.

243

Look at Fig 8.3. Here the true owner of the cheque is C but s.55(2) gives F, in fact a wrongful possessor, the rights of a holder in due course provided the requirements of s.29(1) would have been satisfied if it were not for the break in the chain of negotiation. While D's finding of the cheque and forgery of C's signature breaks the chain of negotiation and title, thereby preventing F from enforcing the cheque against A, B, or C, F can enforce the cheque against E because s.55(2) precludes E from denying that D's forgery of C's endorsement is genuine. C, still the true owner of the cheque, can bring an action in conversion against E or F for the value of the cheque or its return and E is most likely to stand the loss. If C can recover the cheque C can still enforce it against A and B. (Read through this paragraph again, it's complicated but logical.)

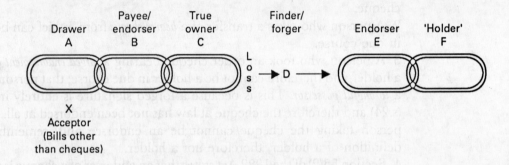

Fig 8.3 The effect of a forged endorsement and s.55(2)

Rights of a holder in due course

If you compare the rights of a holder in due course with the legal characteristics of a negotiable instrument, you will see that they are the practical application of that legal concept. Thus, these rights are the very essence of the concept of negotiability. Specifically, a holder in due course has the following rights.

1 *To sue in his/her own name* any prior party to a cheque (or other bill).

2 *Is unaffected by any defect in the titles of prior parties or from claims arising from previous dealings among them.* An example of the former would be where the issue or transfer of the cheque was obtained by fraud, making the payee or endorser's title voidable. An example of the latter would be where the cheque was taken in payment for faulty goods, entitling the drawer to a counter-claim against the payee in an action by the latter to enforce payment of the cheque. A holder in due course can therefore acquire a *better title* to the cheque than that held by his transferor.

Remember, however, that crossing a cheque 'not negotiable' prevents a person from becoming a holder in due course. Any prior defects in title are transferred with the cheque.

3 *Can transfer his/her title* as holder in due course to any person for value or as a gift, provided that that person was not a party to any defect which affected the cheque.

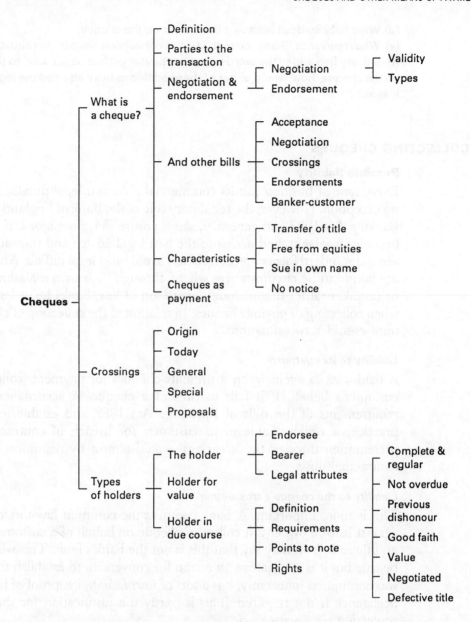

Fig 8.4 Summary diagram of cheques

ACTIVITY 8.3

Barry draws a cheque on Midtown Bank made payable to Graham. Jean steals the cheque from Graham, forges Graham's signature on it and transfers the cheque to David who takes it in good faith and for value. David gives the cheque to Hansa as a present.

(a) Is Helen a holder, a holder for value or a holder in due course of the cheque? Is she none of these?

(b) Who can Helen enforce the cheque against, if anyone?

(c) Who is the true owner of the cheque, Helen, Barry, Graham, Jean or David.

(d) What liability does Midtown Bank incur on the cheque.

(e) What relevance, if any, does the tort of conversion have in this situation?

(f) If Barry had added the words 'Account payee' or 'Not negotiable' to the crossing on the cheque, how would either of these additions have affected the legal position, if at all?

■ COLLECTING CHEQUES

Possible liability

Every type of business has its commercial risks and legal pitfalls. Banking is no exception. However, the regulatory role of the Bank of England, under the Banking Act 1987 and generally, *should* ensure that no major UK bank ever becomes insolvent, and access to the best legal advice and transactions built around standard form contracts should avoid most legal pitfalls. And yet there are bound to be circumstances where, through their own maladministration or mistakes rather than through operation of law, banks incur legal liability when collecting or paying cheques. In relation to the collection of cheques, we must consider two situations.

Liability to its customer

A bank acts as agent when it presents cheques for payment (collects) on its customer's behalf. If it fails to present a cheque in accordance with the requirements of the Bills of Exchange Act 1882 and established banking practice, it will be liable to its customer for breach of contract. Clearly, presentation through the 'clearings' would almost by definition satisfy this contractual duty.

Liability to the cheque's true owner

This is more important. A bank commits the common law tort of *conversion* against its true owner if it collects a cheque on behalf of a customer who has no title to it. You may say that this is not the bank's fault. This will probably be true but it is *no defence* in an action for conversion to establish that the tort was committed innocently, it is a tort of *strict liability*, i.e. proof of intention or negligence is not required. This is partly the justification for the statutory protection we discuss next.

A collecting bank's statutory protection

Banks and the services that they offer are fundamental to modern commerce and industry. This in itself does not entitle banks to a privileged position before the law; they are merely another group of business organisations subject to the same economic forces and legal rules as any other group. However, so important is their function in the collection and payment of cheques that they must receive reasonable protection against innocently incurring liability to the *true owner* of a cheque if the system is going to function efficiently, or even at all. The relevant protection is given by statute. No other general area of banking business receives similar comprehensive protection.

The Cheques Act 1957, s.4

This section provides that a bank incurs no liability to the true owner of the cheque where its customer had either a defective title or no title at all to it, merely because it received payment of that cheque. Although s.4 is almost always invoked in connection with cheques, it also covers 'cheques' drawn 'Pay cash' (these are not cheques remember), most payment warrants issued by government departments, and bankers' drafts.

As with all the other instances of statutory protection we have discussed, certain *conditions* must be fulfilled for the protection to apply.

1 The bank must *act*

- *for a customer,* or
- *for itself* having credited the customer's account with the cheque.

Thus, the protection applies both when a bank collects as an agent, i.e. for its customer, and when it collects for itself (as holder of the cheque).

As you should recall from Chapter 5, a customer is a person who has entered into a contract with a bank for the opening of an account in his or her name. This much is easy, but what is the exact meaning of 'for itself' in s.4? The key is that to be protected by s.4 the bank must *not* have given value for the cheque. Since the usual practice is to credit the customer's account immediately a cheque is paid in for collection, the bank is collecting 'for itself', but because it is purely an accounting entry the bank has given no value for the cheque. It is not collecting 'for itself' in the sense that it has 'bought' the right to enforce payment of the cheque.

Payment in of a cheque at another branch of the customer's bank would seem to be still acting 'for a customer' because the bank is at law a single entity. Payment in at a completely different bank would appear not to satisfy the condition and that 'collecting' bank would not be covered by s.4.

2 It must act in *good faith.* Honesty is required but negligence is not evidence of bad faith.

3 And most importantly, the bank must act *without negligence.* Section 4(3) provides that a bank is not to be treated as negligent *purely* because the cheque collected was not endorsed or was irregularly endorsed, i.e. it failed to concern itself with these things, but in all other cases it must establish that it acted with reasonable care. This is justified quite simply in that s.4 deprives the true owner of the cheque of their common law right to compensation from the bank for conversion.

The obvious question arises. What amounts to negligence in relation to collecting cheques? The only way to answer this is to consider a number of decided cases. These provide *guides*, not hard and fast rules, for the court's use. We can, however, start with a number of general propositions.

- The *standard of care* required is that of an ordinary competent bank.
- The criterion for this is *current banking practice*, rather than decisions dating back fifty or more years – times change – although it by no means follows that current banking practice will never itself be held to be negligent.

247

- A bank can plead contributory negligence by the customer in an action against it for conversion. A successful plea will reduce the damages awarded. The defence would be applicable where the owner of cheques carelessly left them lying around, facilitating their fraudulent use, or where carelessly drawn cheques are fraudulently altered.

Attractive though a plea of contributory negligence would appear to be, it has only been successfully pleaded in one reported case, *Lumsden & Co v London Trustee Savings Bank* (1971). Here Lumsden, the employers of the fraudster involved, had drawn cheques payable to 'Brown' intending the payee to be 'Brown Mills & Co'. A gap had been left before 'Brown' on the cheques. The fraudster inserted initials before 'Brown' and paid the cheques into an account opened in the same name and obtained payment. Although, on the facts, the bank had been negligent in opening the account, its own procedures for taking and checking references not having been followed, the plaintiff was held partly to blame for the fraud and their damages were accordingly reduced by 10 per cent.

The *Rule in Macmillan and Arthur* (1918), which we discuss below, does not apply to a collecting bank. Conversely, the defence of contributory negligence is not available to the paying bank.

Examples of negligence

The case law is considerable. This is not to say that banks are frequently negligent when collecting cheques, far from it; it is simply that in collecting such vast numbers of cheques each day mistakes are occasionally going to be made. Over the years these mistakes have provided categories, of sorts, into which negligent conduct can be classified. However, what is important is that you, as other bankers before you, learn from these past mistakes using the actual decisions as *guides*. Each case is ultimately decided on its own facts but *common themes* have emerged in decisions against banks, specifically:

- *absence of enquiry* where it was reasonably called for; or
- the *unsatisfactory nature of the enquiries* that were made.

1 The classic case of negligence is *failure to make reasonable enquiries* about a person's identity and circumstances before opening an account. Although taking references is no longer the universal practice, the law is quite clear. References must be asked for and taken up before an account is opened although they are probably not required, as a matter of strict law, where the prospective customer is already known to the bank as a suitable person, or introduced by a person of similar standing. Furthermore, unless the referee is personally known to the bank, for example where s/he is an existing customer, the authenticity of the reference should be checked, for example, through the referee's own bankers.

What amounts to reasonable enquiries is a question of fact in the circumstances. The modern leading case on this is *Marfani and Co Ltd v Midland Bank Ltd* (1968), which shows that while basic enquiries must be made, it is impossible to be categoric concerning their nature and extent. It also indicates, perhaps, a more lenient attitude on the part of the courts when compared with older cases. The case concerned a carefully conceived fraud. The office manager of the plaintiff company contrived to make the acquaintance of A, a respectable restaurateur. The office manager introduced himself as E and during the course of the acquaintanceship A became interested in the fraudster's intentions to open a restaurant of his own.

Knowing that Mr Marfani was leaving for Pakistan the following day, the fraudulent office manager prepared a cheque on the company's account for £3000 payable to E, one of the company's suppliers, and obtained Marfani's signature on it. He opened an account at the Midland Bank with this cheque using the name E and as one of his two referees he nominated A who already had a good account with the bank. The other referee did not reply, but A gave a satisfactory reference whereupon the bank issued a cheque book to the new customer. Over the next two weeks the entire balance was withdrawn from the account, following which the office manager departed for Pakistan – and was never seen again. The company sued the bank for conversion, alleging negligence in opening the account.

The Court of Appeal held that the bank was protected by s.4 following evidence by other bankers that the defendants had acted as reasonable bankers. In particular, the following circumstances were held *not* to constitute negligence in the case:

- opening an account after only one reference had been received without making further enquiries, the referee who replied was a respected customer and the second referee's failure to reply was satisfactorily explained by the mobility of the ethnic minority community to which he belonged;
- failure to ask the new customer for his passport; and
- collecting the cheque before receiving the reference.

2 *Failure to obtain the name of its customer's employer* or, in the case of a married customer, the name of the *spouse's employer*. The point in making such enquiries is to avoid being innocently made party to conversion of cheques by your customer. The customer might, for example, steal cheques payable to their employer and pay them in for collection for their own account.

Similarly, a spouse's account could be used to collect cheques stolen by the other spouse payable to or drawn by that spouse's employer and fraudulently endorsed. The customer may even be in a position to draw cheques on behalf of his/her employer making them payable to his/her spouse. In all these cases knowledge of the customer's employment should prevent the fraud. Note, however, that once the account is opened there is no legal duty to keep employment details up to date.

The case law concerns married women customers but there is absolutely no reason why the same precautions should not be taken when a married man seeks to open an account. Indeed, since the enactment of the Sex Discrimination Act 1975, any apparent discrimination against married women (or, indeed, married men) can no longer be maintained.

Both the situations we have outlined occurred in *Lloyds Bank Ltd v E B Savory and Company* (1932). In the case, two clerks, P and S, stole cheques from their employers, Savory and Company. The cheques were payable to various stock brokers or to bearer. They were paid in at City branches of the bank, some by P for the credit of his account at the Wallington branch and some by S for the credit of his wife's account at the Redhill branch and, later, at the Weybridge branch. The 'branch credit' system, as it was then called, entailed the branches where the cheques were paid in sending the cheques through the clearing system for collection and passing on credit slips with a form of banker's payment to the account-holding branches. The credit slips bore no details of the items and thus the account-holding branches remained in ignorance of the payees and drawers of the cheques concerned. Even had this information been conveyed it would have been of no use since details of the employers of S and P had not been obtained. From what we have said already, you will realise that the bank was liable for conversion because it lost the protection of s.4 through its negligence in failing to obtain details of the employers of the account holder, or, in the case of Mrs S, of her husband.

As interesting and important as the actual decision in this case is the fact that it was the direct cause of two important changes in banking practice. First, it became standard practice to ask for details of a customer's employment or the customer's husband's employment and second, full details of cheques had to be recorded on the credit slips used for 'branch credits' so that the division of knowledge between branches, which facilitated the fraud in this case, was avoided for the future.

Current practice among banks and even branches would appear to vary. Case law dictates that enquiries are to be made of a married woman customer while the 1975 Act dictates that separate treatment on the grounds of sex alone is unlawful. Often the problem is avoided by not asking any married would-be customer for details of his or her spouse and his or her employment or, conversely, by asking all married would-be customers for details of their spouse's employment. Whether the courts would accept the former practice as reasonable is uncertain.

ACTIVITY 8.4

What should the bank do where it knows or suspects that its would-be customer is cohabiting – possibly with someone of the same sex. Should enquiries be made of the co-habitee? Case law does not provide an answer. What is your bank's policy? What do you think and why?

The cases above illustrate negligence in opening an account, other instances of negligence (below) involve collecting cheques where the customer has broken their duty of care to the drawer or payee of the cheque.

3 Crediting cheques payable to *a company to the private account of an official of the company or to another company*. This applies even where it is a 'one-man company'. For example, in *Underwood v Bank of Liverpool and Martins Ltd* (1924) the bank was liable to the company for conversion when it collected cheques payable

to the company and endorsed by Underwood for the latter's personal account even though Underwood was the company's sole director and held all but one of its issued shares.

4 Crediting the *private account of an agent or of an employee* with cheques drawn by them on the *account of their principal or employer*. You have already seen an example of this in *Midland Bank Ltd v Reckitt* (1933) in Chapter 5.

5 Crediting an *agent's private account* with cheques expressly payable to the agent in the capacity of an *agent*. For example, in *Marquess of Bute v Barclays Bank Ltd* (1955), the bank was held to have acted negligently in collecting for the private account of an agent three warrants made payable to him because in brackets on the cheques were the words 'for Marquess of Bute'.

6 Although a bank is under no general legal duty to examine for endorsement cheques paid in for collection, a bank is negligent if it collects a cheque which *lacks an endorsement* where one is necessary. This is partly based on the law but mainly on banking practice, specifically a resolution of the Committee of London Clearing Bankers in 1957, which was adopted in spite s.4(3) (*see* above). Examples include:

• cheques paid in for an account other than that of the payee;
• combined cheques and receipt forms marked 'R';
• travellers' cheques;
• cheques payable by banks abroad; and
• cheques made payable to joint payees and collected for an account to which all the joint payees are not parties, e.g. a cheque made payable to Mr and Mrs Patel and paid in by Mrs Patel for a sole account in her name. (Note that cheques payable to one or more of a number of joint account holders may be collected for the credit of a joint account without first being discharged; this includes the accounts of partners and trustees.)

A third category of negligence is where cheques are collected without sufficient enquiry where unusual circumstances demand particular care. We give some examples of this below.

7 Collecting without satisfactory explanation cheques, particularly third party cheques, for *amounts inconsistent with its customer's activities*. For example, in *Nu-Stilo Footwear Ltd v Lloyds Bank Ltd* (1956), the plaintiff's company secretary opened an account in an assumed name, giving his real name as referee. The first cheque paid in was drawn in his own favour (under his assumed name) and for a modest sum, but the second cheque was a third party cheque, apparently endorsed to him, for £550 (a lot of money in 1956). While the bank was held not to have been negligent in opening the account, nor in collecting the first cheque, it was held to have been negligent in collecting the second and subsequent cheques, some of which were also third party cheques, because the amounts were inconsistent with its customer's stated occupation as an agent newly started in business.

8 Collecting *third party cheques*, that is cheques which have apparently been endorsed to the customer, without sufficient enquiry where the circumstances

demand it – but the bank is not expected to play 'amateur detective'. In *Motor Traders Guarantee Corporation Ltd v Midland Bank Ltd* (1937) a bank lost the protection of s.4 when it collected without enquiry a third party cheque fraudulently endorsed by its customer to himself because in the six months the account had been opened 35 cheques drawn on it had been dishonoured.

9 Collecting with sufficient explanation *'Account payee' cheques for someone other than the named payee.* As you already know from our coverage of crossings on cheques, the effect of these words is merely to put the bank on enquiry. If its enquiries are reasonably answered, it retains the protection of s.4.

Note two points here. First, the 1990 White Paper 'Banking Services: Law and Practice' (*see* page 236) proposes that a cheque marked 'account payee' shall not be capable of being transferred at all. Second, that there is no duty on a bank to make enquiries where it collects for a third party a cheque crossed 'not negotiable'.

ACTIVITY 8.5

(a) Make sure that you know sufficient facts about the cases mentioned above to be able to use them in examination answers. Each relevant case you mention will probably gain you one or two marks so there is no point writing a page on each. Although it is always worthwhile to know sufficient of the facts to explain the context of the decision, cases are used as authority for legal principles so it is the legal principle in the case – the *ratio decidendi* – that you *must* know.

(b) Students usually worry about remembering cases, particularly their names, dates are not so important. By the time the examination comes, however, this is usually a 'non-problem' – generations of students *have* remembered the cases. The best advice we can give you is to:

● make sure you understand the decision – understanding is usually the key to remembering; and

● pick a 'keyword' or phrase for each case and learn it. The 'keyword' or phrase will then act rather like a password or file reference on a computer, giving you access to the information you have stored in your memory. An example to illustrate: *London Joint Stock Bank v Macmillan and Arthur* (1918) – '£2'. Think about it.

Adopt this principle for the cases above and others you have difficulty remembering.

Protection as holder in due course
Introduction

The protection of a collecting bank that we have discussed so far – s.4 of the Cheques Act 1957 – is expressly given by the Act but a collecting bank will also gain protection as a consequence of establishing itself as the holder in due course of any cheque that it collects.

Section 4 protects a bank when it acts as agent for its customer, merely receiving payment for the customer's account. If, however, it gives value (consideration) for the cheque, it will be collecting for itself as holder for value of the cheque and not as an agent. Consequently, it will not be protected by s.4 because this requires it to 'receive payment for a customer'. (Crediting the account before receiving the funds is purely a book-keeping entry, it is not giving value, and is expressly within s.4.) Nevertheless, establishing itself as holder in due course of a cheque in such circumstances gives a bank an alternative and perfect defence to an action for conversion of the cheque. At law it is the *true owner* of the cheque and it cannot commit conversion against its own property!

The defence, afforded by satisfying s.29 of the Bills of Exchange Act 1882 (the section that states the required attributes of a holder in due course), has the *advantage* of applying even where the bank may have acted negligently, but it has the *disadvantage* of not being available where the collecting bank took the cheque under a forged endorsement for this prevents the bank from becoming even a holder. As you have seen above, the protection of s.4 of the 1957 Act is not lost in this latter situation.

Quite apart from the defence that it affords, the bank as holder in due course acquires the right to enforce the cheque, if it is dishonoured, against all prior parties, s.4 only affords a defence. An example of this would be where having credited the customer's account and allowed the customer to draw against the uncleared effects (*see* below) the subsequent debit creates an overdraft which the customer is not in a position to repay. The bank could then enforce payment against the drawer and any endorser of the cheque.

Instances of giving value

As you know, to be a holder in due course the *holder* must give value for the cheque, it is not enough that value has been given by a prior party. Thus, in what circumstances will a bank give value for a cheque which it collects?

1 Where it allows the customer to draw against the cheque *before it has been cleared*. There must, however, be an express or implied agreement entitling customer to do so, e.g. following the customer's specific request.

2 Where the cheque is paid in *specifically to reduce an existing overdraft*, and not in the ordinary course of business as an overdrawn account. This would apply where the bank has specifically asked for the overdraft to be reduced and the customer pays in a cheque drawn by a third party in favour of the customer or the customer's own cheque drawn on another bank. The consideration (value) provided by the bank is the existence of the overdraft – past consideration supports a cheque.

3 Where the bank '*buys*' *the cheque*: for example, where it cashes a cheque drawn by a third party for its customer, or where it cashes a cheque drawn on another branch without open credit arrangements. In both cases the bank is acting in excess of its contractual duty and is therefore providing consideration (value).

4 Where the bank has a *lien on the* cheque it is the holder for value of the cheque to the extent of the sum for which it has a lien. A lien arises automatically if a cheque is paid into an overdrawn account providing there is no agreement to the contrary.

Endorsement

The Cheques Act 1957, s.2, provides that a bank is to be considered the holder of a cheque payable to order for which it has given value, or over which it has a lien, although the customer delivered it to the bank for collection without endorsing it. This provision is necessary because an order cheque can only be negotiated by endorsement completed by delivery while the Cheques Act 1957, s.1, removed the need for endorsement of an order cheque paid straight into the payee's account.

Statutory requirements

As you know, a holder in due course is a more complex animal than a holder for value. We have seen what constitutes value, but to be a holder in due course of a cheque received from a customer for collection, a bank must satisfy all the criteria in s.29(1) of the Bills of Exchange Act 1882: *see* above.

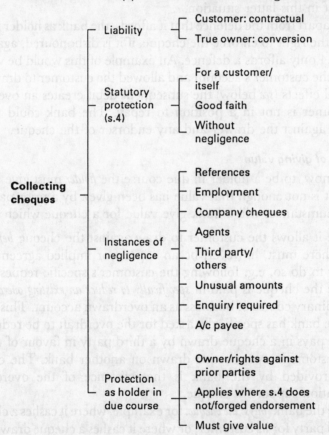

Fig 8.5 Collecting cheques

■ PAYING CHEQUES

What of the paying bank's position? To whom may it be liable, in what circumstances, and what protection does it enjoy? Once again, you will see that a pragmatic compromise exists between the legitimate rights of the true owner of a cheque and the need to give banks sufficient protection for them to be willing and able to fulfil their functions in relation to paying cheques.

Termination of authority to pay

As you already know from Chapter 5, a bank owes a contractual duty to pay its customers' cheques but that this authority is terminated in a number of situations. We considered them briefly then and we are now going to study them in more detail.

Countermand of payment

This is usually known as 'stopping a cheque'. Certain basic rules apply to an effective countermand, it must:

- Be made by the *drawer*;
- Be absolutely *unequivocal*, in effect this means that it must be in writing although there is no *legal* requirement that this should be so;
- Be *communicated* to the *branch on which the cheque was drawn*; and
- Give *complete details* of the cheque, in particular the payee's name, the amount of the cheque and its number. The cheque's *number* is the most important detail and a bank will not incur liability where a countermand gives the wrong number of the cheque and the bank accidentally pays the cheque which the customer intended to stop.

One point to remember, a customer cannot stop a cheque which was correctly backed by a cheque card. This is by virtue of the express terms in the contract made with the bank for the use of the cheque card.

An important decision on the countermand of cheques is *Curtice v London City and Midland Bank Ltd* (1908). Here a telegram countermanding payment of a cheque was delivered after banking hours and left in the bank's letter box. The next day the countermand was accidentally overlooked and was found the following day. By this time the cheque had been paid. It was held that the countermand was not effective unless and until it came to the *actual attention* of the drawee bank. The countermand in the case was therefore ineffective and the bank was entitled to debit the plaintiff's account with the amount of the cheque. (It is interesting to speculate what the decision would have been if the plaintiff had chosen to base his case for breach of contract on the bank's negligence.)

Although we have said that, in practice, a countermand must be in writing, the obvious reaction of many people who wish to stop a cheque is to telephone their instruction to the bank. This entitles a bank to postpone payment or dishonour of the cheque pending the customer's written confirmation of the initial instruction. If, in the meantime, the cheque is returned, the bank must indicate that confirmation of countermand is awaited.

What is the position of the drawee bank where the payee or a subsequent holder of a cheque loses it or has it stolen from them and contacts the bank to stop payment? The bank is in a legal dilemma although usually there would be a simple practical solution. Without doubt, the bank would have no legal grounds to stop payment – only the drawer can countermand payment of a cheque – but it would risk losing its statutory protection under the Bills of Exchange Act 1882, s.60. This is because it would seem clearly not to be 'in

255

the ordinary course of business' and possibly not 'in good faith' to pay the cheque if it is later presented knowing that it has been lost or stolen and therefore, almost by definition, to be in the hands of wrongful possessor. Fortunately, the problem would usually be capable of resolution by asking the payee/endorsee to contact the drawer or by the bank itself contacting the drawer and asking for instructions.

Legal bar to payment

This can take two forms: a garnishee order or an injunction.

Garnishee order. A garnishee order is an order of the court which commands a debtor (in this instance the bank) to pay the debt, not to the immediate creditor (in this instance the customer), but to the court for the benefit of a person who has obtained a final court judgment against the creditor. The order attaches funds standing to the credit of the account at the moment the order is served and, depending on the amount specified in the order, if insufficient funds are left it prevents the bank lawfully paying further cheques drawn on the account.

Since a garnishee order is not made against the judgment debtor but against one of his/her own debtors, such as his/her bank, it is usually an effective yet fairly cheap and simple way of enforcing payment when it is not volunteered. It does, of course, assume that the judgment debtor has not taken the precaution of withdrawing the balance on the account!

Injunction. An injunction is a court order which forbids a person from doing or from continuing to do something. An injunction may be issued against a bank directly or, more usually, against a customer to freeze a bank account where, for example, the ownership of certain funds is disputed. The injunction's purpose is to prevent them from being paid away, possibly abroad and therefore outside the court's jurisdiction, before ownership is determined by the court. Such injunctions are known as *Mareva Injunctions* after a 1975 case involving a company of that name.

The legal effect of an injunction against the customer is that if the customer draws a cheque in breach of it, the customer would be guilty of a contempt of court, and if the bank honoured the cheque it would be guilty of aiding and abetting the defendant's contempt. Thus, once a bank has notice of an injunction affecting money (or goods) in its hands it must not allow anyone to dispose of it except with the authority of the court.

Notice of certain events affecting the customer

Notice of the following events terminates a bank's authority to pay:

- the customer's *death*;
- the customer's *mental disorder*, although the disorder must be such that the customer is incapable of managing their affairs;
- a *bankruptcy petition* or *winding up petition* against the customer. (These steps are the first in making a person bankrupt or putting a company into liquidation.)

Bankruptcy order or winding-up order

Both orders basically have the effect of bringing to an end the commercial activity of a business organisation, the former applying to sole traders and partnerships, the latter to registered companies. The point to note is that it is the *making* of the order, and not notice of it, which terminates a bank's authority to pay. A bank therefore has no authority to pay the cheque even if it acts in complete ignorance of the order.

Third party rights

If a bank either *knows* or *should know* that an account is being conducted fraudulently, it must not pay a cheque which furthers the fraud. Examples include:

- a trustee acting in breach of trust, such as a member of a firm of solicitors drawing cheques on the client account for his or her own purposes;
- agents exceeding their authority; or
- a company official signing company cheques for the purchase of the company's own shares contrary to the Companies Act 1985.

The possible liability of a paying bank
Wrongful debit of an account

A bank is liable in damages to its customer if it wrongfully debits the customer's account. It may do so in one of four ways.

1 *Countermand* – by debiting the account after its customer has countermanded payment (*see* above).

2 *Post-dated cheques* – by debiting an account with a postdated cheque before the proper date for payment. The customer is entitled to stop the cheque before the payment date and an early payment could result in other cheques being dishonoured for apparent lack of funds.

3 *Forgery of the customer's signature* – a forged signature is completely without legal affect: Bills of Exchange Act 1882, s.4. Thus, if its customer's signature on a cheque is forged the bank has no authority to pay the cheque. However, a customer may be estopped from denying the genuineness of the signature, as happened in *Greenwood v Martins Bank Ltd* (1932). Here the plaintiff's wife held the cheque-book for his account at the defendant bank and, over a period of time, drew a number of cheques by forging his signature. The plaintiff subsequently discovered this but did not inform the bank. After the wife's death some eight months later, the plaintiff sought to recover from the bank the amount of the forged cheques. His action was unsuccessful because his inaction after discovering that his wife had been forging his signature prevented him, at law, from denying their genuineness. The bank was entitled to debit his account with the value of the cheques.

4 *Material alteration* – a bank is liable if it debits an account with a cheque which has been materially altered without the customer's consent. A material alteration is one that has the effect of changing the operation of the cheque or the liabilities of the parties. The alteration is usually a fraudulent increase

in the amount but it could be an alteration to the payee's name or to the crossing to enable the cheque to be cashed.

Only parties to a visibly altered cheque who made, authorised or consented to the alteration, most likely by signing over it, and any person who endorsed it in its altered state are liable on it. If the alteration is *not apparent*, a *holder in due course* is entitled to the original amount for which the cheque was drawn. Any other holder presenting the cheque is entitled to nothing.

A bank has no statutory protection if it pays a cheque which has been materially altered, whether or not the alteration is apparent. However, a customer owes a duty to draw cheques with reasonable care to avoid fraudulent alteration of them and the bank may debit the customer's account where the latter's negligence has facilitated the fraud. This is known as the *Rule in London Joint Bank v Macmillan and Arthur* (1918). Here, a partner in the defendant firm signed a cheque payable to the payee or to bearer made out by a clerk for the sum of £2. The amount payable was shown in figures only. The clerk fraudulently altered the figure to read £120, wrote the amount on the cheque and obtained payment from the plaintiff, the firm's bankers. Because of the defendant's negligence, the plaintiff bank was entitled to debit the firm's account with the value of the cheque.

If you reflect on the legal position for a moment, you will see that a bank will seldom be the innocent victim of a fraudulently altered cheque. If a visibly altered cheque is paid without confirmation of the alteration, it has only itself to blame, while most non-apparent alterations will be facilitated by its customer's negligence, thereby enabling the bank to rely on the *Rule in Macmillan and Arthur* (1918).

Recovery of money paid by mistake

If a bank pays a cheque in any of the circumstances described in the previous section, it may be able to recover the payment from the payee as money paid by mistake. In *Barclays Bank Ltd v Simms, Son & Cooke* (1979), for example, a customer of the bank drew a cheque in favour of S in payment of a debt. S went into receivership the following day and the customer telephoned a countermand, confirming it in writing. S's receiver, unaware of the countermand, paid the cheque into S's account and had it specially cleared. By mistake the bank paid the cheque. The court held that the bank was entitled to repayment from the receiver.

If you consider the circumstances above carefully, you will see that they share two characteristics:

- the bank makes the payment under a *mistake of fact*; and
- the bank does not have its authority to make the payment.

These are the two criteria which must be satisfied if funds are to be recovered. Thus, funds cannot be recovered if payment is made merely because the bank mistook the balance on the account (there being no other reason requiring the bank not to pay the cheque) for here the bank still has its customer's authority to pay.

Wrongful dishonour of a cheque

This is unusual, but if it should happen a bank can incur liability under two heads. First, for *breach of contract* and, second, for *libel*. This first needs no further explanations, the latter does.

Libel is a form of *defamation* and the cause of action is based on the statement made lowering the plaintiff in the eyes of right-thinking members of society generally (whoever they might be!), or causing the plaintiff to be shunned and avoided. An action for libel following a wrongful dishonour of a cheque is based on the words used in stating the reason for dishonour.

In *Jayson v Midland Bank Ltd* (1968) J was a garment manufacturer and retailer. The bank returned two of his cheques marked with the words 'Refer to drawer' because paying them would have resulted in his overdraft limit being exceeded. The bank successfully defended the libel action which resulted by showing that the dishonour of the cheques was justified but the jury (defamation cases involve a jury) held that the words were defamatory. 'Refer to drawer' is probably the most common defamatory phrase used when dishonouring a cheque but the phrase 'Not sufficient' has also been held to be defamatory.

The phrase 'Refer to drawer' is defamatory because it has the generally accepted connotation that the drawer of the cheque has no money in their account and this, it is argued, causes them to be lowered in the estimation of others. This is no doubt the case with business persons and was no doubt the case some years ago with individuals when only the prosperous middle classes had bank accounts. Perhaps it could be argued today, however, that the phrase does not always have the required effect as far as individuals are concerned – especially among student communities! Alternatively, and perhaps more realistically today, the phrase could carry the connotation that the drawer has been acting dishonestly by drawing worthless cheques – in so far as the drawer knows that they will be dishonoured – to obtain goods and services. (There is no authority for this proposition, however, and the *Jayson* decision must be taken to have decided the matter until and if the point is judicially reviewed.)

Thus, when banks use the phrase they must be prepared to justify it by showing they were not under an obligation to honour the cheque. The problem is neatly avoided by stating a technical reason for dishonour, if such is the case.

For breach of contract, a *trader* is entitled to substantial damages (reasonable compensation) for injury to reputation and credit without proof of actual damage. A *non-trader* must generally prove actual damage to be awarded more than nominal damages. By actual damage we mean damage measurable in financial terms. If, however, a cheque is returned to its presenter stating a reason for dishonour which is subsequently held to be libellous, a non-trader's claim would not be limited to nominal damages.

Where such an unfortunate situation does occur, litigation can usually be avoided by the bank admitting its mistake and making a prompt apology to its customer and the presenter of the cheque – banks are as anxious to keep their customers as customers are to keep their banking facilities.

Liability to the cheque's true owner

If a bank pays a person who is not the holder (the payee or endorsee of an order cheque or the possessor of a bearer cheque), it is liable at common law for conversion to the cheque's true owner. However, because a paying bank is seldom in a position to know whether the presenter is the holder of the cheque, it is given limited statutory protection against innocently committing conversion when paying cheques. This protection is discussed in the next section but it is worth emphasising here that it will be lost when the statutory requirements for it are not met.

A paying bank's protection
Payment in due course

Payment in due course requires the bank to pay the cheque to its holder in good faith and without notice of any defect in the holder's title: s.59, Bills of Exchange Act 1882. It discharges the cheque and all parties to it, i.e. the promise of payment cannot be enforced against any of them.

Forged and unauthorised endorsements

We know that a forged or unauthorised signature is without effect, and therefore a person in possession under a forged or unauthorised endorsement cannot be the holder of the cheque: s/he is merely a wrongful possessor. However, s.60 of the Bills of Exchange Act 1882, protects a bank against liability to the holder (the true owner) if it pays a cheque (open or crossed) which bears a forged or unauthorised endorsement provided it pays in *good faith* and in the *ordinary course of business*.

For example, A draws a cheque payable to B and B negotiates it to C. D steals the cheque from C, forges C's endorsement on it and transfers the cheque to E who obtains payment. Let us consider the rights and liabilities involved. Look at Fig 8.6 which represents the situation as a chain.

Here, C is the holder and the true owner of the cheque, while E is the wrongful possessor. D and E have committed conversion of the cheque against C, as will the bank if it pays it. The bank, however, is protected by s.60 but D and E have no protection (D obviously deserves none) and are liable at common law to C. If E, who has no right to receive payment of course, has to compensate C, E in turn can seek compensation from D, provided E can find D and D proves to have the money to pay.

However, C can take no action against A or B because the bank's payment within s.60 is deemed to be payment 'in due course' under s.59 and this discharges the liability of parties to the cheque, i.e. A and B. In short, it is a question of which of two innocent parties, C or E, should suffer through the fraud of a third: D.

You will agree that whatever the positions of the other parties involved, a bank will seldom be in a position to know whether an endorsement on a cheque which it is asked to pay is forged – it is almost certain to be the signature of a total stranger – and could not possibly check on an endorsement's authenticity without causing the entire system of paying cheques to collapse.

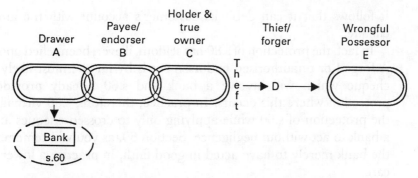

Fig 8.6 Forgery and unauthorised endorsements and s.60

Remember, however, that since only a small percentage of cheques are negotiated, the problems are perhaps more theoretical than real.

The protection of s.60 is not given lightly, it must be earned by a bank. First, payment must be made in *good faith*. Payment of a cheque knowing that an endorsement on it was a forgery would clearly not be a payment in good faith but a *negligent payment* is protected by s.60. Thus, payment in good faith means an *honest* payment. Second, payment must be *in the ordinary course of business*. This means payment according to current banking practice and within normal banking hours. For example, a crossed cheque should be paid only through a bank account and an open cheque cashed over the counter must appear to be properly endorsed. Payment of an open cheque to an 'unusual presenter', for example, to an apparent office junior, particularly if drawn for a substantial amount, would probably not be payment in the ordinary course of business although payment of bills or cheques for large sums over the counter is not in itself outside the ordinary course of business.

The Cheques Act 1957, s.1 (*see* below), has greatly reduced the practical significance of s.60 but it remains important wherever endorsement of a cheque is still necessary. Without s.60's protection, a bank would have to make a second payment to the cheque's true owner (C in Figure 8.4), having already paid the person presenting it (E), but would not be able to debit the customer's account (A).

ACTIVITY 8.6

A draws a cheque on Midtown Bank payable to C. C negotiates the cheque to D but E steals it from D, forges D's endorsement on it and transfers it to F. F obtains payment from Southtown Bank. What are the rights and liabilities of all those involved? Give legal reasons for you answer. (You may find that drawing a diagram helps you to sort out the situation.)

Crossed cheques

The main statutory protection when a bank pays a crossed cheque is given by s.80 of the Bills of Exchange Act 1882. This protects a bank against liability to the true owner if it pays a cheque in *good faith, without negligence and in accordance with the crossing*. Provided these requirements are fulfilled a bank is placed in the same position under this section as if it had paid the cheque's true owner.

261

It follows that it can debit its customer's account with the amount of the cheque.

In fact, the protection of s.80 has seldom, if ever, been relied upon by a bank. A forged or unauthorised endorsement is by far the most likely defect on a cheque which will involve a bank and s.60 already provides adequate protection where this occurs. In practice, therefore, s.80 virtually duplicates the protection of s.60 while applying only to crossed cheques and requiring a bank to act without negligence. Section 60, as you will remember, requires the bank merely to have acted in good faith, in practice a lower standard of care.

However, s.80 also protects the *drawer* if the bank's payment fulfils the requirements of the section – which is almost certain to be the case. (The fact that the section is of little practical relevance to banks does not alter its importance in this respect.) Under the section once a crossed cheque has actually or constructively (to an agent for example) been delivered to the payee, the *drawer* is also regarded as being in the same position as if the true owner had been paid. The drawer is thus discharged from liability on the underlying transaction, the original consideration given for the cheque. In other words, the drawer cannot be made to make a second payment. In fact the situation here is analogous to payment in cash. Once you have paid a debt in cash, your former creditor cannot demand a second payment because the money you paid them has been lost or stolen! Since most cheques are crossed and most payments of crossed cheques within s.80, most drawers are protected if the cheque is lost by or stolen from the payee and payment obtained by the finder or thief. (This principle would seem also to apply to uncrossed cheques.)

Unendorsed or irregularly endorsed cheques

Sections 60 and 80 of the Bills of Exchange Act 1882 deal with endorsed cheques, s.1(1) of the Cheques Act 1957 deals with cheques which are irregularly endorsed or not endorsed at all. Under s.1(1) a bank that pays a cheque drawn on it which is not endorsed or which is irregularly endorsed is deemed to pay the cheque in due course if it pays in *good faith* and *in the ordinary course of business*. In practice, the section means that a bank does not have to check the endorsement. The protection of s.1(1) is necessary because the paying bank will normally have no knowledge of whether the collecting bank's customer is the payee or a third party to whom the cheque should have been endorsed and was not.

Thus, if D in Figure 8.4 opened an account posing as C and obtained payment from A's bank (instead of forging C's endorsement and transferring the cheque to E), A's bank would have a good statutory defence against an action for conversion brought by C. (C's most profitable course of action would probably be to bring an action against the (collecting) bank at which D opened the account. It would then be up to that bank to successfully plead s.4 of the Cheque's Act 1957: *see* above.)

An irregular endorsement must be distinguished from a forged or unauthorised endorsement. An *irregular endorsement* is genuine enough, it merely does not conform to banking practice, while a forged or unauthorised endorsement is one written on the cheque without the holder's authority. Thus, an endorsement on a cheque 'John P Smith' by John Smith when the cheque was payable to him would be irregular, but an endorsement 'John Smith' in the same situation by Tom Jones who had stolen the cheque would be forged and unauthorised.

Section 1(1) means that if a bank pays a cheque on which an endorsement is necessary it cannot rely on the section because it would not be paying in the ordinary course of business. If, however, a cheque is endorsed as required, for example, a negotiated order cheque, but the endorsement proves to be *irregular* it may rely on s.1(1) and, we can add here, if it proved to be *forged or unauthorised* it can, as we have seen, rely on s.60 of the Bills of Exchange Act 1882.

As with the Bills of Exchange Act 1882, s.60, payment under the Cheques Act 1957, s.1(1), is deemed to be payment in due course. Therefore, it protects a paying bank from an action for conversion brought by the true owner of the cheque and entitles it to debit its customer's account. The cheque is discharged and with it the liabilities of the parties to it.

Banks, however, have never fully relied on s.1 of the Act and by the resolution of the Committee of London Clearing Bankers in 1957 (which we mentioned earlier), the following instruments, among others, still require endorsement before payment and the paying bank must examine them accordingly.

- Cheques and other instruments cashed at the counter. (This includes the situation where customers present their own cheques for payment, although the rule is seldom enforced. If, however, the 'cheque' is made payable to 'Cash' or to 'Wages' no endorsement is required – such a cheque is not a cheque remember.)
- Combined cheques and receipt forms marked 'R'. (Although discouraged by the banks, a few customers still insist on the payee's receipt before payment.)
- Travellers' cheques.

Payment of the above cheques without an endorsement would not be payment in the ordinary course of business and the bank would lose the protection of s.1.

The resolution also requires endorsement before payment of:

- bills of exchange (other than cheques); and
- promissory notes.

ACTIVITY 8.7

Harry draws a cheque on Midtown Bank payable to Christopher. Tony steals the cheque from Christopher and posing as Christopher opens an account at Southtown Bank. Southtown Bank obtains payment on behalf of Tony from Midtown Bank.
(a) Would Midtown Bank be liable for the value of the cheque to Christopher?
(b) What would be Christopher's most profitable course of action?

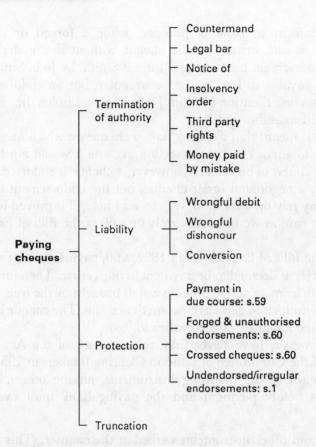

Fig 8.7 Paying cheques

Truncation of cheques

This refers to the practice (at present uncommon) of paying cheques on electronic instructions received from the collecting banks and not on receipt of the cheques themselves. If the practice were to become usual it would have the significant advantage of not requiring the transport of millions of pieces of paper around the country. Legally, however, it is an extremely dubious practice on a par with not taking references before opening an account. Three distinct problems arise.

- The drawer and endorsers will be discharged from liability on the cheque because the bank will not have presented the cheque for payment in accordance with the Bills of Exchange Act 1882. The *collecting bank* will therefore be liable for breach of contract to its customer (the payee) if the cheque is not paid.

- The *paying bank* has no way of knowing whether the drawer's signature is genuine or, where the signature is in a representative capacity, whether it is authorised.

- The *paying bank* will lose the protection of the Bills of Exchange Act 1882, s.60 because the payment will not be in the 'ordinary course of business' as required by the section – s.45 requires that the cheque be presented for payment. Similarly the protection of s.80 will be lost because this section requires the payment to be made 'without negligence'. Paying a cheque without even seeing it would surely constitute negligence.

The 1990 White Paper 'Banking Services: Law and Practice' makes proposals which will facilitate the truncation of cheques – an example of the law having to change to keep up with advances in technology and, possibly, commercial practice. These would enable cheques to be held at the bank branch at which they were paid and the relevant information to permit the debiting of accounts to be transmitted electronically. Banks would be required to keep the original cheques for a reasonable time.

Customers would be protected in two ways. First, in a dispute about a truncated cheque, the bank would have to recredit the customer's account unless evidence of the cheque is produced by the bank within a specified number of working days of the complaint. Second, the customer would have the right to receive within a reasonable time a photocopy of the truncated cheque.

■ CHEQUE GUARANTEE CARDS

What do they do?

The use of cheque cards is now very common. In ordinary retail sales a cheque will frequently not be accepted in payment unless it is 'backed' by a valid cheque card. The main advantage of the cheque card system is that it avoids the need to carry cash and is therefore a safer method of payment. Essentially cheque cards are a means of identification which:

● enable customers to *cash cheques* up to a prescribed limit at branches/banks other than the ones at which they have accounts; and
● *guarantee* that a cheque taken in payment 'backed' by a card will be honoured, whatever the state of the customer's account, subject to a prescribed limit per cheque and provided that the card is properly used.

Three separate contracts

The use of cheque guarantee cards to 'back' cheques, their more important function, involves three separate contracts:

● one between the bank's customer and the supplier (the payee);
● one between the bank and its customer; and
● one between the bank and the payee.

The first contract does not concern us here save to mention that it will most probably be regulated by either the Sale of Goods Act 1979 or the Supply of Goods and Services Act 1982. In the second contract, the customer agrees to use the card in accordance with the conditions of its issue and use and acknowledges that payment of a cheque guaranteed with the card *cannot be countermanded*. The bank for its part *undertakes to honour* any cheque backed by the card taken in payment by the payee subject to the prescribed limit. In the third contract, the bank gives an undertaking to the payee to honour a cheque up to the prescribed limit taken in payment provided the payee takes it relying on the card and according to the instructions printed on it or otherwise made known to the payee. In return the bank receives the benefit of greater acceptability of cheques drawn on itself.

Backing a cheque

If you look at the conditions of use of a cheque guarantee card you will find the following instructions:

- the cheque must be signed in the presence of the payee and the signature must agree with that on the card, or actually be that of the cardholder;
- the card must not be out of date;
- the cheque form must be written on the bank's standard printed cheque and bear the sorting-code number on the card;
- the cheque guarantee card number must be written by the *payee* on the reverse of the card; and
- the cheque must not exceed the stated guaranteed amount.

Remember that the prescribed limit is a limit per *single transaction*. Say, for example, the limit is £100 and the value of the transaction is £175. If two cheques are made out in payment, one for £100 and one for £75, the guarantee will only cover *one* of them. However, it could be argued that drawing two cheques in this way is a breach of the conditions of use which nullifies the guarantee on *both*. If a cheque guarantee card is used to back a cheque, in this case, for more than £100, the guarantee is also nullified, in other words, it does not even apply to the first £100.

Above we have outlined a couple of possible problem situations involving cheque guarantee cards and you may be able to suggest others. The legal position is uncertain in some of them because, in practice, a bank will only question payment of cheques backed by cheque guarantee cards when either insufficient funds are in the account or where unauthorised or irregular use is made of the card. In the latter case, the problem is simply solved by taking back the card, or, ultimately, by closing the account.

Fraudulent use of cheque guarantee cards

Cheque guarantee cards offer great potential for fraud, both by the customer to whom a card is issued and by a thief or finder of a cheque book with the relevant cheque guarantee card. Thus, cheque guarantee cards are not normally issued until customers have proved to be responsible in the operation of their accounts, or their integrity and responsibility is undoubted, or they are willing to provide the bank with acceptable security beyond the potential risk, i.e. the number of cheques multiplied by the prescribed limit. Students are, however, frequently issued with cheque guarantee cards without these requirements being fulfilled, but this is a calculated risk by the bank in the hope of securing their loyalty in future years.

Furthermore, the conditions of use printed on the card or, more likely, contained in a leaflet sent to the cardholder will specify that:

- it remains the property of the bank
- it does not entitle the customer to overdraw the account without prior agreement; and
- the card should be carried separately from the cheque book in order to prevent fraud if one or the other is lost.

These terms put the bank in a strong position as against its customer should the card be misused, although whether action is taken is essentially a practical rather than a legal decision.

We must consider the position of three parties in relation to the fraudulent use of cheque guarantee cards: the payee, the customer and the bank.

ACTIVITY 8.8

(a) How does a cardholder signify acceptance of the conditions of use of the card – expressly and impliedly.

(b) Obtain a copy of your bank's cheque guarantee card conditions of use. Identify the clauses which embody the terms above. Make sure you understand *all* the terms that it contains. (You may need to ask a more experienced colleague or consult your in-house information to do this.)

The payee

Provided that the instructions for the use of the card have been followed, the payee's position is secure because the bank guarantees that the cheque will be paid. The most likely situation where the bank can refuse payment is where the signature on the cheque does not agree with that on the card, for here the possibility of fraud arises and the payee would be wrong to accept the cheque without further enquiry or proof of identity. This, however, does not give the bank a great deal of protection against the determined and professional rogue. Indeed, because of rising losses through fraudulent use of cheque guarantee cards, banks have begun to take a stricter view of their obligations. In such a case they may refuse to pay a cheque because the *signature is not that of the customer*, despite the forgery being indistinguishable from the real thing. Needless to say, retailers are not happy about this change of policy but the evidence is that in the past they have frequently not exercised reasonable care in accepting cheque guarantee cards. In addition, 'cashless banking', if it becomes a reality, will almost certainly require a much more stringent attitude to the use of 'plastic and electronic money'. After all, a forged signature on a cheque is without legal effect, why should the position be different with plastic or electronic 'cheques'?

The customer

The customer's position is also secure where a cheque book and cheque guarantee card have been fraudulently used, for without the customer's signature on the cheque the bank has no authority to debit the customer's account. However, the customer's own behaviour is relevant. If the customer has been negligent in the care of the cheque book and cheque guarantee card and this negligence was responsible for the fraud being perpetrated, the bank would have a counterclaim claim against the customer for the amounts of the cheques which they had to honour. (Whether or not a bank would wish to pursue this course of action is another matter.)

The misuse of a cheque guarantee card by the customer to obtain an unauthorised overdraft is the criminal offence of dishonestly obtaining a pecuniary advantage by deception under the Theft Act 1968, s.16. This was so decided by the House of Lords in *Metropolitan Police Commissioner v Charles* (1976), where the defendant, who had been granted an overdraft limit of £100, issued 25 cheques each of £30 with each properly backed by a cheque guarantee card during the course of one evening at a gambling club. The bank was obliged to honour all 25 cheques, even though the defendant's overdraft now stood at £750. It was held that the issue of a cheque combined with the production of a cheque guarantee card constituted a representation by the drawer that he had authority between himself and the bank to use the card in order to oblige the bank to honour the cheque. If the representation should be false, an offence is committed. (Perhaps we can note here that the Court of Appeal in *R v Gilmartin* (1983), held that issuing a post-dated cheque knowing that there is no reasonable possibility of funds being available to meet the cheque when it is presented, is an offence under s.15: dishonestly obtaining property belonging to another by deception, i.e. the bank's money.)

The bank

We have seen that the bank is obliged to pay if the payee has followed the instructions for the use of the cheque guarantee card. Thus, the bank's interest is in recovering some or all of the money if this is possible. Clearly, it would not be in a bank's interest to try to recover a small sum from its customer when a cheque book and a cheque guarantee card have been either lost or stolen with no blame attaching to the customer. This would hardly be conducive to good customer relations. However, where the customer has been grossly negligent in the care of their cheque book and cheque guarantee card, or has been unnecessarily slow in reporting a loss or theft, the customer has broken the contractual duty of care to the bank and it would be possible to commence a civil action to recover the monies. This would probably be the course of action followed by a bank if the customer has fraudulently used the cheque guarantee card and there appears to be a reasonably cost-effective prospect of the customer being able to repay the overdraft.

■ CREDIT CARDS

The use of credit cards is very widespread. Many people use them instead of money or cheques. They are convenient. Surprisingly, perhaps, there is little case law on the subject and we must rely mainly on our knowledge of basic principles of contract law to understand their specific legal framework. Remember, however, that credit cards are covered by the all-embracing Consumer Credit Act 1974.

The contractual position

In *Re Charge Card Services Ltd* (1988), three separate contracts were identified when a credit card is issued and used.

1 A contract between a supplier of goods or services and the cardholder.

2 A contract between the supplier and the card issuer (often a bank or its subsidiary) under which the company agrees to pay the supplier the amount of the purchase by the cardholder in return for the supplier accepting payment by the card and paying commission to the company. It was held in *Re Charge Services Ltd* (1988) that acceptance of card issuer's card in payment under this contract includes acceptance of the card issuer's promise of unconditional payment. The effect of this is to substitute the card issuer for the cardholder as the debtor of the supplier and therefore to completely discharge the cardholder's personal obligation to pay. The cardholder's obligation to pay is owed to the card issuer. What this means in practice is that if the card issuer becomes insolvent owing suppliers money, the suppliers cannot enforce payment against the cardholders because their debts are owed to the card issuer. (This, of course, is unlikely to happen today in the case of the major credit card companies but it did happen in *Re Charge Card Services* (1988), where a relatively small credit card company dealing mainly with petrol stations became insolvent.)

3 A contract between the cardholder and the card issuer under which the former agrees to reimburse the latter for the payment it makes to the supplier as a consequence of the cardholder's use of the card.

Under the Consumer Credit Act 1974, the card company is *jointly and severally liable* with the supplier for any *misrepresentation* or *breach of contract* by the latter (*see* Chapter 2). Thus, for example, if goods bought with the card prove to be unmerchantable under the Sale of Goods Act 1979, the cardholder may take action against the company as well as or instead of against the supplier. (This latter liability only arises if the goods have a cash price of at least £100.)

The issuer of most credit cards will be either a bank or a finance house owned by the bank. In the latter case, the contract will be with both the finance house and the bank. This presumably means that if the customer has previously deposited security with the bank, subject to a term to the contrary, this is available to cover 'borrowing' on the card. Furthermore, the bank may combine any credit balance it owes to the cardholder with the debt on the credit card account.

You will recall that in Chapters 4 and 5 we discussed the use of standard form contracts and the contrast between the almost vague contract to open a current account and the very formal, detailed contracts used for lending, and issuing cheque guarantee cards and credit cards. The 'conditions of use', which form the basis of the contract between card company and cardholder, are very specific. This is probably a major reason for the paucity of case law on the subject.

Among the conditions of use you should find terms:

- stating that the card remains the property for the company, which enables the company to instruct the holder not to use it and to ask for it back at any time;
- depending on the card, specific rules for the appropriation of the cardholder's payments;
- that the cardholder undertakes to notify the company immediately the card is lost or stolen; and associated with this,
- a statement of the cardholder's liability for the card's fraudulent use by another.

Under the Consumer Credit Act 1974 the liability of cardholders for the misuse of their cards (being regulated credit tokens) by others is limited (at present) to £50.

A typical 'conditions of use' leaflet is reproduced in Fig 8.8.

ACTIVITY 8.9

Read carefully through the conditions of use reproduced in Fig 8.8.

(a) Make sure you understand the meaning and affect of each condition. If you are unsure, ask an experienced/senior colleague at work or discuss it with your tutor. In particular:

- What is the legal reason for including condition 11?
- What type of condition is 12 and what statute is its enforceability subject to?
- For what legal reason is condition 18 included?
- What type of liability is referred to in the second paragraph of the section headed 'Your rights'?
- What statute regulates the boxed section headed 'Your right to cancel'?

(b) Compare these conditions of use with those of use of another credit card. Compare not only the terms and their legal affect but also any statements dealing with repayment, cash advances and the calculation of interest. Also consider the presentation of the leaflet and its information. How does the leaflet compare in this respect with your bank's charge and guarantee forms? *If* its presentation is markedly different, why is this so?

Misuse by the cardholder

We saw above that it is an offence to use a cheque guarantee card to obtain an unauthorised overdraft. In *R v Lambie* (1981), the House of Lords held that it is similarly an offence under the Theft Act 1968, s.16 (obtaining a pecuniary advantage by deception) to use a credit card after the company has asked for its return. Such use again implies a representation by the cardholder that actual authority exists to make a contract with the retailer on behalf of the card issuer to the effect that the company will honour the credit card voucher signed by the cardholder.

Credit Agreement regulated by the Consumer Credit Act 1974

Barclays Bank PLC, Barclaycard Centre, Northampton NN1 1SG.

BARCLAYCARD

This copy for your retention

BARCLAYCARD CONDITIONS OF USE

INTERPRETATION

1. In this Agreement:–
(i) **"You"** are the Account holder and **"we"** are Barclays Bank PLC or its assignee;
(ii) **"Card"** means (as appropriate) the Barclaycard Visa card and/or the Barclaycard MasterCard issued to you or to an Additional Cardholder on your Account, **"Additional Cardholder"** means any person authorised by you to use the Account and to whom we have issued a Card, **"Barclaycard Cheque"** means a cheque issued on the Account, **"Account"** means an account maintained by us in relation to Transactions, **"Transaction"** means any payment made or cash advance obtained by the use of a Card, a Barclaycard Cheque, a Card number or in any manner authorised for debit to the Account;
(iii) **"Credit Limit"** means the maximum debit balance permitted on the Account, **"Charges"** means the charges specified in Clause 4, **"PIN"** means any personal identification number issued to you.

USE OF CARD

2. (i) You must ensure all Cards are signed immediately on receipt and that any Additional Cardholder complies with such instructions as we may give regarding the use and safekeeping of Cards.
(ii) The Credit Limit must not be exceeded. In calculating whether it has been exceeded we may add to the Account the amount of any Transaction not yet debited and any authorisation given by us in respect of a prospective Transaction.
3. You will be liable for the amount of all Transactions and Charges debited to the Account. The amount of any Transaction in a currency other than sterling will be converted at a rate of exchange determined by us. Amounts due to us must be settled in sterling.

CREDIT LIMIT AND CHARGES

4. (i) We will determine and notify your credit limit to you from time to time. Initially it will be not less than £750.
(ii) An Account fee of £8 will be debited when your Account is opened and annually thereafter.
However:

(a) Barclaycard MasterCard
No fee will be charged if you have a Barclaycard Visa Account but your initial Credit Limit may be less than £750.

(b) Barclaycard Visa Card
No fee will be charged if you are a student until you cease to be in full time education but your initial Credit Limit may be less than £750.

(iii) The interest rate is 1.85% per month.
(iv) A handling charge of 1.5% will be made on the amount of any cash advance or Barclaycard Cheque.
(v) The fee inclusive APR is 27.8% except for cash advances and Barclaycard Cheque transactions when it is 28.1%. The fee exclusive APR is 24.6% except for cash advances and Barclaycard Cheque transactions when it is 24.9%.
In calculating the APRs we have not taken into account any change in the Account fee, the interest rate or the handling charge all of which we may vary at any time upon giving you notice.

REPAYMENTS

5. (i) You must repay us within 25 days of your monthly statement date whichever is the greater of 5% of the amount shown to be due or £5 (or the full amount if less than £5).
(ii) If the whole balance outstanding on a monthly statement date is repaid by close of business on the 25th day following that date then no interest

will be charged on any items appearing in that statement. Otherwise interest will be calculated on a daily basis from the statement date on the balance outstanding in respect of cash advances and Barclaycard Cheque Transactions and on the balance outstanding in respect of other Transactions from the date they are charged to the Account.
(iii) Any excess over the Credit Limit, arrears and the amount of any Transaction made in breach of the terms of this Agreement are immediately repayable to us. All payments will only take effect when credited to the Account and may be applied against Transactions and any Charges in such order as we may decide from time to time.
(iv) Subject to any statutory limitation, all amounts due under this Agreement will be immediately payable in full on your bankruptcy or death or, at our discretion, if you breach this Agreement.

STATEMENTS

6. We will normally send you a monthly statement showing all debits and credits to the Account since the previous statement.

WITHDRAWAL OF USE OF THE CARD AND BARCLAYCARD CHEQUES

7. (i) We may without notice refuse to authorise a Transaction or cancel the right to use the Card entirely or in respect of specific facilities or refuse to re-issue any Card without affecting your obligations under this Agreement which shall continue in force.
(ii) Any Card will be cancelled if returned to us by you or an Additional Cardholder.
(iii) We accept no responsibility if a request for authorisation is declined or if a Card is not accepted in payment, nor for any loss or damage resulting from the way in which either is communicated to you or to an Additional Cardholder. We may return Barclaycard Cheques unpaid if payment would result in the Credit Limit being exceeded.
(iv) Cards and Barclaycard Cheques are our property and if requested must be returned immediately to us or to any other person acting for us.

TERMINATION

8. Either party may terminate this Agreement by giving written notice to the other but such termination shall only be effective once all Cards issued on your Account have been returned and all liabilities under this Agreement paid. The Account fee is not refundable on termination. We may re-issue Cards from time to time for use in accordance with this Agreement until it is terminated.

SAFEKEEPING

9. (i) You agree to exercise all possible care to ensure the safety of the Card and Barclaycard Cheques, to prevent the PIN becoming known to any person other than an Additional Cardholder and to keep the Card apart from any cheques. The Card number may be disclosed only for the purpose of a Transaction, when reporting the actual loss or theft of the Card or when we authorise the disclosure.
(ii) If a Card or Barclaycard Cheque is lost, stolen or for any other reason liable to misuse or if the PIN is disclosed in breach of this condition, you must immediately notify **Barclays Bank PLC, Central Retail Services Division, Northampton, NN1 1SG. Telephone: Northampton (0604) 230230** or any of our branches. Notices given by telephone or in person will only be effective if confirmed in writing to the above address within seven days. Until we receive written notification you will remain liable (subject to any statutory limitations) for any use of a Card but, unless the Card has been used by a person who acquired possession of it with an Additional Cardholder's or your consent, your liability in respect of each period when the Card is not in an Additional Cardholder's or your possession shall not exceed £25. After we have been effectively notified, your liability for any subsequent misuse of the Card during each such period will cease.
(iii) You agree to give us all information in your possession regarding the loss, theft or misuse of a Card, Barclaycard Cheques or the disclosure of the PIN and to take all steps we deem necessary to assist the recovery of our property. You agree we may provide the police with any information we consider relevant. Cards and Barclaycard Cheques reported as lost, stolen or liable to misuse must not subsequently be used. Retrieved Cards must be cut in half and returned immediately to the address shown in (ii) above.

Continued overleaf

Fig 8.8 Barclaycard conditions of use

Barclaycard Conditions of Use continued

REFUNDS AND CLAIMS

10. The Account will only be credited with a refund in respect of a Transaction if we receive refund verification acceptable to us. Subject to any statutory rights, no claim by you against a third party may be the subject of a defence or claim against us. You may not assign or otherwise dispose of any rights against us.

VARIATION OF THIS AGREEMENT

11. We may vary your Agreement at any time whether or not a similar variation is made to other Card Agreements. In particular we may introduce a charge for any service provided by us under this Agreement. Subject to the requirements of statute, notification of any such variation shall be given to you either in writing or by publication by such means as we may select and a variation so notified shall be binding on you.

GENERAL

12. We shall not be liable if we are unable to perform our obligations under this Agreement due (directly or indirectly) to the failure of any machine, data processing system or transmission link or to industrial dispute or anything outside of our control, or our agents' or sub-contractors'. If we are unable to produce or send a statement, your liability for interest shall continue and for the purpose of calculating interest and establishing the date on which payment is due we may select a date each month as the statement date.

13. We will charge for stopping and returning Barclaycard Cheques and for any losses or costs we incur as a result of any breach by you of this Agreement. Interest will also continue to be charged both before and after any judgement.

14. You shall immediately notify us in writing of any change in your address or if you or an Additional Cardholder change your name.

15. We do not undertake that facilities and benefits made available to you but not forming part of this Agreement will continue indefinitely. Such facilities or benefits may be withdrawn or varied at any time without notice.

16. We may assign our rights and benefits under this Agreement at any time.

17. This Agreement is governed by English Law.

INFORMATION

18. You agree that any information obtained about you as a consequence of this and any other application and agreement which you may have made to or with a Barclays Group company may be shared within the Barclays Group Customer Information System and used to identify other products and services which may be relevant to you. We may disclose details of the Account to any company which assumes our rights under this Agreement but otherwise no information will be disclosed outside the Barclays Group unless you are in default under an agreement in which case we may disclose this fact to licensed credit reference agencies.

CHEQUE GUARANTEE (VISA CARDS ONLY)

19. The Card may be used by you or an Additional Cardholder to guarantee cheques drawn on a cheque account with Barclays or Mercantile Credit Company Limited provided that;

(i) Barclaycard Visa cards and Mercantile Credit Barclaycards may only be used to guarantee cheques drawn on an account with Barclays and Mercantile respectively;

(ii) only one guaranteed cheque may be issued in respect of any one transaction and for an amount not exceeding the amount shown on the Card;

(iii) no guaranteed cheques are issued in excess of the credit balance on the cheque account without prior agreement;

(iv) payment of a guaranteed cheque is not countermanded; and

(v) this facility is not used outside the United Kingdom and Gibraltar.

The guaranteed cheque may be debited to the account without reference to the drawer and even though the cheque contains irregularities.

You may also use your Card to guarantee Barclaycard Cheques on the above terms provided you remain within the Credit Limit.

IMPORTANT – YOU SHOULD READ THIS CAREFULLY – YOUR RIGHTS

The Consumer Credit Act 1974 covers this agreement and lays down certain requirements for your protection which must be satisfied when the agreement is made. If they are not, the Bank cannot enforce the agreement against you without a court order.

The Act also gives you a number of rights. You have a right to settle this agreement at any time by giving notice in writing and paying off all amounts payable under the agreement. If you have obtained unsatisfactory goods or services under a transaction financed by this agreement, apart from any purchased out of a cash loan, you may have

---

Barclaycard Conditions of Use continued

a right to sue the supplier, the Bank or both. Similarly, if the contract is not fulfilled, perhaps because the supplier has gone out of business, you may still be able to sue the Bank.

If you would like to know more about the protection and remedies provided under the Act, you should contact either your local Trading Standards Department or your nearest Citizens' Advice Bureau.

LOSS OR MISUSE OF BARCLAYCARD

If the Barclaycard is lost, stolen or misused by someone who obtained it without your consent, you may be liable for up to £25 of any loss to the Bank. If it is misused with your permission you will probably be liable for **ALL** losses. You will not be liable for losses to the Bank which take place after you have told the Bank of the theft, etc. provided you confirm any oral message in writing within seven days.

YOUR RIGHT TO CANCEL

You have a right to cancel this agreement. You can do this by sending or taking a **WRITTEN** notice of cancellation to Barclays Bank PLC, Dept H, Northampton, NN1 1SG. You have **FIVE DAYS** starting with the day after you receive this copy. You can use the form provided.

If you cancel this agreement, any money you have paid must be returned to you. You will still have to repay any money lent to you. But if you repay all of it before your first instalment is due – or, if you are not paying by instalments, within one month after cancellation – you will not have to pay interest or other charges.

PAYMENT PROTECTION PLAN

If you have opted for this Plan and illness or accident prevents you from working for 14 consecutive days, your account will be credited with 10% of the balance outstanding on the last statement date before you consulted your doctor. This sum will continue to be credited monthly until you return to work or until 12 monthly repayments have been made. If the illness or accident proves fatal, the remaining balance (up to the credit limit) will be paid off. The maximum cover is £7,500.

The monthly premium which will be automatically charged to your account, is 30p for each £100 (or part thereof) outstanding on your account at the statement date (up to £7,500).

No premium is payable if you owe less than £10.

The main exclusions of the Plan are: conditions for which you have been treated in the 12 months prior to joining the Plan; disabilities caused by pregnancy or childbirth; self-inflicted injuries (including alcohol or drug abuses); injuries caused by war or civil commotion. There must be a one month interval between claims for different disabilities and six months must elapse before making a claim for the same disability or after the maximum benefit has been received.

This Plan, arranged through member companies of Financial Insurance Group, is available to Principal Cardholders aged between 18 and 65 and employed in the United Kingdom, the Channel Islands and the Isle of Man. Full policy details will be sent to you in due course. We reserve the right to vary or withdraw the Plan at any time.

■ ELECTRONIC BANKING

Perhaps it is appropriate that we should finish this book and your studies by looking to the future. In twenty years' time the financial services industry will probably look very different. High street banks as we know them may have become things of the past, both in their appearance and in their functions. They will have new competitors, perhaps even 'St Michael Bankers'.

What of the cheque, will we still be using it? Do we really need to be paying by writing out promises on hundreds of thousands of bits of paper each day?! But the system works! This is not the place to speculate but we can say with reasonable certainty that banks will use, and be driven by, the available technology to offer ever more efficient, more market-oriented and more cost-effective services to their customers. Electronic banking (essentially automated payment by computer) is with us and will increase in importance and volume at the expense of payment by cheque. The problem is that few customers know how to make the most of it.

Electronic banking and the law

There is little directly relevant case or statute law on electronic banking; the present statutory framework regulating payment systems is based on mid-19th century commercial practice and a paper-based payments system dealing with many times far fewer transactions than today. Even the Cheques Act 1957 became law at a time when computers were in their absolute infancy and certainly had not been applied to financial record keeping. Change in the banking industry, particularly advances in and application of technology, has outpaced the law's ability to evolve in parallel.

In addition, and unlike the underlying 'traditional' banker-customer contract, electronic banking is subject to express contracts which comprehensively detail the rights and liabilities of the parties involved. The contracts between banks and their customers covering ATM and debit cards are subject to written conditions of use (incorporating the express terms of the contracts) and the legal relationship between banks undertaking electronic funds transfer (EFT) is governed by the rules of the clearing systems to which they belong, such as BACS and CHAPS. There is therefore less opportunity for disputes to arise which would result in a body of case law and arguably, at least at present, little need for comprehensive statutory intervention and regulation. Note, however, that in this last respect the 1990 White Paper 'Banking Services: Law and Practice' proposes *inter alia*:

- a ban on the unsolicited mailing of all payment cards, including ATM cards and cheque guarantee cards;
- to give the holders of all payment cards the same protection against misuse following loss or theft as currently enjoyed under the Consumer Credit Act 1974 by credit cardholders, i.e. liability to a maximum of £50 up to the point where the cardholder notifies the card issuer of the loss or theft;
- that the card issuer should not be liable for the loss resulting from misuse of a payment card where the cardholder's negligence has enabled a person

to discover the PIN applicable to the card, for example where the PIN has been written on the card(!).

ACTIVITY 8.10

Discover as much information as you can about the operation of BACS, CHAPS and EFTPOS, including diagrams to illustrate the funds transfer paths.

The fact is that electronic banking is very different to paper based funds transfer systems. An example will illustrate this. A cheque commits the paying bank only when it decides to pay, the payee's right of action is against the drawer of the cheque. On-line electronic payments, e.g. CHAPS, ATMs, EFTPOS, involve immediate payment, are irrevocable and only involve the immediate parties – the right to payment of a cheque can be negotiated remember, it is an item of property. Failure to complete an electronic payment is therefore a straightforward matter between the customer and the bank and depends on the terms of a standard form contract; a dispute involving a cheque may involve persons other than the drawer and payee, plus a collecting and paying bank, with their respective rights determined by nineteenth century legislation (as amended). To cite a very specific issue, is an electronic code (PIN) the equivalent of a signature? The law, at present, provides no clear answer although it would seem reasonable that it is.

Ten years hence electronic banking may possibly be the norm and cheques and paper based funds transfers the exceptions. If so, electronic banking will surely feature in the Banking: the Legal Environment syllabus. Indeed, if after successfully completing the Banking Certificate you decide to study for the ACIB qualification, electronic banking forms part of the syllabus for 'Law Relating to Banking Services'. Having completed this course you will at least have a very firm foundation on which to build your professional knowledge and understanding.

■ SUMMARY

1 A cheque is a bill of exchange drawn on a banker payable on demand.

2 A party to a cheque is someone who signs it (the drawer or endorser) and thereby incurs liability on it.

3 A cheque is negotiated when it is transferred in such a way as to make the transferee the holder of it.

4 Cheques differ from other bills of exchange in that:
   ● they are never accepted;
   ● a very small percentage are negotiated;
   ● they are the only type of bill of exchange that can be crossed;
   ● special rules apply to forged and unauthorised endorsements on them; and
   ● they are issued as part of a wider banker-customer contract.

5 The four legal characteristics of a cheque as a negotiable instrument are:

- title is transferable by delivery or by endorsement completed by delivery;
- the transferee can acquire a better title than that held by the transferor;
- the holder can sue in their own name;
- the holder need not give notice to prior parties to establish title.

6 A crossing on a cheque is a direction to the paying bank to pay the proceeds to another bank as agent of the payee and not to the payee directly. Crossings may be either general or special.

7 Adding the words 'not negotiable' to a crossing deprives the cheque of its negotiability, the transferee cannot become its holder in due course. The words 'account payee', while they are often added to a crossing, are not part of it. (Note the proposals in the 1990 White Paper 'Banking Services: Law and Practice'.)

8 A holder is the payee or endorsee of a cheque (bill) who is in possession of it, or the bearer thereof. The holder is entitled to payment of the cheque.

9 A holder for value is a holder of a cheque for which value has at some time been given, not necessarily by the holder.

10 To be holder in due course of a cheque, it must be:
- complete and regular;
- not overdue;
- taken without notice of any previous dishonour;
- taken in good faith;
- negotiated to the holder;
- taken for value provided by the holder;
- taken without notice of any defect in the transferor's title.

11 A collecting bank may incur liability to its customer for breach of contract and to the cheque's true owner for conversion.

12 A collecting bank's statutory protection is provided by s.4 of the Cheques Act 1957. To benefit from it, a bank must act:
- for a customer (which includes the usual situation where it receives payment for itself after having credited the customer's account with the amount of the cheque);
- in good faith;
- without negligence.

13 Most examples of negligence under s.4 involve either a failure to make satisfactory enquiries before opening the account or a failure to make satisfactory enquiries before collecting a cheque.

14 A collecting bank also receives protection from legal action by establishing itself as the holder in due course (the owner) of any cheque it collects.

15 A bank gives value for a cheque where:
- it allows its customer to draw against uncleared funds;
- the cheque is paid in specifically to reduce an existing overdraft;
- it 'buys' the cheque;
- it has a lien on the cheque.

16 A bank's authority to pay a cheque is *terminated* by:

- the customer's countermand;
- legal bar: a garnishee order or an injunction;
- notice of the customer's death, mental disorder, a bankruptcy petition or a winding-up petition against the customer;
- a bankruptcy order or winding-up order against the customer;
- knowledge of third party rights.

17 A paying bank incurs liability to its customer for breach of contract if it wrongfully debits the customer's account or wrongfully dishonours a cheque, with the possibility of liability in tort of defamation in the latter case.

18 A paying bank may incur liability in conversion to the true owner of a cheque if it pays a person not entitled to payment.

19 The Bills of Exchange Act 1882, s.60 protects a bank who pays a cheque bearing a forged or unauthorised endorsement from legal action by its true owner provided:
- the payment was made in good faith; and
- in the ordinary course of business.

20 Under the Cheques Acts 1957, s.1 a bank is deemed to have paid in due course an unendorsed or an irregularly endorsed cheque provided it was paid:
- in good faith; and
- in the ordinary course of business.

21 A cheque guarantee card is used to guarantee payment of cheques up to a prescribed limit and involves three separate contracts:
- one between the bank's customer and the payee;
- one between the bank and its customer;
- one between the bank and the payee.

The card must be used exactly according to its instructions for use.

22 The fraudulent use of a cheque guarantee card is a criminal offence under the Theft Act 1968.

23 A credit card involves three separate contracts:
- one between the supplier and the cardholder;
- one between the supplier and the card issuer;
- one between the cardholder and the card issuer.

The contract between the card company and the cardholder is a good example of a standard form contract.

24 It is an offence under the Theft Act 1968 to use a credit card after the card company has asked for its return.

25 The evolution of law relating to electronic banking has been outpaced by the technological advances it supposedly regulates.

■ SELF-ASSESSMENT QUESTIONS

1 Define a cheque.

2 Why is a bank never a party to a cheque?

3 When and how is a cheque negotiated?

4 State the requirements for a valid endorsement.

5 How does a cheque differ from other bills of exchange?

6 State the legal characteristics of a negotiable instrument.

7 What is the difference between a general and a special crossing on a cheque?

8 What is the effect of adding the words 'Not negotiable, account payee' to a crossing?

9 Distinguish between a holder and a holder for value.

10 What is a holder's basic right?

11 What seven conditions must be satisfied for a holder to be a holder in due course?

12 State the rights of a holder in due course.

13 Give five specific examples of situations which have been held to constitute negligence under the Cheques Act 1957, s.4.

14 Explain why collecting a cheque as its holder in due course may offer better protection to a bank than relying on s.4. of the Cheques Act 1957.

15 In what circumstances will a bank give value for a cheque it collects?

16 State the circumstances in which a bank's authority to pay its customer's cheques is terminated.

17 State the *Rule in Macmillan and Arthur* (1918).

18 What is the protection afforded to a paying banker by the Bills of Exchange Act 1882, s.60?

19 Explain the relationship between the Bills of Exchange Act 1882, s.60 and the Cheques Act 1957, s.1.

20 What criteria must be satisfied for a cheque to be validly backed by a cheque guarantee card?

21 What offence is committed when a cheque guarantee card is used to obtain an unauthorised overdraft?

22 Identify the contracts involved in the issue and use of credit cards.

23 Why is it important for a cardholder to notify the card company as soon as they know that the card has been lost or stolen?

24 Why is much of the present legal framework inappropriate to the regulation of electronic banking?

25 Give examples which illustrate why electronic banking is very different to paper based funds transfer systems.

■ MULTIPLE-CHOICE QUESTIONS

1 In relation to cheques and other bills of exchange, which of the following

statements is true?

A a bill of exchange cannot be drawn on a banker

B the drawee of a cheque never becomes liable to the payee

C the phrase 'Not negotiable' only has significance in relation to cheques

D the rules relating to negotiation do not apply to cheques

2 The most important statutory protection of a collecting banker/paying banker (match the role of the banker with the appropriate) is found in the:

A Bills of Exchange Act 1882, s.60

B Bills of Exchange Act 1882, s.80

C Cheques Act 1957, s.1

D Cheques Act 1957, s.4

3 If a customer's signature on a cheque is forged, a bank:

A can debit the account provided it acts in good faith

B can debit the account only if the cheque is properly endorsed

C can only debit the account if the customer's actions enabled his or her signature to be forged

D can only debit the account if the customer was aware that his or her signature was being forged

4 A bank must make enquiries before collecting a cheque for someone other than the named payee which is crossed:

A 'Not negotiable'

B 'Account payee'

C neither of the above

D both of the above

5 Which of the following statements is *untrue*?

A the drawee of a cheque never accepts it

B all order cheques must be endorsed before they can be paid into the account of someone other than the payee

C an endorsement on a bearer cheque can be ignored

D a cheque may be countermanded by telephone

6 Which of the following is *not* required for the payment of a bill of exchange to be protected by s.60 of the Bills of Exchange Act 1882?

A the bill must be drawn on a banker

B payment must be made in good faith

C payment must be made without negligence

D payment must be made in the ordinary course of business

7 Which of the following statements is true?

A only cheques can be crossed

B banks never accept bills of exchange

C a £50 note is negotiable but a pound coin is not

D an instrument made out to 'Wages' is within the legal definition of a cheque

8 At law, which of the following statements is true?

A a bank is liable to the holder in due course of a cheque

B a forged endorsement on a bearer cheque does not prevent a transferee from becoming its holder in due course.

C all order cheques must be endorsed before a bank will collect them

D a cheque can be countermanded by telephone

9 Smith draws a cheque in favour of Brown for goods supplied to him by Brown. Brown negotiates the cheque to Jones as a gift. In this situation, which of the following statements is *not* correct?

A Brown can enforce the cheque against Smith

B Jones can enforce the cheque against Smith

C Jones can enforce the cheque against Brown

D both Brown and Jones can enforce the cheque against Smith

10 A cheque can be countermanded by the:

A drawer

B drawee

C acceptor

D payee

11 To which of the following will the Cheques Act 1957, s.4 always apply?

A bills of exchange

B promissory notes

C bankers' drafts

D postal orders

12 Which of the following does *not* form part of a crossing on a cheque?

A two transverse parallel lines

B the name of a particular bank

C the words 'Not negotiable'

D the words 'Account payee'

13 A bank would definitely be unable to rely on the Bills of Exchange Act 1882, s.60 where it pays a cheque:

A a few minutes after its advertised close of business

B negligently

C which lacks an endorsement where one is necessary

D which is uncrossed

14 A draws a cheque on X bank in favour of B who negotiates it to C in payment for services provided to her by C. C's bank tries to collect the cheque but finds that A has stopped it. Who can C enforce payment of the cheque against?

A the drawer

B the drawer and the endorser

C the drawer and X bank

D the drawer, endorser and X bank

15 Which of the following statements relating to the use of a cheque guarantee card is not *completely* correct?

A the cheque must be signed in the presence of the payee and the signature must agree with that on the card

B the card must be used in conjunction with the bank's standard printed cheque form and bear the same sorting-code number as on the card

C the cheque card number must be written on the reverse of the cheque

D the transaction must not exceed the stated guaranteed amount

Specimen examination papers

■ MAY 1988: QUESTIONS

Section A

This section contains one question divided into 20 sub-sections: each carrying one mark. Answer all sub-sections.

1 Answer (a) to (e) 'true' or 'false'.

(a) Including the words 'Not negotiable' in a crossing on a cheque prevents ownership of the cheque from being transferred.

(b) When a bank lends money on mortgage, the bank is the mortgagee.

(c) The House of Lords is the highest appeal court for all civil cases brought in the UK.

(d) The Crown Court has criminal jurisdiction only.

(e) A guarantor incurs primary liability for a debt.

Answer (f) to (l) in no more than 50 words each.

(f) Define a cheque.

(g) What is delegated legislation?

(h) State the underlying legal reasons for the decision in *London Joint Stock Bank v Macmillan and Arthur* (1918).

(i) Explain how a bank's ability to recover moneys owed under a legal mortgage differs from that under an equitable mortgage.

(j) Explain, using one example, equity's relationship with common law.

(k) Distinguish between an estate in land and an interest in land.

(l) Distinguish between consolidating and codifying Acts of Parliament.

Answer (m) to (t) by writing *one* of A, B, C, or D in your answerbook.

(m) A charge is best defined as:

    A a conveyance of an interest in property as security for the payment of a debt

    B a deposit of goods, or documents of title to them, with a lender as security for a debt

    C a right to retain another's property until that person has paid a debt

    D an agreement giving a lender specified rights over property used to secure borrowing.

(n) At law, which of the following statements is true?
  A a bank is liable to the holder in due course of a cheque
  B a forged endorsement on a bearer cheque does not prevent a transferee from becoming its holder in due course
  C All order cheques must be endorsed before a bank will collect them
  D a cheque can be countermanded by telephone.

(o) The right of the owner of Blackacre to cross a field in Whiteacre is:
  A a restrictive covenant
  B a profit *à prendre*
  C an easement
  D a right of entry.

(p) Smith draws a cheque in favour of Brown for goods supplied to him by Brown. Brown negotiates the cheque to Jones as a gift. In this situation, which of the following statements is *not* correct?
  A Brown can enforce the cheque against Smith
  B Jones can enforce the cheque against Smith
  C Jones can enforce the cheque against Brown
  D Both Brown and Jones can enforce the cheque against Smith.

(q) the 'Golden Rule' of statutory interpretation is said to be used where the courts:
  A apply the natural meaning of the words in the statute
  B consider documents other than the statute itself to determine what was the intention of Parliament
  C avoid an interpretation which would lead to an absurd result
  D choose not to apply the natural meaning of the words in order to better implement Parliament's intention.

(r) Which of the following is definitely *not* a regulated agreement under the Consumer Credit Act 1974?
  A a loan to a partnership
  B an overdraft
  C a loan to a private limited company
  D a 'Gold Card' credit card agreement.

(s) The decisions of which of the following courts must be followed by all the others:
  A House of Lords
  B Privy Council
  C Court of Appeal (Civil Division)
  D Court of Appeal (Criminal Division).

(t) The concept of negotiability has its origins in:
  A mercantile custom
  B equity
  C common law
  D statute

Section B

Answer at least one question from this section. 20 marks per question.

2 (a) With the aid of diagrams where appropriate, state and explain the types of crossings that a cheque can bear and the effect of each   [10]

(b) Janet found a cheque which had been drawn by John in favour of Toby, on a floor of a bus. The cheque had been preprinted with a general crossing and the words 'not negotiable'. Janet passed the cheque on to your customer Margaret as payment for some records. When she took the cheque Margaret checked that it appeared to have been endorsed by Toby.

In the meantime, Toby had told John that he had lost the cheque, and John had put a stop on it. When the cheque was presented through margaret's account, it was returned unpaid.

What rights, if any, has Margaret on the cheque? Does it make any difference whether the endorsement was genuine or forged?   [10]

[Total − 20 marks]

3 'Third party cheque' is a term often used by banks to describe a cheque which is paid into the account of someone other than the named payee.

(a) Explain the risks that a bank could run by accepting a 'third party cheque' for collection.

(b) What protection does the Cheques Act 1957 offer the collecting bank in respect of such cheques, and what conditions must be met for that protection to be available?

(c) Give four different examples of third party cheques that should not usually be accepted for collection, and indicate why each one should be refused.

[Total − 20 marks]

Section C

Answer at least one but not more than three questions from this section. 20 marks per question.

4 (a) Explain the terms *ratio decidendi* and *obiter dicta* and distinguish between them.   [10]

(b) Explain the terms 'binding' and 'persuasive' precedents and distinguish between them.   [10]

Illustrate both parts of your answer by reference to cases, preferably cases of direct relevance to banking.

[Total − 20 marks]

5 Memorandum

To: A Student
From: Manager

Last time I asked you for your views on a problem and you said you realised how important it was to read the facts carefully, spend time thinking about it and then write a short, concise answer to what you were asked. So here is another one for you.

Mr and Mrs Antonio lived together in a house solely owned by Mrs Antonio. To finance Mr Antonio's sandwich bar business Mr and Mrs Antonio borrowed jointly from Midtown Bank and the loan was secured by a mortgage from Mrs Antonio on her house. Mr Antonio's business was not successful and the bank threatened proceedings for possession of the house. Solicitors and accountants employed by Mr Antonio arranged with the bank for an order for possession and sale of the house to be postponed for one month to enable short-term finance to be arranged.

Fast Loan Finance were suggested by the accountants as a source of finance and an advance of £25,000 as arranged for six months at an interest rate equivalent to 42.5% per year. The advance was to be used to repay the bank and other creditors. Mrs Antonio was to execute a memorandum of agreement for repayments jointly with her husband, a persona; guarantee and a legal charge on her house as security. In a letter to Mrs Antonio, her husband's solicitors explained that she could lose her rights of occupation is she executed the documents and suggested that she should consider taking separate advice from a solicitor. Mrs Antonio did not do this but executed the documents at the offices of her husband's accountants who fully explained their possible consequences to her.

Mr Antonio dishonoured the agreement and subsequently disappeared leaving Mrs Antonio with the whole debt. Fast Loan Finance Ltd is seeking an order for possession and sale of Mrs Antonio's house, and Mrs Antonio is to defend the action.

I would like your opinion in a memorandum on the following points.

(a) What is likely to be Mrs Antonio's defence to the action? [4]

(b) In relation to the facts of the case, what are the questions which the court will have to answer? [8]

(c) What do you think is the likely outcome and why? [8]

If you can refer to relevant case law so much the better but remember that I am a bank manager not a lawyer and I do not want long accounts of the facts of the cases or the legal arguments raised.

[Total – 20 marks]

6   Memorandum

To: A Student
From: Manager

We received this letter yesterday.

Dear Sir

A am now just 17 and I have had an account at your branch since I was 13. I am going to college next month to study a Hotel and Catering Course. I need to spend about £250 on various items of equipment and special clothing before I go. I will not receive my grant for another six weeks and I write to ask for an overdraft until the end of next month. My father believes that I 'should stand on my own two feet' but he is willing to guarantee repayment of the overdraft.

The course will involve some business law and I would be grateful if you would explain to me the legal position regarding loans to students under 18 and guarantees of them.

Yours sincerely
Mark Abbot

We will lend Mark the money anyway but as part of our 'Customer Count' campaign please include in your letter granting the overdraft facility an explanation on the points he raises.

[Total – 20 marks]

7 Memorandum

To: A Student
From: Manager

As you are aware, at this branch we have two accounts for people called J Smith, but one is called Jane and the other Jamie. The similarity between the names has occasionally caused confusion, and at lest twice in the past credits for Jane's account have been placed in Jamie's by mistake. Fortunately our internal checks revealed the errors so that we could correct them before the customers knew about them. Jane is a good customer who conducts her account properly while we have had problems with Jamie and in the past we returned some of his cheques for lack of funds.,

Yesterday a cheque for £150 was presented on Jamie's account which would have overdrawn it by £120; far in excess of what we would allow him. before returning the cheque, however, I double checked his balance and found that last week he had paid in £200 in cash which had been posted in error to Jane's account.

These errors have got to stop, and we must impress on the younger members of staff the importance of putting the right account number on to paying in slips. Please prepare a brief note for circulation in the branch of the legal implications of yesterdays's problem. There are at least two major points that you should concentrate on:

(a) If we had returned Jamie's cheque for £150 when in fact there were funds to cover it, what might have resulted?

(b) If Jane had spent the £200 with which we credited her, could we have insisted on taking it out of her account?

[Total – 20 marks]

8 Banking operations and procedures are constantly being modified in response to changes in the legal framework. Give *four* specific examples of either *legislation* or *judicial precedent* which within the last 15 years have affected banking operations. Explain how banking procedures reflect each of these changes to the law. [Total – 20 marks]

■ OCTOBER 1990: QUESTIONS

Section A

Answer all parts of question 1. Each part carries one mark.

1 *Give* brief *answers to parts (a) – (b) (a few sentences at most; some parts may require only a few words).*

(a) What do you understand by the 'law merchant'?

(b) In which division of the High Court would an action involving a breach of trust be heard?

(c) State one way in which the Minors' Contracts Act 1987 altered the law.

(d) What remedy is available for all types of misrepresentation in the law of contract?

(e) Give a situation in which a bank would be liable for a breach of trust in relation to the operation of a trust account.

(f) State the Rule in *Clayton's Case* (1816).

(g) What is a *puisne* mortgage?

(h) What is a floating charge?

(i) Explain the difference, aside from payment, between an order cheque and a bearer cheque.

(j) State one way in which negotiation differs from assignment.

For parts (k) – (l), write the letter of the part and one of A, B, C or D in your answerbook.

(k) Which of the following best defines the term *ratio decidendi?*
    A The evidence brought before the court on which it makes its decision.
    B The court's judgement in the dispute.
    C The rules of law on which the court makes its decision.
    D The reasons for the court's decision.

(l) How did the office of the Banking Ombudsman come to be set up?
    A By the Banking Act 1979.
    B By the Banking Act 1987.
    C By the Financial Services Act 1986.
    D By the banks without legislation.

(m) An enforceable regulated agreement under the Consumer Credit Act 1974
    A can be made verbally
    B can be made verbally provided there is a sufficient written memorandum of the agreement
    C must be made in writing
    D must be written and in the form of a deed.

(n) A personal representative appointed in a will is known as
A an executor
B an attorney
C a notary
D an administrator.

(o) Title to unregistered land is proved by
A searching the Land Charges Registry
B a collection of deeds and documents
C a land certificate
D the Land Register.

(p) A lien is best defined as
A a conveyance of an interest in property as security for the payment of a debt
B a deposit of goods, or documents of title to them, with a lender as security for a debt
C a right to retain another's property until that person has paid a debt
D an agreement giving a lender specified rights over property used to secure borrowing.

(q) Which of the following statements is true?
A Only cheques can be crossed.
B Banks never accept bills of exchange.
C A £50 note is a negotiable instrument but a pound coin is not.
D An instrument made out to 'Wages' is within the legal definition of a cheque.

(r) At law, which of the following statements is true?
A A bank is liable to the holder in due course of a cheque.
B A forged endorsement on a bearer cheque does not prevent a transferee from becoming its holder in due course.
C All order cheques must be endorsed before a bank will collect them.
D A cheque can be countermanded by telephone.

(s) Which of the following types of contract is required to be evidenced in writing under a Statute of Frauds 1677?
A Legal mortgage contracts.
B Credit card contracts.
C Contracts for the sale of furniture.
D Contracts of guarantee.

(t) If a contractual offer can be accepted by post, the acceptance is effective when
A the offeror acts upon it
B it comes to the offeror's attention
C it is delivered
D it is posted.

Section B

Answer at least ONE *question from this section. Each question carries 20 marks.*

2 (a) Your customer, Janet, draws a cheque for £250 payable to Graham. She uses a correctable ballpoint pen to make out the cheque. When he receives the cheque, Graham skilfully alters it to read £450. Graham then negotiates the cheque to Bill in settlement of a debt and, in due course, your bank pays the cheque.

When Janet discovers what has happened she demands that you credit her account with the amount of the payment. Discuss whether or not this demand would be upheld at law. (You are not required to discuss Bill's position.)

[10]

(b) Janice found a cheque in the street which has been drawn by John in favour of Tony. The cheque had been preprinted with a general crossing and the words 'not negotiable'. Janice passed the cheque on to your customer Alan as payment for some textbooks. When he took the cheque, Alan checked that it appeared to have been endorsed by Tony.

In the meantime, Tony had told John he had lost the cheque, and John had put a stop on it. When the cheque was presented through Alan's account therefore, it was returned unpaid.

What rights, if any, has Alan on the cheque? Does it make any difference whether the endorsement was genuine or forged? [10]

[Total − 20 marks]

3 While on counter duty, the following cheques are presented to you for the credit of the named accounts. State whether or not in law you could accept the cheque for the credit of the named accounts without further enquiry, *giving reasons in each case.* (N.B. You can assume that all signatures are correct.)

(a) For the credit of Jane Smith. [4]

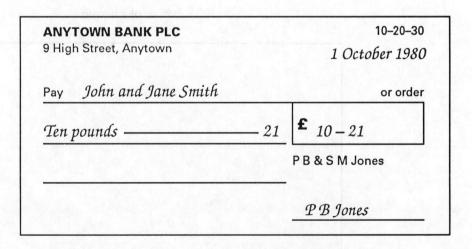

ANYTOWN BANK PLC	10–20–30
9 High Street, Anytown	*1 October 1980*

Pay *John and Jane Smith*   or order

Ten pounds —————————— 21   **£** *10 – 21*

P B & S M Jones

P B Jones

Reverse of cheque

> Jane Smith

(b) For the credit of Josiah Box. [4]

ANYTOWN BANK PLC
9 High Street, Anytown

10–20–30

1 October 1980

Pay   *Josiah Box for Jones Estates*   or order

Four hundred and twenty five   £ *425 – 00*

pounds only   Mrs A Hames

Agnes Hames

Reverse of cheque

(c) For the credit of Tuffbox Ltd. [4]

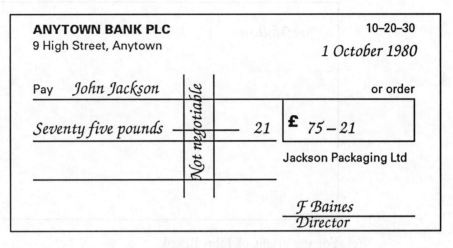

ANYTOWN BANK PLC
9 High Street, Anytown

10–20–30

1 October 1980

Pay *John Jackson*   or order

Seventy five pounds —— 21   **£** *75 – 21*

Not negotiable

Jackson Packaging Ltd

F Baines
Director

Reverse of cheque

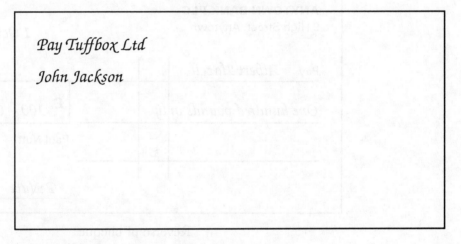

Pay Tuffbox Ltd

John Jackson

(d) For the credit of Arthur Mollison. [4]

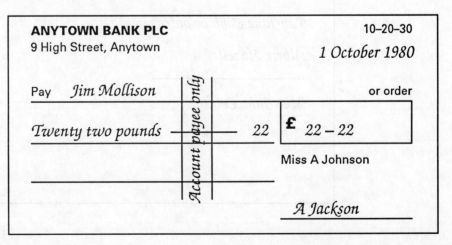

ANYTOWN BANK PLC
9 High Street, Anytown

10–20–30

1 October 1980

Pay *Jim Mollison*   or order

Twenty two pounds —— 22   **£** *22 – 22*

Account payee only

Miss A Johnson

A Jackson

Reverse of cheque

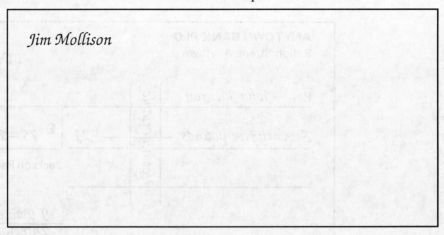

Jim Mollison

(e) For the credit of John Brazil   [4]

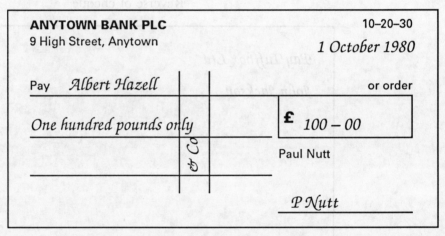

ANYTOWN BANK PLC   10–20–30
9 High Street, Anytown   *1 October 1980*

Pay   *Albert Hazell*   or order

One hundred pounds only   **£** *100 – 00*

& Co   Paul Nutt

                                                         P Nutt

Reverse of cheque

Pay Jane Cobb or order

Albert Hazell
_____

Miss Jane Cobb

[Total – 20 marks]

Section C

Answer at least TWO *questions from this section. Each question carries 20 marks.*

4   Memorandum

To: Student
From: Branch Manager

Re: Account opening procedures

A few days ago, a Ms Jackson came in with a view to opening an account. Since she wanted to think things over she took away one of our current account application forms to fill in at home. She has now written back to us saying that she could not understand why we were asking for some of the information. She has checked what questions other banks include in their application forms! Apparently she is now more confused than ever, since some banks ask for a lot of personal detail, and others hardly any. For example, at least one bank asked for her marital status and spouse's employers (if married), but others did not.

I'm going to contact her myself about this but before I do so I need you to provide me with a briefing note on the points she has raised. I know that part of the reason we ask such personal questions is so that we can offer customers appropriate services, but I'm sure some of the reasons are legal.

Please let me have a note of the legal background to this: what information does the law say we should collect before opening an account? Are those banks that only ask for restricted information running any risks in doing so?

Please also cover the question of references in your note. Is it still a legal requirement to take up references before opening an account, or can we safely stop asking for them?

[Total − 20 marks]

5   Listed below are four Acts of Parliament enacted since 1945

Financial Services Act 1986
Banking Act 1987
Cheques Act 1957
Consumer Credit Act 1974.

For each one

(a) state the main aims of the Act; and   [12]
(b) briefly explain how the Act affects current banking practice.   [8]
[Total − 20 marks]

6   Prepare a factsheet suitable for customers which explains the role and jurisdiction of the Banking Ombudsman. Make sure that the language and layout you use effectively communicates the information in the factsheet.
[20]

7   Briefly explain four of the following aspects of contract law, illustrating them in the context of the basic contract between a bank and its customer:

misrepresentation; undue influence; contractual capacity; express and implied terms; consideration. [5 marks for each aspect]
[Total – 20 marks]

8   Memorandum

To: Student
From: Manager

Last week I received a letter from Mr Patel to say that he intends to form a company to run his three grocery shops. At college he took a business studies course and knows something about company securities. In his letter he states that after forming the company he will want the company to borrow £50,000 to expand the business and is prepared to offer a floating charge as security. On the basis of his accounts and the business plan he showed last time we met, I am happy to make the advance. However, I cannot accept the floating charge as the only security for the loan even though at the moment the value of the company's assets seem to be adequate to cover the advance.

Please draft a memo for me, setting out the drawbacks of a floating charge, prior to my next meeting with Mr Patel so that I have all the facts at my fingertips. If you can suggest any further items of security that we might wish to be offered in addition, please mention them in your note.

[20]

■ MAY 1988: SUGGESTED ANSWERS

Question 1

(a) False

(b) True

(c) False

(d) False

(e) False

(f) You should have quoted the Bills of Exchange Act 1882, s.73 or given a close paraphrase of it.

(g) Delegated legislation is legislation made by a body or person to whom Parliament has given limited law-making powers.

(h) A customer owes a duty to his/her banker to draw cheques with reasonable care in order to avoid them being fraudulently altered.

(i) A correct answer required you to explain that a legal mortgage gives rights against the property itself (rights in rem) in addition to a right of action against the mortgagor for the money (a right in personam). You would probably have scored your mark if you had correctly listed the actual remedies.

(j)   The answer probably required was that 'equity supplements the common law' but you needed to give a relevant example to gain your mark. References to very old cases or history in general were not desirable; you could have cited as examples equitable remedies, trusts or the equity of redemption (mortgages).

(k)   The distinction required was that an estate is a right to the land itself while an interest in land is a right to a claim against the land of another less than possession. Again, you probably would have scored your mark if you answered by listing estates and interests.

(l)   A consolidating Act re-enacts a number of statutes on a given subject in a rationalised way but without making any changes to the law itself. A codifying Act is a new, often different, definitive statement of the law on a given topic derived from both case law and statutes.

(m) D

(n) B

(o) C

(p) C

(q) C

(r) C

(s) A

(t) A

Question 2

(a) A very straightforward question, see pages 235–7.

(b) The answer to this part revolved around the significance of crossing a cheque 'Not negotiable'. Any person receiving a cheque crossed in this way can acquire no better title than the person who transferred it. Since Janet had no rights against previous parties, the cheque had never been negotiated to her, Margaret can therefore have none. Margaret's only recourse is against Janet, if she can find her!

A forged endorsement is a complete nullity (Bills of Exchange Act 1882, s.24) and therefore confers no rights. However, since the cheque is crossed 'Not negotiable' it does not matter one way or the other whether the endorsement is genuine or forged. You should have made this point.

Question 3

(a) The point you should have made here is that a bank could be sued for conversion and be liable to the true owner for its value if the cheque had been misappropriated.

(b) The relevant section of the Cheques Act 1957 is s.4. This protects a bank if it receives payment for a customer or receives payment for itself after having credited a customer's account. The bank must, of course, act in good faith and without negligence.

(c) You could have selected any four examples from those on pages 247–51. Almost certainly marks would have been awarded for examples based more on your bank's internal rules than general legal principles although, again almost certainly, marks would have been lost if all four examples were 'variations on a theme', e.g. all to do with company cheques.

Question 4

Both parts to this question were very straightforward and, as such, made the need to cite relevant cases all the more important.

(a) The *ratio decidendi* is usually explained as the 'legal reason for deciding' a case while obiter dicta are 'things said by the way'. To gain full marks you should have explained each more fully. The ratio is generally said to consist of a statement of the facts, the process of legal reasoning (references to previous cases and interpretations of statutes etc) and the decision *inter partes* (between the parties). *Obiter* remarks are either statements of law made about situations not involved in the case or statements of law on relevant facts where the case is decided on different grounds.

As for examples, you have many to choose from but a case such as *Hedley Byrne* (1963) offers a good, relevant example of both an important *ratio decidendi* and *obiter dictum*.

(b) A binding precedent is very simply a decision which a court must follow when deciding a case involving similar facts. You would have been expected to briefly outline how this principle is related to the hierarchy of courts. *London Joint Stock Bank v Macmillan & Arthur* (1928) (duty of care when drawing cheques) would have been a good example to quote because if you were really up to date and had thought through your answer you could have used the *Tai Hing Case* (1985), which reaffirmed the decision, as an example of a persuasive precedent.

A persuasive precedent is one which a court will pay heed to but is not obliged to follow. Examples are obiter dicta of appellate courts and decisions of the Privy Council, e.g. the *Tai Hing Case*.

Question 5

Despite it's length, an easy question. If you knew the leading case you could have gained high marks while writing comparatively little. Part of the test in such questions is to sort the problem out; once you've done this the answer is almost invariably 'easy'.

The defence involved was undue influence. You would probably have scored two or three marks merely for stating this with an additional mark for a short explanation, e.g. if established it entitles the party influenced to have the contract set aside (rescinded). As to the questions raised, there were basically two. Stating these accurately depended on you knowing the leading case: *National Westminster Bank plc v Morgan* (1985), a House of Lords decision. Whatever other/later cases you might have cited you should have cited this one. The first question was whether Mrs A exercised a free and independent judgment when she agreed to the terms of the loan or did she act under the dominating influence of MR A and/or Fast Loan Finance. The second question was whether the transaction was obviously to her disadvantage, a test stressed by the Morgan decision. To succeed in a plea of undue influence the plaintiff must establish both that s/he could not exercise a free and independent judgment and that the transaction entered into was very much to his/her disadvantage.

Having asked the questions, cited case(s) etc you should have come to a reasoned conclusion. In some ways how you arrive at your 'answer' can be more important than what it actually is. In all probability a plea of undue influence by Mrs Antonio would have failed. She appeared to reject the suggestion of independent legal advice of her own free will, the agreement was after all explained to her, and since she was almost certainly going to lose her home anyway a loan at 42.5% interest while very much more expensive than most loans could hardly be said to be obviously to her disadvantage. It offered her the one remaining chance of keeping her home.

Given the emphasis the syllabus places on communication skills, it's reasonable to assume that marks were awarded for the quality of the actual memo irrespective(?) of its contents.

Question 6

If you knew the Minors' Contracts Act 1987 this question was very easy to score high marks on. If you didn't, you would be struggling to score 8 out of 20! Once again marks would probably have been awarded for the letter – right tone, suitable introduction and conclusion, clarity of explanation, even attempts at cross selling(!) – and probably, merely for stating that the loan would be granted; after all, you were told to do this!

As to the legal position; the Minors' Contracts Act 1987 by repealing the Infants' Relief Act 1874 makes loans to minors unenforceable. Stating this was probably worth at least 5 marks. It follows that a bank cannot recover any such loan unless the minor ratifies it after attaining majority; again worth about 5 marks. The final point to make was that the Act makes a guarantee of a loan to a minor enforceable notwithstanding the unenforceability of the loan itself.

Question 7

This question offered you an opportunity to combine your practical banking experience with knowledge of the law. You probably would have gained an extra mark or two for including suggestions based on your branch experience on how to avoid the situation happening again. Remember, however, it is a law paper and not practice of banking.

(a) Two different types of liability were involved here. First you should have stated that the bank had a contractual duty to pay the cheque because funds should have been available in the account. Thus, the bank would have been liable for breach of its contract with Jamie. Second, it's generally thought that returning a cheque 'refer to drawer' is defamatory (*Jayson v Midland Bank* (1968)), hence the bank could have found itself sued for libel. In the latter action, the quantum (amount) of damages would depend on the court's view of the harm done, whether Jamie was a trader etc. These were points you should have discussed along with, probably, wider factors to be considered, e.g. the bad publicity that could have resulted.

(b) Here the possibility of Jane being able to retain the funds needed to be discussed. The leading case, *United Overseas Bank v Jiwani* (1976), laid down three conditions to be satisfied if funds are to be retained: (i) that the bank misrepresented the state of the account, (ii) that the customer was misled by the misrepresentation, and (iii) in consequence the customer altered his or her position in such a way as to make repayment unfair.

In giving your opinion you should have made the points that a customer owes no duty to check bank statements and that the bank's ability to recover any such mis-credit would depend on whether or not Jane could be said to have realised that she had unexplained funds in her account and what use she then made of the money. Once again, marks would have been given for the quality of the note, e.g. was it presented in such a way as to bring the problem to the attention of the staff, did it explain simply the legal principles involved and was it likely to achieve its objective.

Question 8

Rather more difficult than it might at first seem because knowing the law backwards would probably have scored less than half marks. The essence of such questions is that you must show that you can relate the law to the practical operation of banks. Having said that, if you knew four good examples (within reason anything would have done) and could explain their impact, especially specific procedures or systems introduced as a response, you would have scored very high marks. Chapter 2 contains many examples of both cases and statutes you could have used.

■ OCTOBER 1990: SUGGESTED ANSWERS

Question 1

(a) A body of commercial customs brought to England by foreign merchants which became absorbed into case law and statute.

(b) Chancery Division

(c) Contracts of loan or contracts for the sale of non-necessary goods are now unenforceable not void – they can be ratified. A guarantee of a minor's borrowing is enforceable even though the primary debt is not.

(d) Rescission

(e) For example – where it allows a trustee to use money in a trust account to pay off a personal debt.

(f) In a current account, payments-in are appropriated to debit items in chronological order unless the customer or the bank have taken steps to appropriate particular credits against particular debits (or words to that effect).

(g) A legal mortgage of unregistered land which is not supported by a deposit of the title deeds.

(h) An equitable charge over the fluctuating assets of a company.

(i) A bearer cheque is negotiated by delivery alone, an order cheque is negotiated by endorsement completed by delivery. (Stating that one is payable to bearer while the other is payable to a named payee would not have been awarded the mark.)

(j) An assignee does not take free from equities/defects in title.
Written notice of assignment is necessary to transfer title.
An equitable assignee can not enforce their rights in their own name.

(k) C

(l) D

(m) C

(n) A

(o) B

(p) C

(q) C

(r) B

(s) D

(t) D

Question 2

(a) Three simple points would, if fully made, have gained you the 10 marks on this section. These are, and in order:

- a bank is liable to its customer if it debits its customer's account with a cheque that has been materially altered;
- a customer does, however, have a duty to draw cheques with reasonable care to avoid their fraudulently alteration – which usually affords protection to the paying bank;
- on the facts, it would appear that the customer has probably broken this duty. Therefore the bank is unlikely to have to recredit the account.

(b) The points to make in (b) are that:

- the crossing 'not negotiable' prevents a transferee acquiring a better title than that of the transferor; the transferee cannot become holder in due course of the cheque;
- as Janice had no rights against prior parties, nor has Alan; his only right of action is against Janice (if he can find her!);
- a forged endorsement is completely ineffective and confers no claim. However, since in these particular circumstances Alan can have no rights anyway, it makes no difference whether Tony's endorsement is genuine or forged.

Question 3

(a) The cheque is not acceptable as it is payable to joint payees but is being paid into the account of only one of them. The endorsement of the other party is required to protect the bank under the Cheques Act 1957, s.4

(b) This cheque is not acceptable without enquiry as the cheque appears to be payable to the account holder in the capacity of an agent. Accepting such a cheque without enquiry for the agent's private account is prima facie evidence of negligence: *Bute v Barclays Bank Ltd* (1955).

(c) The cheque can be accepted. There is nothing obviously suspicious in an individual endorsing a cheque over to a limited company. The crossing 'Not negotiable' removes the cheque's negotiability but does not prevent its transfer.

(d) The words 'Account payee' have no statutory significance – they are not actually part of the crossing at all – but banks should make enquiries before collecting such cheques if they are paid in by someone other than the payee. Failure to make enquiries would lose a bank the protection of the Cheques Act 1957, s.4. (Note: some banks refuse to collect 'Account payee' cheques which have been negotiated. This is bank practice *not* the law and would not have gained any marks if it was used as the basis of an answer.

(e) The cheque has been specially endorsed by the payee to Jane Cobb who in turn has endorsed it in blank, thereby converting it into a bearer cheque. Since everything appears to be in order, the bank can collect the cheque.

Question 4

Quite a long question but actually very straightforward. The basis of the answer was application of the Cheques Act 1957, s.4 to account opening procedures.

The first point to make was that it is essential to make enquiries of a would-be customer before opening an account. Failure to do so means almost certain forfeiture of the protection afforded by s.4 should a bank collect a cheque for customer to which the customer has no title. At law this certainly means that references are required but banks may decide that the commercial costs of taking references outweigh the potential losses. If enquiries are made about the employment of the would-be customer's spouse it is because of the possibility of the account being used to collect cheques drawn by/payable to the employer and wrongfully obtained by the spouse – *Lloyds Bank v Savory* (1933) was the case to mention here. Age may be asked to establish that the would-be customer is over 18 and therefore contractually liable for any borrowing on the account.

All this information should have presented in the form of a usable note.

Question 5

A very straightforward question but one which gave you the opportunity to show that you understand how Acts of Parliament directly and indirectly affect the business of banking. You would clearly earn five marks per Act and the mark breakdown would probably have been one mark for each relevant point made about the provisions of the Act, to a maximum of three and one mark for each of two relevant points made about how it affects banking practice.

There are numerous examples to choose from in this book – but the question did stipulate *since 1945* so the Bills of Exchange Act 1882 would not have gained you any marks.

Question 6

Hopefully you bore in mind that you were asked to prepare a factsheet suitable for customers; you would almost certainly have been awarded marks for the effectiveness of your communication skills (although you were not expected to show professional design skills!).

Your factsheet should have contained the following information at a minimum to score high marks.

- Explanation of the Banking Ombudsman's role, e.g. an alternative to the legal process, referral process, funding.
- Jurisdiction:
  - Up to £100,000;
  - Non-corporate customers;
  - No jurisdiction in matters of commercial judgment or policy;
  - Wills, trusts, overseas services etc;
  - Banks must abide by the decision.

Question 7

Misrepresentation
  - Definition
  - Types of misrepresentation
  - Effect on the contract (renders it voidable)
  - For example, misleading advice in security arrangements

Undue influence
  - Definition, including that it must cause loss to the weaker party (*Morgan*), this point for the second mark
  - Effect on the contract (renders it voidable)
  - For example, guarantees or other third party security arrangements

Contractual capacity

- Probably answered by selecting and explaining a couple of examples, minors, partnerships, companies. At least two examples must be used. In each, one mark should be awarded for a general principle and another for the application of this to banking. The fifth mark should be awarded for either a third example or other relevant point made in the two examples given.

Express and implied terms

- Explanation
- Examples from the banker-customer contract, e.g. assumption of joint and several liability, appropriation of payments, rights and duties. One mark for each example to a maximum of three marks.

Consideration

- Definition: each side gives and receives something of value
- Mention of basic principles, e.g. must be sufficient, must not be past
- Additional mark awarded for mention of Bills of Exchange Act 1882, s.27
- Customer receives benefit of banking facilities, bank makes a charge and/or obtains the right to use its customer's money for its own purposes provided it honours customer's cheques.

Question 8

Your answer should have identified the following weaknesses of a floating charge:

- Running down of assets;
- Subsequent fixed charge has priority;
- Postponements: preferential creditors; retention of title clauses;
- Invalidation by Insolvency Act 1986 s.245.

Detailing the weaknesses would probably have scored a maximum of 12 marks.

Alternative or additional security that the bank would probably find acceptable instead of or to augment the floating charge would include: fixed charge on business premises/house; life policies; shares in a quoted public company. The answer should have explained why these are preferred, probably six marks for this explanation with the remaining two being given according to the quality of the memorandum.

Index